Dominion

The Power of Man, the Suffering of Animals, and the Call to Mercy

MATTHEW SCULLY

Souvenir Press

To the memory of my friend Lucky,
and to Farrah, our little stray who found her home

Preface

A strange thing about our animal-welfare debates in both America and Britain is that you never really hear a direct, affirmative moral case for the practices in question – whether it's factory farming, blood sport, experimentation on animals, and so on down the line. Everyone concedes that there is a tradeoff at work, and no one points to such practices as the perfect or ideal way to treat animals. Invariably they are presented as necessary evils, unpleasant things we would rather do without but simply cannot as a matter of economics, custom, or just plain "realism." We really don't have a choice, we're told, and so it's best not to dwell too much on the details.

There's a lot back and forth in the debate, but the basic proposition of today's animal-welfare movement is that we actually *do* have choices, and that these violent practices do not have to go on. The details are everything, and merely looking the other way, or concealing them in euphemism, only makes us complicit. More to the point, the challenge of ridding our societies of cruelty isn't just some onerous obligation, requiring constant agonizing and sacrifice. Viewed in the right spirit, the cause of animal welfare is actually a great moral opportunity. We argue about our treatment of animals because we feel uneasy about it, but no one has ever regretted extending mercy to a fellow creature in need.

This, at least, is the basic outlook of *Dominion*, and I am very grateful to Souvenir Press – and especially to its distinguished founder, Ernest Hecht – for welcoming the book to the United Kingdom and to the Independent Voices series. To acknowledge an even larger debt, *Dominion* is also a book filled with examples, arguments, and ideals of British origin, for in no nation is animal welfare debated with more clarity and conviction. This has been true since the days when William Wilberforce championed the first anti-cruelty statues in Western law, and with fellow reformers founded the Royal Society for the Prevention of Cruelty to Animals. You might even say that like other great reform movements before it, the cause of animal protection began with the decency and good instincts of the British people. And in America, Europe, and beyond, this basic sense of right and wrong is still what carries it along.

To note just a few reforms in recent years, the European Union has codified standards to prevent at least the worst torments of industrial livestock farming. American agricultural policy, too, is beginning to change, less out of any sudden moral awakening than in reaction to electoral defeats wherever animal-welfare reforms are put on the ballot. Consider the scenes of hog farms in Chapter 6 – perhaps the real heart of this book because the man-made miseries recorded there show cruelty at its most extreme, systematic, common, and unjustifiable. At the time, not one of the practices described was unlawful. Today, seven states prohibit the unrelieved confinement of sows, five forbid veal crates, and two have banned battery cages for laying hens. Animal-use industries are very alarmed by the political trends, and for good reason – because animal protection is not only a worthy cause, it is also a winning cause.

The farming issues hit readers closest to home, and comment about *Dominion* tended to linger on those. But really I wanted to convey a certain attitude toward all animals, a spirit of charity and fellow-feeling, a general approach that relies on reason and moral candor instead of excuses and euphemism. In the end, treating animals decently is like most obligations we face, somewhere between the most and the least important, a modest but essential requirement to living with integrity.

A final acknowledgment is owed to a few animals who have come and gone in my own life since the book appeared, starting with an elderly dog named Herbie. At the first sign of frailty, someone dumped him at a Los Angeles "shelter," never knowing what joy they missed in the company of a sweet and noble fellow, in what turned out to be his glorious prime. Then there was Murray, our proud tuxedo cat who so loved his freedom, and was so loved by us; a feline version of the "Independent Voices" series would prominently feature our "Mr. Silky." And then there was Orangeguy, the friendless stray who became my office mate as I wrote *Dominion*, huddled on the back of my chair. Until he left us recently, our dear, pure-hearted Orangeguy was a daily reminder of the happiness that comes from caring for a fellow creature. It is to him, Herbie, and Murray that this new edition is specially dedicated.

CONTENTS

And God said, Let the earth bring forth the living creature after his kind, and cattle after their kind, and everything that creepeth upon the earth after his kind: and it was so.

And God made the beast of the earth after his kind, and cattle after their kind, and everything that creepeth upon the earth after his kind: and God saw that it was good.

And God said, Let us make man in our image, after our likeness; and let them have dominion over the fish of the sea, and over the fowl of the air, and over the cattle, and over all the earth, and over every creeping thing that creepeth upon the earth.

GENESIS 1:24–26

INTRODUCTION

It began with one pig at a British slaughterhouse. Somewhere along the production line it was observed that the animal had blisters in his mouth and was salivating. The worst suspicions were confirmed, and within days borders had been sealed and a course of action determined. Soon all of England and the world watched as hundreds, and then hundreds of thousands, of pigs, cows, and sheep and their newborn lambs were taken outdoors, shot, thrown into burning pyres, and bulldozed into muddy graves. Reports described terrified cattle being chased by sharpshooters, clambering over one another to escape. Some were still stirring and blinking a day after being shot. The plague meanwhile had slipped into mainland Europe, where the same ritual followed until, when it was all over, more than ten million animals had been disposed of. Completing the story with the requisite happy ending was a calf heard calling from underneath the body of her mother in a mound of carcasses to be set aflame. Christened "Phoenix," after the bird of myth that rose from the ashes, the calf was spared.

The journalist Andrew Sullivan discerned in these scenes a "horrifying nothingness,"[1] something about it all that left us sick and sad and empty. More than a year has passed since the last ditch was covered over. But probably you can still recall your own reactions because it was one of those events that made us all pause and question basic assumptions. One knew that something had gone terribly wrong, something deep and serious and beyond the power of vaccines or borders or cullings to contain. We saw in all of their simplicity the facts of the case: Here were innocent, living creatures, and they deserved better, and we just can't treat life that way. We realized, if only for an instant, that it wasn't even necessary, that we had brought the whole thing upon them and upon ourselves. Foot-and-mouth disease is a form of flu, treatable by proper veterinary care, preventable by vaccination, lethal neither to humans nor to animals. These animals, millions of them not even infected, were all killed only because their market value had been diminished and because trade policies required it—because, in short, under the circumstances it was the quick and convenient thing to do. By the one measure we now apply to these creatures, they had all become worthless. For them, the difference between what happened and what awaited them anyway was one of timing. And for us the difference was visibility. This time, we had to watch.

Silent while all of this was unfolding in early 2001 were people usually quick to caution against "sentimentality" toward animals. Looking out upon those fields of burning pyres, no one could claim that mankind is going soft. The images bore witness, instead, to an incredible hardness and abandon. It was an "economic disease,"[2] as one writer put it, revealing attitudes there all along and now, in desperation, grimly carried out to their logical conclusion.

The drama had a familiar feel to it, for in a strange way mankind does seem to be growing more sentimental about animals, and also more ruthless. No age has ever been more solicitous to animals, more curious and caring. Yet no age has ever inflicted upon animals such massive punishments with such complete disregard, as witness scenes to be found on any given day at any modern industrial farm. These places are hard to contemplate even without the crises that now and then capture our attention. Europe's recurring "mad cow" scares have all come about from the once unthinkable practice of feeding cattle the ground-up remains of other cattle. Livestock farmers around the world are becoming "growers," their barns "mass confinement facilities," and slaughterhouses vast "processing plants" dispatching animals—"production units"—at a furious pace of hundreds per minute.

When a quarter million birds are stuffed into a single shed, unable even to flap their wings, when more than a million pigs inhabit a single farm, never once stepping into the light of day, when every year tens of millions of creatures go to their death without knowing the least measure of human kindness, it is time to question old assumptions, to ask what we are doing and what spirit drives us on. "Our inhumane treatment of livestock," as Senator Robert C. Byrd warned in July 2001, in remarks without precedent in the Congress of the United States, "is becoming widespread and more and more barbaric. . . . Such insensitivity is insidious and can spread and be dangerous. Life must be respected and dealt with humanely in a civilized world."[3]

The attitude Senator Byrd describes has already spread into sport hunting, which is becoming colder and more systematic even as the ranks of hunters decline. In our day hunting has taken on an oddly agricultural aspect, with many wild animals born, bred, and held in captivity just to be shot, and even elephants confined within African game parks to be "harvested" by Western sportsmen in a manner more resembling execution. Wildlife across the world live in a state of perpetual retreat from human development, until for many species there is nowhere else to go, as we have seen for a generation in mankind's long good-bye to the elephants, grizzlies, gorillas, tigers, wolves, pandas, and other creatures who simply do not have room to live and flourish anymore.

Even whales are still hunted, long after an international moratorium was declared and longer still after any credible claims of need have passed away. Employing weapons and methods ever more harsh and inescapable, the hunt goes on for many other animals one might have thought were also due a reprieve, as new substitutes are found for their fur and flesh. From Africa to the western United States to the storied rain forest of the Amazon, it is the fate of many wild creatures either to be unwanted by man or wanted too much, despised as a menace to progress or desired as a means to progress— beloved and brutalized all at once, like the elephant and whale and dolphin.

In our laboratories, meanwhile, we see the strange new beings of mankind's own creation, genetically engineered, cloned, and now even patented like any other products ready for mass production. Even with all its possibilities for good, this new science of genetic engineering carries the darkest implications of all for animals, conferring on us the power not only to use them as we will but to remake them as we will. It comes at an inconvenient moment, too, just as research of a very different kind has revealed beyond reasonable doubt the intelligence of many animals, their emotional sensitivity, their capacities for happiness and suffering alike.

The care of animals brings with it often complicated problems of economics, ecology, and science. But above all it confronts us with questions of conscience. Many of us seem to have lost all sense of restraint toward animals, an understanding of natural boundaries, a respect for them as beings with needs and wants and a place and purpose of their own. Too often, too casually, we assume that our interests always come first, and if it's profitable or expedient that is all we need to know. We assume that all these other creatures with whom we share the earth are here for us, and only for us. We assume, in effect, that we are everything and they are nothing.

Animals are more than ever a test of our character, of mankind's capacity for empathy and for decent, honorable conduct and faithful stewardship. We are called to treat them with kindness, not because they have rights or power or some claim to equality, but in a sense because they don't; because they all stand unequal and powerless before us. Animals are so easily overlooked, their interests so easily brushed aside. Whenever we humans enter their world, from our farms to the local animal shelter to the African savanna, we enter as lords of the earth bearing strange powers of terror and mercy alike.

Dominion, as we call this power in the Western tradition, today requires our concentrated moral consideration, and I have tried in the pages that follow to give it mine. I hope also to convey a sense of fellowship that I know many readers will share—a sense that all of these creatures in our midst are here with us, not just for us. Though reason must guide us in laying down standards and laws regarding animals, and in examining the arguments of those who reject such standards, it is usually best in any moral inquiry to start with the original motivation, which in the case of animals we may without embarrassment call love. Human beings love animals as only the higher love the lower, the knowing love the innocent, and the strong love the vulnerable. When we wince at the suffering of animals, that feeling speaks well of us even when we ignore it, and those who dismiss love for our fellow creatures as mere sentimentality overlook a good and important part of our humanity.

It is true, as we are often reminded, that kindness to animals is among the humbler duties of human charity—though for just that reason among the more easily neglected. And it is true that there will always be enough injustice and human suffering in the world to make the wrongs done to animals seem small and secondary. The answer is that justice is not a finite commodity, nor are kindness and love. Where we find wrongs done to animals, it is no excuse to say that more important wrongs are done to human beings, and let us concentrate on those. A wrong is a wrong, and often the little ones, when they are shrugged off as nothing, spread and do the gravest harm to ourselves and others. I believe this is happening in our treatment of animals. The burning pyres of Europe were either a sign to us, demanding an accounting for humanity's treatment of animals, or else they were just a hint of things to come.

After the foot-and-mouth crisis, Matthew Parris, a former member of Parliament writing in the conservative *Spectator,* observed that "a tide of moral sentiment is slowly turning. It turns first in the unconscious mind. We feel—not *opposed* to something, but vaguely uncomfortable about it."[4] I hope he is right. I hope that more of us might pass from moral discomfort to moral conviction. I hope that animal welfare will receive more of the public concern it warrants, leading over time to legal reforms not only in our treatment of the creatures now raised and slaughtered by the billions, but of all within the reach of human recklessness, greed, cowardice, and cruelty. If Mr. Parris is correct, and a spirit of kindness and clemency toward animals is stirring in the world, I hope with this book to encourage it.

THE THINGS

THAT ARE

"And what is this God?" I asked the earth and it answered: "I am not he," and all the things that are on the earth confessed the same answer. I asked the sea and the deeps and the creeping things with living souls, and they replied, "We are not your God. Look above us." I asked the blowing breezes, and the universal air with all its inhabitants answered: "I am not God." I asked the heaven, the sun, the moon, the stars, and "No," they said, "we are not the God for whom you are looking." And I said to all those things which stand about the gates of my senses: "Tell me something about my God, you who are not He. Tell me something about Him." And they cried out in a loud voice: "He made us."

SAINT AUGUSTINE, *THE CONFESSIONS*, X:9

Whether of natural or supernatural origin, the moment that humanity acquired reason and language we were set apart forever from the natural world, and nothing was ever the same. How amazing that for all of our boundless power over the animals, so many of us still care about them, delighting in their companionship, admiring them from afar, and feeling their hurts whenever one of them is actually before us stricken and needful.

I am not, I confess, a particularly pious or devout person. But animals have always awakened something in me—their little joys and travails alike—that, try as I might, I find impossible to express except in the language of devotion. Maybe it is the Lord's way of getting through to the particularly slow and obstinate, but if you care about animals you must figure out why you care. From a certain angle it defies all logic, often involving, as in the case of pets or the strays who find our doors, all sorts of inconveniences and extra worries one could do without. And the only good reason I know to care for them is that they are my fellow creatures, sharing with you and me the breath of life, each in their own way bearing His unmistakable mark.

I know that they do not have reason comparable to ours. I know that their lives and place and purpose in the world are different from ours. I know that theirs is an often violent world, "nature red in tooth and claw" as Tennyson described it. But I also know that whatever their place and purpose among us might be, it is a mysterious one beyond any man's power to know. Whatever measure of happiness their Creator intended for them, it is not something to be taken lightly by us, not to be withdrawn from them wantonly or capriciously.

MERE PAIN

Some readers will say that animals awaken fantasy, if not heresy, in those who attach moral significance to them. Yet often I think it is the more violent among us who are living out the fantasy, some delusion in which everything in nature is nothing and all is permitted.

As sentimentality toward animals can be overindulged, so, too, can grim realism, seeing only the things we want in animals and not the animals themselves. They do us a service if only by inspiring now and then a sense of wonder and humility, for if not even a sparrow falls without His knowing then we are not too important to notice it ourselves. This is probably why many young children have such a natural attachment to animals, seeing things fresh, without the years to refract all the miraculous new images coming at them, all these remarkable animate beings racing and barking and panting and chirping in their midst. Animals also share with children a tie of profound vulnerability. Both, too, are usually the first to feel the brunt of human callousness.

My earliest recollection is of coming upon some rabbit tracks in the backyard snow. I must have been three or so, but I had never seen a rabbit and can still recall the feeling of being completely captivated by the tracks: *Someone* had been here. And he left these prints. And he was alive. And he lived somewhere nearby, maybe even watching me at this very moment.

Four decades later, I do not need to be reminded that rabbits are often a nuisance to farmers and gardeners. My point is that when you look at a rabbit and can see only a pest, or vermin, or a meal, or a commodity, or a laboratory subject, you aren't seeing the rabbit anymore. You are seeing only yourself and the schemes and appetites we bring to the world—seeing, come to think of it, like an animal instead of as a moral being with moral vision. Just one little varmint among billions to be found scurrying and hopping and burrowing all over the earth. Their enemies like the fox and wolf snatch them up in a bloody flash, and that's that. People raise them in cages by the millions for food and medical research, with bigger and more pressing matters on their minds than the meaning of one little rabbit's place in creation. In the grand scheme, not much. And yet, we are told, each one is counted and known by Him, and I believe it.

Desmond Morris in his 1967 bestseller *The Naked Ape* describes seven stages in our human view of animals, all reflecting different phases of our own psychological development. At one end, for example, is the infantile phase, "when we are completely dependent on our parents and react strongly to very big animals, employing them as parent symbols."[1] After this comes the infantile-parental phase, when we perceive smaller animals as symbolic child substitutes. At the other end is the post-parental phase, when animals again figure as child substitutes, followed last by the "senile phase" in which one feels a heightened concern for endangered animals:

> They have to be "saved." The symbolic equation involved here is obvious enough: the senile individual is about to become personally extinct and so employs rare animals as symbols of his own impending doom. His emotional concern to save them from extinction reflects his desire to extend his own survival.[2]

The popularity of animal-protection causes among younger people arose, he theorized, from heightened fear of nuclear incineration, "so that now we all have an emotional need for animals that can serve as rarity symbols."[3]

Doubtless there is some truth to Morris's purely evolutionary and psychoanalytical view that animals serve as symbols for us, and I hate to think what he'd make of my rabbit story. Animals certainly show up throughout our art and literature over the ages, representing everything from temptation to virility to dread to wronged innocence. In place of the imminent threat of human annihilation Morris posited, we might today, I suppose, substitute a widespread sense of estrangement from the natural world as a source of anxiety over "rarity symbols."

Missing, however, from Morris's view of "the naked ape" is man the creature of conscience, the ape who may every now and then catch a glimpse of things beyond his own physical and psychological needs. As in all such theories, Morris could find only scientific or aesthetic reasons to protect any creature or species, by means of "controlled cropping" and the like—the protection in both cases carried out for our own self-interest. I think he overlooked a phase: that empathy stage in our lives when we may begin to see even the commonest animals on their own terms, fellow creatures with their own needs to meet and hardships to bear, joined with us in the mystery of life and death—and frankly, for all of our more exalted endowments, not all that much less enlightened than the sagest of naked apes about the meaning of it all.

That kinship is to me reason enough to go about my own way in the world showing each one as much courtesy as I can, refraining from things that bring animals needless harm. They all seem to have enough dangers coming at them as it is. Whenever human beings with our loftier gifts and grander calling in the world can stop to think on their well-being, if only by withdrawing to let them be, it need not be a recognition of "rights." It is just a gracious thing, an act of clemency only more to our credit because the animals themselves cannot ask for it, or rebuke us when we transgress against them, or even repay our kindness. We are going to need a little mercy ourselves one day. The way I figure it, I cannot expect mercy if I am unwilling to give it.

I felt a similar sense of wonder—to share a less heartwarming story—when I was twelve or so and killed a bird. I was strolling along one day with our family dog when suddenly I heard a peeping noise. Looking over a bridge railing, I saw in the stream below a little robin splashing and flailing about. Just a fledgling, he was badly injured, bleeding from a severed wing and, as I assumed, not long for this world. Perhaps a cat had done it. The memory of what I did then still comes back to me sometimes. I lifted him from the stream and set him on an embankment, I tried to stroke him, I talked to him a bit, telling him how sorry I was for what I had to do, and then to end his misery I crushed him with a large rock.

The stone must have weighed twenty pounds. In the splatter I saw his little heart, and was horrified at the bluntness of what I had done, obliterating this beautiful tiny creature so finely made who tried so hard to live. At the time my action seemed the only alternative, as it often does when man brings his crushing force into an animal's world.

I have always seen pets from this angle of abject dependence upon the master's forbearance. The first pets were probably the young of our prey captured in the hunt and led back to camp, for not even those first bold slayers were immune to the bleats and whimpers of the orphans. Today, for many of us our last real link to the animal world, these pets still seem to me like ingratiating foreign visitors to our world (or, as they themselves often seem to think, foreign dignitaries), comically out of place, pretending to fit in, to be one of us, trying not to be found out and deported. I still laugh sometimes when I see dogs trotting purposefully around city streets, as if they really had any business at all being there in the middle of civilization, or zipping by in cars with their heads poking out the window in unbounded glee at the scents and the wind.

We are urged by some animal rights advocates to avoid such words as "pet," but I think pet is a perfectly worthy and honorable title, exactly right in capturing the creatures' utter reliance on our goodwill, and indeed their sheer, delightful uselessness to us apart from mutual affection. "Companion animal," the suggested alternative, has a slightly false ring, as if our dogs and cats, if the relationship wasn't working out, could go out into the world and set up for themselves somewhere else. That dependence and the trust it instills are the whole point, the fun of it.

Exactly what the world is like for a robin or rabbit or wolf or elephant or any animal we can only guess, a mystery that science may approach but never really grasp, like the mysteries of our own heart and mind. Those creatures given longer lives, such as the ape and elephant, do seem to have some sense of their own mortality, though to say they had an understanding of it would be a stretch. Surrounded everywhere by human achievement and progress, human striving and brilliance, our fellow creatures just go on as they always have, rarely looking beyond the day to take command of their fates, untroubled, so far as we know, by any of the deeper problems of existence and just as clueless about its deeper meanings. For animals, except in the starkest evolutionary terms, there is no such thing as history and no such thing as progress. Theirs is a world of fear and desire, equally raw, and for them whatever happiness life offers seems to lie in those intervals between danger when they can feed, play, or be at peace. We ourselves call these the creature comforts. It is part of their charm, this contentedness with the things of the moment, and how often do we look upon them and recognize something of ourselves.

Many scientists and philosophers still insist that such similarities are an illusion. In ascribing any conscious thought or emotion to an animal, we are guilty of "anthropomorphism," the attribution of exclusively human characteristics to animals. Even dogs, primates, and elephants, as author Stephen Budiansky contends in his study of animal intelligence, are programmed to "mimic" pain and enjoyment alike. Observing the unconscious neurophysiological reactions of animals to external stimuli, we are deceived, he believes, into supposing they actually had any thoughts or feelings at all. In the current jargon, it's all "hardwired," and the creatures themselves haven't the foggiest idea what's happening to them. Whatever pain they might display, argues Mr. Budiansky, a former nature writer for U.S. *News & World Report* and a defender of such practices as commercial whaling and elephant hunting, is "mere pain," not meaningful and profound like *our* pain, intriguing as a scientific matter but morally negligible.

If true, this would certainly simplify matters on the ethical end of dominion, for if there is no such thing as animal pain then there is no such thing as cruelty to animals. "The premise of animal 'rights,'" Mr. Budiansky argues,

> is that sentience is sentience, that an animal by virtue above all of its capacity to feel pain deserves equal consideration. But sentience is not sentience, and pain isn't even pain. Or, perhaps, following Daniel Dennett's distinction, we should say that pain is not the same as suffering. . . . Our ability to have thoughts about our experiences turns emotions into something far greater and sometimes far worse than mere pain. . . . Sadness, pity, sympathy, condolence, self-pity, ennui, woe, heartbreak, distress, worry, apprehension, dejection, grief, wistfulness, pensiveness, mournfulness, brooding, rue, regret, misery, despair—all express shades of the pain of sadness whose full meaning comes only from our ability to reflect on their meaning, not just their feeling. . . . Consciousness is a wonderful gift and a wonderful curse that, all the evidence suggests, is not in the realm of the sentient experiences of other creatures.[4]

Of course, this is the kind of theory a man advances in academic journals and conferences before going home at night to fall to the floor in joyful reunion with his own dog or cat. If we followed Mr. Budiansky around for a day, doubtless we would find him contradicting his own theory with every animal he encountered, bestowing pats and praise and scoldings and other tacit acknowledgments of conscious life in animals. We all do this. Anyone who in the light of day tried putting this theory of consciousness into practice—as some do, like the occasional monster caught torturing cats or burying live puppies in the backyard—would be shunned, reviled, and reported to the authorities.

The theory, in any case, goes back well beyond Professor Dennett, though the phrase "mere pain" could have come only from the modern behaviorist laboratory. C. S. Lewis in *The Problem of Pain* makes the similar point that animals experience "a succession of perceptions" but not "a perception of succession" to confer meaning upon suffering. Lewis adds, however: "How far up the scale such unconscious sentience may extend, I will not even guess. It is certainly difficult to suppose that the apes, the elephant, and the higher domestic animals have not, in some degree, a self or soul which connects experience and gives rise to rudimentary individuality."[5]

We might also ask how many of our own pains are felt on that grand, Shakespearean scale of tragic suffering that Mr. Budiansky describes. A kick in the shorts does not send a man into an existential crisis or exquisite agony of the soul. It just hurts, and like animals, we scream. When injured or abused, animals shriek, squeal, squawk, bark, growl, whinny, and whimper. Some shake, perspire, and lose breath when in danger. Others get listless and refuse food in abandonment and separation. For all we know, their pain may sometimes seem more immediate, blunt, arbitrary, and inescapable than ours. Walk through an animal shelter or slaughterhouse and you wonder if animal suffering might not at times be all the more terrifying and all-encompassing without benefit of the words and concepts that for us, after all, confer not only meaning but consolation. Whatever's going on inside their heads, it doesn't seem "mere" to them.

Never mind, too, how this bloodless theory goes against our own everyday assumptions about animals. The very industries clinging to such theories employ cats and dogs and chimps and so many other animals in laboratory tests of analgesics and surgeries, a useless exercise unless they experience physical pain comparable to ours. Likewise, no one who works with animals feels the least hesitation in making such statements as "That dog is happy," "This elephant is sad," "The chimp is bored," or "The horse is lonely." Part of the skill in tending and training animals is to understand precisely these emotions and each creature's particular disposition and personality, as witness the stablemates kept close at hand to soothe racehorses and to comfort sheep during their shearing.

On top of that, we have many statutes prohibiting cruelty to animals, lightly enforced yet reflecting a consensus that of course animals feel pain and, of course, it is wrong to needlessly harm them. The owner of the largest factory farm or animal laboratory, were he to accidentally step on his own dog or cat's tail, would wince and probably offer a verbal apology: "Sorry, boy!" No one needs language or some elaborate theory of consciousness to understand what internal feeling or thought those shrieks or yelps are conveying: "Ouch—that's my tail!"

The clearest evidence for animal emotion, noted by everyone who cares for a pet, without need of further data to back it up, is that many creatures dream. What more proof could we require that the dreamers have memory, feeling, and some sort of inner life? Perhaps, as I suspect, the dog we see stirring in his sleep is dreaming not only of past adventures and play but of things hoped for, of returns to haunts of old or reunions with companions long departed. This gets dismissed as "anecdotal" evidence, unscientific, mere speculation. No one who has seen a creature in its reveries or nightmares, however, has the least doubt about what's going on. Elephant calves, after seeing their mothers slain, have been observed waking up in convulsions, crying. Outside Jakarta a few years ago some thirty elephants surrounded two of their fellows caught in traps, standing guard over the pair for days and blocking any human approach, at risk to themselves.[6] We tend to discuss animals in the abstract, but the stakes are not at all abstract. Once such data about elephants, for example, are admitted into evidence, where would that leave the slayers in our moral estimation and treatment under law?

Jack London had a good sense of what their lives must be like, here describing human beings through the eyes of White Fang:

> In fashion distantly resembling the way men look upon the gods they create, so looked White Fang upon the man-animals before him. They were superior creatures, of a verity, gods. To his dim compre-

hension they were as much wonder-workers as gods are to men. They were creatures of mastery, possessing all manner of unknown and impossible potencies, overlords of the alive and not alive—making obey that which moved, imparting movement to that which did not move, and making life, sun-colored and biting life, to grow out of dead moss and wood. They were fire-makers! They were gods![7]

Such terrifying powers we possess, but what a sorry lot of gods some men are. And the worst of it is not the cruelty but the arrogance, the sheer hubris of those who bring only violence and fear into the animal world, as if it needed any more of either. Their lives entail enough frights and tribulations without the modern fire-makers, now armed with perfected, inescapable weapons, traipsing along for more fun and thrills at their expense even as so many of them die away. It is our fellow creatures' lot in the universe, the place assigned them in creation, to be completely at our mercy, the fiercest wolf or tiger defenseless against the most cowardly man. And to me it has always seemed not only ungenerous and shabby but a kind of supreme snobbery to deal cavalierly with them, as if their little share of the earth's happiness and grief were inconsequential, meaningless, beneath a man's attention, trumped by any and all designs he might have on them, however base, irrational, or wicked.

This credo in its way is far more subversive than anything to be found in the manifestos of environmentalism or animal rights, for it asks us not only to conserve and manage and protect the creatures, but to reserve a little bit of love for them too. When a man slays an elephant, or ensnares a wolf in his leg-hold traps, or loads his livestock in and out of trucks as if hauling trash, to call him merciless is a far graver accusation than to call him a violator of rights or squanderer of natural resources. He will take far greater offense at the charge, and he should.

For a snapshot of "the gods" in action today we need only turn from *White Fang* to the *Wall Street Journal.* You find similar stories in the newspapers on almost any given day. Something about this one captured the spirit I see at work in the world, the horrific combination of ancient cruelty and modern consumerism. It is not given to the creatures to be bystanders in our human affairs, especially our economic affairs. Run off, killed off, or fenced off in prosperous times by development and recreational hunting, in economic tribulation the animals are typically dealt with even more summarily.

In Indonesia, reports *Journal* correspondent Peter Waldman, once-protected zoos and wildlife refuges are being ransacked, even monkeys and tigers and Sumatran elephants sold off to exotic hunting ranches or food markets or laboratories:

> For foreigners on shore leave, the exotic delicacies are a steal in Indonesian currency. Takeout orders sail up by dinghy: One captain of a big tuna trawler orders a dozen young crested black macaques— an endangered species of primate—delivered to his boat, alive.
>
> The request is relayed over palm-studded hills to the village of Bingaguminan, on the edge of Tangkoko Nature Reserve. Trappers there trek days in the jungle refuge to bag the rare animals. To take baby macaques alive, mothers are shot.
>
> Aboard the trawler, galley hands bind the monkeys' hands and feet. Then, using sharp bamboo sticks, the Taiwanese puncture the babies' soft skulls. As the convulsions ebb, brains are served raw.[8]

There is really just one force on earth, save physical restraint, that could have stayed the captain's hand in this trawler scene. If we could have convinced him the monkey and its mother had rights, that wouldn't have done it. If we explained to him that this particular species of macaque is endangered, and may soon perish from the earth, and there are only a few hundred of the creatures left, and couldn't the captain maybe search the ship's galley for something else to tide him over—no, that would not have satisfied him either. Only conscience, perhaps only the fear of God Almighty, could make such a man draw back.

How many scenes like that unfold every day, unnoticed, unreported, all over our world? Even more bewildering, at the same time in our history many people are more solicitous than ever about animals and their well-being. While this monkey and his fellows are meeting their fate, for example, elsewhere other primates are communicating in sign language, thumbing through magazines, and astounding researchers with other endowments like elementary math and problem-solving skills. It is true, of course, that even these creatures we have all read about have a few eons of catching up to do, but something big is going on here, and it is clashing ever more violently with harsh practices still widespread in our world. There is a disjuncture here between understanding and application, the perceived and the permitted.

Until we address it in our laws, our debates over the protection of animals will grow only more bitter.

INTO YOUR HANDS

In a way, the euphemisms of cruelty do convey a certain blunt candor. They imply an acknowledgment, however obscured, that something has gone wrong. However adamantly we might care to defend certain practices, to press on requires a certain hardness, and it sounds more and more strained to describe the things we do and permit in the language of morality. That doesn't prevent many people from trying, from ascribing their every whim and pleasure gained at the expense of animals to the Divine Order. But theirs is a dominion only of power, with them and not God at the center, all grandeur and no grace.

How very different the spirit we find in those words where, in our Western tradition, dominion is first entrusted to mankind. Many people seem to remember only the "go forth and subdue" part, but, whether read as literal truth or enchanting allegory, no other passage has ever quite captured the drama of it all, the mystery we share with these other creatures, all of us called forth from the same darkness by the same Voice. "Into your hands are they delivered," says Genesis. Delivered alive. "And God formed man of the dust of the ground, and breathed into his nostrils the breath of life." Of that same dust came the creatures, breathing the breath of life. "Be fruitful and multiply." The animals are given the same instructions. "And God blessed them." The animals, too, were sent forth with a "blessing" of their own.

We have always felt the conflict. However much a man might relish his lordship over the beasts, few among us can ever quite shake the sense of empathy. To do so requires a special act of will, often followed by a special kind of regret. "I am a hunter," as we will hear General H. Norman Schwarzkopf say in the next chapter, addressing Safari Club International, "and I can either pull the trigger or choose not to pull the trigger. And I am never more a hunter than when I choose not to pull the trigger. I have an obligation to train myself to shoot straight and clean. I have an obligation to avoid inflicting suffering on that animal. And when I stand over that animal that I love so much, I shed a tear, and I don't know why."

Most of us know the feeling, though it makes us refrain from such pastimes altogether. Whatever abstraction of science or theology we apply to animals, we know they are not like us, and yet we know they are not just objects, either. And when we see them treated as nothing a part of us hurts with them, recoiling at their cries and attempts to escape. So, too, we often rejoice when we see one get away, escaping even the natural dangers of the wild into which all are born and by which all must perish.

"Only man," said Viktor Frankl, is capable of "noble suffering, suffering that you cannot be spared and cannot change. . . . No animal can do this. No animal can do anything like this. No animal can ask the question of whether its life has meaning or not. No animal is even capable of turning a predicament into an achievement—man alone. But if he does so, then he has reached the peak of whatever man is capable of."[9]

Of course this is true—though it is not true that for a life to have meaning that meaning must be understood. An animal cannot, so far as we know, transcend its suffering. A helpless elephant hunted by sharpshooters waiting by the water hole, a deer fleeing the hunter or dying on a highway, a pig or lamb or calf trapped amid the bedlam—they cannot draw meaning from their hardship, or find refuge in God, or pray for deliverance. That still leaves the *enduring* of it, the deprivation and fear and panic and loneliness. We know those feelings too.

The term *dominion* carries no insult to our fellow creatures. We were all sent forth into the world with different gifts and attributes. Their gifts, the ones their Creator intended for them, are good for many things—governing just isn't one of them. Someone has to assume dominion, and looking around the earth we seem to be the best candidates, exactly because we humans are infinitely superior in reason and alone capable of knowing justice under a dominion still greater than our own.

Some animal advocates are wary of religious terminology, sharing with the noted animal-liberation theorist Peter Singer a suspicion of any assumption that mankind may claim a singular place in the world with special authority. "The Bible tells us," writes Professor Singer, "that God made man in His own image. We may regard this as man making God in his own image."[10] Dominion, he believes, is the prime example of human selfishness cloaked in spiritual vanity—the wolf dressed not in the sheep's clothing, but in the shepherd's.

That surrenders far more ground than it gains, and from a strategic standpoint, at least here in America, it is worth noting that no moral cause ever got very far that could not speak to religious conviction, drawing on the deeper sensibilities that guide public opinion even in our more secular era. Here, if anywhere, the creatures actually have a case.

Serious and respectable people warned against cruelty to animals long before there was ever an animal rights cause. Usually they were the more religious-minded people, from Francis of Assisi to Moses Maimonides and others in the Jewish tradition. Today we tend to view it the other way around, the secular rights activists concerned about animals, and the more religious-minded folk standing guard over sound, sensible tradition and the moral wisdom of the ages. I was amazed to come upon this prayer from Saint Basil, the bishop of Caesarea, circa A.D. 375:

> Oh, God, enlarge within us the sense of fellowship with all living things, our brothers the animals to whom Thou gavest the earth in common with us. We remember with shame that in the past we have exercised the high dominion of man with ruthless cruelty so that the voice of the earth, which should have gone up to thee in song, has been a groan of travail.[11]

I once asked a friend who is prominently involved in the animal rights movement what it was that got him started. He said that from the time he was a child, he could not bear the thought of animal suffering, of the helplessness of any creature subjected to cruelty. He is not a religious fellow, traces his thinking on the subject to Peter Singer and other theorists, and shares with other rights activists a general skepticism of traditional religious ideas regarding animals. And yet that original motivation, that basic conviction common to so many people in the rights cause, perhaps runs deeper than any theory they might profess. Another age would have recognized in such feelings the signs of a vocation. It was never better expressed than by Saint Isaac the Syrian, a mystic writing in the seventh century. "What is a charitable heart?" he asks:

> It is a heart which is burning with love for the whole creation, for men, for the birds, for the beasts . . . for all creatures. He who has such a heart cannot see or call to mind a creature without his eyes being filled with tears by reason of the immense compassion which seizes his heart; a heart which is softened and can no longer bear to see or learn from others of any suffering, even the smallest pain

being inflicted upon a creature. That is why such a man never ceases to pray for the animals . . . moved by the infinite pity which reigns in the hearts of those who are becoming united with God.[12]

It is true that you have to look hard to find such passages in the history books and religious texts of old, yet find them you will. There is a long tradition of benevolence to animals lost on us today as we haggle over the rights and science of animal life.

Islam has its principle that "Whosoever is kind to the creatures is kind to Allah,"[13] and Buddhism its credo of "Peace to all beings," counting benevolence toward animals with tolerance, truthfulness, liberality, and purity among the virtues.[14] Plutarch, the first-century Greek philosopher, wrote of the farm animals of his day that "For the sake of a little flesh we deprive them of sun, of light, of the duration of life to which they are entitled by birth and being."[15] In Saint Thomas More's *Utopia* the slaughtering is left to the slaves in fear that when citizens do it "the practice of mercy, the finest feeling of our human nature, is gradually killed off."[16] Sport hunting in *Utopia* is forbidden as "unworthy of free men."[17] The Utopians "would not believe that the divine clemency delights in bloodshed and slaughter, seeing that it has imparted life to animate creatures that they might enjoy life."[18] Tolstoy in *Resurrection* envisions a world of people trapped in prisons of their own making, unable to see that "every man and every living creature has a sacred right to the gladness of springtime."[19]

John Wesley, the founder of Methodism, outdid them all, finding "a plausible objection against the justice of God, in suffering numberless creatures that had never sinned to be so severely punished." In his sermon "The General Deliverance," Wesley even wondered if some divine mercy might await mistreated animals on the other side: "But what does it answer to dwell upon this subject which we so imperfectly understand? It may enlarge our hearts towards these poor creatures to reflect that, vile as they may appear in our eyes, not a one of them is forgotten in the sight of our Father which is in heaven."[20] As late as a century ago we find Cardinal John Henry Newman, counted among Catholicism's great figures, asking:

Now what is it that moves our very hearts and sickens us so much at cruelty shown to poor brutes? . . . They have done us no harm and they have no power of resistance; it is the cowardice and tyranny of which they are the victims which make their sufferings so especially touching. Cruelty to animals is as if man did not love God. . . . There is something so very dreadful, so Satanic, in tormenting those who have never harmed us, who cannot defend themselves, who are utterly in our power.[21]

When did you last hear any Christian minister caution against cruelty to animals? It comes up about as often as graven images, even though animal welfare actually began, in both the United States and Britain, as the cause of nineteenth-century Christian reformers who founded the Royal Society for the Prevention of Cruelty to Animals and its American counterpart. Often they were the same people, such as William Wilberforce, Anglican priest Arthur Broome, Cardinal Henry Edward Manning, and Anthony Ashley Cooper, behind the abolition of slavery and child labor. "I was convinced," wrote Cooper, known as the Earl of Shaftesbury, "that God had called me to devote whatever advantages He might have bestowed upon me to the cause of the weak, the helpless, both man and beast, and those who had none to help them."[22]

Religious thinkers rightly caution against the ideas of theorists like Peter Singer. They might also ask themselves what alternative they profess—what their own standards are for the care of animals, and whether these standards are taught and applied. Our laws concerning animals are inconsistent and permissive. Behind these laws are religious and moral standards almost as empty. They are prescriptive, too seldom prohibitive. They are lofty generalities, admitting of easy and endless adaptation, so that, as we will see in the next chapter, even the commonest gut-shooter may today call himself a "Christian sportsman" without fear of correction.

The catechism of the Catholic Church declares, for example, that "Animals are God's creatures. He surrounds them with his providential care. By their mere existence they bless him and give him glory. Thus men owe them kindness. We should recall the gentleness with which saints like Saint Francis of Assisi or Saint Philip Neri treated animals."[23] The Creator, however,

entrusted animals to the stewardship of those whom he created in his image. Hence it is legitimate to use animals for food or clothing. They may be domesticated to help man in his work and leisure. Medical and scientific experimentation on animals, if it remains within reasonable limits, is a morally acceptable practice since it contributes to caring for or saving human lives.

It is contrary to human dignity to cause animals to suffer or die needlessly. It is likewise unworthy to spend money on them that should as a priority go to the relief of human misery. One can love animals; one should not direct to them the affection due only to persons.[24]

A lot there for everyone. But how to apply it in the particular? If, for example, it is legitimate to farm animals, is it also legitimate to factory-farm or genetically alter them for agricultural purposes? What are the limits? And what exactly are the reasonable limits to scientific experimentation? Where in Catholic teaching might we find them defined? Are these limits being observed, say, in the case of identical pain experiments done thousands of different times by thousands of different researchers? And where disregarded, is that a moral wrong? An evil? A sin?

Does hunting for sport or trophies or profit qualify as inflicting needless suffering? Are modern Western economies, with today's multibillion-dollar hunting industry, discharging this debt of kindness to animals? Are there moral wrongs being committed here, and if so why do they not warrant pastoral condemnation?

And finally, since *any* money we spend on animals could as a priority go to the relief of human misery, why isn't it always unworthy to spend money on animals? Yet if applied in earnest, how would this principle square with the preceding one declaring it is contrary to human dignity to cause animals to suffer and die needlessly?

That passage from the catechism is Catholic doctrine, almost in its entirety, on the matter of animal welfare, elaborated in the occasional papal statement like the quite powerful one quoted below. Absent specific prohibitions requiring specific judgments, anyone can find in the passage just what he or she wants to hear. It declares broad and worthy aims, and cautions against broad and unworthy errors, with none of the rigor one would expect of Catholic teaching on every other conceivable moral topic. *The Catholic Encyclopedia* does describe cruelty as sinful, at least "wanton" cruelty:

In imparting to the brute creation a sentient nature capable of suffering—a nature which the animal shares in common with our-

selves—God placed on our dominion over them a restriction which
does not exist with regard to our dominion over the non-sentient
world. We are bound to act towards them in a manner conformable
to their nature. We may lawfully use them for our reasonable wants
and welfare, even though such employment of them necessarily
inflicts pain upon them. But the wanton infliction of pain is not the
satisfaction of any reasonable need, and, being an outrage against
the Divinely established order, is therefore sinful.[25]

This is helpful. The great problem, however, is that while Catholic tradition and the tradition of every other major religion all deplore "wanton" cruelty, we define "wanton" rather loosely when we pause to define it at all. We
think too little about the "reasonable want" and "reasonable need" that distinguish necessary animal pain from needless, reckless, and willful conduct at
their expense.

The result, in the doctrines of so many churches, is an array of options
without obligations, two worlds often bearing no relation at all to one
another—as in a place described in Chapter 6, in North Carolina, where you
can find a factory farm, a captive hunting ranch, and a Baptist church literally
neighboring one another. For many Christians, there is this one world in
which man made in the image of God affirms the inherent goodness of animals, feeling himself the just and benevolent master. And then there is this
other world, the world of reality in which people and industries are left free to
do as they will without moral restraint or condemnation, without reproach or
even much in the way of self-reproach. There is the stirring world of "All
Creatures of Our God and King," the lyrics written by Saint Francis himself
and often sung by Catholics filing out of Mass. And then there is the world of
the Easter feast of lamb or ham or veal, to be enjoyed without the slightest
thought of the privation and misery the lamb or pig or calf endured at human
hands.

Doubtless one reason for this silence on the subject is that many minis-
ters detect in modern environmentalism and rights talk a hint of pagan
nature-worship, and avoid the subject altogether in fear of confusing the
flock. But even as a peripheral point to larger themes like pride, avarice, and
above all gluttony, one would expect that a proper regard for animals might
get more pastoral attention. Many Episcopal and Catholic churches have an
annual blessing of the animals on October 4, a tribute to Saint Francis and an

echo of the blessing bestowed on them in Genesis, but that's about it. Godly dominion may not be among our highest callings. But it is, at least in the Judeo-Christian tradition, our first calling. That fact alone might inspire a few more sermons.

I think of a fellow I know, in many respects devout and conscientious, who recently tried to shock me with a story about a laboratory (in Indiana, as I recall) where, to silence the yapping of some sixty dogs, the researchers cut out the vocal cords of each one. The dogs still try to bark, my colleague told me, as if relating some hilarious punch line, only it looks like someone has pressed the mute button, and now the scientists can go about their work in peace and quiet.

Where does this spirit come from, that can laugh at such a thing? It seems so contrary to everything else he believes. For him as for many other Christians, the rights cause with its more extravagant claims has become a convenient foil, a pretext for disregarding the subject of animal welfare altogether—as if they themselves had been muted. Ever fearful of threats to human dignity, many religious people today must examine more closely what, in practice, they are actually defending.

One may regard animal welfare as an entirely secondary matter. One may view the creatures as morally incidental, as soulless beings for whom no bell ever tolls and to whom one has no direct moral duties. What one may not do under the guise of religious principle is deny that we have at least certain basic obligations of kindness, and that these obligations impose limits on our own conduct that today are simply not being observed.

It is worth recalling as well the maxim that hypocrisy is the homage that vice pays to virtue. For even our inconsistencies in the care of animals may be taken as evidence that our hearts are in the right place, that we extend leniency where there seems room for leniency, as in the conspicuous case of the creatures we know best, our own pets. I recently came upon a touching instance of this on a Web site called "Brand of the Cross Ministries" for rodeo fans. "We believe it is God and not man who initiates ministry," says their credo. "We believe that God . . . calls us to 'ride for the brand' we belong to: the Brand of the Cross." If ever there were a completely gratuitous abuse of animals, and often baby animals at that, all done for the sheer thrill and bravado of it, it is rodeo. But at Brand of the Cross they are quite certain that God approves, Jesus the Cowpoke "right behind the bucking chutes" to guide and inspire. At the group's prayer site, however, there was this exchange:

DARLENE: I AM NOT HAPPY . . . my dog is being put to sleep. God didn't heal our dog. The vet is putting her to sleep because she is suffering. I am crying and I am sad FOR MY HUSBAND LOVED HER SO!!!!!!!!!!!!!!!

NORMA: I am so sorry that you have lost your beloved pet. I too had to have the only two dogs that I had put down, I know what it feels like. . . . I know both of my pets are in doggy heaven and romping around happily like they should be.

This leads to a discussion about canine immortality:

CAROL: Hi Darlene, I have been where you are. I had a beautiful Lab who died last year. He was fine one moment and the next he fell over and could not get up. I read Psalms and Proverbs to him all night until we could get him to a vet. He had to be put to sleep. Some of the ladies at our church were consoling me by telling me I would see him again. Our pastor said, he didn't want to shock us but there is no Biblical basis to believe that. One of the ladies drew herself up and said oh yes there is. God will wipe every tear from our eyes. Don't you think being reunited with a good and loyal companion qualifies. He said yes, it does. He stands corrected. Lean on the Lord for comfort.

CHRISTINE: I'm so sorry Darlene. Your dog has a place in heaven too. I [have] been there with my dog and it hurts but remember that you and your husband will see your friend again. God bless you!

I find this very beautiful, but the obvious question is why the Lord might care about one creature, this dog who died while Psalms were read, and not at all about others, like all those rodeo animals terrified and tormented while crowds cheer. Even Darlene's friends and the good pastor with their kind assurances assume that God cares about that creature only because she did, that *we* decide what God values and what he doesn't, where his mercies may extend and where not.

Suppose it is true, as many Christians have maintained (C. S. Lewis and Billy Graham among them), that when the Lord comes to collect his own a few exceptions might be made for those furry friends we loved and cared for in life. One would think this only further reason to spread our care as far and wide as possible, to be His instrument in a loving concern for all creation. Indeed, if human involvement is the deciding factor here, how strange to assume that He might care for those of His creatures who meet with human kindness but not for those who meet with human cruelty.

Studying our Bibles and other sacred writings, examining what dominion truly means and then comparing it to our actual conduct, is perhaps a belaboring of the obvious: Fallen man is abusing his powers. I make no claim, moreover, to being any sort of expert in scriptural exegeses, still less an exemplar of the Christian virtues, of which kindness to animals is just one. But these texts carry weight, expressing the fundamental principles and aspirations of our entire civilization. We turn to them for moral guidance in so many other ways, but so seldom in this matter. Many of today's cruelties come at the hands of people quick to identify themselves as good Christian folk. It is galling. If the exercise of examining the words of the Bible will at least spare us the sanctimonious airs of those who wantonly kill or mistreat animals, as if beckoned ever onward into field, forest, or factory farm by the Good Lord himself, that would be a small victory. It is time we inspected that original warrant to "subdue the earth" in both letter and spirit. "How is it possible," asked Malcolm Muggeridge, "to look for God and sing his praises while insulting and degrading his creatures? If, as I had thought, all lambs are the *Agnus Dei,* then to deprive them of light and the fields and their joyous frisking and the sky is the worst kind of blasphemy."[26]

PRACTICAL ETHICS

Animal advocates sometimes speak a language of liberation bearing little resemblance to the world that animals actually inhabit, or to our own world for that matter. Dogs and elephants and pigs are not just so many interest groups barking and trumpeting and grunting to have their demands met and liberation granted. Much as I admire anyone who bothers to take the matter seriously, some theorists, at least in their more abstract arguments, miss a crucial point by assuming that to be cared for a creature must somehow be made our equal, which isn't even true in our human affairs, where often those we love most are the weak and vulnerable.

The best known and most vilified of all liberation theorists is Peter Singer, known to critics as "Professor Death." An Australian appointed in 1999 to a prestigious chair on the faculty of Princeton University, he has become exhibit A in the case against animal-related causes. Here is a sample of the reasoning that earned Professor Singer his sobriquet, quoted from his book *Practical Ethics*:

> If the fetus does not have the same claim to live as a person, it appears that the newborn baby does not either, and the life of a newborn baby is of less value to it than the life of a pig, a dog, or a chimpanzee is to the nonhuman animal. . . . In thinking about this matter we should put aside feelings based on the small, helpless and— sometimes—cute appearances of human infants. . . . If we can put aside these emotionally moving but strictly irrelevant aspects of the killing of a baby we can see that the grounds for not killing persons do not apply to newborn infants.[27]

Let nobody fault Professor Singer for extravagant sentimentality. Although his 1975 manifesto *Animal Liberation* has been enormously influential in the modern debate over the status of animals, Professor Singer does not, as many critics assume, actually believe in or argue within a framework of rights. Today's animal rights cause owes more to philosophers Tom Regan, Mary Midgely, the Reverend Andrew Linzey, and others who argue, in a variety of ways, for the inherent moral worth of animals. For Professor Singer there is no such thing as inherent worth, leaving all moral claims to be weighed by a utilitarian calculus of pleasure and pain: Pleasure is the ultimate good defining existence. Humans and animals alike are capable of pleasure. Therefore, all creatures are equal in their right to existence. The general idea, writes Professor Singer, is "that the most obvious reason for valuing the life of a being capable of experiencing pleasure or pain is the pleasure it can experience."[28]

All sorts of things follow from this theory, including Professor Singer's contention that a baby, having not yet attained full self-awareness, may in good conscience be disposed of if this execution increases the sum total of pleasure on the parents' end. Handicapped babies, needless to say, do not add up to much in this moral arithmetic, nor do the comatose, terminally ill, or mentally retarded. Only if humans were uniquely spiritual beings would this change the math, and Professor Singer has ruled that out.

It doesn't even seem a wise theory given Professor Singer's own concern for animals. If no life, human or animal, has any inherent moral worth, then there are no moral absolutes to guide us in anything we do. If everything in the end is a contest for power, each species pitted against the other in an assertion of self-interest, guess who's always going to come out ahead?

I read *Animal Liberation* when it first came out, and even at age sixteen recognized in Professor Singer the combination of a good heart and an overly abstract turn of mind. My dog didn't care much for his theories either. Try as I might, I could not discern in his furry face any desire at all for Liberation. He just wanted to go for a walk around the lake once or twice a day and then come back with me, where our Total Sum of Pleasure lay in each other's companionship. We didn't worry much about Equality, either. And so it is with domesticated animals generally, who look to us only for creaturely respect and whatever scraps of love we have to offer. In fact it was Lucky who, among many other feats of valor, all by himself refuted utilitarian theory by climbing up a three-level staircase one unhappy evening—stairs he had not climbed for six months, all alone, unbidden, age fifteen, severely arthritic and soon to leave us—to come offer solace. I can still see that brown-and-white muzzle poking in through the door. He was putting my "right" to pleasure above his, and I still appreciate it.

The problem with such power theories is twofold: They are theories. And they are about power. Any time a modern intellectual goes down that road, we're in for trouble. "Mr. Singer," wrote Naomi Schaffer in the *Wall Street Journal,* "supports all forms of euthanasia, voluntary or not; abortion and infanticide; and rights for animals. And who decides which lives are pleasurable? Presumably people as enlightened as Mr. Singer."[29] "Presumably," added conservative columnist Don Feder of the *Boston Herald,* "one must be a bioethicist to see selfishness in parents who would spare their disabled child or in children who won't pull the plug on parents on life support":

> The two halves of Mr. Singer's philosophy (animal rights and the denial of rights to human "non-persons") are symmetrical—fewer people, more room for animals. As Los Angeles talk-show host Dennis Prager puts it, "Those who refuse to sacrifice animals for people will end up sacrificing people for animals." Mr. Singer proves Mr. Prager's thesis.[30]

I don't see it that way. I think that from both right and left, they are all bringing to fairly simple questions of human love and duty and kinship a preoccupation with human power. Professor Singer sees human power and he hates it. So he drags it into his bioethics lab and turns the terror back on man himself. Mr. Feder and Mr. Prager (a theologian) see human power and love it—a little too much. So with other conservatives they invent, as we'll see, unfeeling creatures and "generic beings" and false dilemmas, lest any animal get in the way of man's designs, caprices, or commercial aims. Fixated on power, they would all abuse power, in Professor Singer's case by killing off the two things that not only infants and unborn children but our fellow creatures, too, depend upon most in the human heart—reverence and mercy.

Such thinking is all of a piece, arising from the same impatient and imperious spirit affecting mankind's treatment of animals and of vulnerable, inconvenient human beings. Where animals are concerned, many of us follow a utilitarianism of our own that is almost as ruthless. A good description of this spirit in action comes from Pope John Paul II, who in a 1990 encyclical warns of a disordered relationship with the natural world:

> In his desire to have and to enjoy rather than to be and to grow, man consumes the resources of the earth and his own life in an excessive and disordered way. At the root of the senseless destruction of the natural environment lies an anthropological error, which unfortunately is widespread in our day. Man, who discovers his capacity to transform and in a certain sense create the world through his own work, forgets that this is always based on God's prior and original gift of the things that are. Man thinks that he can make arbitrary use of the earth, subjecting it without restraint to his will, as though it did not have its own requisites and a prior God-given purpose, which man can indeed develop but must not betray. Instead of carrying out his role as a cooperator with God in the work of creation, man sets himself up in place of God and thus ends up provoking a rebellion on the part of nature, which is more tyrannized than governed by him.[31]

Conservatives praise John Paul II for his moral stances against the trends of the day. They pay less attention when he turns his critique to the sins of capitalism, viewing it as a papal eccentricity to be indulged. Many would be surprised to hear his call to follow the example of Saint Francis, who "looked upon creation with the eyes of one who could recognize in it the marvelous work of the hand of God. His solicitous care, not only towards men, but also towards animals is a faithful echo of the love with which God in the beginning pronounced his 'fiat' which brought them into existence. We too are called to a similar attitude."[32] "It is necessary and urgent," said the pope in marking the eight-hundredth anniversary of the saint's passing, "that with the example of the little poor man of Assisi, one decides to abandon unadvisable forms of domination, the locking up of all creatures."[33]

Those who construct elaborate theories based on rights or liberation risk pulling animals out of the world where affection and creaturely goodwill are possible. People who deal harshly with animals, using them cruelly and cavalierly, pull them too far the other way, out of creation itself, as if our fellow creatures were just unfeeling raw material for commerce, human appetite, and will, to be assigned value only as we see fit, bereft of even the smallest measure of dignity or trace of their Maker's hand.

RECKLESS DIVINE CRUELTY

I suppose I am an unlikely friend to the animal advocates of our day in that I count myself a conservative, and conservatives tend to view the subject with suspicion. But the whole matter can also be understood within the conservative's own moral vocabulary of ordered liberty and abuse of power. Are many people prone to abusing their power over the natural world and its creatures? Of course they are. This certainly happens in human affairs when the powerful forget the source of and justification for their authority. The power is corrupted, the abuses multiply, the governed suffer.

Even the folks at People for the Ethical Treatment of Animals (PETA) and other such groups, so frequently derided for their solicitude for mink and pigs and chickens, are, as a practical matter, usually just pointing out obvious and rectifiable wrongs even if one does not accept their whole vision of the world. Nobody, least of all the conservative, should be shocked or offended to be told that we are abusing dominion, the first and greatest power given to man on earth. It would be shocking if we didn't abuse our power.

My brand of conservatism also brings with it a basic realism, accepting that there is a certain amount of suffering in the world beyond our power to avoid or spare, especially in the case of animals. C. S. Lewis thought animal pain a serious enough topic to give it a whole chapter in *The Problem of Pain*, noting the *"appearance* of reckless divine cruelty" since no animal, in any moral sense, can either deserve its suffering or be improved by it.[34]

It is likewise true that when we look out upon the natural world, "mercy" is hardly the first word that comes to mind. Most animals in their natural state are born precariously, live in perpetual danger, and often die in horrible ways. One recoils from the sight of human cruelties, but then again one recoils from many sights in the wild, the world of parasites and disease and death, of sick dolphins beaching themselves by the hundreds, of zebra dragged down by lions, wolves in pursuit of fawns, seal pups in the jaws of orcas. "Death by violence," as Theodore Roosevelt observed in his safari diary, "death by cold, death by starvation—these are the normal endings of the stately and beautiful creatures of the wilderness. The sentimentalists who prattle about the peaceful life of nature do not realize its utter mercilessness."[35]

The problem with this outlook is that it obscures our own singular capacity to make choices, for good or evil. It doesn't refute the demands of mercy, it renounces them, choosing instead violence and conquest and self-aggrandizement, like Roosevelt himself composing those very words during a lull in a full year of his life devoted only to killing. It sees in nature's violence an invitation to compound nature's violence. It is the outlook of men who can see terror and cruelty and malignancy everywhere—everywhere except in their own hearts.

Suffering in general is a mystery we live out with all temporal creatures, and is obviously beyond the aim or presumption of this book to explain. But gratuitous cruelty cannot take cover behind the fact of inevitable suffering. Skeptical readers may fault me many times over for sentimentality toward animals—typically, in my experience, the accusation of people defending their own sentimental attachment to one or another practice involving the use of animals. I never knew how deeply sentimental people could be until I saw Safari Club in action. Cruelty has its own rites, cherished lore, myths, and attachments. These attachments, far more than any needs of ecology or economics, are what drive those who fight attempts to improve the lot of animals in our world.

At times the whole debate over animal welfare strikes me as a clash not between reasoned arguments but between rival mythologies: animals as Victims, oppressed by Man, versus man the Conqueror, guided by God. Human beings tend to be sentimental about animals one way or another, if not in the delight and wonder of seeing them alive then in the ignoble rituals accompanying their torment and death. If it is a choice of myths, I'll take man as the Creature of Compassion. It is better to be sentimental about life.

For my part, any sentimentality I might bear toward my fellow creatures seems to arise from a realism about the very violence of the world that sport hunters and their kind are always citing as justification for bringing more violence into the world. More than any work of philosophy or holy book, I think it was good old Lucky who taught me, in his twilight months, to appreciate the beauty of animals, their dignity and vulnerability and the bond of mortality they share with us.

For me it was a simple moral step of extending that vision out into the world, for what are dogs but affable emissaries from the animal kingdom? Here, in this one creature, was a gift given to me and to my family, bringing so much life and happiness. What gifts they all are if our hearts are inclined in the right way and our vision to the right angle—seeing animals as they *are* apart from our designs upon them, as fellow creatures on their own terms, some glorious and mighty like the elephant, some fearful and lethal like the tiger, some joyful and gentle like the dolphin, some lowly and unprepossessing like the pig, but not a one of them, however removed from our exalted world, hidden from its Maker's sight.

One doesn't have to pull them from their place and demand perfect equality to care for them, to see in animals the moral dignity only man can perceive, and to refrain wherever possible from harming them, as only man the rational and moral creature can do. Here again this rhapsodizing about the beasts will be dismissed by some as fantasy. The truth is that realism doesn't come any harder to swallow, literally, than this. Go into the largest livestock operation, search out the darkest and tiniest stall or pen, single out the filthiest, most forlorn little lamb or pig or calf, and that is one of God's creatures you're looking at, morally indistinguishable from your beloved Fluffy or Frisky.

Talk like this in my conservative circles, and there's no surer way to bring conversation to a throat-clearing silence. For many of my friends it has the scent of Far Eastern mysticism, some eerie New Age creed alien to their own moral outlook, not a part of our own Western tradition. But if you want to get scriptural about it, that very same Bible always invoked for harsh dominion insistently calls mankind in just this spiritual direction, as in the post-Flood Second Covenant—right after the creatures are delivered into our hands— when we are told:

. . . I will establish my covenant with you; neither shall all flesh be cut off any more by the waters of a flood. . . . And God said, This is the token of the covenant which I make between me and you and every living creature that is with you, for perpetual generations. . . .

And it shall come to pass, when I bring a cloud over the earth, that the bow shall be seen in the cloud . . . and I will look upon it, that I may remember the everlasting covenant between God and every living creature of all flesh that is upon the earth.[36]

I don't know how much preachin' and teachin' I have heard over the years about all of the covenanting between God and man. I do not recall ever once hearing that our fellow creatures were included, too. Yet there it is. The whole "fear and dread" scene is an act of leniency toward man, with quite explicit reminders to extend that spirit of clemency all around. When He says "the fear of you and dread of you shall be upon every beast of the earth," it is not exactly our proudest moment and He is not bidding us to pursue that vision. The drama, an epoch of renewal unfolding even as the dove debuts as symbol of peace, comes in the context of a divine concession to our incorrigible weakness and taste for violence. Echoing throughout the Old Testament is a call to rapprochement, at least in our hearts—as when Hosea, pausing in his rebuke of Israel, reminds us of the restoration to come:

And in that day I will make a covenant for them with the beasts of the field, and with the fowls of heaven, and with the creeping things of the ground; and I will break the bow and the sword and the battle out of the earth, and will make them to lie down safely.

And I will betroth thee unto me forever; yea, I will betroth thee unto me in righteousness, and in justice, and in loving kindness, and in mercies.[37]

Isaiah, hardly the maudlin type, prophesizes that one day

The wolf shall also dwell with the lamb, and the leopard shall lie down with the kid; and the calf with the young lion and the fatling together; and a little child shall lead them.

And the cow and the bear shall feed; their young ones shall lie down together; and the lion shall eat straw like the ox. . . .

They shall not hurt nor destroy in all my holy mountain: for the earth shall be full of the knowledge of the Lord, as the waters cover the sea.[38]

Granted, that doesn't seem like one of Scripture's more practical sayings. The wolf and lion are going to need a lot of convincing. It's a mysterious image. So also are many other images in the Bible mysterious and wildly impractical, like beating swords into plowshares or loving both your neighbor and your enemy, or, when a man asks for your coat, giving him your cloak, too. That doesn't prevent us from seeing the general idea, which here as throughout the Bible would seem to be the way of peace toward man and beast alike, bringing closer the promised age when there is no more bloodshed and no more death. Why, when it comes to dominion, are we always stern literalists in the subduing parts and scornful skeptics in the peace-bringing parts?

THIS LOVELY WORLD

I debated long and hard with myself about whether to include farm animals in this book. Holding off on that topic for another day would certainly spare me a lot of trouble, and maybe even gain me a wider readership ("Oh, good, at least he's not one of *those* people"). It is always easy to stir up indignation in defense of dolphins and elephants and ill-treated dogs. Most everybody likes them. In the end, though, there is no avoiding the abattoir, to use the euphemism of choice, and to do so would be an act of selective abandonment—the very thing I am faulting others for. If there were ever forgotten "extras" in the background of our human story, here they are. I guess I am one of *those* people. I really do care about those creatures. I hope that after reading this book you might care too.

I think using animals for milk and wool and the like is perfectly acceptable provided they and their young are treated humanely, as they are on smaller farms. This is probably a good example of what Saint Francis (not himself, I should note, a strict vegetarian) meant by dominion as domestication, like pruning the tree to make it grow. Indeed such animals would never know life at all were it not for these small businesses.

That is not the way of the future, however. Our vast factory farms are the future. It is no one's favorite topic, a matter we prefer not to dwell upon, but I have a hunch that even before the farm crises of recent years most of us who live in the more developed parts of the world have paused now and then to reflect on the lot of farm animals, feeling a little sad that it has come to this even for these doomed ones. Already the sight of them grazing and sniffing and clucking about outdoors instills feelings of nostalgia. There was a time when these creatures rated a certain respect from those who reared them for slaughter—unsentimental, and yet shown in a minimal attentiveness to their needs. Gazing upon those long rows of sunless concrete and steel barns into which our farm animals are now disappearing, one doesn't have to accept the notion of animal rights to feel a sense of regret. We cringe when things go wrong at the farm and they all have to be shot, incinerated, and buried. But it is just as hard to watch when things are going right.

Giant livestock operations become unavoidable as human population grows and economic competition accelerates. Four companies now produce 81 percent of cows brought to market, 73 percent of sheep, half our chickens, and some 60 percent of hogs.[39] From these latter, the 355,000 pigs slaughtered every day in America, even the smallest of mercies have been withdrawn. In 1967 there were more than a million hog farms in the country; today there are about 114,000, all of them producing more, more, more to meet market demand.[40] About 80 million of the 95 million hogs slaughtered each year in America, according to the National Pork Producers Council, are intensively reared in mass-confinement farms, never once in their time on earth feeling soil or sunshine. Genetically designed by machines, inseminated by machines, fed by machines, monitored, herded, electrocuted, stabbed, cleaned, cut, and packaged by machines—themselves treated like machines "from birth to bacon"—these creatures, when eaten, have hardly ever been touched by human hands.

Take a few other numbers. Across the world agricultural production, including meat production, doubled between 1820 and 1920, doubled again between 1920 and 1950, again between 1950 and 1965, yet again between 1965 and 1975, and continues to grow exponentially. All of this, of course, to accommodate an increase in human population from about a billion in 1800 to 6.5 billion today. Farming at the same time has become more automated. Before World War II, 24 percent of the American population was employed in agriculture, as against 1.5 percent today. In 1940, one farm worker supplied every eleven consumers. Today it's one for every ninety.[41] Dennis Avery, a director of global food issues at the conservative Hudson Institute, lays out the big picture for pork:

With the Third World's rising incomes, the world's demand for pork is soaring. And, despite fervent hopes among environmentalists, there's no vegetarian trend in sight. Asia has already increased its pork consumption by 18 million tons in the 1990s, and its pork imports by 30 percent. The world currently has a stock of about 900 million hogs. By 2050, there are likely to be 2.5 billion hogs living somewhere. For the sake of the environment, we'd better hope those hogs are raised in big, efficient confinement systems.[42]

In America, says Mr. Avery, our total porcine population remains the same, but "we're producing 50 percent more meat per hog, partly because the hogs are becoming healthier and happier as more of them move indoors."[43] Elsewhere, in a commencement address to a new generation of agricultural scientists, Mr. Avery predicts a time when an annual three billion hogs will be needed to meet global demand, adding that of course mankind cannot possibly spare the land it would take to raise all of them outdoors.[44]

Economically, it makes such perfect sense. But think what he is saying here: Three billion of these creatures—"sociable, loving" animals, as one defender of modern farming admits[45]—locked up at any given moment, every pig condemned to the life of a veal calf. Eight million of them, slaughtered every day across the planet. That is an awful lot of pigs, an awful lot of killing. You would think such figures would make a man draw back, question a premise or two and ask where it all leads. Mr. Avery, like the industry he speaks for, displays no such doubts. And I wonder what his projections are for global pork demand still further into the future—say, for the year 2100. Sixteen million per day, out of five or six billion to be kept in confinement? Twenty million? What's the stopping point? How much misery, how much death, can we extract every day in the life of the world before it is enough?

For Mr. Avery it is a problem only of land use. And that's easily enough dealt with once we realize that pigs and other farm animals never really cared much for the outdoors anyway. Everything's going to work out very nicely for all concerned. We will get the meat we demand and the animals the confinement they prefer. Even the birds, he assures us, yearn for the warmth and security of our factory farms: "We are . . . told by urbanites, who don't raise livestock or poultry, that confinement feeding is cruel for the birds and animals, and bad for the environment. Yet birds and animals are more comfortable in confinement [and] grow faster on less feed."[46]

The short of it, even if we do not share Mr. Avery's excitement over "the greatest surge of meat and milk consumption ever seen,"[47] is that livestock agriculture is still being industrialized. This is an entirely rational and predictable economic stage, except that it involves a massive and deliberate disregard of animal suffering to which the same squeamish consumers demanding and buying all this meat are not fully reconciled. At our corporate farms they have accepted these severities, embraced them, cast aside all doubt, and they are counting on you to do the same. They know that the world has changed and farming will never be as it was. They know that providing meat for billions requires very different methods from providing meat for millions, and that today's factory farming is only the beginning. The reality is just this simple. Unless consumers rebel against factory farming, unless our personal choices condemn these cruelties and our laws forbid them, then in a generation or two people will no longer even speak of "factory farms" because there will be no other kind of farms from which to distinguish them.

These places are not only relevant to my argument, but front and center. Whenever we pause to think on animals and their lot, somewhere in the back of our minds are those afflicted creatures way off in the darkness of those factories. The question is a radical yet perfectly reasonable one at this point in the human story: Is all this *necessary* anymore? Is there no better way? Three quick news stories illustrate the point.

In January 1998, two pigs escaped from a slaughterhouse in Malmesbury, England. Soon all of Britain was following the drama, with sky-cam helicopters scouring over field and thicket in search of the fugitives. A reporter for Reuters picks up the story:

> Even after being cornered in a garden, "Sundance" refused to go quietly. It took eight persons and two dogs to bring him in. . . .
>
> The famous fugitives' escapade began eight days ago when they fled from a slaughterhouse by scuttling under a fence and swimming an icy river to freedom.
>
> The porkers' feats have saved their bacon. The two will be

spared the butcher's knife and will spend the rest of their days at an animal sanctuary. . . . [48]

You have to see the accompanying picture to really appreciate the story. I will be accused of projecting, here as elsewhere, but as one of the pigs is being handed over across a barbed-wire fence to the authorities—unaware he has been pardoned—you can see in the creature's hanging head the travail of the world. He thinks they're taking him back.

What I hate about that story is the jokey sentimentality accorded the animals, now an object of delighted amusement: They've been named "Butch Cassidy and the Sundance Pig," the reporters boast of "world oinksclusive" interviews, etc. What I love about the story is the thought of the two pigs arriving at the refuge, sleeping and snuffling and rooting around for a day or two until slowly, in some inarticulate way deep in their porcine hearts, it dawns on them: "We did it!"

A similar thing happened one morning in the fall of 1998 when some people in suburban Maryland woke to find a truck full of hogs parked in their neighborhood. One hundred seventy-one of them, four already dead from stress, in a single truck. No one could explain it. The driver just left the truck there. A local animal-rescue group, the Poplar Springs Animal Sanctuary, offered refuge, and after some grumbling from Hatfield Quality Meats, the Pennsylvania slaughterhouse to which they were being shipped from a North Carolina factory farm, the pigs were reprieved. Again the picture, appearing in the *Washington Times,* captured the moment: One of the pigs was being hosed down, cleansed of the filth and stench of the factory farm, unbearable for any creature. The sun was out, probably the first time he had ever felt it. He is leaning his face into the water, just lapping it in, the cool water. You can *feel* his relief.

The last story, again from late 1998, has the usual cutesy headline, "Pig, Soooie! Weeping Porker Rescues Mistress."

This is the story about a pig that won't ever grow up to be bacon.

Jo Ann Altsman of Pittsburgh, suffered a heart attack in the bedroom of her vacation trailer on Presque Isle in Erie, Pa. . . . "I was yelling [to neighbors], 'Somebody help me. Please help me. Call an ambulance,'" recalled Mrs. Altsman. . . .

"LuLu looked at my head. She made sounds like she was crying. You know, they cry big fat tears," she says.

The porker pulled herself together, and headed outside through the door and into the fenced-in yard. Never before had LuLu left the confines of the yard, except for a walk on her leash. She pushed open the gate and walked into the road. . . .

Witnesses told Mrs. Altsman that LuLu waited until a car approached and then walked onto the road and lay down in front of it. Several times she returned to Mrs. Altsman only to leave again and try to get help. . . .

Finally a motorist stopped for the prone pig and got out. LuLu knew just what to do. She led the man to the house and the rescue. . . . [49]

Here the pig has saved the woman, by her own account shedding tears and crying frantically at her call for help. Yet still they make those trite "porker-saves-his-bacon" cracks. What would the creature have to do before it's not all a big joke anymore—drive the ambulance herself, and wipe the tears away with a handkerchief? Probably even that wouldn't do it. We can write the headline ourselves: "Hog Hits the Highway, Sobbing Sow Saved from Scrapple."

I detect nervous laughter in these giddy little jokes one hears whenever some creeping thing has crept off the production line into the light of day, and a little bit of moral self-indulgence in these grand displays of clemency. Like America's annual presidential turkey pardon, like saving one calf from the death pits of England last year, they are the modern, inverted version of the animal sacrifice: We raise a live one up to the gods, and then kill all the rest. A similar rule obtains in today's wildlife "conservation" ethic: Save the species, liquidate the members.

The argument I will make in Chapter 7 is a familiar one—we have alternatives now and no longer need to subject these creatures to such misery. Here I am asking only why we take such delight in these occasional escape stories.

Why, for that matter, given our operative assumptions about the creatures, did the pigs escape at all, spotting the fence and making a run for it, instead of marching automaton-like forward under the shouting and prodding and momentum of the production line? Here is a creature, one little pig, who came into the world as livestock, wrung from creation in a vast godlike system of inscrutable darkness and clattering machinery infinitely beyond his understanding. Yet even he, who has never known the warmth of the sun and the breeze and the cool water, yearns for them. He liveth, yearning for the things of life. He was deprived of companionship, sunlight, a name, any concern whatsoever as a fellow creature, allowed only the breath of life until that, too, would be abruptly withdrawn. Then the moment came and he was herded out into the somber procession, poked with electric prods, hit, yelled at, driven toward the devilish clattering and godawful squealing, losing control of his bladder from the horror of it, everywhere around him the smell of death and panic and, as even an uncomprehending little pig or calf or lamb must feel it—utter damnation.

No, they cannot draw higher meanings from it all. But we live in that world of physical enduring, too, after all. They cannot know our world in all its complexity, grandeur, spiritual nuance, but we know *theirs,* we who live off these giant factories we cannot even bear to look at or see on film, today getting bigger and bigger as production rises and rises, and now abrim with waste and sewage flowing into our rivers and water supplies, so that just one 50,000-acre factory farm in Milford, Utah (owned by the Smithfield company we will visit in Chapter 6), produces every year 1.2 million hogs and more waste than greater metropolitan Los Angeles. Can glorious man peer into these places of stinking, nightmarish bedlam, down to the creatures that creepeth therein, into their brutish hearts to grasp their suffering? Not only can we grasp it—it is our own worst nightmare.

Likewise, the delight we take in these escapes reflects our own deepest yearnings for deliverance. That reaction comes from the best thing in us. Of course we feel happy for them. They are spared. Now they can live. Now they can feel the sun and the cool water and the breeze and freedom and fellowship with their kind. Spiritual grandeur always brings with it the risk of spiritual snobbery, treating those less endowed as nothing. But what would *we* most yearn for if we were locked away in dark little pens and stalls and ignored or shouted at and treated like garbage? I for one would yearn most for the sun and the cool water and the breeze and freedom and fellowship with my kind. I would yearn to be seen, feeling that if only others saw me they would try to help. A few of us would emerge from the tribulation to compose great masterpieces of poetry and music and inspirational literature, something man alone can pull from the extremities of suffering. For myself, I would just want the whiff of Dachau out of my nostrils and relish again the simple things and rejoice in having my life and freedom back again. That strikes me as kinship enough with my fellow creatures, and reason enough to spare them the travail.

And frankly, even if they are all doomed, their suffering unavoidable, their bleats and squeals and whimpers unnoted even in heaven, I only love them more. But I think that their cries are noted. As we often remind ourselves in other contexts, His ways are not our ways. There is, as the old hymn goes, a wideness in God's mercy greater than the mind of man. And who among us is so imbued with divine wisdom as to be certain that His mercy cannot reach down even to them? Here, more than anywhere, the animals can teach us a lesson in humility. Take man in all his glory, man in all his brilliance and power and conquests, and what are we to Him but what they are to us?

The escape story reminded me of *Charlotte's Web* by E. B. White. Children's books often have a profound realism to them—the reason so many sport hunters have been sneering at *Bambi* these past sixty years, because the story (the book at least) in its simple depiction of life and death in the woods is an enduring indictment of perverse and gratuitous pleasures. So too *Charlotte's Web* captures something about the lives of animals, the fears and contentments and flashes of happiness available even to them. It's the scene where Charlotte, the spider, is bidding farewell to Wilbur, the pig she saved from the butcher shop, telling her bereaved friend to go on without her, to live and savor his days on earth:

> These autumn days will shorten and grow cold. The leaves will shake loose from the trees and fall. Christmas will come, then the snows of winter. You will live to enjoy the beauty of the frozen world. . . . Winter will pass, the days will lengthen, the ice will melt in the pasture pond. The song sparrow will return and sing, the frogs will awake, the warm wind will blow again. All these sights and sounds and smells will be yours to enjoy, Wilbur—this lovely world, these precious days.[50]

Lest I be accused of making too much of a children's tale, consider a memorable image from real life. The novelist Stephen Crane toured a coal mine near Scranton, Pennsylvania, in 1894, describing the condition of the men and boys who labored there, enduring the heat and noise and risks of explosions and methane gas, and also of the mules used to pull the coal and slurry. The animals were kept in the mine for years at a time, such was the effort involved in dragging them back, appearing to Crane in the dark gloom like "giant rats":

> Usually when brought to the surface, the mules tremble at the earth radiant in the sunshine. Later, they almost go mad with fantastic joy. The full splendor of the heavens, the grass, the trees, the breezes, breaks upon them suddenly. They caper and career with extravagant mulish glee. A miner told me of a mule that had spent some delirious months upon the surface after years of labor in the mines. Finally the time came when he was to be taken back. But the memory of a black existence was upon him; he knew that gaping mouth that threatened to swallow him. No cudgellings could induce him. The men held conventions and discussed plans to budge that mule. The celebrated quality of obstinacy in him won him liberty to gambol clumsily about on the surface.[51]

There is nothing fanciful here. It is hard realism, facing facts about suffering both human and animal. Whenever any animal is locked away, or treated cruelly, or hunted or trapped, that is what we are taking away, the grass and trees and breezes and the sun. Whenever we reach down in mercy to spare one, as only we can do, that is the gift we are giving back, and what a beautiful gift it is.

TASTY NIBBLES

Such matters are rarely debated in the open, but it does happen. One memorable exchange took place a few years ago on the floor of the British House of Commons, perhaps the first time that the ethics of meat consumption in the industrial age has ever been disputed in such a forum. In 1999, the United Kingdom banned fur farming throughout the realm, effective in January 2002. "The Government," declared Minister for Agriculture Elliot Morley, "believes it is wrong for animals to be farmed and slaughtered for their fur. It is not consistent with a proper value and respect for animal life."[52] There was no debate about whether animals stuffed into tiny cages and killed by gassing or electrocution actually suffer. Indeed it was a Conservative MP, Alan Clark, who challenged a fellow Tory's use of the word "harvesting" in describing the fate of the animals. "In describing the killing process," said Mr. Clark, concurring with the preceding speaker,

> will he also express his contempt, which is widely shared, for the euphemism that was deployed by my right honorable Friend the member for Teignbridge when the mask slipped for one minute and he referred to 'harvesting,' which is an ad man's euphemism for the process that the right honorable Gentleman has described? What is interesting is that that term conceals the innate guilt and distaste that is felt by everyone who is associated with the process.[53]

Debate turned to rabbits, leaving Maria Eagle, the Labour member for Liverpool and sponsor of the bill, to rebut conservative opponents demanding to know why, if fur farming is to be abolished as needless cruelty for the sake of a luxury garment, the law should not then go further to ban the farming of animals for luxury food items. Why is it wrong to raise animals for fur, asked David Maclean, a Conservative MP, yet morally acceptable to raise the identical animal, in identical conditions, for food?

> MR. MACLEAN: I suggest that, if rabbits are currently being farmed in cages that are no doubt suitable and appropriate, providing the right conditions, they can also be farmed safely for fur. What is the moral difference? Certainly there cannot be a welfare difference. Angora rabbit must surely enjoy the same welfare conditions as an identical rabbit.
>
> MS. EAGLE: Does the right honorable Gentleman recall the Second Reading debate, when I tried, as the promoter of the Bill, to make it plain that I did not wish to include rabbit?
>
> MR. MACLEAN: The honorable Lady may not wish to include rabbits. The Bill does not include the ordinary or common garden rabbit, of which there are millions too many. It does not include pet rabbits because they are not usually farmed for their fur. However, if people get into the business of farming Angora rabbits solely for their fur, will they be covered by the Bill?

MS. EAGLE: [Indicated assent.]

MR. MACLEAN: The right honorable Lady indicates that those people will be. If it is her view and that of the Government that Angora rabbits that are kept in cages will be banned because they are being farmed primarily for the value of their fur, will someone please tell me the moral, ethical and welfare difference between Angora rabbits in a cage that are bred for their fur, which is 60 percent of the profit, and other members of the family that have a different name and are of slightly different style, which are being bred for their meat and whose fur is worth only 49 percent of the profit per rabbit? The animal with the slightly more expensive fur is banned and the other is not. . . .

MS. EAGLE: Just to clarify the point, I hope that I have not been inconsistent. The point that I have been trying to make is that I see a difference . . . between keeping animals in intensively farmed conditions for food, which is a necessary part of life, and for adornment, which is not necessary. I accept that the right honorable Gentlemen do not think that that is a sufficiently large difference to matter, but I do.

MR. MACLEAN: I am grateful to the honorable Lady and I respect her view. She sees an ethical distinction between rabbits in a 2-feet-square cage that are reared for expensive titbits in restaurants and those other rabbits.

Rabbit is not a staple diet of the British population. The last time I had rabbit was downstairs in the Churchill Room of this building as an expensive starter. It is not an essential requirement of life. However, I do not see the distinction between keeping rabbits in a 2-feet-square, or a 1.5-meter-square cage—whatever the size is; I will not bore the House with the figures—merely so that we can have them as tasty nibbles in the Churchill Room of the House of Commons, and keeping other rabbits, identical in almost everything but their covering, in the same size of cages, fed and watered the same way to the same welfare standards. The latter would be illegal and liable to a 20,000-pound fine because we have determined that those rabbits are being kept purely for the adornment of women, or men. I see that, in the latest fashions, men are into fur as well. If the honorable Member for

Garston takes that view, I can equally say that the bit of rabbit that people eat is not essential to our lifestyle either, as we have ample food supplies of all other types available.[54]

Of course Mr. Maclean's logic is flawless. And of course he is right that Ms. Eagle's reasoning is inconsistent. If subjecting a rabbit to misery for the sake of sartorial vanity is morally indefensible, so is the same treatment indefensible for the sake of one's little morsels down in the Churchill Room. He sees the arbitrariness of it, but for him that is further reason to leave things alone, whereas for her it is reason to extend the scope of human compassion. Mr. Maclean's argument amounts to this: As long as we're going to be arbitrary about it, better to be arbitrarily cruel rather than arbitrarily compassionate.

Nor, obviously, are rabbits alone at issue. Once we have asked whether it is cruel and unnecessary to raise rabbits for food, the next question is what about lambs and pigs and so on, each creature in turn. This is just the kind of logic people fear in the agenda of animal rights, rarely noticing how it works just as relentlessly the other way: If we can raise chickens and other fowl like so much produce, with little or no regard to their miseries, why not also pigs and cows? If pigs, cows, and other sentient mammals can be treated as nothing, why not also wildlife—deer and tigers and elephants? What standard is left to limit our claims on any animal?

It fell in the end to MP Mike Hancock, a Liberal Democrat for Portsmouth South, to reply, delivering as fine a defense of the animals as they have ever received in any modern legislature. It is a model of grace and clarity, of reason and compassion working as one, and ought to be preserved somewhere outside of *Hansard,* so allow me to quote him at length. The Dispatch Box to which Mr. Hancock refers is a red leather briefcase, symbolic of Britain's economic might, that sits in Parliament next to the royal scepter:

The first argument [against the bill] is that the measure is an infringement of the individual's right to conduct business and that fur farmers are law abiding. The response to that is that people do not have the right to do lots of things that are considered inhumane. For that reason alone, there is reason—it is time—for the decision to be taken.

We have progressed as a society and become more intolerant of many inhumane practices, which are legion. Over the past hundred years or so, we have successfully passed laws to end many of those practices. Our attempt to ban fur farming, once and for all, is the latest example of the progress that we are trying to make. . . .

The four key arguments leveled against the Bill are easily and remarkably quickly dispatched. Sadly, it is a lot quicker to dispose of them than to dispose of the animals that those people continue to torture.

The dimensions of the cages in which the animals are held are not much larger than the Dispatch Box. Do advocates of fur farming honestly believe that those are the proper conditions in which to keep any animal—especially an animal that should develop and flourish—for any longer than a few minutes? . . .

I cannot believe that even the most hardhearted honorable Member would want to go home and tell his or her children that he or she is in favor of animals—100,000 of them every year in the United Kingdom—being caged in such conditions for long periods, simply so that they can be put to death and more than 1,000 fur coats can be made, so that people can prance around feeling that they look a little more attractive than they might in a man-made alternative. It is not reasonable for the House to allow the trade to continue.

The consequences of our vanity are all around us. For centuries, we have used and abused animals to satisfy our own vanity. But there is no excuse for us to continue exercising that right, if it is a right. . . . It cannot be right, and must not be thought to be right, to allow animals to be so mistreated and abused.[55]

"A preposterous impertinence," wrote Mark Daniels of the *Western Morning News*. The bill was further evidence of New Labour's "blend of Puritanism, urban ignorance of the realities of country life, autocracy and envy."[56] A mere thirteen licensed fur farms remained in England, critics noted, raising at most a hundred thousand animals per year, and what would become of these businesses? One Tory MP suggested the farmers might even take their case to the European Union's human rights commission on the grounds of being unjustly denied their livelihoods. Owen Patterson, MP for North Shropshire, rose to note the absurdity of banning domestic fur farming when furriers abroad in Europe would simply increase production and import their furs into England: "In Denmark and Holland they will be laughing all the way to the bank."[57]

In what other area of moral concern would the fact that *others* are doing the same thing be held out as reason to continue the practice in one's own country? Doubtless in Denmark and Holland they once talked about British furriers laughing all the way to the bank, which now, at least, they can no longer do. Such arguments are just an extension of the same kind of reasoning, permitting the worst cruelties to serve as our standard and tradition to stand as its own justification. Mr. Patterson, Mr. Daniels, and Mr. Maclean cannot even bring themselves to consider the matter as a moral question at all, something to be decided on its own merits and according to the moral claims of the animals themselves. It all seems like perfect nonsense to them. They have more important matters in mind, the great and enduring values of the ages, timeless moral goods like fur coats and tasty nibbles.

Traditions can ennoble us, or they can enslave us, leaving human beings a little too comfortable and settled in our ways. Traditions can be changed and replaced with better ways that in time become traditions themselves, as witness that very bill Mr. Hancock and the others were debating in Parliament. "Lifetime peers," as reports described the scene, "sat swathed in fur-trimmed scarlet robes as Queen Elizabeth II read out the government's legislative program."[58] I find the language of the bill very touching, the full majesty of the law here reaching down even to those afflicted creatures huddled in their cages, just as the merciful judgment that every human being will need must come in a way and from a place as far from our understanding as the halls of Westminster are to them:

> BE IT ENACTED by the Queen's most Excellent Majesty, by and with the advice and consent of the Lords Spiritual and Temporal, and by the Commons, in this present Parliament assembled, and by authority of the same: It shall be an offense for any person to keep or knowingly cause or permit to be kept for production of fur any mink, fox, or other fur-bearing animal.[59]

That is now the law of England, and yet somehow or other the kingdom has actually survived.

℮

As reforms come about in the care of animals, it will be the doing of people like Mike Hancock, who speak not in the language of some alien ideology or liberation movement, but in the simplest terms of reason and common decency we all understand. One can empathize with the men and families and rural communities for so long dependent on raising or trapping fur animals. They have never known anything else, and to be told that change is coming is alarming and galling. But what happens, what changes, if one accepts that attitude? Nothing ever changes at all. Everything is pushed off, closed to debate and moral inquiry. That alone is usually a telling sign—anger and resentment at the "impertinence" of merely raising the subject.

We can challenge farming practices today without passing judgment on the whole of human experience, just as we can reflect on the hardships of mules in the coal mines of another time without faulting the miners. Once, men like those miners had no choice except to use the mules, dragging them down into the heavenless pit—and yet even then, as Crane describes, giving them a break sometimes, feeling for them as comrades in toil and misery. One needn't condemn the practice. How could you? Hard necessity demanded it. It is part of the story, the animals' and ours, and both good and ill came of it.

Now, in the more developed world, the mule is free at least of that assignment. His services are no longer needed. So too have many other animals served us well over the ages. It was the use of livestock that first freed us from the chase, allowed man to settle and civilize himself, slowly rendering the hunter a useless and ever more ridiculous figure engaged in what the name itself, "game," implies. Meat and dairy products undeniably furnished a wide array of protein sources, like the soybean today as we discover its many uses and superior protein value. It was the labor of the mule and the horse and the ox and the elephant that allowed man to turn his energies to greater work, building his earthly life over the ages up from savage squalor to the world we live in today. It was the fur-bearer whose pelt shielded us from the elements, the oil of the whale that lighted our lamps, the ivory of the elephant and bones and antlers of other animals that gave us tools and adornments. And so on through the story of civilization, leaving today, in many cases, only customs and habits and industries surviving on the momentum of vanished necessity. For ages people needed furs to survive in the severe elements we faced. Women who today keep the fur industry thriving, in order to be seen swathed in mink on a 60-degree December evening in Beverly Hills, or in Manhattan making the harsh winter trek from Saks to Tiffany's, do not have the same excuse.

When substitute products are found, with each creature in turn, responsible dominion calls for a reprieve. The warrant expires. The divine mandate is used up. What were once "necessary evils" become just evils. Laws protecting animals from mistreatment, abuse, and exploitation are not a moral luxury or sentimental afterthought to be shrugged off. They are a serious moral obligation, only clearer in the more developed parts of the world where we cannot plead poverty. Man, guided by the very light of reason and ethics that was his claim to dominion in the first place, should in the generations to come have the good grace to repay his debts, step back wherever possible and leave the creatures be, off to live out the lives designed for them, with all the beauty and sights and smells and warm winds, and all the natural hardships, dangers, and violence too.

If we take Isaiah at his word, maybe the moment prophesied is arriving, an unexpected turn in our human story, not an onerous moral demand but a wonderful moral opportunity. Perhaps we are getting uneasy about our mistreatment of animals because we should be uneasy about it. Maybe we wonder about these practices because we are supposed to be wondering about them. There comes a time when the service is no longer needed, and the master, if he is just, will turn to the suffering creatures in his dominion, from the mink to the pig to the elephant to the great leviathan, and say, "Dismissed."

I understand the staggering complexities of reforming our treatment of animals, though the "conservation" imperatives where wildlife are concerned are wildly exaggerated. Here I only put to you one simple proposition about the animals we raise for fur and flesh. If, in a given situation, we have it in our power either to leave the creature there in his dark pen or let him out into the sun and breeze and feed him and let him play and sleep and cavort with his fellows—for me it's an easy call. Give him a break. Let him go. Let him enjoy his fleeting time on earth, and stop bringing his kind into the world solely to suffer and die. It doesn't seem like much to us, the creatures' little lives of grazing and capering and raising their young and fleeing natural predators. Yet it is the life given them, not by breeder but by Creator. It is all they have. It is their part in the story, a beautiful part beyond the understanding of man, and who is anyone to treat it lightly? Nothing to us—but for them it is the world.

The economic complexities? The world is complex no matter how you arrange it. Take one impulse, your hankering for a hot dog. Multiply it a hundred million times over and follow the lines as they meet in Utah at that 50,000-acre facility, housing all those hogs never once allowed outside. That is the complex world one craving creates. Most people can't even face the details behind it.

Now take another impulse, your compassion for a fellow creature. Multiply that a hundred million times over and see where it leads. It is a world and an economy employing just as many people now called to produce the substitute products. In all the complexities required by change, that world you can at least look at without cringing. Indeed, if Genesis is any guide, it bears a much closer resemblance to the world meant for *us*. In those pre-Fall days, after all, animals were off the Garden menu:

> And God blessed them, and God said unto them, Be fruitful, and multiply, and replenish the earth, and subdue it: and have dominion over the fish of the sea, and over the fowl of the air, and over every living thing that moveth upon the earth.[60]

In the very next breath man is told to keep his mitts off the critters (and vice versa) and be content with the herbs and the fruit of the trees:

> And God said, Behold, I have given you every herb bearing seed, which is upon the face of all the earth, and every tree, in which is the fruit of a tree yielding fruit; to you it shall be for meat.[61]

If any passage in Scripture lends credibility to the writers, it is this, for of course they were not themselves vegetarians. The alternative vision must simply have seemed inconceivable—a world in which it actually pleased our Maker to see His creatures stalking and slaying and absorbing one another. The Catholic "meatless Friday" as a sign of penance, purity, and peace came to us (via a papal boost to the fishing industry, with the Friday of course symbolizing something else) from this same idea of predation as a consequence of the Fall and corruption of the world, as does the "grace" before meals. Indeed there was a time when Christians fasted from animal products throughout all forty days of Lent, a form of self-denial still found among the orthodox and matched in Islam by the prohibition on killing game while on pilgrimage. Certain Jewish dietary laws, such as the prohibition against mixing milk with flesh—in effect basting the animal in the milk of his or her mother—carry a similar sense of meat as bearing the stain of violence and needing sanctification.

The next step seems obvious to me. If sanctity is the goal, and flesh-eating a mark of the Fall, the one is to be sought and the other to be avoided. Why just *say* grace when you can show it? Maybe, in the grand scheme of things, the life of a pig or cow or fowl of the air isn't worth much. But if it's the Grand Scheme we are going by, just what is a plate of bacon or veal worth? The skeptical reader can write me off as misguided, if not mad. I am betting that in the Book of Life "He had mercy on the creatures" is going to count for more than "He ate well." The Reverend Andrew Linzey, a profound writer on the subject, puts it this way: "Whatever the difficulties in conceiving of a world without predation, to intensify and heighten—without any ethical necessity—the parasitical forces in our world is to plunge creation further into that darkness from which the Christian hope is that we shall all, human and animal, be liberated."[62]

Whenever we are called to decide the fate of an animal, the realism comes in at least facing up to the price of things whenever man with all his powers enters the picture. It requires discernment and care and humility before Creation. It means understanding that habits are not always needs, traditions are not eternal laws, and the fur salon, kitchen table, or Churchill Room are not the center of the moral universe. It means seeing "the things that are" before we come marching along with our infinite agenda of appetites and designs and theories, and not covering it up with phony science or theological niceties or the unforgiving imperatives of tradition or economics or conservation.

But man *is* a part of nature, say the furriers and factory farmers and hunters and whalers, and so on down the line. Man belongs here too, playing a crucial and perfectly natural role in ecology. I'll leave that question for later, except to point out that we cannot have it both ways. We cannot stand proudly above nature—man the creature of reason and conscience—while using the violence and predation of nature as our moral example, and that in defense of customs and commercial products most of us now freely admit are no longer needed.

A further problem with this "They do it too" line of reasoning is that we, unlike any animal, have both unlimited appetites and unlimited means to pursue them. We have steel-jaw traps, guns, grenade-tipped harpoons, industrial trawlers and drift nets stretching miles, and an ever-expanding array of technology with which to search and destroy. Against these, the creatures stand utterly defenseless.

Realism is seeing reality. And the two hardest realities are life and death. We share with animals in the fellowship of both, and there never was a better reason to be kind and merciful than the leveling death which will find us all. "For that which befalleth the sons of men befalleth beasts. Even one thing befalleth them: as the one dieth, so the other; yea, they have all one breath; so that a man hath no pre-eminence above a beast: for all is vanity. All go unto one place; all are of the dust, and all turn to dust again."[63]

And now away from the lofty realm of moral speculation and theory to see how dominion is actually practiced. If you are looking for the noblest impulses in the human heart, Safari Club International is not the best place to start. But if you would understand the world that many of our fellow creatures actually inhabit today, the place to be is Reno, Nevada.

God of my fathers, Lord of mercy, you . . . have made all things by your
word, and in your wisdom have formed man to have dominion over the
creatures you have made, and rule the world in holiness and justice.

WISDOM 9:1–3

It all depends on your budget," says Johnny Vivier. "Everyone's got a budget.
You want an elephant, we can get you one. You want lion or buffalo, that's
easy. We had a guy who came up here and bought two rhino at $35,000 a
rhino. Didn't even ask the price. He just said 'I'll take two rhino.' Look, we're
not salesmen. We're professional hunters. You tell us what you want."

Johnny owns and operates Johnny Vivier Safaris, one of eleven hundred
hunting, guide, and outfitter concessions here in January 1999 for the twenty-
seventh annual convention of Safari Club International (SCI), the world's
largest gathering of the trade. We're standing at his booth in the Reno-Sparks
convention center in Nevada. South Africans in their mid-thirties, he and
wife Bev have been in the business thirteen years. Bev works another
prospective customer, one of five or six thousand Safari Club members
milling around the 370,000-square-foot facility, as I tell Johnny thanks but no
rhino for me, not in the budget, let me take a brochure and think it over. "Elephant, then. We've got some fine ones. Big tuskers. Eighty inches." The big
tuskers run at $10,500 apiece.

Over at Trophy Adventures, an outfitter based in Washington State,
rhino are going for a song. Not just plain old rhino, either, but "Gold Medal-

lion Rhino." I am craning over the shoulders of two other conventioneers looking at the trophy pictures. Proprietor Skip Clemens assumes we're all together: "That's the best deal in the room you're looking at. You guys got your rhino yet? They just included it in this year's Big Five, you know. You get that and you got your Grand Slam. You shoot 'em at close range. And the thing is, they don't go right down. They get up. And now they're pissed."

Africa over the last few decades has witnessed a mysterious disappearance of rhinos. Market forces have responded with the "Rhino Dart Hunt." You can still hunt them for keeps in Zimbabwe for $23,000 and up. Skip's got a "Big Five Special" there: rhino, elephant, leopard, lion, and buffalo. Here in this particular South African game park, you don't get to keep your rhino—just really piss 'em off. You sedate the rhino from a jeep, hit fifth gear, hover a bit, then during his unscheduled nap rush up for some posing, measuring, and high fives. "It counts," says Skip. "You get just as many Gold Medal points." The cost of this excursion is $6,500.

A crowd has formed around the booth of Qwatali Productions, where the proprietor has just flipped *With Deadly Intent* into the VCR. Qwatali is a mail-order sportsmen's video company out of Delaware, Ohio, competing here with some five or six rivals with total annual sales in the millions. *With Deadly Intent* is from "The Classics" series, a big-tusker trilogy including *Elephant Trails* and *Double-Barreled Zambezi Adventure*. Following professional hunter Johan Calitz, says the dust jacket, "You're right there to see four dramatic brain shots. See how the searing .500 Nitro Express stops a raging bull's charge at 10 steps."

The video begins with Johan and company whispering to each other in the jeep. Through an opening in the trees, some 75 yards away, we see the elephants. The herd is agitated. Two females are bookending a calf. The bull turns to face us. He charges and then stops, flapping his ears. He trumpets again and again, as the crowd thickens at Qwatali. The standoff lasts 20 seconds or so. Johan has seen this before and doesn't move an inch. Then the action starts, Johan wildly narrating the whole thing for us, something like "Here he comes! Now! Now! I got him! He's still coming!" He seems to hesitate, almost stopping, just before the first shot. The second one staggers him yet he keeps coming. Johan has his back to the jeep when he takes the third and fourth brain shots. The last drops the elephant in a scene of dust and mayhem and jubilation and little calf trumpets from the herd in the background.

This costs $29.95, or you can get The Classics set for $89.95.

Skins and Bones

These booths, manned by more than three thousand guides and outfitters serving the 13,554 naked apes attending the convention, run in eighteen rows, each about sixty yards long. Stuffed deer, caribou, zebra, wildebeest, elk, eland, dik-dik, kudu, and impala are everywhere, some displayed in prone positions as if caught or being devoured by the stuffed leopards, hyenas, and cougars. Stuffed rabbits and fawns are stuffed into the mouths of stuffed wolves. A stuffed baboon at the Boskoppie Game Reserve & Lodge sports a ranger hat and little "Game Warden" uniform complete with badge. A lifeless moose is fighting off two lifeless wolves, little blood-painted bits of its limbs already in their jaws. An elephant head hangs from the rafters over row 12, "Elephant Walk." An aisle over are perched two stuffed specimens of *haliaetus leucocephalus*: the American bald eagle. At the center of the hall towers a giant grizzly, "Stalker of the North," his mighty claws extended forward as if sleepwalking.

These are just the full-sized trophies, and in three days I only got as far as row 14. There are unnumbered heads, tails, teeth, paws, skins, bones, horns, tusks, and sets of antlers. At the Skins and Bones boutique, a Houston firm specializing in curios and trinkets, a giraffe-skin day planner goes for $189, a zebra-skin purse for $149, impala-skin gun cases for $249, giraffe rugs for a few hundred, golf bags crafted of silver and finest Cape buffalo hide for a grand and up.

Thousands of birds are placed anywhere and everywhere like little household knickknacks one hardly knows what to do with—on counters to greet customers, as centerpieces on the roundtables where deals are struck and checks cut, as doorstops, bookends, paperweights. If all the stuffed ducks, geese, pheasants, and doves suddenly sprang back to life, feathers would fill the convention hall as if some mass pillow fight had broken out.

A few of the grizzly's arctic kin have joined us from the northland wild. Congress in 1998 lifted a ban on the import of polar bear trophies from Canada. This is one of several legislative victories Safari Club is celebrating here. These bears—one identified as Canadian—wasted no time in coming to Reno to mark the occasion. "Yes, it is legal to import Polar Bear into the United States from Canada," says Ameri-cana Expeditions, Inc. "All our Polar Bear hunts occur in the areas where you can take your Polar Bear home after acquiring your import permit from U.S. Fish & Wildlife."

Your bruin costs $20,000. Down at D&H Safaris they've got a "polar bear special"—$12,000. In both cases you pay up front, and the money, in the standard proviso of guides and outfitters, is "nonrefundable in cases of animals wounded or lost." Adventures Northwest, a Canadian outfitter, will do it for $19,500—satisfaction guaranteed. Borne onward by a dog team, guided by local Inuit tribesmen, you'll track that bear down for as long as it takes. "Extra hunting days can be arranged 'on the spot.'" If you're on a tight schedule, Adventures Northwest will charter a two-seat Piper Supercub plane to and from the Inuit village—in the shorthand of Safari Club, a "same-day airborne."

Bow hunters are welcome, too, says the brochure. While bows are less reliable in arctic conditions, this presents few problems as "it is extremely unlikely that a wounded polar bear would ever be lost, but it could happen if there was open water nearly and the wounded bear succeeded in getting to it and swimming away." That's when the dog pack comes in handy: "When the bear is in sight and it looks as if it might escape into open water or rough ice, the dogs are cut loose so that they can bring the bear to bay. The hunter and his guide have to follow quickly."[1] Very quickly, or you will be taking home one sorry-looking trophy. The frenzied hounds want a piece of the action too.

Ameri-cana is cutting-edge, on the newly legalized polar bear front and in the growing field of big-game archery. There are sixty or so firms here specializing in bows. A seminar on the subject covered the finer points of effecting maximum internal hemorrhaging. ("Remember," explained archer Gary McDonald, "we don't kill an animal with shock; we kill it with bleeding.") "Imagine," beckons Ameri-cana's brochure, "hunting in an area that has been archery-only for the last 12 years and the professional hunters are all avid bow hunters and know what it takes to provide a quality archery hunt." They are talking about African big game. Not only are you going to get your Big Five— by God you're gonna take 'em with a bow. Here, too, no fear of wounds, escapes, and losses. It is a private, secluded, fenced-in archer's paradise.

Down at Tanzania Safaris they're talking about the art of "cat baiting." There are competing schools of thought. A hunter at Nolte Safaris, dismissing conventional wisdom, asks why bother killing an impala for bait when "dog food" will do the trick. At Tallgrass Safaris of Tanzania they actually describe baiting techniques in the brochure: "Baiting for the big cats is one of the most exciting parts of a good safari. The haunch of a buffalo or zebra hung in a tree at the proper height will almost always produce a lion."

At New Zealand Wildlife Safaris they're discussing the challenge of hunting sheep by helicopter. Climb aboard the chopper with Kulu Hunting Company of Magadan, Russia, and you can shoot at brown bear ($11,000) and rare snow sheep ($14,900). Another service here will transport the creatures themselves by helicopter. They are bought from other ranches or from circuses and zoos and airlifted into game parks to be shot.

Norzaim Bush Tracks of Zimbabwe is designing a package to meet the needs of a client wondering what his chances might be of taking big game with a pistol: "Well, pistol shooting is illegal—but we could make a plan. Like, if it's in a competition, we could make it happen, for one day maybe in certain areas."

At Jeff Neal, Inc., of Tulsa, Oklahoma, a female customer worries that elephant hunting might be too dangerous. "You can just put a bag of peanuts out the window," a guide explains. "Actually, you can shoot from the car if you want to." With Atcheson's Hunting you can hunt an elephant "from horseback or even from the backs of trained elephants!" These trained elephants are the calves orphaned and captured in previous hunts. Atcheson's employs Namibian hunting guides, gifted, their brochure says, with "a Teutonic flair for organization," as witness the construction of fences and a "rancher-developed water supply" that brings the game into range without fail.

At Berlin Game Ranch Safaris the Teutonic touch is evident in a full-color picture of a slain giraffe. The creature lies on his stomach and folded legs, the neck forming an arch off to the side, providing an elbow rest for the posing hunter, a woman. The dangers she braved are best captured in the brochure of Borton's Overseas, offering purely photographic safaris at a place called Rothschild Manor: "Kenya's Rothschild giraffe were moved to the grounds and now, years later, offspring still remain as the focus of the manor. Don't be surprised if a giraffe pokes its head in for breakfast!"

Nimrod Safaris of Namibia invites you to its private 60,000-acre spread in the Kalahari "with game fencing for those who do not mind ranch hunting." Plenty of "the big stuff" here, including giraffe at $1,850, which you can take by rifle or bow: "Everything Is Lined Up: All We Need Is You."

Now showing at Alaska's Glacier Guides, Inc., *Silent Stalkers of the North*, filmed from behind two men whispering just before dispatching a grizzly bear, who is seen alone in a grassy field munching on something, then running away at the first shot, then doing a complete flip on the momentum of his gallop when the third shot brings him down.

In the Reno-Sparks lunchroom, eight or nine hundred people are settling in for drinks on the house while perusing the day's offerings. The bar is open and the afternoon auction has begun.

TAKE CHARGE

"Good evening, ladies and gentlemen, and now it's time to buy some diamonds!"

Our emcee for the first evening's banquet is a professional announcer whose cheerful voice and manner recall Bob Eubanks of *Dating Game* fame. As he opens the diamond sale, the Grand Ballroom of the Reno Hilton goes dark and spotlights follow a dozen sparkly sirens, showgirls on loan from the hotel cabaret, performing some sort of willowy swan dance as they disperse into the crowd bearing treasures. "Diamonds are Forever" is playing in the background. A banner over the stage declares "Take Charge"—this year's convention slogan. Next year's theme is "Thundering into the Millennium."

The girls, beckoned here and there for a sale, slowly reunite on the stage, joining the stuffed lion and buffalo. Gazing across the ballroom from 23 feet up is a stuffed giraffe on sentry duty to the left of the stage. He has journeyed here from someone's private collection. The beauty of it, Safari Club's Dave Coldwell explains to me, is that "old Joe Schmo sitting over there at his table can point up and say to his friends, 'Hey, that's my giraffe.'"

When the diamond dance is over, the nightly auction will begin. There is a day auction, running from noon to six, and an evening auction from ten to midnight. Up for grabs are wild animals from around the world donated by owners and lessors of the reserves and game parks in which those animals live, along with jewelry, nature paintings, and other donated goods. Earlier this evening we heard from Pennsylvania governor Tom Ridge—a Republican, as most Safari Club members seem to be—and before his speech some tunes from the Oak Ridge Boys. Only about sixteen hundred people are here tonight. The big events are tomorrow night's speech by retired general H. Norman Schwarzkopf and Saturday's keynote address from former American president George Bush.

Ridge, a Medal of Valor–winning infantry sergeant in Vietnam, is here to accept Safari Club's "Governor of the Year" award. He seems to represent the larger of two categories of hunter. There are the ones who can afford the faraway expeditions year after year, carting home rhino, elephants, giraffes, and—the must-have item of late—Argali ram from remotest China at

$26,000 per rack. Not many of these hunting high rollers live in rural Pennsylvania, nor do they fit easily into any of the usual sociological slots.

And then there are the hunters that Duane Allen of the Oak Ridge Boys probably had in mind when he thanked "all you fine folks at Safari Club" before going to "American Made." No $20,000 brooches, $90,000 rifles, or $35,000 rhinos for them. They just want a deer or two every season, maybe an elk or a bear too. Their fathers and grandfathers hunted, they're teaching the kids to hunt, hunting's fun, a part of life, and that's just the way it is. Most of them would probably look with contempt on someone shooting game, for example, from a helicopter.

The divisions aren't always so clear, though, at least not here. At Safari Club it seems to be a difference in cash flow. I chatted at my banquet table with a retired pipe fitter from Idaho named Wilbur. He once played minor-league ball with Stan Musial and was incredulous about the recent auction of Mark McGwire's seventieth home-run ball for $3 million. "The guy's got more money than sense." I agreed. But then, in the next breath, here's old Wilbur himself talking about his life's ambition to bring home the Big Five, which is going to run him a hundred grand at least unless he wins tonight's "Hunt of a Lifetime" raffle offering a Big Five safari ("varmints included")—the proceeds, at $250 a ticket, going to Safari Club's PAC. They had sold 740 tickets when I inquired about it.

"I was in Africa last year," Wilbur tells me, "and they kept trying to get me to take a giraffe. But I wouldn't do it. The Big Five—that's what I'm after. Just never been interested in giraffe myself. Where's the challenge in it? I guess some people want 'em for rugs, but it's too easy. But hey, if that's what they want. It's all in what a person wants."

He seemed like a nice guy, and joked that his wife had spent the afternoon in the convention hall "putting me in the poorhouse." The men here are in no position to gripe, however. The average Safari Club member owns eleven rifles, six shotguns, five handguns, and a bow. He spends $14,000 a year on hunting, compared to $1,500 for the average American hunter, for an annual half a billion dollars spent by the entire membership. Two-thirds hunt more than twenty-six days a year, and a quarter of them more than fifty days, typically in fenced ranches and game parks. Half of them, like Wilbur, have hunted in Africa at least once. Over 50 percent of members report an annual income exceeding $100,000, as against 6 percent of hunters nationwide.[2]

Probably what unites all hunters here from all classes and backgrounds is

Wilbur's conviction that it all comes down to what a person wants. You want a deer, that's fine, and if it's giraffe or elephant a man wants, and he's got the money, why then that's fine too. The important thing is not to let a lot of outsiders start laying restrictions on things. Then you're fiddling with basic rights, above all the constitutional right to firearms, as the National Rifle Association is here to remind us at its booth. Nothing unites like a common enemy, and they've all got one here: Give an inch to the enviros and Bambi lovers, all those urban types who know little about firearms and even less about wildlife, and it won't end there. It won't end with elephants or giraffes or the Big Five or wolves in Arizona or bison near Yellowstone. Before long it'll be deer. If anyone in this convention hall feels uneasy about any display, they keep it to themselves. Here, the mildest qualm or fugitive doubt is heresy. Let them take away our helicopters and next it'll be our guns.

A curious angle here. This touchiness about the sport has lately led many hunters to search for higher ground, to ultimate meanings and spiritual self-justification. The result is a mix of feel-good moral relativism, infomercial-type self-empowerment, and half-baked mysticism resembling the sort of "deep ecology" literature they scoff at. For sale here, and later to be recommended to us by General Schwarzkopf, is a 1995 book, *In Defense of Hunting,* by James A. Swan. "A truly spiritual person," writes Swan, "does not judge others if they are following an honest path of the heart, and among those paths of the spirit there is that of the hunter."

> "And what about the poor animals?" the critics of hunting scream. Anyone can declare an animal to be special, even sacred. But a thing can become truly sacred only if a person knows in his or her heart that the object or creature can somehow serve as a conduit to a realm of existence that transcends the temporal. If hunting can be a path to spirit, unhindered by guilt, then nature has a way of making sure that hunters feel compassion.[3]

Like, wow, is that deep or what? Things are "sacred" only when the hunter in his heart has made them so. The wanting of something confers validity. The creature becomes a "conduit" to the transcendent. Guilt now becomes a *hindrance* to compassion, which is achieved in the very act of killing, and so on further up into holy realms unattainable, one assumes, to the non-hunter. I kill, therefore I am. Elsewhere Mr. Swan informs us that to abstain from venison "is to deny our nature" and biochemistry:

> I am like the cougar; I need to eat meat. I once tried a vegetarian diet for nearly a year; the East Indian holy man I was studying with at the time told me to stop, because it was running against my nature and making me ill. He was right. I was having trouble sleeping and felt weak. Within a week after returning to my [venison] diet, my symptoms were nearly gone.[4]

So hunting is not only a path to the sacred—it is a health imperative. Mr. Swan also describes hunting, during three hundred pages of scattershot self-justification, as an outlet for repressed anger, "a spiritual act of love," "a great teacher of love," a grim conservation duty, "an obsession," a test of manhood, a source of "self-esteem," a patriotic obligation, a "numinous" experience, "a path to self-actualization," a family unifier, a quest for enlightenment, a form of therapy, "a primal energy" force, an inhibitor to aging, an antidote to urban "alienation," a factor in keeping down violent crime—etc. "Like his predecessors," Mr. Swan explains,

> the modern hunter hunts for meaning, to express himself as a member of the human race. . . . The experience of hunting is so special, so different from most other aspects of life today, and so filled with what Jung called "the numinous," that hunting really must ultimately be seen as a spiritual practice by those who sincerely follow the spirit of the hunt. When you participate in someone's home and he offers you a wild game meal, know that you are participating in a sacrament.[5]

I knew that "venison" and "veneration" come from a common root, but this is still an awful lot of baggage to lay on one deer. It is the sort of eco-deep-think that Schwarzkopf, Wilbur, and probably Swan himself would recognize as incoherent drivel were they to encounter it as a defense of any other practice. Indeed, a booklet by one Tom DeWeese given to us at the Safari Club prayer breakfast warns against "The Pagan Roots of Environmentalism," tracing everything from the United Nations to the Endangered Species Act to "New Age religions that include deep ecology, eco-feminism and the worship of Gaia—Mother Earth."[6] The New Age conspiracy may be worse than Mr. DeWeese imagines: It has come to Reno, where guns offer not just sport and sustenance but spiritual affirmation; where "conservation" has replaced good works; where the Big Five has become a kind of Trinity, and racks, horns, and tusks are the holy relics.

The typical American hunter, in any case, never goes to Africa—or to Reno or Las Vegas, for that matter, to shell out hundreds of dollars for a Safari Club convention. Pennsylvania, says Governor Ridge, "issued over a million hunting and fishing licenses last year, contributing $2 billion to the Pennsylvania economy." We must safeguard that right and "pass on that tradition to future generations." This is a sacred right and solemn conservation duty, for here and the world over "what we're really doing with our license fees is building those animals a better home." Hunting, "as Theodore Roosevelt said, 'is one more chance to be a boy.' We live in a complicated age, full of pressures and demands, and there are few things more enriching and peaceful than being with friends in the glory of God's creation. Let us have the youth and strength to pursue our great adventures and to 'be like boys again.'" He leaves us with reflections on the joy of seeing his children picking up their first bows, and a touching story of helping to rescue an orphaned bear cub, though just how the cub was orphaned we never learn.

FAIR CHASE

Day two at the convention began with a post-breakfast *Death on the Run: The Greatest Buffalo Charge Ever Filmed*. Watch this video, and you won't need your morning coffee.

He's in standoff position in the thick of some brush. He's surrounded, snorting, staring. A professional hunter narrates each shot. The second levels him. "He's down! We got him! Unbelievable!" But no, he's up again! He lunges with a final snort. Two more shots, and he falls in a big black dying heap. Looks like a hundred-pointer. The tape is brought out for exact measurements.

For the uninitiated, let me explain this business of point sizes and "Gold Medallions" and "Grand Slams." They've got these contests at Safari Club. Founded in 1972 by trophyman C. J. McElroy just as trophy hunting around the world was waning, the entire 32,000-member club could itself be herded into the convention center with room to spare for all the stuffed animals. Yet already they have compiled *The Official Record Book of Trophy Animals,* a

Manhattan directory–sized volume—yours for just $195—in which are immortalized the exploits of winners in some twenty-nine categories of achievement and hundreds of subcategories. (A companion volume, *Trophy Rooms of the World,* goes for $100, and I am told features the room of one determined fellow who got himself an entire orca.)

Each category is based on species. There is the Bears of the World Grand Slam, for instance. To achieve this the hunter must bring home an Alaska brown bear, a grizzly, a Eurasian brown bear, and a polar bear. An African Big Five Grand Slam requires an elephant, a rhinoceros, a Cape buffalo, a lion, and a leopard. Within each grand-slam category are still more distinctions and honors conferred according to weight, tusk length, horn size, fur color and quality, and so on.

A still loftier realm of human aspiration is the "Inner Circle." Entry is gained according to sheer volume, raw numbers, and even within the Inner Circle are ascending circles winding up to the summit. First comes the "Copper Level"—requiring some seven or eight different species. Next is Bronze—another dozen species of trophy animals. Next, Silver—ten creatures from ten species. Then Gold—a dozen more trophy animals. Finally, Diamond Level. By then you will have slain a minimum of seventy-six creatures. Now you must go forth and subdue eighteen different species of Asian and African animals such as black wildebeest and fallow deer.

By the time you have attained all of Safari Club's awards in all categories, collecting that most coveted honor of all, the "Crowning Achievement Award," you will have extinguished the minimum-required 322 animals. One fellow who picked up this year's "Intercontinental Award" "already has 369 species." It is work, and they don't give prizes for all the wounded ones left along the way.

This year's Crowning Achiever was one Marvin Hill, Sr., of Texas, a one-man forest fire who did us proud in every category. After much fanfare, a drumroll, and Oscars-type buildup running late into evening, darkness falls on the banquet room and we see a video narrative of the victor's life and triumphs. Then, filmed in a quiet moment in his trophy room, surrounded by these monuments to his life on earth, Mr. Hill describes the vision that has kept him going all these years, never wearying, never quitting. To "harvest" these animals is "such a privilege," and let us never forget that. "We need to teach *respect* for animals. We need to be *responsible.* Contribute to wildlife—don't take too much. Don't *waste* them. Don't take more than you need."

As he searches for words, the camera withdraws to wider angle, revealing above and around Mr. Hill the full dimensions of his trophy room: a shag-carpeted hell of dead animals. The lights come on, and to a standing ovation he comes forward to accept the prestigious "Bronze Buffalo," as I believe it was called. (They give trophies for trophies at Safari Club.) Is he done yet? Ready to pack it in, call it a career? Not for one damn minute: Safari Club, he reminds us, has lately made some inroads in Mexican trophy hunting, now restricted, and when those game ranches and parks open up Marvin Hill, Sr., won't be far behind. "Maybe one day, if we can dream big enough, we'll be able to harvest those spectacular cats in South America."

With 503 different awards and citations to be presented this year, it seems like everybody's being honored for something except me. Winners in other categories deserve brief mention. Lois Sharboneau has claimed "South Pacific—Estate-Taken" honors with a canned wapiti, a large deer. Lois looks like a good bet for next year's "Diana the Huntress Award." Rex Baker has wrapped up his Silver in the "Ibex of the World" division—this on top of his "African Big Five," "Gazelles of the World," "African 29," and Grand Slam in wild sheep. That puts Rex at the "Fourth Pinnacle of Achievement."

Wade Boggs, the future baseball Hall of Famer, got himself a Diamond Grand Slam; wife Debbie was not far behind with her "Top Ten Award." Wade, at this rate, might wind up in Safari Club's own pantheon. (I forgot to mention they also have a "Hunters Hall of Fame.") Skipping on through the awards program (eighteen pages, ten in small print), Anne Dodgson snatched Bronze in "Chamois of the World" as husband William Dodgson V reached for the Gold in Africa. Gabriela Bankmann is dominating the "Wild Pigs and Peccaries of the World" division, and Bob Lee—"with a trophy collection of 140-plus record-class animals from 17 African countries"—walked away with this year's "McElroy." For "his 11 Grand Slams, 273 hunts on six continents, and 369 species" one Wayne Picius was enshrined in the Hall of Fame. The 1998 "Diana Award" went to Barbara Sackman of Pennsylvania in recognition of her 116 entries in *The Official Record Book of Trophy Animals*.

Assume an annual average take of ten animals per SCI member, the Hills and Piciuses with their ten or fifteen kills in a good year picking up slack for the idlers with their three or four. Multiply that by 32,000. A safe guess would put the total yearly kill by Safari Club alone at over 300,000. But oddly enough, even with all those charging buffalo and Silent Stalkers and "monster moose" and close-call brain shots, you don't hear of many casualties. In fact, none. No moments of silence for Safari Clubsmen lost in action since the last convention. No memorials. No collections taken up for the wounded or widowed. Not even any special prizes or plaques named for those lost to the unforgiving wilds. If there were ever a single fallen hero at Safari Club, I'm betting they'd have an award named for him.

So that's why racks and horns are everything back at the convention center. The fascination and scorekeeping extends even to water buffalo. Rhino and elephant—now that, from a certain angle, even the uninitiated can grasp. Harder to figure is the hushed reverence, the unbounded rapture, occasioned by the humble buffalo.

"Once you've shot a buffalo, it's like a disease," explains professional hunter Clint Taylor of Kibuko Hunting Safaris. "You've got to come back and shoot another." What kind of rack points are we talking at Kibuko? "Oh, we've got some fine buffalo for you. See that one over there?" He directs a little red laser dot to a poster-sized photo of himself and a client posing with an ex-buffalo. "He was forty-eight and two-thirds inches. But he goes down in the book as a hundred."

In the book, you multiply by two and round the number out at the top. How close can we get? "See that one over there? He was shot from ten feet. That close. You come there seven days, you'll get a buffalo. I'll see to it. I'll get you there."

The tone of it all is not easily captured. One thinks of adolescents whispering and giggling over a *Penthouse.* Or the crazed concentration of a video arcade. You get the feeling that the animals are merely extras in a deeper psychodrama, capable of drawing even serious people like Schwarzkopf under its trance, some sort of ass-backward coming-of-age rite that, as Governor Ridge puts it, makes boys of men. Nature, in this holy rite, is transformed into an endless theme park, and the creatures into so many animatronic figures ingeniously designed to jump and flee and fall for the giddy delight of the boys.

Sometimes the psychodrama takes an introspective turn, and we get dark, tormented soliloquies such as this from one George N. Wallace in a collection called *A Hunter's Heart: Honest Essays on Blood Sport,* here wrestling with the question of how to kill mercifully without marring one's trophy. Mr. Wallace is sitting beside a dying elk. "If elk could scream," he reflects, the woods would have fewer hunters. I thought, 'I've never shot an elk this big; what a trophy. If I shoot him in the head, I'll ruin that mount. My God, man, he's suffering, shoot him. No! To hell with the trophy, you're just like the hunters you despise.'[7]

Time passes while Mr. Wallace ponders his dilemma, until, at last,

I shot him at the base of the brain. He quivered, looking ahead wide-eyed, straining, then slowly all the life force slid from those eyes and his muscles lost their tension. He took one last, long, slow breath and died. I cried inside and out. . . .

I want to sit here for another half-hour with the elk, as if at the bedside of an old friend. Just sit as I have done before and try to fig-ure out why it is I do this. Kill and then mourn.[8]

There is a whole genre of this stuff, always with this same theme of killing and bereavement, killing and self-revulsion, killing and emptiness. The idea that just maybe *killing* is the problem, and it might be best to work it all out at home, take a little break from the blood sports to "figure out why it is I do this," never seems to occur to them. Read enough hunting literature and you begin to suspect a deeper kind of self-display, the spiritual version of pos-ing with one's trophies.

It was a mistake, in any case, to schedule the "Fair Chase" seminar in room B-10 while "Judging Trophy Animals" was going on over in B-13. "You need to have *respect* for the animals, respect for the institution of the hunt," explained hunting ethicist Jim Posewitz, a former parks and wildlife official in Montana, author of *Fair Chase*, and winner of this year's Safari Club Educa-tor of the Year award. He then proceeded to tell us about some buffalo-hunting opportunities in his state, where last winter many of the thirty-four hundred or so wild American bison still with us were slaughtered by hunters as they wandered from the legal protection of Yellowstone Park in search of food.

"Respect" at Safari Club always means the courtesy of leaving enough behind for the next hunter, just as compassion always means helping the less fortunate who cannot hunt (they've got new "Hunting for the Disabled" and even "Hunting for the Blind" programs), and generosity always means sharing the fruits of the hunt ("Hunters against Hunger"). They practice a socially conscious sadism here. Ethics at Safari Club is ordered libertinism, like teaching cannibals to use a table napkin and not take the last portion.

But no matter. Mr. Posewitz's ethics lecture was delivered to me, eighteen hunters, and 112 empty chairs. "Look for the spiral ridge circumference of the horn, tip to tip," explained antler expert Bill Stratton, pointer in hand, to a standing-room-only audience in B-13. "Look for the width of the boss. If the ear is *just* coming out from under the horn, that's a good sign."

But, hey, you never really know, like there was that crazy time Bill's professional hunter egged him on into "harvesting" an idu so they could inspect the antlers. "I didn't really want to take him but my PH wanted to see the rack up close. I shot him and it turned out he wasn't as long as I'd like to have seen." *Damn.* But it all worked out well and guess what, "You'd be amazed. He turned out to be a Gold Medallion rack!"

What the idu lacked in length he made up for in spiral ridges. So this creature slain to satisfy one man's curiosity had some value after all.

Back on the showroom floor, Cal Yates of Newfoundland Moose Hunts, catering annually to some three thousand Americans, explains regional variations in moose racks. "We have a success rate of about eighty-five percent. Now, our moose aren't as big as moose in Alaska. Up that way you get 50-to-60 point moose. Ours are more in the range of 30-to-40, like this one over here. . . ."

At Gilroy Hunting Lodge of New Zealand, owner Jim Hunter, who runs a 14,000-acre private game park, is disputing a rival lodge's claims of superior rams. "Anyone who tells you he went to New Zealand and shot a fourteen-pointer—first of all, that's bullshit. Ours are as big as they get, and in winter they come right out where you can shoot 'em."

At Tourngat Wilderness Adventures they're advertising the biggest caribou racks anywhere. What if they don't come near the lodge? "You will be transported over our scenic land by our privately owned aircraft. . . . This will offer positive hunting results at no extra expense to you." An exciting, cost-efficient, and fair chase: one caribou, one plane.

The theory is that the longer and bigger the rack or horn, the longer that animal has endured upon the earth. Therefore the tougher an adversary that animal must have been. Ergo, the more enduring and powerful the testimony that rack or horn bears to your courage and prowess—and never mind the "ecological" necessity of sport hunting to spare weak animals from lingering death by cold or starvation.

And of course it is a perfectly reasonable and valid theory—indeed, irrefutable—if you are a moose or ram or caribou regaling youngsters in the herd with tales of triumph over other moose, ram, or caribou. The high-powered guns and bows, one would imagine, change things a bit—as do the professional hunting guides, native guides, trackers, aerial and satellite photography services, static-free two-way radios with headsets, binoculars, barbed-wire fencing, infrared lights, motion detectors, heat sensors, "bionic ear" sound systems, herd transport and engineering, small aircraft and helicopter piloting, snowmobiles, all-terrain vehicles, thermal boots and camouflage, dog teams, baits, lures, decoys, mating callers, cub callers, high-powered scopes, and armor-piercing bullets that all these same sports are here to buy and sell.

The Deer Factory

You begin to wonder, walking around this place, if there is a wild creature left on the good earth that is not for sale in someone's brochure, a single plain or forest or depth of sea that is not today being turned to profit. As Gander Outfitters of St. John's, Newfoundland, explains in its brochure, hunting is "like visiting a used car lot. You have to choose from what we have in stock. We do our best to show you what we have this week, [and] more units are arriving all the time. But you have to see it and shoot it to take it home." The non-human inhabitants of the world are hardly granted the dignity of fellow creatures anymore. They're units now, priced competitively, available on demand, and even made to customer specifications:

> Mustang Creek Ranch is proud to offer *exceptional trophy white-tail bucks* . . . produced through our intensive game management program and game fencing. We attribute our exceptional growth and superior antler development to the professional managing of Dr. James Kroll, 'Dr. Deer,' as well as to our *highly improved genetics*, various enhanced pastures, naturally occurring mineral licks, and high protein program.

Get your deer made and developed by a professional. "The bulls at Velvet Ranch are truly Trophies for this coming hunting season. We anticipate the best year ever with the quality of 6 × 6's and 7 × 7's and even larger bulls at Velvet. Last year was a banner year again with *100% hunter success*."

Why settle for some second-rate 5 × 5er when you can have the brand spankin' new 7 × 7 model? The "ingredients" for trophy whitetails, says Massive Northern Whitetails, Inc., include "quality genetics and a plentiful high protein diet." At Massive, these ingredients combine "to secure the Oakcrest herd as some of the finest whitetails in the hunting world."

Another ingredient seems to be that four-wheel drive truck custom-made for shooting, pictured in Massive's brochure as a happy client fires at a deer. In the exhibit hall I actually heard Dr. Deer himself describing Mustang to a customer as "the Jurassic Park of deer." Apparently a scientific gadfly in the canned hunting community, he turns up again in a recent issue of *North American Whitetail* advocating, in a piece entitled "Building Your Own Deer Factory," his theory that the doe "crop" can be minimized and the buck crop maximized. "[A] proper harvest can produce more and bigger bucks with fewer total deer in the herd," he explains. "This is a win-win scenario: more bucks and better nutrition, meaning bigger bodies, bigger antlers, and higher fawn survival to keep the pipeline full of bucks for the future."[9]

So competitive is today's "deer industry," as they call it at the Texas Deer Association, that sometimes all pretense of sportsmanship is abandoned. The Galloway Exotic Game Ranch in Pearsall, Texas, boasts of its "beautiful high-fenced ranch." In Wimberly, Texas, the Pico Ranch No. 1 offers "2,000 High-Fenced Acres," enclosing deer engineered under the "Texas Scientific Breeder Program." Lest anyone worry that the deer might have the least chance of escape, Pico's brochure has pictures of three startled-looking creatures standing right next to these barbed-wire fences. Oddly, though, no fences in the background of Pico's posed kill shots, only close-ups of proud and solemn men kneeling by their kill, their guns resting on the carcasses. Two of these characters are done up head-to-toe in leafy camouflage—in their imaginations, so it seems, at Normandy or in the jungles of 'Nam instead of inside a large pen where they have just ambushed two trapped animals.

This is what sport hunting looks like in modern America. Your typical trophy hunter today is hunting captive animals, and for all the skill and manhood it requires might as well do his stalking in a zoo. Indeed, many of the "exotic livestock," as they're now termed in the industry, actually come from zoos. Often they're sold off to hunting ranches by roadside zoos to be found throughout our country, businesses hardly noticed by the law and rarely subject to inspection. It is legal, and not all that rare, for even our larger zoos to sell off their older or sick animals to hunting concessions—the reward for a lifetime in one cage to be transported to another cage, released, and, as in the case of one aging tiger caught on film by ABC's *Primetime Live,* executed on the spot for the trophy. The *San Jose Mercury News,* in a two-year investigation, found that "of the 19,361 mammals that left the nation's accredited zoos from 1992 through mid-1998, 7,420—or 38 percent—went to dealers, auctions, hunting ranches, unidentified individuals or unaccredited zoos or game farms."[10]

Zoos were also found to be advertising surplus animals in the *Animal Finders' Guide,* a newsletter of the exotic trade where hunting-ranch owners post notices of sales and auctions. Any trophy animal you want, the *Finders' Guide* will get you—from private owners, from zoos, from their native habitat however remote. Many hunters today actually prefer killing zoo animals because they tend to make better-looking trophies. The mane of a zoo lion, for example, is cleaner and fluffier than that of a battle-scarred wild lion. British television's *The Cook Report* in 1997 ran an exposé on a hunting ranch in South Africa where the lions were not only confined but drugged, prompting the rare police investigation. Among the evidence was a letter to the ranch from an American firm, Safari Headquarters Ltd. of South Carolina: "Late this afternoon had request for two canned lion hunts. One is a doctor and the two hunters want to go at the same time and both want good heavy-maned lions, preferably black mane. Can you get a couple of zoo lion and what will be the price? . . . I don't like these canned hunts, but hell it's part of our service I suppose." The South African outfitter replied that, not to worry, "the canned hunt is done so well, nobody will know."[11]

There are capture services, too, like Chase Net, Inc., of Texas and Wildlife Services, Inc., of Michigan, which find and trap wild animals on demand. Every year thousands of deer, wild sheep, boars, big cats, wolves, or even larger game like grizzly bears and moose are tracked down by helicopter, shot with a tranquilizer, caged, and transported hundreds or thousands of miles to a game ranch, all so that they can be cornered and shot again by trophy hunters. Incredible as it seems, a few animals may still be imported from abroad—sika deer from India, for example, or rams from the far reaches of Manchuria—to be bred for sport hunting and then hunted themselves. Picture the poor beasts on that journey—captured from their native land, encaged in the bowels of a cargo ship, and destined for delivery to some auction block or 100 percent guaranteed–kill ranch across the world.

How could anyone hunt a trapped animal? "The appeal is the concentration of the game," explains hunter Ray Baxter, a patron of the Wood's Mountain Hunting Ranch, to the *Arkansas Democrat-Gazette.* When the animals are all trapped in one place, "You get to see a lot more and get a lot more action. You know you can go off and get a chance to kill an exotic animal. . . . It gives people who live hurried lives an opportunity."[12] He's a busy man, says Mr. Baxter, a lawyer with only weekends to spare for hunting. He has a bad back, too, which makes any kind of lengthy stalking a hardship; plus, he likes to bring his kids along, and they are easily bored. These are his needs, his demands as a paying customer, and of course all things of the earth must be reordered to meet them—whatever creature Ray Baxter desires located, seized, trucked to Arkansas, and brought before him for a quick and convenient shot. Mr. Baxter's most recent trophy, says the *Democrat-Gazette,* was a $1,000 lion slain at the ranch, where "he says the ranch hands took him to an elevated stand and told him to wait while they turned the lion loose nearby."[13]

The elevated platforms are also standard equipment nowadays, often accompanied by the use of a "feeder." There is actually a company in Pearland, Texas, called Ambush Outdoor Products, which sells the feeders, feed, and blind boxes from which to shoot. You erect an automatically timed feeder on a tripod and wait a few weeks until the deer become accustomed to being fed at a given hour. A little ways from that, on another tripod, you set up your "Hideaway," a carpeted box with dark windows, a gun perch, and comfortable chair ("approved by our staff of physical therapists"). The "feed"—formerly known as *bait*—is called "Trophy Builder," a compound "formulated to meet the demands of the Texas hunter. Mix 5 lbs. of our concentrated mineral, vitamin and protein pellet with 50 lbs. of corn, and let the results of our acorn and molasses flavored attractant bring the wall-hangers to you."

Just keep the wall-hangers comin', that's the important thing. What matters is *quality.* What matters is customer satisfaction. What matters is product availability, so that every Texas sportsman can have an enjoyable and comfortable ambush experience.

Some products are always in "the pipeline," in constant surplus, and may be appropriated at will to serve as rugs or knife-handles or purses or golf bags or lamp shades or fur coats or trims or mittens or earmuffs or—to acquire bigger products—as bait. Other products must be harvested, with prices and quotas fixed according to production rates. When one area is running low, more animals are transported in to meet demand, or else the consumer is transported to where supply is greater. Sometimes the inventory drops suddenly, the product is endangered, and then it is time to start conserving again, until such time as supply and demand are again in balance, whereupon the harvesting must resume. All purchases are subject to availability, all payments must be made before entering the forest or savanna, and, attention shoppers, all customers are responsible for items broken, wounded, or lost.

It is our modern consumer culture meeting old traditions, taking from them whatever there was of decency or moderation or honor. There are no limits. They're all there for the taking, all across the world. Have at it, and remember, No Kill, No Pay. Just leave enough for the next guy. Be *responsible*.

It's a "win-win scenario," if we share with Dr. Deer and his kind the assumption that all the power and technology of modern man should be placed at the service of every hunter who thinks that every moving thing in God's creation was put here to satisfy his or her pleasures. The audacity of this genetic tampering for bigger "racks" is beyond belief. Not only has modern man now taken it upon himself to re-create his fellow creatures; in a kind of metaphysical hat trick, he is re-creating creatures for recreation. It can only be a matter of time before the Dr. Elephants and Dr. Buffaloes and Dr. Lions come along bringing new and improved tusks, horns, and manes to market, if they were not somewhere in Reno already.

Wildlife, we are constantly told, would run loose across our towns and cities were it not for the sport hunters to control their population, as birds would blanket the skies without the culling services of Ducks Unlimited and other groups. Yet here they are breeding wild animals, year after year replenishing the stock, all for the sole purpose of selling and killing them, deer and bears and elephants so many products being readied for market. Animals such as deer, we are told, have no predators in many areas, and therefore need systematic culling. Yet when attempts are made to reintroduce natural predators such as wolves and coyotes into these very areas, sport hunters themselves are the first to resist it. Weaker animals in the wild, we hear, will only die miserable deaths by starvation and exposure without sport hunters to control their population. Yet it's the bigger, stronger animals they're killing and wounding—the very opposite of natural selection—often with bows and pistols that only compound and prolong the victim's suffering. And now even bows are not quite challenging and primitive enough for some. Safari Club president Skip Donau boasts of harvesting his smaller game with "a slingshot," and even proposes this as "a new category in the Alternative Weapons section of the Record Book."[14] What's the next new conservation tool, one wonders. The whip?

MEN OF INFLUENCE

"I am a *hunter,* and I don't apologize to anybody."

This opening line from General Schwarzkopf brings such loud applause you half-expect the giraffe to bolt from the grand ballroom. "I don't say that in a belligerent way," he continues. "I simply don't feel obliged to explain to anyone why I am a hunter, and frankly I'm not sure I could. I don't apologize for being a hunter because hunters have done more to protect and increase animals and habitat than any other organization or group. Plain and simple, hunting is in my heritage, and it's in the heritage of every American, and frankly no one is going to take that away from me."

A Safari Club regular, Schwarzkopf used the line to similar effect at last year's convention in Las Vegas. This time he has come with a warning to the hunters themselves. The Tucson, Arizona–based Safari Club has 32,000 members, each paying $250 in annual dues. With projected gross revenues of $13.2 million for this year, half of which will come from this convention, and a tax-exempt charitable status granted after some dispute in 1985, Safari Club has an office in Washington and is today the foremost hunters' lobby, pressing for ever more vigilant "conservation" on every conceivable front.[15]

Safari Club's man in Washington is Ron Marlenee, a former congressman from Montana who during his service distinguished himself by supporting the slaughter of buffalo near Yellowstone Park—regretting only, as he told reporters, that official business prevented him from joining in the fun with his .44-magnum pistol.[16] Mr. Marlenee reports progress in the past year's legislative session, including a big breakthrough in the Arctic. In one of "13 solid wins for sportsmen last year, SCI succeeded in opening up another major Polar Bear area." On other conservation fronts, he writes in a memo to members, there had been some complaints about canned hunts—hunting enclosed and often drugged animals—but not to worry, it's all been taken care of. SCI "prevented the issue from attaining widespread support."[17] Some notable wins in Africa, too. SCI lobbyists secured renewal of congressional support for an international elephant "conservation" program known as CAMPFIRE, under which the creatures are sold off at $10,000 and up in Zimbabwe and elsewhere, the local revenue from trophy hunting serving as an incentive to safeguard the big tuskers from ivory poaching.

CAMPFIRE (Communal Areas Management Program for Indigenous Resources) satisfies a need hunters have had ever since Theodore Roosevelt published *African Game Trails* in 1910—to feel themselves a part of some grand and glorious purpose beyond mere butchery. It's a very American thing. British and German hunters had been in Africa long before T.R. got there, filling their own safari journals with breathless romantic drivel but sparing us, at least, any pretense of altruism. To Roosevelt we owe the notion of the safari as a form of public service and the rich American trophy hunter as a sort of missionary, there to uplift the natives and instruct them in the ways of game management.

In our day, these good works are supported in large part by American taxpayers. Altogether, the U.S. government has paid $28 million to fund CAMPFIRE. Safari hunters operating under the program may now claim that by hunting elephants they are actually saving the elephants from a worse fate at the hands of ivory hunters, while also boosting the local economies with their license fees. The elephants thus "pay their own way," in a motto of the hunting trade. And it's a very practical idea, provided you assume (1) that the fraction of humanity that hunts big game can bring more tourism revenue to Africa than all the rest who don't—a claim disproved by Kenya, which prohibits sport hunting and has by far the highest tourism revenues on the continent; (2) that the only thing of economic value African villagers can possibly offer the world is "the Big Five," and the best they can hope for is to go on forever serving as trackers, skinners, and lodge boys for Western sportsmen; and (3) that it is ecologically and morally acceptable under any circumstances to, in effect, farm elephants like cattle for the sole purpose of slaughtering them for trophies. It appeared very suddenly, too, this outpouring of concern for local villagers. "One moment," as Douglas Chadwick writes in his 1992 *The Fate of the Elephant,* "Zimbabwe was simply a great place for trophy hunters to shoot themselves a giant. The next moment, the Zimbabwe safari industry was a caring community of white people devoted to improving native communities while saving species."[18]

There are no coldhearted killers here, in any case, just 13,554 really committed "conservationists." Still, Schwarzkopf is concerned that Safari Club isn't doing enough to improve the image of the sport. Not enough time is spent on outreach, on "creating a new image for hunters." The general has brought along *In Defense of Hunting,* Swan's meditation, and reads from an appendix called "How to Save Hunting," colorfully expanding on each proposal:

"'*Support the men's movement and women hunters—either or both may help save hunting.*' We need more women hunting in this country. I mean, you just look at the women that hunt in this organization here and they do an awful lot to counteract the crotch-scratching, tobacco-chewing image of the hunting slob, *okay*? We need them with us, and these women will also bring their children to hunt. . . .

"'*Create more opportunities for hunting that don't require large cash outlays.*' This is a great organization, but today I heard some startling figures on the amount of money—all the average amount of money that individuals within this organization spend each year on hunting. It's a lot, okay? *A lot.* . . . It's important that we let everybody have opportunities, not just the people who are rich.

"'*Create a new image for hunters.*' Let's face it—I know people in this organization that are the worst kind of slob hunters. *Kick their ass out,* I'm telling you that right now! . . .

"'*Safeguard hunting yourself.*' . . . Blow the whistle on the poachers, *okay*? . . . I am a hunter and what I hunt I consume. I am a hunter, and I can either pull the trigger or choose not to pull the trigger. And I am never more a hunter than when I choose not to pull the trigger. I have an obligation to train myself to shoot straight and clean. I have an obligation to avoid inflicting suffering on that animal. And when I stand over that animal that I love so much, I shed a tear, and I don't know why."

The crotch-scratching stuff causes a mixed reaction. The kick-their-ass-out part leaves a stunned silence. At the head table, outgoing Safari Club president Skip Donau, a bearded, fiftyish trial lawyer, now in tuxedo and grinning tightly over a glass of Cuvée Dom Pérignon, looks like some ready-to-ship masterpiece from the taxidermy shop. To everyone's relief, however, the general comes through with a stirring call "to be leaders in the hunting industry." There are larger pro-hunting groups, says Schwarzkopf, but SCI has a unique obligation because "Within this organization there are more people of influence and there are more people of affluence than in any of the other organizations by far. Because the future of hunting, quite frankly, is right in the hands of people in this room. If hunting survives in this country, it will be because of you. But if hunting fails in this country, it will also be because of you."

Donau is Inner Circle, and certainly the kind of leader in the "industry" (as it is now routinely called, never mind "conservation") in whose able and caring hands Schwarzkopf is placing his hopes. Back in July of 1998 Donau and two Safari Club colleagues landed themselves some rare prizes in the Mozambique province of Cabo Delgado. Accompanied by former SCI president Lance Norris and Crowning Achiever Kenneth Behring, a California realtor and onetime owner of the Seattle Seahawks football team, it seems the threesome had made a contribution of $20,000 to a Cabo Delgado hospital among other benefactions distributed to local authorities before embarking upon their—wink wink—"surveying expedition."

That's the way conservation, Safari Club–style, works at its best: Three white guys from across the world show up, pick out the local chieftains, and throw some money around while hinting of bigger favors to come in exchange for the privilege of looting the local forests. Before this became "conservation," we used to call it colonialism. Here is how the surveying expedition went, as relayed by editor Dan Causey of the *Hunting Report,* a newsletter serving the trophy-hunting elite: "A delegation from Safari Club International on a special-invitation safari has taken three elephants, two of them very good and one of them absolutely stupendous. The largest of the three weighed a mind-boggling 92 pounds [per tusk] and is thus one of the biggest takes in Africa in recent years."[19]

Mozambique banned elephant hunting for sport in 1990 after the herds were destroyed by ivory poachers in a decade of civil war. The surveyors, reports the *Johannesburg Mail and Guardian,* killed not three but five "problem elephants," and "local communities say the hunting party used a helicopter to drive the animals and to drop off the hunters." Interpol, according to the paper, "is investigating what happened to two tusks which appear to have gone missing after the hunt."[20]

Asked about the incident by the Humane Society of the United States, Safari Club claimed in a press release that the elephant hunt had been authorized. Mr. Donau tersely informs us that while some hunting did indeed take place, "Some of us were successful; some of us were not. . . . I, however, did not harvest an elephant."[21] Whoever played what role, the threesome were apparently unaware of Mozambique's unambiguous regulations regarding elephant hunting: "It is hereby declared that, in terms of Ministerial Diploma No. 60/90 of 4th July 1990, the trophy hunting of elephants in Mozambique is forbidden, as also the export of ivory."[22]

A footnote to the adventure is a letter from the local wildlife reserve manager noting that the surveyors had also shot "3 lion, 5 buffalo, 1 eland, 3 kudu and 6 impala. . . . The Reserve game guards also heard reports from throughout the area that wounded animals were dying along the river. Specifically, 1 impala and 2 kudu were found with gunshot wounds, and an eland with gunshots in its chest had been found alive in the river, struggling to avoid being eaten by crocodiles."[23]

"Lord Jesus, come into my life. Occupy the throne of my life. Help me to change my pursuits. Purify my heart from all unrighteousness."

It is the Christian Sportsmen's Fellowship breakfast, a Safari Club tradition, Skip Donau sitting at the head table as we bow our heads in this opening prayer after some hymns from the Sons of Mercy. The fellowship's motto is "On Target to Catch Men for Christ." Their logo depicts a deer head beneath a cross. About 250 people are here. There is a raffle: hanging in the balance, a camouflage-covered Bible. When we leave, the tables will be cleared and the room prepared for the afternoon auction.

Our main speaker is Joe Foss, governor of South Dakota back in the 1950s, commissioner of the old American Football League, ex-president of the NRA, and host of the '60s show *American Sportsman* back when a man could have a good elephant or lion hunt with Robert Stack on network TV without anyone making a big hoo-haw over it. Like Schwarzkopf and former president Bush, he is also the sort of man who commands enormous respect, and complicates any impulse to judge all hunters by the sins of some. He is featured in Tom Brokaw's 1998 book *The Greatest Generation*. A former Marine Corps captain, he earned the Medal of Honor with extraordinary valor at Guadalcanal, where he shot down twenty-six enemy aircraft. For Foss, hunting was always just a part of life. "As a kid I'd take my gun to school, put it in the back, and then hunt on the way home." The family would eat the pheasant that night. "We didn't have all these freezers and stuff back then."

They didn't have "all these anti-gun people," either, says Foss, "all these animal people. And that's why SCI is so important, because it protects our right to hunt. . . . But the antidote to the woes of our day is prayer. You have to say, 'Lord Jesus, come into my life, forgive my sins.' It involves a simple Yes or No— it's that simple. If you have the Lord on your side, you'll win. If you don't, you'll lose. And hunting and fishing—if you're involved in that, it's tough to go wrong. . . . I believe in the Bible and everything in it. Every one of you is a miracle. Every human being is a miracle. It's hard to believe—there are so many of us—but it's true. Think about it. A miracle, the world created for you. You're it."

"Five thousand, do I hear five thousand? Five five five, do I hear five five five?
Five thousand, in the back of the room! *Fifty-five hundred, anyone? Fifty-five*
five five, I'm sellin' for fifty-five five five. . . . "

In the balance now, two hours after we have given thanks for the miracles
of creation, is a polar bear "donated" to Safari Club, the proceeds again going
to its PAC. Even if you could explain it to him, the bewildered bruin—living
up there as far from man as nature could put him—would still have trouble
comprehending that his fate has just been determined in a convention hall in
the Nevada desert.

The auctioneer is a professional renowned on the cattle-show circuit. His
assistants have fanned out into the crowd, signaling bids with red, handheld
lights. It goes on like this hour after hour, as pictures of each particular
species up for grabs are projected onto the big screen. Any distinction there
might once have been between a domestic animal and a wild creature roaming the remotest corner of the planet has vanished. It's all livestock, and
everything's for sale.

". . . . Anybody? Anybody? Sold, for five thousand dollars!"

A Spot of Plains Game

The flashing cameras and commotion in the exhibit hall signal former president Bush's arrival for a tour. He was here at the 1997 convention (his vice
president, Dan Quayle, was the keynoter last year) and stops first to buy a
necktie at Fred Hoppe Studio, where the proprietor greets him as an old
friend. Escorted by Schwarzkopf and three or four Safari Club sub-dominant
males, he passes under the elephant head and straight past all the low-rent
booths with hardly a glance, pausing in what seems to be a strict itinerary at
various clothiers and sunglass shops and finally at Holland & Holland gunmakers, where the former president dons a tweed jacket and tries out some
binoculars.

Strictly a wingshooter, back during the 1988 campaign Mr. Bush caught
grief from all sides when he went quail hunting in Texas. "These aren't animals," he explained to reporters, "these are wild quail. You've got to eat. Our
forefathers ate by harvesting game. . . . I don't think I could shoot a deer.
Quail, that's something else again. You get up tremendous excitement."[24]

The animal people were upset about the hunt, the hunters upset about
the deer remark. Here in the exhibit hall, wearing a necktie with little green

elephants and trees on it, Mr. Bush seems a man not quite comfortable with his surroundings yet determined not to offend. As the former president walks by without breaking stride, the grizzly with outstretched paws looks deflated, like some hefty precinct committeeman who had been waiting hours for a handshake.

Suddenly Bo Derek appears. She and Mr. Bush chat and pose for pictures a little past the grizzly. What brings Bo here? "I haven't actually had my first hunt, but it really interests me." Doesn't she have some little horse ranch or stable back in Malibu? Seems like I saw her on *Lifestyles* or the *E!* channel not long ago, showering affection on her horses. "You know, I love horses and animals, and I know it seems like a contradiction being here. But these people—they do so much for conservation." Before she can finish the thought, a Safari Clubber whisks her away ("Miss Derek has an *appointment!*").

Just then Schwarzkopf comes back to me. We had been talking a few minutes earlier at the tie shop about his speech last night. He tells me not to judge too quickly or harshly, that "there's a lot of goodness in this place—you just have to look for it." People have been coming up to him all morning telling him his speech was right on the money. That goes to show that the slobs are a small minority. Sure, there are excesses among hunters, he says, but that's true of just about everything. "Where don't you find excess today?"

I lingered at Holland & Holland. Owned since 1989 by the French perfume company Chanel, Inc., with offices in New York, London, and Paris, they are clearly the standard setter here. Probably they're a good example of both the excessive cash outlays the general was talking about, and also of the influence and high standards upon which the future of hunting depends. They cater to "the gentleman hunter," not the hunting slobs, not the lowlifes, not the sort who bait or poach or stand around gawking at video kill shots, and their establishment is respectable enough to rate a presidential visit. Even their booth is not a booth at all but a mirrored, multi-roomed, wood-paneled little haven from the hurly-burly of the convention floor.

It has the feel of Brooks Brothers, lending an air of grace and refinement even to the elephant guns handsomely displayed on the green felt countertops. "Winning all classes in the Field Trials of 1883," says the H&H magazine, the *Shooting Field*, "Holland & Holland was established as London's premier rifle makers, and went on to design and develop a range of sporting rifle calibres that revolutionized the hunting world, particularly African big game hunting. Around 1898, one of Holland & Holland's first introductions was the .500/.450 3¼ Nitro Express. This round was favoured by President Theodore Roosevelt. . . ."

Costing $105,000, ten times the price of the elephant itself, the fabled Nitro Express is fashioned from "magnificent, centuries old trees." Three-fourths of the raw wood is discarded. The rest is carved and polished in "120 hours of craftsmanship," with a sterling silver "game scene" of your choice affixed to its side. A splendid piece of equipment, the gentleman's choice, the favorite round of T.R. himself—the very weapon Johan Calitz used to give us those "four dramatic brain shots" in *With Deadly Intent*.

"There is little to match the anticipation of a good day's shooting," says an essay in the *Shooting Field* entitled "An Ideal Shooting Day." "Even if the day's quarry has been nurtured throughout the year by a gamekeeper, the more the guns remember that these are essentially wild creatures that can surprise and delight in their wild unpredictability, then the better they will enjoy the day." A gentleman or gentlelady is patient, waiting until his or her assigned birds have been properly "presented"—the term of choice for birds released for the first time in their lives from the cage. "A greedy shot in line is tiresome and an ideal day requires participants to be considerate about which birds they attempt to shoot." As the keeper grabs hold of the fowl of the air and hurls them heaven-ward, "experience the exhilaration of hearing all the familiar sounds of the beaters urging the birds on their way, and relish the challenges ahead."[25]

The *Shooting Field* has also favored us with a "safari diary" by one Richard Gallyon. He is the owner not only of a .500 Nitro, but of what is surely the most formidable title in Reno this week, by far overshadowing even those of Bush and Schwarzkopf. Mr. Gallyon is "Past-Master of the Worship-ful Company of Gunmakers and East England Representative for Holland & Holland." Back in 1997, he recalls, "a chance conversation at the Burgley Horse Trials revealed that my friend Keith Massingham and I were hankering after a spot of plains game shooting in Africa. . . . We were to be allowed twelve animals between us. Permitted species would be impala, warthog, wildebeest, kudu, eland, and zebra together with any number of jackal. . . . In true explorer style, I kept a diary on the trip, a day-by-day record of the excite-ment and adventure."[26] A few snippets from the Past-Master's journal give us the flavor of it, and a snapshot of two gentlemen hunters afield with their native tracker, Amos:

Sunday: Up at 6:00 A.M. to meet our professional hunter, Alec Friend, over tea and toast by the campfire. . . . Saw a lot of game—giraffe, elephant, wildebeest, impala—but there was no chance of a shot. Back to camp for lunch at noon and a siesta at 3:00. . . . *Monday:* In the afternoon Keith went with Amos, our tracker, to stalk and shoot an impala. . . . *Tuesday:* Ruth provided the most wonderful wildebeest pie for lunch! Josh shot an impala and called a jackal within 10 ft of the land Rover, just as we do with foxes. . . . *Wednesday:* I shot a prize warthog boar with enormous tusks. . . . *Saturday:* Josh wanted a zebra for its skin, and after an hour in the bush he shot an old female. Late in the afternoon, I shot a wildebeest but it moved off. . . . [27]

And so to bed. What became of the wounded wildebeest that "moved off," hunted, one surmises, for another spot of pie, we may only guess. Maybe they sent Amos after him. Nor is it quite clear just why the pair were even *looking* for a shot at the giraffe and elephant, as he seems to suggest, having both been given specific instructions to take only impala and the like.

The .500 Nitro is not even the fiercest weapon here. At another booth they've got an elephant gun that looks like something confiscated from the mujahideen during Soviet days. I walk up to inspect another gun, thinking it must be a large telescope. Selling for $118,000, it needs a tripod for support and can pierce armor. They make special bullets for it at $100 apiece that will annihilate with internal hemorrhaging while leaving just the slightest little rip in the target's thick gray skin.

I test her out, pivoting around to train it on the elephant head hung over Elephant Walk. He could be drinking at the water hole now, or bathing, exactly as most of these rampaging menaces are found and taken. How could anyone find pleasure in shooting an 8,000-pound mammal who has been walking the earth for fifty-odd years, who lives in a complex family structure, needs fourteen or fifteen years to rear the young, charges only in defense of the calves or of the herd, has been observed bringing food to sick members of the herd and even aiding the young of other species, and who on his best day is about as hard to nail as Bullwinkle wafting down Fifth Avenue on Thanksgiving Day? Hold this baby in your hands, or even those $100 bullets, and you begin to understand the sheer malicious power of it.

Holland & Holland, reports columnist Jim Carmichel in the February

1999 *Outdoor Life,* will soon bring forth a .600 Nitro Express, directing "a thumb-sized, 900-grain slug at nearly four tons of muzzle energy."[28] There's a .700 Nitro in the works as well, with an .800 Nitro expected after that, and apparently no theoretical limit to the violent power one man can direct at one elephant.

In the woods, every man is a big shot, noticed, regarded, feared. Apparently the sense of satisfaction only grows with the size of the animal within one's power to terrify. For Mr. Carmichel himself, hunting elephants has become "a consuming passion."[29] He likes it especially "when a brain-shot elephant thunders to the ground [and] its buddies sometimes run in screaming, panicky circles."[30] He has come to appreciate the sensitivity of elephants too, for "no wild creature on earth is as fascinating or as intelligent—or as dangerous."[31] One day, for example, he and his professional guide came upon a herd in Africa, feeding on some trees. "Suddenly," in that dramatic turn of all safari stories, "all hell broke loose." In fact, hell had just arrived. "There was a great thundering of earth, a crashing of brush and the shrill trumpeting of an elephant stampede. . . . [A] smallish elephant broke through the trees and came charging directly at us! . . . This beast meant deadly business. . . . The damn thing meant to destroy us just as it had the tree!"[32] After a flurry of shots from both men, "the vast form became motionless, and then it was very silent":

> It seemed so uncomplicated, I later remembered thinking, *the power of a trigger finger challenging the might of an elephant.* . . . But why did it happen? That was answered minutes later when our trackers discovered the still-born calf the cow had been guarding. The crashing stampede we'd heard earlier was the cow chasing other elephants away from the dead calf she'd been guarding. We'd come between her and her calf and her rage was the most protective instinct in all of nature.[33]

This was Jim Carmichel's contribution to the world that day—to terrify and kill a mother elephant who had been watching over her dead calf. "The damn thing" was grieving. From that day to this, recapturing the experience has been "my true hunting passion." The big tuskers "are in my blood and they won't leave my dreams."[34] He'll keep going back for more, too, says Mr. Carmichel, because under today's CAMPFIRE program African villagers have so much to gain. "Everyone benefits, especially the human population, because the price of an elephant license will now pay for a desperately needed schoolroom, or a teacher's salary for a year."[35] That's one possible explanation for what inspires men like Mr. Carmichel—they're concerned for the world's poor, they just want to help all of those African children and schoolteachers. A somewhat more plausible explanation was offered long ago by Joseph Wood Krutch in his book *The Modern Temper*:

> Killing "for sport" is the perfect type of that pure evil for which metaphysicians have sometimes sought. Most wicked deeds are done because the doer proposes some good to himself . . . [but] the killer for sport has no such comprehensible motive. He prefers death to life, darkness to light. He gets nothing except the satisfaction of saying, "Something that wanted to live is dead. There is that much less vitality, consciousness, and, perhaps, joy in the universe. I am the Spirit that Denies."[36]

THE CURATORS

It has been a good convention for jewelers, too. I wander by Status Diamonds as Nina Popkins has just sold a $20,000 emerald brooch. "Usually we don't get our big sales until the last day. The wives always come up and say 'I'll be back when he's done lookin' at safaris.'" The priciest merchandise in the place seems to be the white rhino package at $210,000. And that's not even counting preparation and shipment back to the States.

The taxidermy bills here are unbelievable—costing so much precisely because, in the end, you are not getting the animal itself but its dried, dipped, and treated skin fitted around a urethane molding. Tusks, horns, antlers, and skin are kept, the bones and all the rest left behind. The job takes months, says C. Larry Quinn of American Sportsman Taxidermy, based in Tallahassee, Florida. His goal is "satisfying the discriminating sportsman, offering an alternative to the mass production of mounted animals. Each piece is custom mounted and every effort is made to achieve accuracy and detail of the live animal." No second-rate rush jobs—the whole thing has to be reconstructed. Mr. Quinn is a specialist in African trophies; his "sculpting abilities allow him to take photographs, measurements, death masks, and skeletal parts, and transform them into a lifelike mannequin of any animal."

It would be cheaper, when all the costs are tallied up—skinning, shipping, trophy fees, veterinary inspection, customs, insurance, taxes, and taxi-

dermy—to have sent the live elephant or giraffe off with a ticket on the Con-
corde. A lion at American Sportsman Taxidermy—just the reconstructing—
costs $3,595. A zebra: $3,795. A buffalo: $7,495. An elephant head: $13,500.
An entire elephant: $45,000 and up. A rhino: $19,800. A hippo: $21,985.

That giraffe back at the Hilton? From habitat to hotel, you're looking at
upwards of $60,000 just to obtain that one creature, haul the "lifelike man-
nequin" across the earth, and resurrect him here in Reno where he now
graces us in the Grand Ballroom.

They've got the tax angles all figured out too, as we learn at a seminar entitled
"SCI, the IRS, and You." With this, the reduction of all creatures of the earth
to commodities is complete.

There comes a time in every sportsman's life when he must look to posterity, ponder his own mortality, plan ahead, prepare his or her will. When
that solemn hour comes, Safari Club International hopes you will remember
that it is a 501 (c)(3) tax-exempt charity. It is an entity, as the Internal Revenue Service determined in 1985, after several SCI appeals, "organized for
exclusively charitable and educational purposes."[37]

Death's harvest must come to all, the Reaper's quarry is always in season,
but the work of conservation goes on, the work of educating people about
conservation, lobbying for conservation in every state capitol and in Congress
and the White House, conserving for future generations the same bounty of
wildlife we hunters enjoy today. Oh, sure, getting all those trophies and
Bronze Buffaloes and McElroys is an honor, but *conservation*—that's what it's
all about.

Bequests to Safari Club offer many advantages, even before your last
shot has echoed across field and forest. Just name SCI as the beneficiary of
your estate. You get to write it off as a charitable donation for years to come,
under a device in the tax code known as a charitable remainder trust, or a
CRT. When you pass on, everything then goes to SCI. Safari Club lawyers are
standing by in the back of the room. They'll handle it for you on the spot. All
the forms are ready. You can have your estate in order before lunch. (Just one
downside, as it fell to a young hunter in the audience to point out: "So, what
you're really saying is that with a CRT, when you die there's nothing left for
your kids.")

Then there is the "trophy museum" angle, outlined in a Safari Club members-only advisory.[38] The way this works is, you "donate" your trophies, often hundreds of them, for eventual shipping to SCI's own International Wildlife Museum. You agree "to store and maintain the collection within museum standards until such time as the initial use within our tax exempt function is determined." Never mind shipping off the stuff now. Just hold on to it. Meanwhile, explains the document, consider yourself a "curator" sharing in SCI's 501 (c)(3) charity status.

Step one: *"Establish public museum space and other facilities (Sensory Safaris, etc.) across the country to preserve museum quality mounts."* Translation: Declare all or a portion of your house a "wildlife museum."

Step two: *"Utilize these museums and other facilities to educate the public about pertinent wildlife and conservation issues."* Invite your hunting buddies over to the "museum" for some drinks and story-swapping, making sure someone has "donated" a bottle or two of Cuvée Dom Pérignon.

Step three: *"Provide a source of revenue to further the goals and the mission of SCI."* When you get around to writing up your will, don't forget who gave you all the good tax advice.

What is a "sensory safari"? A sensory safari is a safari for the blind, one of the "outreach" programs that Swan and Schwarzkopf commend. Just off the main hall in the convention center is a full-sized stuffed rhino, a giraffe from the shoulders up, a lion, and sundry other "mounts." Blind or partially blind children are ushered in for a chance to touch and stroke the animals, the idea being to share with them the wonders of nature and wildlife. "Ever touch a giraffe?" says the curator of this display. "Now's your chance."

It is a new program that SCI is now broadening around the country. Of course, with all these new sensory safari centers opening up, it becomes all the more urgent and vital to keep the wildlife coming. And of course, hunters obtaining animals for display in sensory safaris are engaged in a charitable enterprise. It's only right that these altruists should be able to write off expenses involved in the acquisition. SCI lawyers will help you with that, too. It's all for the kids.

A still more intricate savings plan is explained by R. Bruce Duncan, president of the Chicago Appraisers Association, in "Secrets of Tax-Deductible Hunting," a handy little insert provided in the brochure of Jeff C. Neal, Inc., whose guide we heard earlier explaining the peanuts-out-the-window technique of elephant hunting.

In Mr. Neal's brochure we find one client, Ken Behring, pictured with an elephant in Botswana, a lion in Zambia, an ibex and Gobi Argali sheep in Mongolia, another sheep in China, a bear and a moose in Russia, and a tiny deer in Nepal—even in this last pose looking so triumphant, so thoroughly pleased with himself, that you'd think Mr. Behring had just scaled Mount Everest in pursuit of the deer. All this on top of the elephant and assortment of other animals that Ken, Skip, and Lance went forth and subdued in Mozambique, shooting up the place and making the crocodiles' lives easier with those wounded, ready-to-go meals.

Mr. Behring gets around. Money's no problem, either. With an endowment of $100 million the man has lately managed to turn an entire wing of the Smithsonian Institution into his personal trophy room—the "Kenneth E. Behring Family Hall of Mammals." Most hunters have to be more cost-conscious, though, and Mr. Duncan, the self-described "father of game mount appraisals," is there to help. The "Build Your Own Museum" route is one possibility, he explains in "Secrets of Tax-Deductible Hunting." Another popular option is to donate trophies for commercial display:

> Restaurants, bars and sporting good stores have written off the cost to obtain trophies for display either through outright prorated expense or depreciation. Automobile dealers have cleverly done so, too. Rams (Dodge), Cougars (Mercury), and Impalas (Chevrolet) are eye-catching displays next to their namesake car. One manufacturer named every one of his products after a game animal and put the appropriate trophies next to it in the company showroom. Today many shopping centers are using wildlife displays for traffic builders. A future trend.[39]

Then there is the "Keep the Monster" technique—a "Monster" being one's prime target as opposed to miscellaneous animals killed along the way. Using this device, advises Mr. Duncan, you "donate everything collected on your hunt but the one animal you really need. Very popular among sheep hunters and advanced rare species."

Alternatively, you can "Give Away the Monster": "Donate your record book animal for the mouth watering tax deduction and have your taxidermist obtain a second cape and cast fiberglass horns from your original. . . . Use the tax savings to go on another hunt. Used more often than you think!" Still another big saver is to simply "make a check out to your local museum for the cost of the hunt, then have them pay all the costs." All expenses are thus "a charitable contribution."[40]

The general idea is to make each hunt pay for the next, a sort of frequent-slayer program. This is needed, explains Mr. Duncan, because "hunting costs double every ten years."[41] Why are costs rising? Because availability is declining. Why is availability falling? Because demand has overtaken supply. Why is demand so overwhelming? In large part because of these very tax techniques which have put even endangered big-game animals within the means of more hunters than ever before. It is a vicious cycle of depletion and depredation, leaving fewer (and younger) animals at ever higher prices, the barriers on the hunters' appetite artificially removed by political lobbying and creative manipulation of the tax code.[42]

Might be time for the Internal Revenue Service to set forth on a little safari of its own. If there are any IRS agents among my readers, drop everything and come to Reno next season. Some real Monsters out this a-way, and you can keep 'em.

NIMROD.COM

Mr. Bush's keynote address this evening, the final night, turns out to be a routine affair extolling the wonders of nature and duties of conservation while congratulating an astonished Skip Donau on leaving Safari Club "with over a million members, and still growing. I understand members have flown in from all over the world, from all over Asia, and Africa, New Zealand, Russia, as well as our neighbors to the north in Canada and in the south, in Mexico—which leads me to thank the Sada family for bringing me up here in the charter plane." Adrian Sada Gonzalez, a 1998 Crowning Achiever and chairman of Mexico's eighth-largest corporation, the Vitro SA glass manufacturer, can be found in one brochure posing with a $23,000 Argali ram from his latest sheep safari in Mongolia. From his estate in Monterey, Sada is heading up SCI's cutting-edge conservation efforts in Mexico, trying to get those big-cat preserves opened up for business.

They like to keep everything very *presidential* here. A few years ago former Argentine president Carlos Menem was here. In 2000 the guest of honor will be former French president Valéry Giscard d'Estaing, and in 2001 it will be Mr. Bush again. Apart from the payment he has received for this visit, in the form of two Baretta rifles, what this great and kindly man himself gets out of it is hard to say. He seems ill at ease with his hosts except for Schwarzkopf. This is the same president, moreover, who to his lasting credit invoked in June 1989 the African Elephant Conservation Act signed by Ronald Reagan to ban the importation of ivory into the United States—a ban Safari Club opposes on the grounds that one legal protection for elephants will only lead to others.

"The fact that there's such a strong international presence," Mr. Bush continues, "is a tribute to the hard work of the SCI staff—that they help educate and promote conservation and ethical standards through more than 165 chapters in over 16 countries around the world. . . . Back when I was president we called this kind of neighbor-helping-neighbor spirit being one of 'a thousand points of light.'"

From "points of light" it's on, inevitably, to "the Rough Rider." Roosevelt, says Mr. Bush, "was another accomplished outdoorsman of unquestioned repute and a personal hero to me. He was always exploring the wonders of the outdoors, noting later in his life that [the forests] 'can tell the hidden spirit of the wilderness, that can reveal its mystery, its melancholy and its charms.' . . . The lesson we take from T.R. is that those who hunt and fish can be the best defenders of our precious natural resources and defenders of our wildlife. Indeed, Roosevelt said it best when he noted, 'Game butchery is as objectionable as any other form of wanton cruelty or barbarity. But to protest against all hunting of game is a sign of softness of head and unsoundness of heart.'"

Why there is no Theodore Roosevelt Award at SCI is a mystery. A fitting honor in his name might recognize, for instance, excellence in the total number of orphans and wounded left behind in a single year. "There was a young one," T.R. recalls in a typical passage after killing a female elephant, that "ran off as soon as the mother was felled." The calf would be fine, though, appearing "quite able to take care of itself."[43] A rhino ambushed by Roosevelt and his son "halted and half wheeled. . . . Kermit putting in a couple of bullets as she went off. A couple of hundred yards away she fell, rose again, staggered, fell again, and died. The calf, which was old enough to shift for itself, refused to leave the body, although [we] pelted it with sticks and clods. Finally a shot through the flesh of the buttocks sent it off in frantic haste."[44] The next time, after killing a rhino mother, "we shot the calf, which when dying uttered a screaming whistle, almost like that of a steam engine."[45] Other heroics follow, as one elephant falls dead and another, "hit hard," escapes. "If we had been only after ivory, we should have followed him at once; but there was no telling how long a chase he might lead us; and as we desired to save the skin of the dead elephant entire, there was no time whatever to spare."[46]

Maybe there is no award named for our twenty-sixth president because even he, who could kill the young without any need or remorse and leave the wounded to "shift for themselves," professed at least minimal standards and despised captive hunting. Whereas the virtues of hardihood and self-reliance are instilled by hunting in the wilderness, he wrote, "Shooting in a private game preserve is but a dismal parody," and "I should much regret to see grow up in this country a system of large private game preserves, kept for the enjoyment of the very rich."[47] The twenty-three hundred roughshod riders listening to Mr. Bush either own, lease, equip, or patronize exactly the kind of fenced-in, "No Kill, No Pay" game parks that Roosevelt had in mind when he denounced as beneath contempt the "game butchery" of hunting captive animals. As for competitive hunting, Roosevelt wrote, "to let the desire for 'record' heads, to the exclusion of all else, become a craze, is absurd."[48]

Before departing I wanted to talk again to the professional hunters themselves. Safari Club on the last day was on my trail anyway, demanding to know why I had not come as a member of the press (because they do a lot of "harvesting" in reviewing press applications), opting instead to cough up the money for member admission. After my chat with Bo and Schwarzkopf in the exhibit hall, I could see lots of little Safari guys eyeing me and talking into cell phones, and from then on I might as well have been strolling around with a set of sixty-point antlers on my head. I figured it was time to make tracks out of the "Biggest Little City in America," but not before asking a few of the professional hunters what the business was like on their end.

They have something, the African ones especially, you find yourself admiring. For starters, they have skill. They are the ones who actually track and find the animal, all but tying the creature's paws and feet behind its back before clients step up to crown themselves in glory with the kill shot. Even game-park hunting between fences takes a little work and know-how, and without the professionals doing the mapping and driving and whispering most of the clients would wind up being harvested themselves.

You can see this dependence in the clients' faces in the endless photos on display in the convention center and in the brochures. They're all smiles, aglow with surprise and excitement over their kill, like big, round-faced kids who have just ripped off the blindfold to see the smashed piñata. The hubris of it is staggering, but they hardly seem serious enough souls to deserve such a weighty word, guilty at worst of a dopey arrogance we might call boobris.

Next to them, in the photos on display at the booths, are the professionals. (In the clients' home photos, one imagines, no professional hunter is in sight.) Their expressions are hard to read. A little bored, maybe. Tired. Distracted. Glad the day's expedition is over with so they can order the skinners to work, get in the Rover, and head back to the lodge. Another day, another kruger.

In a few pictures they seem ill at ease, diffidently stepping away from the hero or heroine of the hunt: They know who *really* found and killed that lion or giraffe or elephant. Not always: In some pictures you wouldn't know the professional hunter from the customer but for the leaner, calmer, more self-assured aspect of the former. These seem to be the younger professionals.

So what did they make of Reno, I wondered. What did they think of all these Americans coming over to throw money around for an easy shot at the big boys? Did they ever tire of it? They actually live in Africa and know these animals, as the rubes who come and go never can. Did they ever feel just a little sorry for the animals, knowing them only as the true hunter can know the hunted?

One professional hunter, a friendly, freckled, red-haired fellow in his mid-twenties named Vlam Myburg, has been hunting for Madabula Safaris for three years. He says he does feel some regret at killing, for example, an elephant, and so do many clients. "You'd be surprised. I'd say two of every five clients we take on an elephant hunt cry when it's over and they are actually standing by the animal. They've been chasing it and chasing it, and when it's over it's a very emotional experience."

I'm not sure we mean the same thing by "regret." He is certain, in any case, that all this is necessary and serves a good purpose, culling elephant herds that are today pressing up against human populations, especially the "crop raiders" that menace local farms. "You do feel some regret at killing this beautiful and majestical animal," he continues. "I feel that way about all big game. They're like us in many ways, the elephant especially. On the other hand you [the hunter] know how much damage the elephant does. You have to control the population. And yes, I enjoy it. It's exciting. I love it. You never kill two critters in the same way. Some are smarter. They all have different strategies."

At Tanganyika Wildlife Safari, Frederic Blochet, a handsome, thirtyish native of Nice, France, offers me a hunt package in the Selous Reserve, so named for Frederick Courtney Selous, a hunting partner of Theodore Roosevelt. Blochet spent his childhood in Tanganyika and has now returned as a professional hunter, he tells me. He pulls out his Macintosh PowerBook and clicks on "December 1998" to show me an elephant hunt by one Pat Bollman, chief of the Safari Club awards committee whose wife, I notice in the brochure, also got herself an elephant in November of last year. The Bollmans wanted a His-and-Her set. You can even call them for references along with a dozen or so other Americans. The moment after the video starts, Blochet realizes I am not interested, but it's too late—the show has begun.

We see the elephant drinking from a water hole some fifty yards from client and camera. "I studied in Limoges for a year," he tells me, "but then decided to come back. To tell you the truth I don't really enjoy hunting that much." The elephant is lifting his trunk toward the hunters. He's caught the scent. He knows. "Swordfishing is my real passion. Hunting, that's just business." He starts to run, falling with a great splash into a kneeling position, his trunk and head under the water, stilled just like that as if in freeze-frame. No need even for a second shot. The skinners, charged with moving him, will earn their pay. "I don't like hunting at all, really, especially this"—pointing to the PowerBook. "It's just business."

It wasn't the moment for career counseling, but Blochet seemed embarrassed so I asked if there aren't other ways of making a living, maybe photographic safaris and the like. "Yes," he replied, holding up his fingers, "but you know what they make? Zero." On the silent video there is wild backslapping as the assassins emerge from the bushes to inspect their prize.

Next I talk to John Sharp of John Sharp Safaris ("Hunt on Foot—The *Real* Way"), a lean, formidable-looking character of fifty or so with a bandanna over his long, graying blond hair. With none of the droopy-dawg jowls or paunches of his American counterparts, the ones offering "Monster Moose" hunts and "Elk Crazy" adventures, he looks a little like the actor Paul Hogan of *Crocodile Dundee*. Not the sort of fellow I'd want to look back and find on my trail.

I found Sharp just as he was completing some forms for an elephant-hunt package, his specialty, judging by the posters displayed at his booth. He seemed to welcome the chance to set aside his price lists and contracts and to talk about the creatures themselves, surprising me with his eloquence. "Elephants, yes, I always feel regret and sadness. Especially the old bulls like this"—pointing to the picture on his desk. "Everybody wants the big tuskers.

But they're very intelligent, very sensitive animals. They even know when the hunting season begins and ends. I have seen elephants who wandered into the hunting areas running back into the protected areas, and you can see them visibly relax [now imitating a body relaxing] when they've crossed the road, as if they know they're safe. And they'll begin grazing again.

"There have been studies recording the subsonic sounds they make, and when they're played back the elephants respond accordingly. They understand, and they can communicate danger. When one elephant is shot, the word seems to get out, and you can see whole herds gravitating together in small protected areas.

"And yes, I, too, have a special place in my heart for an elephant, especially the older ones—like this one here, fifty years old—because you know when you look at an old tusker that one day there won't be any more, and when you shoot one you lose a little something here [he points to his heart]. But, you know, that's life."

Sharp adds that the governments of Africa are so hopelessly corrupt and incompetent that this is the only way, trophy hunting, to maintain some sort of stability among animal populations. The theme is picked up by Pieter Stofberg of Komasam Safaris, a professional hunter in his mid-forties whom I encounter at the main exit from the convention center. He too welcomes the interview, directing me to take down every word he says, pausing for puffs on his cigarette as I transcribe. A bearded, diminutive native of Namibia, who goes by "Nimrod" in his e-mail address, Stofberg is going to explain to me the basic principles of trophy hunting as conservation. He describes his prey using almost exactly the same words as Sharp. He is a practical man and has had it with all this sentimentality about animals, elephants in particular, and wants me and my readers to get this straight once and for all:

"You see, elephant has no predator. It has been scientifically proven that eventually, if not predated upon, they will get sick and die out. So I am the predator. Because we hunt them, there are now about 40 percent more animals in Africa than there were sixty years ago. Because we hunt, we give that animal a value—say for elephant $10,000.

"It is like cattle: If they had no value, the farmer would come in and wipe them out. Of course—because they have no value. . . . So now trophy hunting has given that animal a value, especially since there's a hell of a lot more hunters than twenty years ago.

"Here's a herd of elephant. There's a population explosion. We've got to take out that bull. But nobody benefits. But now we bring in a hunter from America, and now that bull is worth thousands. Do you see the synergy here? The guy with the money from America and the guy with the knowledge, the hunter."

Photographic safaris? "I have no problem with that if the guy's going to pay the same game fees. I will take him to the same places, I will take him right up to the animal so he can take his picture, *if* he pays the same fees. . . . But here, this is where the money is. It's these people who give the animal value. It's the way it is. That's our nature. You can't take away my nature. Screw with nature and you'll fuck up the world."

I agree to look Stofberg up if I am ever out his way, asking him before we part to tell me what elephants are like before he and his clients give them value.

"Elephants are like us," he answers. "They live to be eighty and they are sexually mature at, what, eighteen or twenty. When you kill them, like when they have to cull the herds from helicopters, it's terrible because you can't just kill some individuals. You have to kill them all. Men just cry like babies. I have been there."

You have to kill them all because we have lately discovered the intricate family relationships at work in the herd. The calves, without their mothers' care, will become rampaging, asocial juveniles, and so they, too, must go.

"Elephants are very sociable animals—when you kill the adults the younger ones become dysfunctional. Africa is full of wild, dysfunctional elephants. . . . They're smart. They know where the hunting areas are. They know, and they can communicate that to each other. Where I am in Namibia, we have a road that divides the hunting area from the protected area. The water is in the hunting area. And I see the elephants come into the area, rushing, to get a drink. And then they rush back. And when they're across the road you can see them relax. You can see the relief. They know."

THREE

MATTERS OF
CONSEQUENCE

Is it not sufficient for man to absorb the useful labors and lives of the inferior creation, without superadding excessive anguish, want and misery? When his own cup of suffering is full and overflowing, desperate resort to revolution sometimes rids him of his cruel tormentors and taskmasters. But of the inferior animals, generations and generations suffer and expire without any chance of relief or redress, unless it be granted by the generosity and justice of man.

—JULIUS AMES, *THE SPIRIT OF HUMANITY*[1]

I don't know about you, but all of this is not my idea of wise dominion over the natural world and its inhabitants. You didn't have to be the fainthearted type to take in a scene like Safari Club and feel that something has gone horribly wrong, something involving our own human dignity every bit as much as the animals'. You look at these pictures here, all the brochures and catalogs I've been citing, and it's just beyond belief. I've got sixty pounds of the stuff here on my desk, the pornography of bloodlust, and like other obscenities today a multibillion-dollar industry. The gun and the camera—perhaps only in combination have the blood sports reached their full potential for iniquity.

Here is the slain giraffe courtesy of Berlin Game Ranch Safaris. Why could this woman possibly want to kill that giraffe, a beautiful and graceful creature who did her no harm, isn't overpopulated, isn't causing environmental damage anywhere, and inhabits an enclosed ranch unable even to escape? Why?

Here are three guys sitting next to a grizzly that has been propped up in seated position. They're all laughing and pointing at him, as if at a drunken bar mate who has passed out. The mighty "Stalker of the North" deserves *this*?

Here is Brother Wolf, as Saint Francis called him—five of his kind hanging from a rope like so much laundry. Were these marauders harassing ranchers, killing livestock, threatening innocent people, terrorizing a town? No. Like those polar bears being torn to pieces by packs of dogs, they were minding their own business in the frozen wilds of northern Canada, where in all likelihood the first humans they ever saw were these miscreants now posing with the carcasses.

Here is a face I recognize—Lee Bass of Fort Worth, heir to one of America's biggest fortunes and chairman of the Texas Parks and Wildlife Department. Mr. Bass doesn't appear in this picture to be there on official business, unless it is to inspect potential new stock for Texas's six hundred or so hunting parks—of which Mr. Bass himself owns three, totaling nearly 100,000 acres[2]—overseen by the department. Here he's holding a leopard in the standard full-nelson pose, flashing a grin that could not be more maniacal if the cat were alive and still fighting back.

Then there are all these dreary pictures of elephants, hundreds upon hundreds of them. Here's one with the elephant on his side, bleeding from the neck. How long did his death agony last? His tongue is hanging out, and, ducking down so as to be framed by the elephant's tusks, is some grinning little bantamweight in a polo shirt.

If all this is dictated by practical economics, then maybe we'd all better start being a little less practical. Who among my readers is content to accept as a fact of life or economics this image of an elephant—a smart, sensitive animal by the professional hunters' own account—rushing frantically to and from the water hole knowing what might be waiting there? This is the best humanity can offer him? How did Johan Calitz's big tusker feel in *With Deadly Intent* when the bastard showed up with camera in tow, taunting the herd until the great bull charged to give us those four thrilling brain shots? How must the elephant calves feel, these little ones who have nightmares, when they are being led away by the slayers (for sale to circuses, as often happens) or left with the herd to go on alone with only their aunts to care for them? What kind of man takes delight in causing such torment, much less filming it all for the delight of others? What kind of economic reasoning is it that can ascribe value to these creatures only by leaving them in a bloody mess? Even if all these things were necessary, as we are assured—the grim and unavoidable business of conservation—what a living nightmare.

Yet it goes on today, and on and on, in the name of dominion, conservation, and other high-sounding aims, and all too often justified by the few who even bother to take any notice at all of these abominations inflicted on animals. Whenever anyone ventures criticism, it is always the creatures themselves and their defenders who are called up for cross-examination in the moral docket, often to justify the animals' very existence—as if they had to prove the negative, that they are *not* unfeeling beings, *not* immune to pain, *not* just "broken machinery" as René Descartes described the screaming of tortured animals. Are they, we still ask, conscious, fully sentient, self-aware, thinking, feeling, emotive beings? Do they *really* feel pain or does it just look that way? And even if they *may* have emotions, are these "emotions" really and truly meaningful emotions like *ours*?

Those are questions for later. They go to the heart of things, and one way or another must shape our whole understanding of dominion and its duties. In this chapter I just want to examine the thinking of many skeptics, especially my fellow conservatives and the lengths to which they often go to avoid animal welfare as a serious moral issue. Typically this involves three points of attack: A glorification of economic imperatives; a summary dismissal of the matter as sentimental, morally trivial and probably subversive; and a little Scripture thrown in for our moral uplift.

Best to take the religious points separately and then move on to the question of economics and emotionalism. On this biblical score more than any, it is about time the Nimrods and Dr. Deers and Christian gentlemen hunters and Safari Clubbers of the world took the stand themselves and explained to us where on earth they got this idea of dominion as a relentless, merciless merchandising and pillaging of our forests and their inhabitants. And let's begin at the beginning.

Go Forth

A reading from the Book of Genesis:

> And God said, Let the waters bring forth abundantly the moving creature that hath life, and fowl that may fly above the earth in the open firmament of heaven.

And God created great whales, and every living creature that moveth, which the waters brought forth abundantly, after their kind, and every winged fowl after his kind: and God saw that it was good.

And God blessed them, saying, Be fruitful, and multiply, and fill the waters in the seas, and let fowl multiply in the earth. . . .

And God said, Let the earth bring forth the living creature after his kind, and creeping thing, and beast of the earth after his kind: and it was so.

And God made the beast of the earth after his kind, and cattle after their kind, and everything that creepeth upon the earth after his kind: and God saw that it was good.

And God said, Let us make man in our image, after our likeness; and let them have dominion over the fish of the sea, and over the fowl of the air, and over the cattle, and over all the earth, and over every creeping thing that creepeth upon the earth.[3]

That is what the Bible says, and that is what the folks at Safari Club think they are doing: the relentless, rewarding, natural, and praiseworthy work of dominion. Quite literally, as we saw at the SCI prayer breakfast, not a one of them is burdened by the least doubt that they are bringing God's will to nature, with every shot proclaiming His glory. Go hunting, as Governor Joe Foss told us, and it's tough to go wrong.

Explain, then, that "blessing" the animals received, and further explain where in their own conduct is that spirit so evident in the words of Genesis— a loving, kindly, and merciful spirit clear to anyone capable of recognizing those qualities. *And God said, Let the waters bring forth abundantly the moving creature that hath life, and fowl that may fly above the earth in the open firmament of heaven.* How did we get from there to stuffing the fowl of the air into cages for the leisurely shooting of gentlemen hunters? *And God said, Let the earth bring forth the living creature after his kind, and creeping thing, and beast of the earth after his kind: and it was so. And God made the beast of the earth after his kind . . . and God saw that it was good.* How did we get from there to ten-grand-apiece pops at the water hole? *And God said, Let us make man in our image, after our likeness: and let them have dominion. . . .* Where in that whole sorry spectacle of auctions and frenzied marketing and giraffe-adorned ballrooms do you find man made in the likeness of God?

My copy of the Good Book doesn't say, "Go forth to selleth every creature

that moveth." It doesn't say you can baiteth and slayeth and stuffeth everything in sight, either, let alone deducteth the cost. What's more, I don't see
anything here that says you can manipulate genes for bigger racks, or control
food supply for the sole purpose of recreational killing, or anything of the
kind. Oddly enough, no mention here of the "Big Four," either, or of Inner
Circles and Pinnacles of killing achievement and competitive hunting as
godly pursuits. Believe it or not, nowhere in all of God's holy word did He
even think to mention the "point size" of any creature, and the closest thing
we find to any "big boy" is the hart that thirsts after cool streams.

In Genesis, the creatures as they come to *life* receive names, not in being
killed as in the sport hunters' grisly rituals: "And out of the ground the Lord
God formed every beast of the field, and every fowl of the air; and brought
them unto Adam to see what he would call them: and whatsoever Adam
called every living thing, that was the name thereof."[4] This distinction offered
by man in addition to that little blessing from the Creator, bestowed again
even in the fear-and-dread scene of the Second Covenant as the animals—
"two and two of all flesh, wherein is the breath of life"[5]—emerge from the Ark
as the earth is renewed. "The Lord is good to all: and his tender mercies are
over all his works."[6]

Reading these familiar passages, it is easy to forget what a radical depar-
ture they mark in mankind's outlook on animals and the natural world. Animals in the pagan religions were less than extras in the drama; they were
props, objects of fantasy, superstitious symbols, figures of myth, the embodi-
ments of departed souls or divinities in disguise. Judaism gave the world
monotheism and a vision of the God who loves and cares for each person, and
with that vision a view of the creatures as individual beings also known by
Him, sharing with man not only in the earth's bounties but also—a still more
intimate bond—in its punishments and suffering. For the first time animals
are not only significant in themselves, belonging to Him and not to us; they
are players, however lowly, in the story of our own moral development. The
God of Israel delights in all that He has made. All creatures sing their Creator's praises, and are dear to Him for their own sakes.

Even slaughtering and sacrificing were, in doctrine at least, a pious homage to creature and Creator alike, requiring, in the case of hunted animals,
the Levite priests to sanctify the kill. Moses, we are told, was chosen because
he rescued a stray lamb: "You who have compassion for a lamb shall now be
the shepherd of my people Israel."[7] To say this is mere symbolism only begs

the question of why saving a little lamb would symbolize mercy. When the prophet rebukes David for contriving to kill Uriah and steal his wife, he uses a story of a man slaying and eating the beloved ewe of a poor man. To Balaam, the false teacher, God actually speaks through an animal, the mistreated mule who sees the angel of heaven even before his master, asking "What have I done unto thee, that thou hast smitten me these three times?"—a question the angel then repeats before rebuking Balaam's cruelty and unfaithfulness.[8]

The Old Testament has few admonitions about animals, yet they are quite direct and specific, like the saying never to yoke an ox and ass together since the latter would suffer, or never to muzzle oxen when they're threshing grain, since the creatures will desire the food but be unable to eat. And how strange, in our age of the factory farm, to hear in the commandments that even cattle are to be given rest on the Sabbath, for "a righteous man regardeth the life of his beast: but the tender mercies of the wicked are cruel."[9]

If anything, it is the hunters in the Bible who are treated warily, folks like Nimrod and Esau who also have trouble living peaceably among their fellow human beings. There was sport hunting of lions and elephants in those times, all right: It was the recreation of Pharaoh, of the oppressors, just as it later became the entertainment of Caesar, Herod, and the kings and debauched elites of other ages.

Judaism was the faith of the powerless and hounded and persecuted, looking beyond earthly tyranny to the Lord of justice and mercy, the God who opens His hand "and satisfiest the desire of every living thing."[10] For our fellow creatures, no longer just objects, no longer just background, but now bound up in the world and its sorrows, God at times seems to reserve a special solicitude, a providential care bordering on the embarrassingly sentimental:

> He sendeth the springs into valleys, which run among the hills. They give drink to every beast of the field: the wild asses quench their thirst.
>
> By them shall the fowls of the heavens have their habitation, which sing among the branches. He watereth the hills from his chambers: the earth is satisfied with the fruit of thy works.
>
> He causeth the grass to grow for the cattle, and herb for the service of man: that he may bring forth food out of the earth; and wine that maketh glad the heart of man, and oil to make his face to shine, and bread which strengtheneth man's heart.

The trees of the Lord are full of sap; the cedars of Lebanon,
which he hath planted; where the birds make their nests: as for the
stork, the fir trees are her house. The high hills are a refuge for the
wild goats; and the rocks for the badgers.[11]

It will be objected that in ancient Judea the men who wrote these words
and described these visions themselves raised and ate the flesh of animals.
There were exceptions to this, various ascetic movements that swore off
meat, and there is a tradition that Christ refrained from flesh. But it is best
not to try fitting Him into our own categories, be it Jesus the Gamekeeper or
Jesus the Vegetarian, and the point in any case only cuts the other way. What
is clear is that in all of their prophetic visions, in straining to describe God's
goodness and plan for the world, the seers could see no more killing and prey-
ing and violence. In these they saw only the corruption of man, even in meat
eating the mark of sin, all things to be washed away when we see with new
eyes "the last things, for which the first were made."

Whether we regard their visions as inspired or not, the Bible expresses
something fundamental in human experience: that in glimpsing the realities
of our own condition, we begin to feel sympathy for the animals. In understanding our own dependence and weakness and perishability, we begin to
understand theirs. And sometimes, like Isaiah with his visions of peace, it is
only when we have grown sick of our own predations, sick of our own killings,
sick of our own wars and acts of violence and cruelties to one another that we
begin to look with gentleness upon the animal world, to see things in the light
of grace and truth, things as they are and were meant to be.

Ernest Hemingway conveyed this sense of revulsion and regret in *The
Garden of Eden,* in which the killing of an elephant is a symbol of evil. My
favorite image of the experience comes in *The Deer Hunter* when Robert De
Niro's character has just come back from Vietnam and sets out with his old
hunting buddies into the woods. While his friends are back swilling beer and
shooting from the car, De Niro, the true hunter, is on the trail of a large buck
with a huge rack. Finally he has a 16-pointer, or whatever, caught in his
sights, and through his scope we see the creature looking back at him, scared
yet serene. At the last moment, De Niro fires into the air, shouting something
like "Just this once." The idea is not that he has suddenly converted to the
animal rights cause. It's just that something has changed him, and after all he
has seen even the life of a deer now seems worth sparing.

THE LORD OF MERCY

Nothing supports dominion, Safari Club–style, in the New Testament, either. Never do we hear the Lord say, "Kill this in remembrance of me." His is a quite different message, blurred over the centuries by the doctrines of man that have often reduced animals to nothing, as if to hide them from God's sight. In his own words I detect only a theme of gentleness, the assurance that not a sparrow falls without His knowing, the "humble ass" bearing Jesus into Jerusalem, and the lamb as symbol of guiltless suffering—fairly high honors for all three creatures.

True, the Gadarene swine don't fare so well, which Saint Augustine took as evidence of divine indifference to animals. They didn't make the Beatitudes, either, unless you count "Be ye, therefore, merciful, as your Father also is merciful," and the Lord himself doesn't have much to say on the subject.[12] On the other hand his personal example is worth something, and though we know he was not a vegetarian we also know he was not a glutton, eating what he pleased without regard to moral costs. And if he ever went hunting, or raised any weapon against man or animal, the moment went unrecorded.

Typically he points to animals to illustrate some larger point, as in likening himself to the hen gathering her chicks, or when he says the birds have their nests and the foxes their dens but the Son of man no place to lay his head, or when he asks, "Are not five sparrows sold for two farthings, and not one of them is forgotten before God? . . . Fear not, therefore, ye are of more value than many sparrows."[13] He asks a similar question in his encounter with the Pharisees who scold his disciples for picking grain on the Sabbath, divine solicitude for animals here again the premise for a reminder of His love for us: "What man shall there be among you, that shall have one sheep, and if it fall into a pit on the sabbath day, will he not lay hold on it, and lift it out? How much, then, is a man better than a sheep? Wherefore, it is lawful to do good on the sabbath days."[14]

Helping the creature is not just a protection of property, as many a biblical scholar still insists—it's an opportunity to "do good." Mercy for a mere creature takes precedence over the law against work. We are "of greater value" than the animals, "better," but they do have value, a value all their own, and they are not forgotten. How could he of all men forget them, having been born in a stable, the sounds and smells of living creatures all around him, attended by shepherds, the protectors of lambs from predation, beginning his ministry, as Mark tells us, in the wilderness "with the wild beasts,"[15] and ending his journey at the cross, where he was led "as a lamb to the slaughter"?[16]

I have always loved that old medieval depiction of his birth. There is Mary looking in wonder at her baby. There are the shepherds and wise men with their offerings. And there, just barely muzzling into the frame, are the lowly cattle and lamb poking their heads in to see what's going on, as if even they had some stake in the events unfolding. Everything is in just the right order: God in all His mystery, man in all his hope, our fellow creatures in all of their dependence. They had no offerings to give except, if quaint lore is to be credited, their breath to warm the infant, and of course when all the excitement was over they had to go back to their pens and stalls and existence as livestock serving the ends of man. There would be no reprieve from that. But there they are, part of the story, and without them something important and beautiful would be missing.

We hear the sacrificial worship of those times cited today as evidence of the hardy and godly spirit of ancient Judea. This ignores the whole story line. Part of his work in the world was to end those very practices and lift our minds to better things. This mission was foretold by Hosea—"For I desired mercy, and not sacrifice; and the knowledge of God more than burnt offerings"[17]—and repeated by Jesus himself when he tells the Pharisees in the grain field: "I will have mercy, and not sacrifice."[18]

It was this mission that brought him to the Temple. The Temple cleansing, as I read the story—the animals here again extras in a human drama, off in the background cowering and fluttering—is about the closest thing he ever witnessed to the Reno prayer room/auction hall. His sole aggressive act on record comes when, seeing the merchants slaughtering and selling thousands of animals, he drives off the lot of them, merchants, oxen, sheep, yearling, and doves alike, and calls the whole place a den of thieves.

Though I have no biblical authority for this, I like to think some of the animals escaped in the confusion. We do read in the gospels that Jesus saw the Temple the night before and "looked round about upon all things."[19] It is a moving image. What could he have seen but the creatures shuffling, stirring, and sleeping in their cages? Everything we know about him tells us that along with his indignation at seeing the holy place defiled, he must have felt some compassion for the creatures being slaughtered and sold by the defilers. I think he did. Why else would he, who came to save the world, who showed

us the way of Christian manhood, take for himself the names of the Lamb
and of the Good Shepherd?

> The hireling fleeth, because he is an hireling, and careth not for the
> sheep. I am the good shepherd, and know my sheep, and am known
> of mine. As the Father knoweth me, even so know I the Father: and I
> lay down my life for the sheep.
>   And other sheep I have, that are not of this fold: them also I
> must bring, and they shall hear my voice; and there shall be one fold,
> and one shepherd.[20]

Of course the sheep are here a metaphor and the chief point is not solicitude to animals but man's own salvation. But what kind of mind was it that
went back again and again to the lamb and other animals like the birds and
fox to convey images of gentleness and suffering and providential love? And
why a helpless, harmless creature to illustrate the Christian way instead of a
proud and violent predator?

Mercy, too, when the Lord speaks of it usually consists in very practical
things. Everything is laid out in the most tangible terms. I've always thought it
worth noting that when he describes how the kingdom of heaven is gained, by
sharing food and drink, by visiting the captive, welcoming the stranger, and
clothing the naked, all of them except for the last are things that animals can
suffer too—hunger and thirst, loneliness and imprisonment.

A friend of mine well versed in Catholic doctrine, though not really sharing
all of my views about animals, points out that in the story of mankind's spiritual growth there are three stages of sacrifice. First, she observes, it was man
who sacrificed man. Then it was animals sacrificed in place of man. Then, in
the Christian account, God takes the place of both man and animal on the sacrificial altar, the Lamb who offers himself up for the world like the sheep to
slaughter. There might be something there applying to our own treatment of
animals. The whole logic of Christianity is one of condescension, of the higher
serving the lower, the strong protecting the weak, the last being first, and all
out of boundless love and generosity, "rights" having nothing to do with it.

I confess, in any case, that I have often wished he had been more explicit
on this score, somewhere along the way encountering a four-footed equivalent of the woman about to be stoned, fleeing its persecutors, finding refuge
beside him, prompting some saying for the ages about laying hands off the

innocent creature and dealing mercifully with them all. It didn't happen, at least not in any record we have. There were no factory farms or 100 percent guaranteed–kill ranches in first-century Palestine on which to pass judgment, and we are left only with his simple and constant theme of provision and gentleness and the divine mercy we are to emulate. To stretch the text any further, enlarging the place of animals in the biblical narrative, would be as egregious and presumptuous as the "conservation" hirelings at Safari Club with their camouflage-covered Bible and idolatrous deer head beneath the cross.

He does, for some reason I have never heard explained, dispatch the disciples with instructions to "Go ye into all the world, and preach the gospel to every creature."[21] There are images in the end-time books of all creatures in heaven, the earth, and the sea coming before their Maker to give thanks, and John's vision has them joining in the heavenly chorus—while the hunter, when last we see him in the Bible, is thundering into the millennium in the form of the Antichrist.[22] But that's about all we have, a spirit of love, caregiving, and forbearance about as far from the Safari Club convention as the Twelve Apostles from the "Inner Circle," or the cross at Calvary from the "Pinnacle of Achievement."

Obviously that story of the temple, too, is not about the animals. It has to do with man's defiling of a holy place and his being called to throw off the habits and practices of six hundred years—the time that temples had been used for slaughter and sales—not for the creatures' sake but for the sake of man's own immortal soul. Safari Clubbers do not install their bear, elephant, or giraffe trophies in churches, though I have not the least doubt that given the go-ahead from their local pastor, most of them would think it a fine idea and a perfectly fitting offering. Without making too much of the comparison, there is a common thread here in the confusion of the things of God and the things of man, the ready conversion of everything on earth to merchandise and profit or bloody recreation.

In contests of scriptural quotesmanship, the violent have their favorites too, as in Genesis when God is said to dwell with Ishmael the archer, or when Paul seems to scold the vegetarians of his day, or when Jesus feeds the five thousand. Drawing inspiration from Ishmael, a modern bow hunter writes that "when I am in the outdoors hunting, I'm comforted to know that God is with me"—the Lord as all-knowing hunting guide leading him from kill to kill.[23] And maybe the central idea in the Bible regarding animals is to refrain from just this kind of cloddish presumption. Kindness to animals is a small yet necessary part of a decent and holy life, essential if only as a check against human arrogance and our tendency to worship ourselves, our own works and appetites and desires instead of our Creator and His works.

Indeed, listen carefully to hunters describing their debaucheries, and beyond the sheer vulgarity of it you find something bordering on willful defiance of any moral code at all, what the poet Samuel Taylor Coleridge termed a "motiveless malignity" that glories in destruction. "Strictly speaking," wrote José Ortega y Gasset, the Spanish philosopher whose 1942 *Meditations on Hunting* is still the canon of "spiritual" hunting, "the essence of sportive hunting is not raising the animal to the level of man, but something much more spiritual than that: a conscious and almost religious humbling of man which limits his superiority and lowers him toward the animal."[24]

In the mere photographing of a wild animal, Ortega observes, "instinct is cheated and mocked, and thus its total extinction is encouraged. To its demand for real and tangible capture, which alone would satisfy it, man responds by carrying off an image of the animal, a view of it."[25] Hunting is *"an imitation of the animal,"* "a mystical union with the beast."[26] Man is "a fugitive from Nature" before whom animals flee, "surly," "unsubmissive," "unobtainable."[27] *"The only adequate response to a being that lives obsessed with avoiding capture is to try to catch it."*[28]

A contemporary sportsman describes the chase and kill as "intercourse with nature."[29] Another, an American bow hunter, picks up the rape theme in this lyrical masterpiece of the genre directed at a deer, a passage the Marquis de Sade might have composed had he discovered the blood sports:

> To see the soft and devious approach of the wary thing; to see the lifted light head turned sharply back toward the evil that roused it from its bed of ferns; to feel the strong bow tightening in my hand as the thin, hard string comes back; to feel the leap of the loosened cord, the jar of the bow, and see the long streak of the going shaft, and hear the almost sickening "chuck" of the stabbing arrow. No one can know how I have loved the woods, the streams, the trails of the wild, the ways of the things with slender limbs, of fine nose, of great eager ears, of mild wary eyes, and of half-revealed forms and colors. I have been their friend and mortal enemy. I have so loved them that I longed to kill them.[30]

Some very formidable spiritual power seems to be at work there, but it is not the Prince of Peace. The passage lends a certain credibility to James Swan's argument in his *In Defense of Hunting* that killing animals provides an outlet for criminal urges that might otherwise be directed at people.[31] Sport hunters operate in a subculture, like pornographers, and are tolerated by the 93-to-95 percent of folks who don't hunt for much the same reason. In conservatives, even the more religious conservatives, questions of animal welfare bring out the libertarian streak.

LAISSEZ-FAIRE

We all know these things are complicated, involving many intricacies of ecology, economics, and ethics, and citing the Bible chapter and verse doesn't prove much except that fallen man has once again made a mess of things. Bullies and cowards are taking out their problems on animals, and some folks will do anything for money, and the general public has lots of other things to worry about, and it's a crying shame: So what else is new? As General Schwarzkopf asked, "Where don't you find excess today?"

What's new is the scope of it, today covering all points of the planet. The people you least want looking after wildlife now have a near-complete monopoly on it. The same kind of money we saw in Reno buying diamonds and giraffe and pachyderms and charitable tax status also buys influence at state wildlife agencies and at the U.S. Fish and Wildlife Service as well. "It's our mission to serve hunters," says one state parks official, "much like welfare agencies serve welfare recipients."[32]

These folks run the show, they have the money and the profit incentive, they have the power, and you have seen the results. Just as hunter Sharp says, you can prepare to say so-long to the elephant as we once knew him. Driven, decimated, dysfunctional, hunted, and in places tormented almost beyond recognition—gone forever, unless we help him, this noble creature that has lumbered the earth all these millions of years. The whole natural world is becoming an archipelago of game parks and shooting ranches and outdoor laboratories for the likes of Dr. Deer to test their cutting-edge theories and innovations, with our zoos and biologists left to preserve and protect remnants of the type, all the species now being assembled in a new ark of science.

Conservatives come at the matter from the basic standpoint of freedom, human self-advancement, and what they take to be our Western religious tradition. If anyone is likely to invoke "dominion" by name, it is the conservative. Whatever the issue might be—wildlife in the way of development, big-game trophy-hunting, the treatment of animals raised for food, fur, or other uses—conservatives are wary of any pleas made on behalf of the creatures.

They like animals as much as anyone—indeed some half of the seven million members of the Humane Society of the United States are Republicans, and where animal issues are concerned you can never quite predict who stands where. Conservative Republicans Chris Smith of New Jersey and Ed Whitfield of Kentucky are great friends to animal causes. So are Representatives George Miller and Peter DeFazio, liberal Democrats from California and Oregon, respectively. Likewise, it was the support of Republican senator Bob Dole, despite a strong Kansas agricultural lobby, that won passage in 1978 of improvements in the Humane Method of Slaughter Act and in the 1985 Animal Welfare Act. In the Senate today animals have no better friends than Republicans Bob Smith of New Hampshire and Wayne Allard of Colorado (a veterinarian), and Democrats Barbara Boxer of California and Robert Byrd of West Virginia. In the United Kingdom some of the most ardent defenders of animals are Tories like Mike Hancock and the late Alan Clark, both members of Parliament, along with Labour MPs like Maria Eagle and Elliot Morley, the minister for agriculture.

In general, though, among conservatives the beasts and their well-being seem to come lower in the moral hierarchy than the rights to property and free enterprise. And of course, up to a point, there is much wisdom in their concern for these rights. I myself, as an occasional Republican speechwriter, have toiled many hours to convey this credo of human aspiration and creativity unhindered by the presumptuous and meddlesome state. The problem to guard against is that this very same outlook can at times cut against the conservative's own belief in man as a fundamentally moral and not merely economic actor, a creature accountable to reason and conscience and not driven by whim or appetite. Often, too, we find conservatives and libertarians bringing to animal and environmental issues their own unique brand of sentimentality, invested in the conquest of nature instead of in nature itself.

Habits, customs, and impulses, just because they are ancient, are not necessarily venerable. And conservatives above all should see in modern dominion the eternal question of earthly power and its abuses, the corruption to which any power in the hands of man is prone. Where our fellow creatures are concerned, in any case, the conquest is complete. Not only are they conquered and subdued in most parts of the world; where not protected in government-owned preserves (and even there routinely trapped and poached), they are fenced in and up for sale. Conservatives are wary of environmentalism and its more radical strains of nature-worship. They would do well, however, to examine their own beautiful abstractions, their laissez-faire outlook toward animals and where it sometimes leads.

Consider, as a microcosm of this attitude in action, one of the occasional newspaper stories that first got me thinking about writing this book. It was a 1997 *Washington Post* item about a fellow in Great Falls, Virginia, not far from where I lived at the time, who had a problem with a flock of Canada geese who had taken up residence on a small island in a man-made pond by his $1.4-million property.

Geese are majestic and lovely birds—from a distance. When you get closer they are more like winged dogs, and wherever they go they leave their calling cards. The neighbors, according to the *Post,* actually liked having them around, but, what with all their honking and traipsing across his finely manicured lawn, they were driving this man nuts.

Finally he could stand it no more. The owner of a public relations firm in Washington with various political clients, he arranged through some connections to have a team of trappers from the U.S. Department of Agriculture come by while he was away and take care of things. They did. Not bothering to consult his neighbors, this man had them all trapped and killed, sparing not even the goslings. The meat was then donated to a Washington homeless shelter, in true Safari Club style, lending an air of benevolence and charity to the deed.[33]

I picture this man coming back that evening, walking out on his patio, looking over the now silent pond, and breathing a deep sigh of relief. *Ahhhhh, peace!* Now at last he could enjoy the beautiful view.

But think about it. Here we have a guy lucky enough to be living in a very nice neighborhood, making a handsome living and probably enjoying every comfort we could name. Then this little disturbance comes along. It is unbearable. Never mind that by building the lake in the first place he and the developers might as well have sent off engraved invitations to each and every goose within a fifty-mile radius to come and live there. This man wants things *his* way. He wants the beauty and tranquility of nature without, well, nature. He wants a pretty lake without those foul geese that lakes usually attract.

So, one fine morning he has them exterminated, while he is away at the office and spared from the unpleasantness of it all. An entire flock of geese, gone, just like that.

A hundred perfectly practical reasons could be found to do as he did: It was his property. He paid for the trappers. The creatures were a nuisance, an aggravation. They were adding to his gardening bills. And so on. Basically, he had dominion.

There was only one good reason not to do it: Those were the fowl of the air, his fellow creatures, and what rank selfishness to begrudge them their little pond.

Another item that caught my attention was an advertisement in *Outdoor Life,* the sportsman's Bible, offering something called the "Wayne Carlton bear call." Hunters, as we saw earlier, employ an endless array of technology out in the field, and this gadget, for sale in Reno, makes the spot-on sound of "the frantic squalling of a terrified cub."[34] The adult bears hear it and come running—while the intrepid sportsman waits.

It is the old practice of bear-baiting, new and improved by modern innovation. A company in Maine makes a similar device called the "Phantom Whitetail," digitally reproducing "12 different sounds proven to arouse the curiosity of Whitetail Deer," including the "estrus bleat" and "fawn distress."[35] And here again every free-market justification can be found for such products. People freely buy and sell them. Government should stay out of it. The manufacturer needs to make a living. They're a time-saver, and on and on. But we're left with the same moral question. What sort of dominion is *that?* What kind of person would use such a thing, drawing in animals by the sounds of their helpless young?

A final illustration hits closer to home for many Americans—the deer problem faced by suburban communities. In the Washington area, we are always hearing about it. The main complaint is the danger they pose to traffic. I wrote a piece on the subject for the *Washington Post* and received a flurry of letters from people angry at my seeming indifference to human safety, one woman telling me about her friends' daughter who had died in a deer-related car accident. Among the lesser complaints is that the deer are known to avail themselves of shrubbery adorning people's finely kept gardens, remorselessly nibbling away at the petunias and azaleas.

It is a serious and complicated situation, and I don't claim to have all the answers. The first question a reasonable person asks is why are deer suddenly darting into highways, like the one I saw writhing on an icy Route 267 in northern Virginia a few years ago. It's not as if they are irresistibly drawn to busy roads and terrifying cars and lights. If you were a deer, you would stay as far clear of highways and busy roads as you could, and that's exactly what deer do when left the alternative. That deer I saw had simply been looking for food, water, and other deer, having been frightened off from somewhere else by trucks and dynamite and bulldozers. Or, as in the case of a friend of mine who collided with a deer further out near Leesburg, Virginia, the deer spring into busy unfenced roads in flight from hunters—about as sorry a picture of dominion as I can imagine. Indeed, a study in Pennsylvania found that car insurance claims for deer-related accidents increase fivefold during hunting season.[36]

The second question is, who are the chief complainers? The developers and the hunters, ever quick to exploit the safety hazards they themselves have caused. I am all for measured development. I am not writing this from some tiny cabin in a forest. I live on developed property. I live in civilization, and I am glad of it. But when you take and develop land you have to confront the simple fact that it causes the deer to scatter. You, the developer and renter or buyer, are therefore the morally responsible parties, just as you would be if the project left falling-rock hazards near busy roads.

The developers don't want to pay for fences, road-light systems alerting the deer to approaching cars, or vaccines to prevent fertilization (administered by treated feed or darts), all of which would serve the purpose quite well, and indeed are working already in places where they have been tried such as Gaithersburg, Maryland. Their line is "fences don't work," as if northern Virginia's bionic deer can scale any height—a claim easily enough refuted by noting how fences somehow seem to work when the aim is to *make* money by keeping the deer captive. Those fences back at the Velvet and Mustang hunting ranches seem to be doing the trick.

In an animal version of the Andy Warhol saying about fame, every species today gets fifteen minutes of pity, and Washington's local deer got theirs one day in 1997 when dawn found three of them at the corner of Seventeenth Street and Pennsylvania Avenue. One was caught in the iron fence between the Treasury building and the White House as he tried squeezing through onto what must have seemed the lush safety of the North Lawn. He was so scraped and bloodied that, after trying to calm and free him, Secret Service officers covered him in a blanket and euthanized him. "We lost him," said one officer."[37]

Local political authorities don't want to foot the bill for fences, road reflector systems, and a more rigorous enforcement of speed limits, nor to antagonize the developers who contribute generously to their campaigns. It seems cheaper to all parties concerned to just kill the deer. And why not make it fun, too, for the sportsmen, who inevitably have begun promoting "the suburban deer bowhunt."[38] As it turns out even these managed hunts are problematic: The more deer they kill, the more space and food is left to the other deer, yielding over time more deer than before. The females reproduce in greater numbers, a phenomenon known as compensatory reproduction and observed in human populations, too, during wartime. To solve the problem with hunting alone, they'd have to wipe the creatures out by the thousands, and it may come to that. Here, as reported by the *Post,* is how this question of dominion is being resolved:

> The first of eight managed hunts—designed to help winnow a deer population estimated at 25,000—got Fairfax County's animal-control effort off to a slow start yesterday. . . . "It was a very nice day in the woods," said Don Gantz, 53, of Fairfax, who bagged two deer—the only ones he saw. Gantz . . . said he was about to give up at noon when two does cautiously came up to him, heads down. He shot both—a 108-pound pregnant doe and a 67-pound doe.[39]

So there is our menace. Two does with their heads bowed. Approaching cautiously. "A very nice day in the woods." Twenty-five thousand of these marauders supposedly inhabit the county, yet when the day was done 150 hunters (selected by lottery) could find only ten of them. A few weeks later Fairfax County hired sharpshooters for the job, sending them in at night to avoid public notice. This time they could find just 107 deer in six days' worth of slaughter.[40]

Wouldn't it be a lot easier, at least on one's conscience, to put up the roadside fences and lighting systems? We're talking about developments usually making the owners millions of dollars in sales or rental profits. Northern Virginia, home of America Online and the entire Internet corridor, is the picture of modern prosperity, and few are prospering more than real estate developers and their clients. They can't spare a little of that wealth to protect the deer whose forest homes they have appropriated, make a little room in all their big designs and master plans for creatures who, before the development, weren't causing any harm to anyone?

As for the homeowners, are azaleas really worth that scene described above? Are there really people so touchy about their gardens and flowers that, seeing a doe with her fawns feasting in the backyard, they feel compelled to call in the sharpshooters? And where will *they* be when the job is done? Indeed all these "managed hunts" are now done in secret. What does that tell you?

The solution is always the gun, or poison, or traps, and the divine mandate always money. Geese getting on your nerves? Wipe 'em out. Want a stuffed bear for the living room? Go forth then to bait and slay the beast— bring along the "Wayne Carlton," and don't forget the keg. Wildlife hindering new development? Bring dominion to field and forest, exterminate the creatures, and raise up thy new strip mall.

Conservatives should recognize here a familiar figure from their own critique of modern culture. It is the Imperial Self, armed and dangerous. Indeed dominion today is a little like the U.S. Constitution, stretched to cover all kinds of abuses done in its good name. It is the same fundamentally vulgar vision of man that conservatives elsewhere so earnestly worry about—man the perpetual victim, man the whiny special pleader, man the all-conquering consumer facing the universe with limitless entitlements and appetites to be met no matter what the costs.

Even when the complaints are legitimate, as with lethal driving hazards to people, there is an utter refusal to accept human culpability, as if the deer were to blame and not the developers. It is as if the whole natural world existed for no other reason than to please the appetites of man, however ignoble, irrational, and reckless. Anything that is there is there to be taken. If it's in the way, level it. If it dares distract or inconvenience, run it off. If it adds to costs, kill it.

It is a vision that looks upon our fellow creatures to find only an infinite array of pests, threats, resources, obstacles, targets, livestock, roadkill, racks, and "wall-hangers." Nowhere in this vision is there any room for animals with their own purpose in the world apart from the designs of man. Never is a deer just a deer, the thirsty hart needing a place of its own, an unoffending creature in need of a break. It fell to a deer hunter, in *A Hunter's Heart: Honest Essays on Blood Sport*, to ask the basic question of fairness:

The more we eliminate the wet and wild places from our farms and ranches, the more we dice and cut, spreading our homes and business deals over first the farms, then the hills above them, along the lake shores and streams and into the forest, the less we will be able, in good faith, to pick up the shotgun or rifle to take to the fields that are left. Even if we do find a few derelict patches that look healthy, we must know that the game we seek is cut off and more vulnerable to our presence now. We must wonder, at some point, if we still have the right.[41]

We often hear the animal rights cause dismissed as "politically correct." But really it never has become PC, perhaps because more than allegiance to any idea or doctrine the cause requires a conscious act of will and a change in personal habits. A regard for animals requires actually giving up a few things, be it a fine fur, a trophy-hunting safari, a coveted building site, or a pristine lawn unsoiled by noisy geese.

At least in troubled economies like Indonesia, where we have seen once-protected monkeys and other animals being auctioned off wholesale, or in Rwanda and Congo where chimps are sold in marketplaces like so many chickens, or in other parts of Africa where every time some rebel group needs cash for new weapons they kill a few hundred more elephants and sell the ivory on the black market—at least in these places human beings have the excuse of desperation. In the affluent West it is just whim and habitual arrogance, King Consumer having his way with nature, to hell with the costs. The fashion magazines have lately been heralding that "fur is back," which is only fitting. Often, too, furs are now dyed in an array of pinks and purples and yellows, as if to push the creatures further back from our consciousness, and conceal with bright colors the origin of each product and the ordeal behind it.

My *National Review* colleague Jeffrey Hart, a professor at Dartmouth College, captured the attitude nicely, noting indifference among some of his students toward environmental and animal-welfare causes. "It is depressing," he writes, "to hear cigar-smoking young conservatives wearing red suspenders take a reductive view of, well, everything. They seem to contemplate with equanimity a world without lions, tigers, elephants, whales. I am appalled at the philistinism that seems to smile at a future consisting of a global Hong Kong."[42]

IMPERATIVE COOKING

Each side of the animal debate is always psychoanalyzing the other—the hunters and their kind detecting an effeminacy and softness of heart in the animal lovers, the animal lovers detecting in hunters a mix of maladjustments from bloodlust and impotence. I will try to steer clear of that temptation, or at least not rest any arguments upon such probings. But there is one little facet on the conservative end I have never quite figured out, something in the tone of voice.

Conservatives bring to the whole matter not only philosophical doubts and debatable economic points, but a kind of exasperated snobbery, as if they should not even have to bother with such trifling questions, and who are all these petty little activists distracting them from the great moral questions of the day? It leads to a dogmatism rivaling anything among the animal rights crowd, if not worse in its stern uncharity toward our fellow creatures, its lazy disdain of moral inconveniences mixed with high talk of moral virtue, and its rigid faith in the Prosperity Bible, that all-consoling assurance that somehow the free market will right all things and any cruelty will be redeemed by the miraculous workings of capitalism. A gem of the first genre came in a 1998 column by conservative Auberon Waugh of the London *Daily Telegraph*, commenting on the hunting issue:

> What distinguishes these nice people [opposed to hunting] from unpleasant ones holding the same opinions is the latter's element of self-righteousness. Unpleasant, sanctimonious people are to be avoided because they are boring. What distinguishes the merely unpleasant from the fascists is the latter's desire to stop anyone from hunting. These people—the fascists—should be insulted, kicked, and thrown into the nearest river whenever possible.[43]

This from a veteran commentator who spent his entire adult life telling people how to think and act. Maybe those *boring* activists don't have columns and other means of influence at their disposal. So they assemble in protests to convey their objections. What's wrong with that?

A similar outpouring came recently from American Walter Williams, one of my favorite columnists and a conservative economist known for his usually analytical mind and fine sense of humor. He has had it with the anti-fur activists, here commenting on a 1999 Beverly Hills, California, initiative (unsuccessful, as it turned out) to put labels on fur products describing their provenance. The labels would have read:

> CONSUMER NOTICE: This product is made with fur from animals that may have been killed by electrocution, gassing, neck-breaking, poisoning, clubbing, stomping or drowning, and may have been trapped in steel leg-hold traps.[44]

Dr. Williams's reaction:

> Tyrants never reveal their true agenda up front. They always start off with something relatively benign and sometimes quite reasonable. Then they incrementally become more oppressive. . . . Animals are killed far more humanely than ever before. . . . These people [advocating the consumer notice] are useful idiots for animal rights wackos like PETA, who are evil people who sabotage experimental laboratories and assault people wearing furs. I own a beautiful shear skin coat, and Mrs. Williams has a full-length mink coat. The animal rights wacko who would toss red paint on us had better be prepared to meet his maker.[45]

How does Dr. Williams know the animals "are killed far more humanely than ever"? The folks at the "Fur Commission USA, an association representing mink and fox farmers," told him so.[46] That is all the evidence he cites. Unlike those useful idiots blindly following the animal rights agenda, Dr. Williams has done his research, accepting nothing less than the personal assurances of the public relations firm financed by the fur industry. And just in case *that* doesn't convince us, he invokes his own wardrobe, those exquisite furs we touch at our peril.

Fending off the "food fascists"[47] on the culinary front is Digby Anderson, another Brit and my fellow contributor to *National Review*. He is both a social commentator and food columnist, often mixing his essays on animal matters with recipes. His London *Spectator* column is called "Imperative Cooking." A particular favorite is rabbit, for Digby the symbol of our age, "soggy as it is with animal sentimentality and ecological obsession."[48] "It is silly and sinful, and ungrateful to the Almighty, not to eat rabbits," he writes:

> In a civilized society rabbits are shot (or snared or ferreted) and eaten. They are not shot grudgingly, as vermin, and eaten grudgingly, to use up what had to be shot. They are to be eaten enthusiastically with mustard sauce (Dijon mustard) or an English parsley sauce— the sauce should be based on a stock from the head, ends of the front paws or other fleshless pieces.[49]

"Very elderly rabbits," he continues,

> if one has been remiss enough to let them live that long, are finely chopped or minced. . . . Younger rabbits, babies and teenagers, can be quickly fried with just parsley, black pepper and garlic thrown on at the last minute. . . . They are particularly economical to shoot. The wary shooter gets up early in the morning and walks his land till he espies a family of young rabbits. They will, as young people are wont, be playing, making little leaps and dodging about. The gun waits for the crucial moment when three or four are suddenly alone together, and fires. With luck, it is three or four rabbits and only one cartridge.[50]

Without luck, it is two or three wounded rabbits left to run off and bleed to death somewhere. As a regular reader of Digby's fare, I note that he has never once expressed concern for any animal on or off his menu, be it a rabbit, dog, dolphin, whale, or elephant. Equally contemptuous of all creatures, he has never had much to say on questions of animal intelligence or emotion, believing as an article of faith that in the killing of animals "their value is recognized. Wild animals need to be invested with economic value."[51] Any trace of emotion toward animals (live ones, anyway) he regards as a sign of weakness and moral confusion to be scorned and rooted out. Hence the relish with which he describes interrupting the bunnies' play with gunfire, and that bit about being "remiss" in letting any of them get old.

"All children," Digby advises, "by age 10, should have killed at least rabbits (chop the back of the neck), chickens (wring the neck), and ducks (cut the head off). Other anti-sentimental exercises include handling slimy things such as eels and plunging their little hands up the bottoms of fowls to pull out the entrails."[52]

There are big and important principles underlying this outlook. Animal-welfare advocates are passionate about animals. Digby is passionate about, well, pie: "For it is not just rabbits which the modern generation, especially intellectuals, have severed from their proper connection with the pot," he writes in an essay entitled "Why Get By Without Our Rabbit Pie?" It is "Nature" from which we are estranged:

> [An] earlier generation of children and adults knew that rabbits and other animals had to be killed before they served their proper vocation on the plate surrounded by rich gravy. . . .
>
> In this older England, Nature was neither sentimentalised as snuffling bunnies or theoreticised into balancing eco-systems. It was something whose ways had to be mastered in order to provide in the kitchen. Even when increased affluence meant this was not necessary to survive, some cultures, especially France, retained this understanding.
>
> Maybe you can get enough food to survive today without a realistic and traditional view of Nature, but you will eat much better with one. In France, wild rabbits are scarce and prized and so are wood pigeons, wild duck and even squirrels. Not in England, any more.[53]

This brings us to the big picture:

> But the end of rabbits, though temporary, hinted at a wider threat which is coming true. The end of a kitchen intimately linked to Nature. The end of the notion that wild creatures are placed there by the Almighty for man to study, follow, hunt, kill, cook and eat.
>
> With the passing of that traditional view of nature, the way is left wide open for the animal sentimentalists who will make pets out of a good dinner and the eco-loonies who would take man from the pinnacle of creation and enthrall him as a cog in a system.[54]

Granting Digby that one can be too emotional about animals, it seems fair to ask if one cannot also be a little too emotional about food. Why is it excessive sentimentality to see rabbits as our harmless fluffy tailed friends, but not excessive sentimentality to go on and on about rabbits soaked in rich gravy with the parsley and Dijon mustard and stock from the paws and head and old England and all the rest?

Whether or not we accept his view of Nature and the kitchen and man at the pinnacle of creation, it is not exactly the light of pure reason one detects here. These are not principles he is defending; they are pleasures, by his own account "not necessary" anymore. Nor is it Nature and our ties to it that are in question (obviously bread and fruit and vegetables also come from nature), but his own particular vision of nature and our moral place within it.

All of which would be fine, if only Mr. Anderson would spare us this insufferable blather about the Almighty whose sole purpose in sending forth every creature on earth was to furnish unbridled epicures like himself with things to shoot, wound, strangle, or disembowel. If only he would look up from his plate long enough, perhaps he would discern some even grander design at work in the world.

As if to show us where his own vision leads, lately Digby has taken to setting off the word "creatures" between quotation marks.[55] Apparently even *that* concedes too much, as if for the sake of his all-important stews and pies he must now stamp out the very idea that they are living beings created by God—and never mind all those "creatures" running around Old England's King James Bible.

DEEPER THAN CHOICE

Hard to beat for sheer snobbery is the case of British philosopher Roger Scruton, a Tory intellectual who fled the cities in middle age, discovered the joys of country living and in particular fox hunting, and now sees in the eclipse of his new pastime all the lights going out across Western civilization. His 1999 book *On Hunting* offers a variation on the familiar "primal urge" mysticism with a modern conservative flavor to it, informing us, like Mr. Anderson, that hunting is not only a noble pursuit but that "God intended that we should live in such a way."[56] As with most conservatives, his argument comes in the form of a high-minded scolding. "Sentimentality over animals is rather endearing," writes Mr. Scruton,

But it is also a vice. Animals cannot answer back. They cannot punc-
ture our illusions. They allow us complete freedom to invent their
feelings for them, to project into their innocent eyes a fantasy world
in which we are the heroes, and to lay our phony passions before
them without fear of moral rebuke. They are the easy option for the
morally deprived.[57]

A few pages later, after warning us against ascribing personalities or even
names to animals, Mr. Scruton strains to describe the deep yearnings at play
in the hunt:

[R]eligion and erotic love are the deepest of our poor resources; but
hunting, however distant on the surface, lies adjacent to them in the
depths. What else explains the mysterious and soul-shaking chem-
istry that Wagner works in the second act of *Tristan*, as Isolde sings
out her impatient love above the distant sound of hunting? Listen
carefully to this passage, and you will hear something that cannot be
put into words, but which lies as deep in you as it does in me.[58]

Though I have my doubts about Wagnerian music as an inspiration for
the healthiest human passions, the composer himself, as it happens, was a
vegetarian who wrote that "the same thing breathed in animals as in mankind," and described blood sport as "a bottomless pit of cruellest misery."[59] So
whatever Mr. Scruton hears in Wagner, it doesn't seem to be what Wagner
actually intended.

Leaving musical interpretation aside, however, the obvious question here
is this. If hunting is such a profound, fundamental, and indeed "soul-shaking"
part of us—ranking right up there with our religious and erotic yearnings—
why do so few people do it? In America just 5 to 7 percent of us are succumbing to the charms of Isolde—or Tristan, or Wagner, or God, or whoever
is encouraging us to hunt—considerably fewer than display an interest in
spiritual and erotic pursuits. In Britain fewer than 4 percent hunt—"a substantial minority," he calls it in his 1996 *Animal Rights and Wrongs*.[60] Mr.
Scruton's fellow fox hunters come to all of 0.5 percent of Her Majesty's subjects. In fact that's why he's so worked up about the issue—because as he was
composing this ode to the foxman, Parliament was very close to banning the
sport, Prime Minister Tony Blair himself favoring abolition.

Later in *On Hunting,* as Mr. Scruton describes the pleasures of hunting, we learn what we are missing. Looking quite the "hero" himself, with that special pink button denoting membership in the "Vale of the White Horse" (fox hunting, Mr. Scruton proudly informs us, even has its own "Inner Circle"), he is now astride Sam, his noble steed, surrounded by the hunting dogs, accorded snooty names like Sonorous, Sanguine, and Saviour, all of them experiencing "the unique love that grows between the hounds and hunter."

The hounds, whose "individual vices and virtues" he knows, are unleashed in frenzied pursuit of "Charlie," the traditional name, we're told, accorded the fox by English fox hunters. Ever "crafty" and "wanton," Charlie is suddenly endowed with "beliefs and strategies, vulpine strengths and weaknesses." "The hunter now works side by side with animals whom he treats as individuals, in hot pursuit of the prey whose individuality is lent to it only temporarily, as it were, and because it has been singled out by the chase."[61]

. Finally comes the delight, that "blood-filling joy," of the kill. Charlie "jumps from the barn at Maunditts Park Farm, and stupidly runs downhill into the wind. We encourage it in the opposite direction, but it insists on the gorse, where it is instantly cornered and killed. This pleases the hounds, and therefore the huntsman."[62]

I guess it's an acquired taste. Typical of writers recounting their punitive expeditions in field and forest, in this case the gentleman's version of cock-fighting, Mr. Scruton has no trouble at all ascribing vivid emotions and personalities to animals when it serves the purpose. In a wave of sentimentality evoked by the ritual of the kill, all the horses and hounds and foxes spring dramatically to life in his imagination, displaying not only vulpine craftiness and fatal "stupidity," but canine "love" and equine "joy."

And talk about laying our "phony passions" before animals: Mr. Scruton has laid before the late Charlie not just his own peculiar passions, but an entire new theology in the form of something called "the species-soul." Animals have no capacity for individual suffering, existing only as "generic beings."[63] Charlie, for example, "will survive its death."[64] When Saviour and the other dogs have finished with him, he "returns to his archetypal condition, resuming his nature as The Fox, whom the huntsman knows and loves, and whose eternal recurrence is his deep desire."[65]

What a comforting thought. So Charlie didn't feel a thing. And now he lives up there in archetypal realms, eternally loved and desired. It sure sounds better than "Charlie got mauled."

Pets, with their clearly distinctive traits and personalities, pose a challenge to this generic-being theory, a problem Mr. Scruton has solved as follows:

> We relate to one another as individuals, and the soul is the animating principle which makes a person who he is. In the case of human beings, therefore, the soul is the self. In the case of wild animals, to which we relate as interchangeable members of their species, the soul-idea becomes attached to the species. . . .
>
> This way of relating to animals is less familiar to those who know only pets. For domestic animals have a kind of personality bestowed by our daily dealings. We treat them as individuals and they learn to respond as such.[66]

This won't quite do it, though. It is true, of course, that our human dealings with animals do bring out certain traits of personality that would never emerge in their natural state. But whatever traits of personality emerge in an animal through human influence must obviously be traits latent in the creatures themselves. We can "bestow" only the training and influence, not the qualities. These are *revealed* through our contact with a given animal. The potential must be there, in the nature of each animal. Pets in this way actually draw us closer to the reality of animal life than do beasts of the wild—a transformation vivid to anyone who has ever taken in a stray or feral, and observed the creature slowly shedding the primal fear and voracity of its former life. The tame animal is in a sense the most natural of all, displaying qualities hidden within his or her own nature that only human kindness can elicit.

Even assuming that foxhunting served a vital ecological purpose—in the thrall of his own poetic vision, Mr. Scruton never even gets around to the practical questions—what a strange sight. Here is a right-thinking conservative intellectual designing, to suit a taste for gratuitous violence, his own little monogrammed morality, this value-free universe of victimless hunts and killing without costs. In *Animal Rights and Wrongs*—charmingly dedicated to "a bull calf called Herbie, which has now been eaten"[67]—he has written his own indictment, here explaining in more detail why sentimentality is a vice:

> A sentimental emotion is a form of self-conscious play acting. For the sentimentalists it is not the object but the subject of the emotion which is important. Real love focuses on another individual: it is

gladdened by his pleasure and grieved by his pain. The unreal love of the sentimentalist reaches no further than the self and gives precedence to pleasures and pains of its own, or else invents for itself a gratifying image of the pleasures and pains of its object. . . . It consumes our finite emotional energies in self-regarding ways and numbs us to realities.[68]

It never occurs to Mr. Scruton that such sentimentality can accompany the killing of animals as much as the care of them. Like others who revel in violence to animals, the man leads almost a double life in this respect, one moment engaging in serious moral reflection and a moment later lost to reason in the thrill of the kill. Here he is in his man-of-reason mode diagnosing in *National Review* the lure of modern pagan cults such as the "wiccan" and "deep ecology" movements. Members of these groups are drawn by "enchantment," he explains.

> Science has disenchanted the universe and deprived us of our place at the center. Human beings cannot live in this demoralized world. They need to see their environment as their tribal forbears saw it: as an enchanted place, which mysteriously returns our glance. The spell answers directly to this need, since it enables the witch to reanimate her universe. . . . Rituals, spells, and incantations are deliberate defiances of reason. They place nonsense at the center of people's lives and ask them to unite in believing it.[69]

Change a few words, and it could be another of Mr. Scruton's raptures on the enchantments of hunting. For all of his erudition, he simply cannot see how hunters themselves might be in the grip of some spell, some mania in need of rational moral scrutiny.

This self-delusion leaves only the problem of guilt. Hence his inevitable lashing back at the "vice" of others, that 96 percent or so of the British population too soft for the hunt. He has abolished his own vice by abolishing cruelty, abolished cruelty by abolishing suffering, and abolished that by, in effect, abolishing the fox. The wind at his back aboard Sam, Mr. Scruton physically corners and kills the fox, first "lending" him individuality in the act of hunting, then finishing him off with a theological death blow, taking from the creature its very status as a particular being. And he's worried about other people living in a fantasy world.

People have always found justifications for cruelty to animals, but never with that imperious disdain of Mr. Scruton's, this odd mix of primeval desire with utter theoretical certainty, or frankly, as I detect in his tone, such pure spite. The big picture for Mr. Scruton is "stewardship." Writing in the *Los Angeles Times* he lays it down as a guiding principle of modern dominion that "We are now stewards of the animal kingdom. Henceforth, no species exists without our permission. We therefore have some difficult choices to make."[70] This leads to another principle, the holy dogma of modern conservation, namely that "we can provide for the animals only if we have sufficient motive":

> And "we" does not mean pampered intellectuals but rural primitives, rednecks and the kind of person who would like to keep a pit bull. Fortunately, the motive exists. There is no better way of protecting the habitat of a species than by systematically hunting it. . . . [I]t is big-game hunting that will save the safari parks of Africa and whaling that will save the whale. Elephants may be threatened by ivory poachers, but not so much as they would benefit from ivory farmers, who would have an interest in protecting them. As it is, however, the shortsighted ban on the trade of ivory will probably lead to the extinction of the elephant.[71]

Defended over the ages as necessary to human survival, now all of a sudden hunting is necessary to the animals' survival, at least those favored species deigned fit to exist. But think about what he is saying. What a jaded, selfish view of the world and our place within it—a kind of reverse Genesis in which every species shall now be summoned before almighty man to justify their existence or be banished from creation, man the Unmaker of all things.

And what do *we*, the stewards, have to justify? Mr. Scruton speaks of "difficult choices," in that familiar tone of the realist resigned to life's hard duties. But duties are usually more complicated than that, involving some sort of hardship or self-denial. Here, in the end, all the stewards and those they serve get exactly what they want, their duties always bearing such an uncanny resemblance to their desires. No human appetite goes unmet. The ivory hunters and carvers get their ivory. The hunters get their trophies. Presumably even Asian inamoratos get their aphrodisiac "cures" from the horns and ivory (their desires, alas for them, only to meet with disappointment later on).

It doesn't even matter to Mr. Scruton that these are each fundamentally irrational desires, indeed vanities and superstitions—false goods, as we would call them in ordinary moral reasoning. It was observed when Viagra came along that this might actually save the tiger and rhino and some species of ape, rendering obsolete the market for traditional Asian aphrodisiacs which require parts from these animals. What a sorry state of affairs when the fate of the ape and the rhino and even the great tiger—all five thousand wild tigers left on earth—should hinge on such a thing.

As with so much of modern "conservation," Mr. Scruton's entire scheme is nothing but an elaborate evasion of duty, leaving us to make hard judgments about the creatures and none about ourselves, to deny them their lives and habitats while denying ourselves nothing. The standard in all of this would be decided, in Mr. Scruton's vision, not by any fixed moral code, not by the example of people who protect and care for animals, but by the "primitives" and "rednecks" who shall inherit the earth. Lest we forget, here are the sort of stewards Mr. Scruton has in mind, two typical American sportsmen doing some deer conserving as described in a 1998 *Washington Post* profile:

> Inch by inch, she'd moved nearer. Inch by inch, he'd positioned himself for the shot. . . . Tensing, crouching, watching—he'd been ready. All was quiet except for the occasional wail of a sika buck. . . .
>
> "Please," he said to himself, "let her turn."
>
> As if she'd heard, the doe turned—a perfect target.
>
> He shot.
>
> The arrow strikes with a resounding whack, followed by a mad thrashing as the wounded deer gallops in a wide splashing arc to the hunter's front. In 20 seconds, the noise stops abruptly. There's a small wet gurgle.
>
> "I whacked her!" Forster roars. "She went down! That deer is down!" He's so excited, he's dancing. Another hunting pal . . . hearing the commotion, walks up.
>
> "Hey, Mike, I whacked one! Man, I'm so pumped!"[72]

Borrowed from the jargon of the Mafia, the term "whacking" was popularized by Ted Nugent, the rock star, leader of United Sportsmen of America, and self-described "master whacker" of deer who lately has been showing up at political events such as the 2000 Republican National Convention. His motto: "Whack 'em and stack 'em."[73] He's a conservationist too, says Mr. Nugent, proudly discharging "the moral obligation of resource stewardship."[74] Indeed, in culling deer, bear, and other creatures that might otherwise perish in the cruel winter, "I am almost Mother Teresa."[75] In his popular video *Down to Earth,* as one critic, a fellow hunter, describes it, Mr. Nugent "kneels and sarcastically asks for 'a moment of silence' while the viewer is treated to close-up, slow-motion replays of the hits, including sickening footage of some animals that clearly are gut shot or otherwise sloppily wounded."[76] Into these hands, people who dance around their kill, inflicting unmitigated torture on a deer, just plain "pumped" by the twang and thrashing and gurgling and gut shots, Mr. Scruton would have us deliver the world's remaining wildlife.

Of course he would resent any comparison of his own pleasure in hunting with the likes of Mr. Nugent, this creepy little vulgarian with a following of hundreds of thousands. Mr. Scruton's is a more refined version of the experience, the gentleman's "pump." "My life," he tells us, "divides into three parts. In the first I was wretched; in the second ill at ease; in the third hunting."[77] This was presumably offered as jocular overstatement, though reading on, one wonders. "In those centaur hours . . . real life returns to you. For a brief ecstatic moment the blood of another species flows through your veins. . . ."[78] Hunting, in a parade of florid phrases, is also a return to "the matrix of primeval desire."[79] "An act of worship."[80] "An act of communion."[81] "The therapy for guilt involved in guiltless killing."[82] An "absolution in the blood," as in the tradition of drinking the blood of the animal one has killed— "a barbarous practice, say some, but one which engages with the most vital of human needs, the need for social membership that goes deeper than chatter and deeper than choice."[83]

Now there is an interesting turn of phrase: "deeper than choice." One would like to know just how it squares with the rational moral choices he has elsewhere been discoursing about, all of those "difficult choices," "duties," and "principles" of modern dominion. How is man to exercise rational dominion over nature while submerged into nature with all of this phony primal playacting? Mr. Scruton never explains, and in the end the pleasure and profundity of it all are beyond even his own lyrical powers: "If you wish to know what fox hunting is, and why it is beyond measure beautiful and compelling and obsessing, then you should read the novels of R. S. Surtees—*Hadley Cross*, and *Mr. Sponge's Sporting Tour*—novels that do not merely capture the deep emotions that focus on this sport, but provide an inimitable record of the society which grew around it in the nineteenth century."[84]

If Mr. Sponge is anything like Mr. Scruton, I'll take a pass on both books. I have had my fill of blood rites, obsessions, centaur hours, and sickly brooding on the meaning of it all. G. K. Chesterton had a good term for such enjoyments: "the devil's sentimentality."

THE PROSPERITY BIBLE

It all adds up to exactly the kind of intellectual puffery that Mr. Scruton elsewhere debunks. In Walter Williams's tantrum we see exactly the kind of attitudinizing, unreliable data, and capricious reasoning that his columns routinely assail. In Auberon Waugh's scolding we see the very kind of posturing and moral hamming he usually poked fun at. All around, too, one notes the ready claim to victimhood, with Mr. Waugh detecting "fascism" in the concerns of animal advocates, Dr. Williams standing in defiant guard over his closet, and poor Mr. Anderson sounding like some sniveling sybarite in danger of losing his pie. Even their writing grows labored and pompous at the mention of the subject. What is it about the question of animal suffering that makes such ordinarily reasonable people fly off the handle?

This always surprises me. If you express concern for the fur bearer in question, his or her paw all but severed by the time the trapper comes along for the forking and bludgeoning, or huddled for its entire life in a tiny cage in 32-degree temperatures—why, then, you must be one of those ridiculous, killjoy fanatics. A bore. But rise in furious defense of a coat—now there's the mark of a serious man. Likewise, express qualms about some little delicacy like foie gras—fifteen thousand tons of the stuff eaten every year in France alone,[85] all of it obtained by forcing a metal pipe down the ducks' throats and pumping in pounds of food until their livers are grotesquely enlarged—and that makes you petty and trifling and sentimental, and why don't you have your mind on bigger things? But reach for the knife and crackers, never mind the damned duck, and then you're thinking straight. *Now* you've got your priorities in order.

Nobody likes being preached to, especially about meals and clothing. I sure don't, and most of us who worry about animal welfare have learned to let the point go. But spare us the haughty airs. If moral seriousness is the standard, I for one would rather be standing between duck and knife than going to the mat in angry defense of a table treat.

In fact, let us just call things what they are. When a man's love of finery clouds his moral judgment, that is vanity. When he lets a demanding palate make his moral choices, that is gluttony. When he ascribes the divine will to his own whims, that is pride. And when he gets angry at being reminded of animal suffering that his own daily choices might help avoid, that is moral cowardice.

Conservatives in particular would do well to examine the huffy impatience they sometimes bring to questions of animal welfare. We are talking, after all, about some fairly simple connections here, and after a while it becomes perverse not to make them. I think for example of some wrenching footage aired in late 1998 by the NBC News program *Dateline* documenting the use of some two million cats and dogs a year by Chinese fur manufacturers for export mostly to the West. Filmed by undercover agents for the Humane Society of the United States, on the video we saw the dogs tied down while being skinned alive, whimpering for mercy, actually licking the hand of the skinner, and the cats stuffed into little cages, huddled in terror as one after another was strangled to death—literally noosed and hung inside the cage, this to avoid bleeding or other damage to the fur.

A horrible scene for any American (and still going on throughout China and Korea) because, of course, we don't do that with cats and dogs. We protect cats and dogs. We like cats and dogs. We only allow that to happen to other animals. It's okay to stuff millions of other creatures like mink and beaver and fox into cages and torture and terrify and electrocute them—precisely the method, despite those comforting assurances the furriers gave Walter Williams. Indeed, the very fact that Dr. Williams thought it necessary to seek such assurances is an admission of the moral relevance of the question. Only he doesn't seem to really want the facts, which threaten upheaval of his world and wardrobe.

Whatever motive is at work there, it is not reason. What principle of reason or morality permits us to disapprove of one kind of fur trade and not the other? It's easy for us to look aghast on the Chinese. How uncivilized of them! Yet all they are doing is applying our own logic and economics to the fullest, with none of the arbitrary and dainty moral distinctions we bring to the matter.

℮

You can see the Prosperity Bible working its wonders every time the subject of one or another endangered species comes up for debate. Typical was a *Wall Street Journal* op-ed challenging international bans on whale hunting— the subject of our next chapter. Though "unquestionably extraordinary animals," possessing "a certain intelligence," argued the author, whales and their fate are an issue best left to "natural resource managers" within the whaling industry. Moreover, whaling is integral to the economies of Japan, Greenland, and Norway, and "given the abundant world-wide [whale] populations, there is no reason to penalize the many in these countries who choose to toil—skillfully and at high risk—to hunt a few thousand whales per year." Accompanying the column is a drawing of a hunted whale with the caption, "There's plenty more where he came from."[86]

Leave it all to the natural resource managers—they'll take care of everything. Let them handle the moral nuances. And so the great leviathan, these grand mammals of "a certain intelligence" about which we learn more every year, creatures with no natural predator, not causing any environmental damage or harm to anyone, hunted to the point of annihilation in a single century after millions of years swimming the seas, are consigned to more years of hunting long after humanity has any need for any product derived from them.

The same kind of reasoning has cast the elephants of the world in their starring role as marauding big tuskers in *With Deadly Intent* and thousands of similar, unrecorded scenes of mayhem carried out in the name of resource management. For years they were poached on every side by ivory hunters. Then, seeing a "conservation" opportunity as elephant populations began to stabilize, along came good old Safari Club and all those entrepreneurial professional hunters and outfitters with an offer to local African villages: You safeguard the elephants from illegal ivory hunters, leave the hunting to us, and we'll pay $10,000 or more per elephant. The elephants thus become a "cash crop."[87] Instead of being slaughtered all at once for ivory, they would now be slaughtered in a more orderly fashion for trophies.

The few conservatives who even noticed this turn in the plight of the elephant (our own GOP symbol, for goodness sake) immediately liked it. Now, as one writer put it in the *Weekly Standard*, the creatures could start "paying their own way." We must, he urged, avoid the "emotionally appealing arguments" and "counterproductive do-goodism" of those trying to protect the

African elephant. Under the CAMPFIRE program ("doing so much to help those elephants," as a Safari Club banquet speaker put it), the elephants are converted from an economic "liability" into an "asset." A valuable resource is "deregulated." "Rights" to the elephants "devolve to the empowered peasants," all along "the rightful owners of the game," and market forces prevail.[88] We hear similar arguments today for a resumption in legalized ivory trading. Elephants, declared the editors of *New Scientist* in April 2000, "must earn their keep if they are to compete for land."[89] "Forget Trade Bans," the magazine urges in a familiar refrain. "Just Make Animals Pay Their Own Way."[90]

They are talking about a species of intelligent mammal whose population across Asia and Africa stands at 5 percent of what it was a century ago; whose numbers were halved in a generation; who suffered casualties of more than 700,000 just in Africa during the 1980s, facing Nitro Expresses on one side and, on the other, swarms of paramilitary poaching gangs armed with AK-47s, radios, and spotter planes. In Africa there is hardly such thing anymore as a middle-aged wild elephant with fully grown tusks, which for illegal poachers still at work has meant twice the killing for the same amount of ivory. In 1979, as Douglas Chadwick writes in *The Fate of the Elephant*, "it took 54 elephants to get a ton of ivory. Now, with mature tuskers all but non-existent and females the prime target, it took 113 elephants and left an average of 55 orphaned calves and young juveniles to die later."[91] It has been so bad for the big tuskers that in India, Sri Lanka, and even in Africa, where both male and female elephants have tusks, scientists have lately noticed a strange frequency of elephants born with no tusks at all. By a genetic quirk a tiny percentage of male elephants have always been tuskless. Now, as if evolution itself were trying to spare these creatures from human avarice, that gene is spreading because the tuskless ones are often the only ones left to breed.[92]

In view of such details, one would have thought the elephants had already "paid their own way," with a security deposit for decades to come. In truth, if the market alone is our measure, they can never pay enough.

Another conservative, my friend Tom Bethell in his 1998 book *Noblest Triumph: Property and Prosperity through the Ages,* makes the case for reopening the ivory trade on the grounds that only "privatized elephants" can flourish. If the ban on ivory is successful, he writes, "the animal is deprived of most of its economic value. Trying to preserve it by such methods is like trying to conserve cows by banning the consumption of beef."[93]

Usually a very astute writer, and a person of deep moral sensibility, Tom doesn't seem to have pondered the full implications of his position. It is a completely amoral vision of nature and our duties of dominion, making none of the distinctions that he, as a conservative and a Catholic, would make in any other area of human activity between licit and illicit appetites, just and unjust behavior, moral and material values. He simply layers this rational system of economic value upon a fundamentally irrational and perverse demand for trophies and ivory trinkets, which would make perfect economic sense were it not for that fact that by the terms, at least, of his own faith there are indeed questions of morality to be considered.

Nothing in the natural world, he seems to be saying, is of value unless someone owns it. We can save the world's elephants and tigers, but only by consigning them all to elephant and tiger farms, each creature in due course to be possessed and killed and thereby accorded value—a way of reasoning that reminds me of the businessman in Antoine de Saint-Exupéry's *The Little Prince,* who thinks that by counting each star he assumes possession of it, until they're all added up and in time he may lay claim to the universe. "And what good does it do you to own the stars?" asks the little prince:

"It does me the good of making me rich."

"And what good does it do you to be rich?" . . .

"It makes it possible for me to buy more stars, if any are discovered."

"How is it possible for one to own the stars?"

"To whom do they belong?" the businessman retorted, peevishly.

"I don't know. To nobody."

"Then they belong to me, because I was the first person to think of it."

"Is that all that is necessary?"

"Certainly. When you find a diamond that belongs to nobody, it is yours. When you discover an island that belongs to nobody, it is yours. When you get an idea before anyone else, you take out a patent on it: it is yours. So with me: I own the stars, because nobody else before me even thought of owning them."

"Yes, that is true," said the little prince. "And what do you do with them?"

"I administer them," replied the businessman. "I count them

and recount them. It is difficult. But I am a man who is naturally interested in matters of consequence."[94]

In the same way, one might well ask what good it does us to keep the elephants alive at all if their sole value on earth is a hunter's fee. Why even *bother* if we think so little of these creatures, after all that they have endured at the hands of man, that we are now willing to let them be farmed and administered in this nice, systematic way by the very people who have already done them so much evil?

What the free market touches, it blesses. If the profit incentive points that way, why then that must be the right thing to do. Let one and all pay their own way. And so the trophy hunters are now strutting about as big-hearted humanitarians, doing their bit for the "empowered peasants," while the noble elephant, beset by helicopters, trapped in game parks, his water supplies controlled by hunting outfitters, uncounted orphaned calves being raised for labor or circuses, today lives in a nightmare world of ceaseless attack by the likes of Kenneth Behring and Skip Donau.

I find nothing in the conservative moral tradition remotely resembling this sacrifice of every creature in sight before the almighty dollar. It is a different spirit entirely. It isn't rooted in conservatism, or Christianity, or Judaism, or classic capitalism, or any other tradition of honorable origin. It is much closer to what, in conservative big-think circles, they call "the modern spirit." Friedrich Nietzsche, despite a personal abhorrence to animal cruelty, would today fit right in at one of our libertarian think tanks with his notions of human morality: "Life is essentially appropriation, injury, overpowering what is alien and weaker, suppression, hardness, imposition of one's own forms . . . exploitation."[95]

The free market could just as easily be brought to the aid of villagers and elephants through non-hunting tourism and indeed the non-tourism industries Africa needs most. There are a thousand people in this world who would pay to see elephants and tigers alive for every one person with a taste for killing. The situation is complicated because those of us who live in the more developed world are dealing with other countries and with our fellow human beings living in poverty. But if there is to be American and Western involvement, why this and not another approach—the most obvious being to help purchase land for elephant reserves? That would require some ingenuity and some regard for elephants on their own terms, as assets all by themselves, not just as big fat privatized "resources" or commodities, but as creatures of beauty and value and moral worth regardless of how many thousands of dollars some wretch will pay to shoot them.

Their fate spells very bad news for the animal kingdom, for there are probably no beasts on earth, save our canine and feline friends, who command higher esteem from humanity. Yet, in our laws, we let this happen to them. In private game parks across Africa the elephants have been delivered into the hands of their worst enemy. Their only enemy.

BACK AT THE RANCH

Here I must take to my soapbox and megaphone again outside the factory farm. It would probably be better for the elephant and other wild creatures not to bind them in my argument with the doomed livestock who command so much less sympathy. Even the mink and fox will eventually get a hearing if you press the point and show the evidence. They are coveted by an affluent but small market or, more understandably, by working-class folk who see in a fur coat the symbol of their economic struggle upward. But the lamb and pig and cow—where is our heart for them?

At some point we began to lose sight of the distinction between wildlife and livestock. That fellow arguing in the *Weekly Standard* that the elephant must "pay his own way" and become an asset, one Ike C. Sugg, was at the time a "wildlife and land-use expert" at the libertarian Competitiveness Enterprise Institute in Washington. A self-described "free-market environmentalist," he has since found his true calling as executive director of something called the Exotic Wildlife Association in Kerrville, Texas, the trade group of those fenced-in, guaranteed–kill hunting ranches we saw in Chapter 2 which, in the thirty-odd states where canned hunting is still legal, are permitted even to import African animals to America for the sole purpose of being shot. ("Introduced Trophy Animals," as this award category is known at Safari Club.) Mr. Sugg is also, it turns out, from a prominent ranching family in Texas. What is he doing but applying the economics of livestock to African wildlife? The trade group's Web site is explicit about it, using the term "exotic wildlife" interchangeably with "exotic livestock" or "alternative livestock,"[96] and posting notices of upcoming auctions where deer, big cats, big-horned sheep, and other wild animals may be purchased by hunting ranches just like cattle.

At Safari Club we heard hunter Pieter Stofberg express this same out-look, as does Tom Bethell with his notion of elephant preserves as privatized ivory farms. How fitting, too, that the wildlife auctions in Reno should be conducted by professionals from the cattle-show circuit. The elephants of Africa have it better than the animals we raise in our intensive livestock oper-ations. But little by little, in spirit at least, the factory farm is coming to them.

I understand that many people today depend upon animals for their livelihood, and don't take kindly to sermons on the topic. If the wolf under-stood the sheep, as Abraham Lincoln is said to have observed, he would die of starvation. Wild animals, too, are caught up in the cultural ways of many regions, as in parts of America where a man's social life can be divided into three basic activities: talking about the last hunt, hunting, and planning the next hunt. I understand as well that some people who work on farms or deal every day in animal trades, particularly small farmers I have met, are perfectly sensible and decent folk who would be as repelled by the likes of Safari Club as I was and in their way are kind to the creatures in their dominion. One such man is Iowa hog farmer Larry Ginter, the rare farmer today who will have no part in intensive agriculture. "It's unnatural to me," he told an Associ-ated Press reporter. "They [the factory farmers] view the sow as a machine. It's not a machine. It's an animal, and it needs care."[97]

Small farmers like Mr. Ginter are themselves a vanishing breed. The future lies in the factory farm. In some European countries they have "Green" butcher shops where the meat comes from animals raised by relatively humane standards, and here in the States we have similar options through various sellers like the Fresh Fields natural-food chain. I think that's a useful practice and I'm glad to see people caring enough to buy only "ranch-raised" flesh. This consumer option, however, only attests to the fact that meat from ani-mals raised with any compassion at all has now become a sort of specialty food one has to look for. By far most pork or veal or beef for our burgers comes from the large-scale enterprises. Soon there will be even fewer facto-ries of even greater size and scope.

They confront us with a choice we have been putting off for a while now. The only way of winding down the factory farms is by withdrawing our weight, each person, one act of conscience after another, from the momen-tum of consumer demand.

As it is, I see in those factory farms a spirit not much better than that we observed in Reno, a casual willingness to subject animals to suffering without

end for the sake of little things we could do without. I cannot think of a better image to capture the fruits of this spirit than those massive runoffs of
waste and filth and toxins seeping into our own water supply—now, as the
public takes note, suddenly causing "environmental concerns" and a "public
hazard." A public hazard? My Lord, what about the creatures inside those
places?

Few adults have any illusions about our modern factory farms and packing plants, or about the tender mercies accorded the creatures that creepeth
therein: the bright, sensitive pig dangling by a rear hoof as he or she is
processed along, squealing in horror; the veal calf taken from his mother,
tethered and locked away in a tiny dark stall for all of his brief, wretched
existence. If you could walk all of humanity through one of these places, 90
percent would never touch meat again. We would leave the place retching
and gasping for air. We cringe at the thought of it, and that cringe is to our
credit.

But there's a little bit of Safari Club in us all. We fall back on the lofty-
sounding justifications. And so demand for the product only gets more furious. We push the image away, smite it, command it to leave, shrug it off,
trusting that somehow it all comes out even, it is all redeemed by need, it's all
a part of the natural order. And of course everyone else is doing it so what's the
big deal? Only a few cranks question the necessity of it. So we tell ourselves.

Then, adding to the fantasy of it all, when it suits us we pour on the sentimental mush. With that distinctively modern mix of sentimentality and
ruthlessness, we get all weepy over movies like *Babe,* while, back at the ranch,
the intensity of consumer demand leaves no time for the least modicum of
mercy. "What happened to Babe's mother?" the kids always ask. We make up
some nice, comforting story because the little ones aren't ready for that yet.
But if the movie itself suddenly flashed to Babe's mother hanging up there in
the shackle squealing in agony, adult viewers would be as mortified as the
children.

Not *important,* we keep telling ourselves. No, it is only important enough
to hide, lock away, bar from filming, forget about, laugh off, deride, belittle,
and at all costs avoid discussing in detail. The factory farm is an economic
necessity, cuts costs for the consumer, unavoidable in the global economy, a
fact of life, a way of life, a livelihood, blah blah blah, all this to justify an obvious moral evil so sickening and horrendous it would leave us ashen, produc-

ing goods now replaceable, and employing people who could be making those alternative products instead. All this so we can have our accustomed veal or lamb or fried chicken or pork chop or hot dog at the ballpark. Talk about sentimentality.

Yes, I include here the fowl, too—all the little creatures we cram six or eight per cage, cage upon cage, in giant windowless sheds. Recall the mad frenzy of killing in Hong Kong a few years back following an outbreak of avian influenza. Tens of millions of the creatures shoveled into trash bags, gassed, and buried in a landfill, thousands of tons of feathered garbage, in what then became a worldwide cleanup operation. It was the same in 1996 when England had its "mad cow" scare, repeated in France, Belgium, Germany, and other countries since then. Both were just glimpses into the hellish world of mass livestock production upon which most of us feed today.

Pretty radical, but to his credit the conservative British historian Paul Johnson, in his 1996 spiritual memoir *The Quest for God*, has topped me:

> Great saints like St. Francis, St. Cuthbert and St. Philip Neri, who were particularly close to animals, and specially sensitive to the way in which they manifested God's will and love, saw this coming and were ahead of their times. The understanding of animals they individually and intuitively acquired is gradually becoming more general as we use all the resources of modern science to get closer to them. We are indeed beginning to understand how animals think and why they do things, and that understanding makes us appreciate them far more and treat them more intelligently.
>
> The more we understand about life in general, the more we value the lives of all creatures. Vegetarianism is spreading, inexorably I believe. God allowed us to live off the beasts of the field and the forest because there was no other way, then, for humankind to survive and prosper. But our technology is now such that we can produce endless varieties of nourishing and delicious foods without resorting to animal flesh. Gradually this realisation will take hold of us. The rise of factory farming, whereby food producers cannot remain competitive except by subjecting animals to unspeakable deprivation, has hastened this process. The human spirit revolts at what we have been doing.[98]

THINK A SECOND TIME

Even among people whom one cannot imagine deliberately harming an animal, there remains some sort of mental block, an utter inability to see how their very own moral insights—and more than that, their own sense of life as a moral drama full of trials, temptations and false choices—might apply to man in our dealings with the other creatures.

One commentator dismissive of animal rights is Charles Colson, a great Christian voice of our day and a man for whom I have enormous admiration. He's the Watergate figure who went on to found the Prison Ministry, bringing hope and fellowship into the lives of hundreds of thousands of prison inmates and their families. He has a radio program, has published many books, and often writes columns commenting on public affairs from the evangelical standpoint. In both modern environmentalism and animal rights, Mr. Colson reflects in *How Now Shall We Live?* (co-authored with Nancy Pearcey), lurk the evils of a naturalistic worldview, a view that neglects the unique dignity of man made in the image of God:

> In that naturalistic worldview it is only logical to place the goal of population control above the dignity of human life and to resort to any means available in order to preserve Mother Nature from being depleted and despoiled. From this perspective, humans are often seen as aggressors against pristine nature. Of course, Christians believe we are responsible to protect God's creation, to be good stewards, and to exercise dominion.[99]

A paragraph later:

> The same logic drives the animal rights movement, as it denigrates human life in its efforts to make the human species equal with all others. These attempts often turn nasty, with animal rights activists throwing paint on women wearing furs; nasty and destructive, strapping explosives around tree trunks to blow up loggers and save the spotted owls; nasty, destructive, and sometimes silly, raiding restaurants to liberate lobsters.[100]

So Christians are called to be good stewards. And just what might that mean? What is good dominion? What is godly dominion? What is bad or irresponsible or wicked dominion? We never learn, though there is hardly any shortage of human depravity in the picture they paint of modern culture.

The whole subject comes up only as an occasion to rebuke the radicalism of environmental and animal rights causes with the platitudes of evangelical Christianity, this useless pabulum about being good stewards of the earth. In the absence of animal rights activists to criticize, one doubts the subject would have come up at all. Here are two Christians earnestly asking *How Now Shall We Live?*—in a 470-page survey of modernity and all its woes, of all the sins they seek to cure with their Christian message. Yet never once do they pause to note a single example of how that duty of Christian stewardship is being abused or even how it can be abused. Ask them to explain any other form of human cruelty or neglect or exploitation, and they, like all the Christians they speak for, would have a ready answer: Evil has a name and it roams the world. On the problem of cruelty to animals, one hears only silence.

Another influential commentator often heard warning against environmental and animal rights causes is Dennis Prager, the Jewish theologian and popular radio talk-show host. I have never heard the show, but his books are full of good sense and sharp but kindly moral counsel. He has a question for animal rights advocates, here posed in his 1995 *Think a Second Time* by way of describing one of "three 'minor' events that had a big impact on my thinking." Mr. Prager was on an airplane:

It was mealtime on a flight somewhere over the United States. I noticed that both the middle-aged woman seated next to me and I had ordered special meals. I had a kosher meal, she a vegetarian one.

"Are you a vegetarian?" I asked the woman.

"Yes," she responded.

"Why?"

"Because we have no right to kill animals. After all, who are we to claim that we are more valuable than animals?"

I vividly recall my thoughts. When she said that we have no right to kill animals, I felt a certain sympathy for her and her position. After all, I thought, here I am eating a kosher meal, and I have always understood kashrut to be Judaism's compromise with vegetarianism.

But when she delivered the second part of her explanation, I couldn't believe what I was hearing. In fact, I was so certain that she was engaging in hyperbole that I said, "I certainly understand your opposition to killing animals, but you can't really mean what you said about people not being more valuable than animals. After all, if an animal and a person were both drowning, which would you save first?

I was sure I had posed a rhetorical question. So, when I received no response from the woman, I asked her if she had heard me. "Yes," she responded, "I'm thinking."

That was a bombshell. I recall my reaction as if it had happened last week: She's "thinking"? What on earth was there to think about?[101]

Well, for starters, we can think about the fact that Mr. Prager has just described his own position on the matter of meat eating as a "compromise," whereas this woman is simply acting consistently with her own principles. If we're going to be purists about it, find me the passage in any holy book, Christian or Jew, in which it is laid down that anyone *must* eat meat. It is permissible, not mandatory. A concession, not a commandment. The laws of the *kashrut* are themselves a ritual reproof for the practice of killing and eating animals, as Mr. Prager acknowledges. But without the practice, there is no need for the ritual, and indeed many Jews today have become vegetarians for just that reason.

The next question might be how, in reality, kosher meats—requiring unanesthetized killing and blood draining—are actually prepared for today's mass-market consumption, at a pace of hundreds of animals per hour, in plants mostly supervised by non-Jews. This is a delicate matter, and I am wary of commenting any further on Jewish traditions or practice. If Mr. Prager can freely criticize vegetarianism, however, then I am free to describe the objective facts behind his own position, a typical account of which we have from a consultant to the livestock industry, here describing a kosher meat plant. The throat slashing, she writes,

resulted in vigorous reactions from the cattle during the cut. The animals kicked violently, twisted sideways, and shook the restraining device. Cattle which entered the poorly designed head holder in an already excited, agitated state had a more vigorous reaction to the throat cut than calm animals. These observations indicated that the head holding devices must be designed so that the incision is held open during and immediately after the cut. Occasionally, a very wild, agitated animal went into a spasm which resembled an epileptic seizure immediately after the cut. . . . Since animals cannot communicate, it is impossible to completely rule out the possibility that a correctly made incision may cause some unpleasant sensation.[102]

This is a "compromise" with the cruelties of ordinary slaughter. In *Think a Second Time* Mr. Prager also tells us that one measure of a civilized society is "holiness—the amount of distinction between the society's behavior and that of animals; the closer a society's behavior is to the animal kingdom, the less developed it is."[103] Which, here again, strikes me as a concise case for vegetarianism.

Then he says something even more striking, recalling a second minor event that shaped his thinking. Throughout the book he has mentioned all the familiar animal causes, adding all the familiar disparagements: "In our liberal age, the intellectual and moral norm is to regard a baby seal as of more worth than a human fetus."[104] The rights activists display deep moral confusion in trying to liberate "a killer whale held 'captive' in a huge aquarium."[105] It was shameful of the folks at PETA, he writes, to compare the suffering of our factory farms with the Holocaust.[106] Two pages later comes this story, a description of a cockfight Mr. Prager happened upon in Bali when he was a young man:

Men were cheering on animals that were trying to scratch out each other's eyes, and wagering on which one would die first.

Two powerful realizations came to me.

One was how bestial human nature is. The Holocaust is what first made me aware of humanity's enormous potential for doing evil. But it was this visit to human ugliness amid natural beauty that confronted me in a less threatening way than the Holocaust with what lurks in people beneath the veneer of civilization.

The other, more powerful realization was what a tremendous moral revolution ethical monotheism had wrought. I imagine what sort of a world it was over three thousand years ago, when the first

Jews introduced a universal invisible God who demanded goodness. It was far more than cockfighting that had to be fought: Human sacrifice was commonplace.[107]

I could not describe any better my own sense of the wicked desires people reveal in their hearts by mistreating animals. But if Mr. Prager believes this, why do we so rarely hear about it? Here is an obviously gifted commentator, a wise and decent man with an audience of millions. In all his columns and books and radio discourses, however, the only time he ever comments on animal welfare is by way of denigrating the animal rights cause. Perhaps it is by default that Peter Singer and others with no religious faith are left to champion the cause of animals, precisely because men and women like Mr. Prager and Mr. Colson have so little to say on the subject—on practices they themselves, when they happen to notice them, will often concede are wrong or indeed evil.

Moreover, as long as we're making stern judgments here, what is to prevent those men in their enjoyment of cockfighting and similar cruelties from saying that they have made a compromise too? Objectively speaking, if we simply compare harsh realities with actual needs, the suffering inflicted with the pleasures gained, is their position so different from one's insistence on having fowls obtained in factory-farm conditions? Your chicken from McDonald's, Tyson Foods, or Perdue Farms spent most of its life stuffed in a cage with three or four others, occupying a space about the size of this page you are reading.[108] Your foie gras came from a duck treated far worse than any champion rooster. And your lobster, if Mr. Colson wants to bring that up, was boiled alive. And now, in certain trendy restaurants, it is the craze to eat lobsters alive.[109] Explain to me why cockfighting is unconscionable, but those other practices aren't.

And if, on Mr. Prager's own account, the sport of cockfighting is shameful and unworthy, then what does he make of the sports of rodeo, or bird shooting, or bearbaiting, or canned hunting, and so on down the line? Maybe the whole problem here is that too many people have made too many compromises, so many that we can hardly tell the compromises we make from the principles we hold.

As for his question to animal rights advocates—whom to save first from drowning, a human being or an animal—this sounds like one of Peter Singer's hypotheticals, with that same fundamentally negative outlook, the same perverse knack for starting with hard cases. One answer might be that we would save the person but mourn the dog. Or we could answer the dilemma on its own terms by asking Mr. Prager whom he would save first if two people were drowning, a stranger or his own child? Most of us would probably save our child or wife or husband or friend, though by doing so we could not rationally claim that the stranger's life was any less valuable. Even less could we claim that the stranger's life was of no value at all, though by the terms of this dilemma we may be compelled to let that person die.

His question forces us to affirm one value by essentially negating another, when in fact, just as in our human affairs, we usually have the third option of affirming them both, as witness his own scenario: Having saved first the drowning person, we might well ask why try to save the drowning animal second? Why save the creature at all, especially if there is some risk or sacrifice involved?

His answer would probably be that the creature's life does indeed have some lesser value than the person's life, that we care about the dog and don't want him to suffer. Less philosophically, he might reply that it is just the decent thing to do. And it's a good answer. But then we must ask again what that value might be, from where it arises, how it applies elsewhere, and why it should not be applied consistently. In our farms and laboratories and hunting ranches, what is the decent thing to do?

MILD QUALMS

A final sample of the conservative's suspicion of animal causes comes from my friend Joseph Sobran, the syndicated columnist. At his best, Joe is for my money among our finest writers of political commentary, and far and away the funniest. What I admire most about him is his independence. He does his own thinking and doesn't just go along with the crowd, though on animal issues he tends to be pretty orthodox.

Joe kids me now and again about my moral indignation over animal welfare. When I told him I was a vegetarian of twenty-five years' standing, he said "A conservative, with a Catholic upbringing, *and* a vegetarian? Boy, talk about aggrieved minorities!" Here, in a column he wrote a few years back, Sobran offers us an amusing little riff on the animal right cause. "In the first place," he writes, animals "do not even claim rights for themselves. They certainly don't recognize each other's rights. So any rights they have would be exclusively man-made, at least until we could raise their consciousness, which might take millions of years":

> This would put us, the human race, in the position of policing the entire animal kingdom, making sure they don't violate each other's rights. After all, if they have rights, these are not just rights that inhibit us humans in our dealings with them, but rights against each other. We could reduce our workload by allowing each species to police itself, but we'd still have to protect the weaker species against predators: the antelope against the lion, the rabbit against the fox, even (if we mean business) the fly against the spider. If we suc-ceeded, the predatory species would become extinct. This would be a pretty self-defeating victory for animal rights. One way around it might be to put the predators on a different diet, which it would be up to us to produce. We're talking a lot of soybeans.[110]

He goes on to suggest commissioning "a feasibility study from the Department of Agriculture" for the soybean program, his basic point being that any notion of moral status for animals ends in absurdity—as witness, he adds, the concern over dolphins caught in fishing nets but not over the poor tuna. "All they care about is a few dolphins, which whimper pathetically when they get caught in the net. If there was ever a case of the squeaky wheel get-ting the grease, this is it."[111]

Like other conservatives, Joe raises many quandaries for anyone con-cerned about the lot of animals. He also leaves a few problems to be explained by libertarian conservatives and other skeptics—beginning with that dolphin, an advanced mammal, whimpering in the net.

It is logically true that creatures without duties cannot be said to exercise rights in precisely the same sense that we do. On the other hand, it doesn't follow that because they have no rights we bear the animals no obligations. Any rights they have are the mirror image of those human duties. They can't "claim" rights (though that whimper's good enough for me), but it comes to the same thing: They are owed dutiful human care. And so we're back to the question of what those duties might be. This classic distinction that conser-vatives always make to prove animals don't have rights, typically with a tri-umphant air as if that settles the matter once and for all, is a classic distinction without a difference.

We all know, likewise, that the natural world is vicious and predatory, with most animals winding up as meals for other animals. There is a gentleness there, too, easy to overlook if all you're going by is *When Predators Attack* and other such videos popular in America today. This truth about the lives of animals was immortalized by Gary Larson in a "Far Side" cartoon showing, in frame one, the hunter killing a bear from behind while the creature is quietly lapping water from a pond, then in frame two the stuffed bear in the guy's living room baring fang and claw—Stalker of the North. It's always easier, when we think of animals as ruthless and predatory, to be ruthless and predatory toward them.

But, yes, in many ways nature is harsh and unruly and unforgiving and we all know that. A raw fact. This does not, however, lay to rest the matter of our own ethical conduct toward animals. The whole point of dominion is that the animal kingdom is not our moral example—that in a sense we are in the natural world, but not of it. The non sequitur running through the animal rights debate is that because the creatures cannot themselves grasp or act upon moral concepts, we are not obliged to act morally in our conduct toward them.

As our powers are unique, it would follow too that our ethical obligations are unique: A lion when he's hungry pounces on a zebra and that's the end of it. He can't raise zebra in captivity or construct vast factory farms for zebra. He can't take out the herd all at once, or build a fence and charge other lions to come in for an easy kill, or bait zebra with contraptions imitating the frantic squalling of young zebra, or tape the kill and sell it for the vicarious delight of a libertine lionine market. All predators are limited in the kind and duration of suffering they can inflict (though cats stretch the rule a bit with their practice of keeping prey alive for the instruction of cubs, as do foxes and weasels with their habit of surplus killing), and in the level of moral degradation of which they are capable. We are not.

A very kindly fellow himself, Sobran earlier in his column describes feeling "mild qualms about eating ham ever since I read an article saying that pigs are highly intelligent animals which, given a chance, are as affectionate as dogs. I wince at the lobster tanks in swanky restaurants. . . . All creatures great and small have their place, as far as I'm concerned."[112]

That's probably the position of most people: We feel a natural regard for and at times even kinship with animals, especially the more affable ones like the dolphin or elephant or chimp. But we're pulled in the other direction, too.

If we grant some special moral distinction to the dolphin, what then? Who comes next and where will it end? Mammals only? Pigs, too? Chickens? Lobsters? And so on down the slippery slope until the whole inquiry seems silly and dangerous and we draw back, leaving things as before. We'd like to help our figurative dolphin, still squeaking and thrashing in the net. But to do so, it seems, would overthrow the whole moral universe.

Along with this hesitation comes a suspicion common even among people basically well disposed to animals. Many of us, when we pause to think on animals, fear that as our concern for them extends, our concern for each other shrinks. We hear this fear in the familiar complaint about all those Greenpeace types up there trying to protect baby seals, or out on the high seas throwing themselves between whaler and whale, and so on, but who don't seem to care about people. Where is their compassion for the poor, or homeless, or handicapped? Anything we give the creatures must be extra, the unwanted scrap tossed from our moral table. The French philosopher Jean-Paul Sartre put this suspicion best: "When one loves animals and children *too much,* one loves them against human beings."

Surely the interesting thing in that maxim is the inclusion of children, who, though a world apart from the animals, are also vulnerable to human caprice and who seem to share with animals some natural bond, an instinctive kinship beautifully captured in William Blake's poem "The Lamb." The other interesting thing is its complete misunderstanding of love. Since when does love ever diminish as we spread it around? Among humans it usually works the other way. So too in our dealings with the animals we know best.

When you bring a dog into the house, is he absorbing love and attention that would otherwise go to household members? Typically, if we treat the creature right, he or she has something to give back, and indeed many parents get pets in the first place so that the kids might learn to think beyond themselves and to care for other beings. Neither you nor the dog are ever confused about who's running the show or who has dominion, except maybe when you're away. You do not ask more of him than he can give, nor do you think less of Scruffy because he can't rake the leaves or handle the family finances. You don't even think of him as having "rights" and yet, useless as he is to the practical affairs of the household, over time he comes to fill a crucial place. He's just sort of *there,* this furry, funny, needful, affectionate, and mysterious being creeping around the house. Everybody in the end gains something, and when he or she is gone a little bit of love has been subtracted.

It is the same with animals generally. I once saw a television show called *Wild Rescues* in which two men of twenty or so were out deer hunting when they came across a doe drowning in a muddy river. Their videotape of the rescue showed them struggling for over an hour to save her. Finally they dragged her out and she darted off into the woods. On their own terms it was a completely irrational act—she could wind up in their gun sights the next day. And yet they seemed enormously pleased at the deed—"just knowing," as one of the men put it, "that we gave her one more day of life."

On the same program you can see people rushing to the aid of beached whales and dolphins, orphaned seals, oil-covered gulls, penguins, and other sea creatures. The striking thing is how satisfied they all feel afterward. None of them ever describes embarrassed feelings of wasted time or of having cared *too much* about the stricken animal. A variety of programs have been devised in recent years involving the care of animals by troubled children, violent criminals, the handicapped, and the lonely aged. Far from stealing away charity and compassion from the human heart, we are just now discovering the gift many animals have for bringing those qualities back to life.

The best answer to our whimpering-dolphin dilemma comes from the dolphin. Marine biologist Kenneth Norris in his 1991 book *Dolphin Days* recounts the escape of one creature from the closing net controlled by speedboats circling round it. When the dolphin jumped the cork line at the edge of the net, "It *knew* it was free. It burst forward, propelled by powerful wide-amplitude tail strokes . . . [it] then dove, swimming at full speed . . . down and away into dark water, only to burst from the surface in a high-bounding series of leaps."[113]

Forget rights and even duties for a moment and think of the delight we would feel seeing that in real life, just this one creature's boundless joy at deliverance from the net. What a glorious thing it would be to spare them all.

Whatever we think of animal causes like banning drift nets and traps and the like, we should not condemn any animal with a zero-sum vision of compassion that assumes a fixed and finite reserve of available love. What is this but another version of Peter Singer's hard utilitarian calculus, choosing who rates love and who doesn't, guarding and hoarding love, leading in his case to a theoretical defense of such abominations as infanticide?

Likewise, what is our reflexive compassion for the dolphin and other animals in need but the natural extension downward into creation of the same impulse we feel to defend a child neglected, threatened, or deliberately harmed? Don't both reflexes come from the same place in our hearts?

For his part, Professor Singer would have us "put aside these emotionally moving but strictly irrelevant aspects of killing a baby"—a grievous project. Those who belittle or write off animal-welfare causes would have us put aside emotionally moving aspects of animal exploitation. That isn't a project to be proud of, either, and is all the more shameful for the money and bloodlust and phony spiritual airs they throw onto the moral scale against creatures who need only our forbearance and respect.

I myself do not even believe that extending more protections to animals would bring the unrest and economic disruption that some envision. Maybe it is not really so complicated and we are just dragging our feet a bit, buying time and making excuses like the whalers we're about to meet. We can do away with all the harpoons and drift nets and traps and trophy hunting and, yes, even the industrial farms, and the world will be just fine after all. The moral universe may even come to seem clearer and our place within it grander still, as our religious traditions with their visions of peace among all creatures so often hint. Our economies might actually prosper more, as usually happens when human creativity shakes off inertia and looks for better ways. We'd be wincing a lot less, too.

—e—

RICHES

OF THE SEA

*Oh Lord, how manifold are thy works! In wisdom thou hast made them
all: the earth is full of thy riches. So is this great and wide sea, wherein
are things creeping innumerable, both small and great beasts. There go
the ships; there is that leviathan, whom thou hast made to play therein.*

PSALMS 104:24–26

It comes down to this," says Steinar Bastesen, a whaler from Norway explaining to me the hard facts of life. "If we accept that mankind's resources should be utilized, why should the whale be excluded? If we have meat, you have to kill an animal. Killing animals is not nice at all—to kill any animal is not nice. And of course it goes into your heart to see a whale harpooned or a seal pup clubbed. The same for a lamb, to see it killed and butchered. And it should not be shown in an emotional way, a way that provokes people. If these things were shown in the same way that whaling is shown in films, the entire meat industry would be crushed. People would not like what they see. But you know, that is reality. People today, especially in the cities, are too much away from nature. They don't see reality anymore. They don't see the red in the beef. But the red color is blood."

We are chatting in July 2000 during a coffee break at the fifty-second annual meeting of the International Whaling Commission (IWC) in Adelaide, Australia. Bastesen hasn't whaled full time since the early 1980s, when his own industry was nearly crushed by the world's sudden burst of sympathy for whales. Twenty years ago, just after he had bought a new boat to expand his business, the IWC placed strict quotas on whalers, finally fixing a quota of zero in 1986, in effect a ban on commercial whaling, or at least an official request for one and all to stop killing whales. The IWC doesn't really have any enforcement power. But for Norway and Japan, the last nations to whale for profit and in the open seas, there is the fear of public disapproval, consumer boycotts, and trade sanctions. So, once a year, all interested parties meet for what Bastesen wearily calls the "media war."

These IWC conferences are the one time of year when public attention turns briefly to the fate of the whale, so it seemed like a good idea to come and see how things are going. This time around everyone's talking about an Australian proposal to create a new sanctuary in the South Pacific, where about a million and a half whales were killed in the last century and where two-thirds of all whales are found today. "The first step in our campaign for a truly global whale sanctuary," as Australia's minister for the environment, Senator Robert Hill, describes the plan. It's a nice idea, though of doubtful practical effect. There is already a Southern Ocean Sanctuary, established in 1994. The Japanese fleet routinely hunts there, and will set forth again within weeks of this conference.

SAVE THE WHALES FOR DINNER

Killing a thousand or so whales a year under various loopholes in the ban, Japan and Norway are here with their allies to expand quotas and one day resume commercial whaling. Everyone else is here to restrict quotas and one day abolish commercial whaling entirely—if not in law then, it is hoped, by moral suasion. Adelaide's main newspaper, the *Advertiser,* runs a typical plea on the day of the sanctuary vote: "It is not just the raucous, belligerent and frankly unsympathetic environmental extremists who are against you. It is the children, those children who have been so distressed by the images of the way the whales are killed and butchered, who cannot understand why grown-ups should permit this cruelty."[1]

Such appeals will not move Steinar, who was eight when he took part in his first expedition and who has wanted ever since only to whale and to teach his own children to whale. "I remember the first time I saw my father kill a sheep," he tells me. "I did not like it. He clubbed the sheep. I did not like it the first time I saw a whale harpooned. But you get used to it. You learn that that's what life is."

Now, at fifty-five, Bastesen must spend many of his days just defending his livelihood against the "protest industry." He's an IWC regular and seems to know everybody in the room—the Eskimo whalers over there, the Japanese delegates conferring a few tables away, the folks from Greenpeace International, the Humane Society of the United States, Friends of the Earth, Friends of the Whale, Friends of the Whaler, everybody from everywhere who today claims a stake in the fate of leviathan. A few years ago he formed his own coalition, the Coastal People's Party, and running on the slogan "Save the Whales for Dinner" got himself elected to the Norwegian parliament. Now and then he makes the news outside of Norway, like the time Greenpeace protesters boarded his boat in 1995 and Steinar hurled one of them overboard. Or the time in 1998 when Keiko, the killer whale of *Free Willy* fame, was flown from Oregon to Iceland to be returned to the waters from which he had been captured in 1979, and Steinar called it a giant waste of time and money, telling reporters that Keiko "would have been more suited as hamburger on a plate."[2]

He is also involved in something called the High North Alliance, representing animal-related industries from around Europe, and publishing such magazines and newsletters as the *International Harpoon* ("The Paper with a Point"), and in a still larger group with the prolix name of the International Wildlife Management Consortium—World Conservation Trust, a self-described "union of all wildlife hunters."[3] Whales, in the 1970s, became the martyr for all environmental and animal-protection causes, a symbol of everything that was wrong in the world. Today, for Steinar and his allies, whales have become a symbol of everything wrong with environmentalism and animal-protection causes, and once whaling is stopped then next it will be trapping, or trade in exotic animal parts, or safari hunting, or who knows what else. Groups representing these interests are here too, spreading the good news of "sustainable use."

A bulky fellow who still looks like he could handle any two protesters, he has an appealing way about him, punctuating his worldly observations with an endearing little cackle, and somehow we seem to have hit it off. There are hard men and there are cruel men, and Steinar strikes one as the former. He is a whaler and proud of it. Whaling for him is a demanding and decent and

honorable vocation, something worth preserving against the weepy, free-Willy
sentimentality he despises. He is also one of those men who has got just
about everything figured out, and with little prompting will explain to you
How The World Really Works.

I ask him about the protest industry. "I'll give you the basics," says
Steinar, leaning forward and folding his hands on the table as the discourse
begins. "You've got this commission, this international body with all these
diplomats. And you have the NGOs," the non-governmental organizations
like Greenpeace on the one side and the High North Alliance on the other.
"They represent the extreme right in each country and the extreme left. For
the left, it's some kind of religion, the New Age and all that.

"And then you have people who live off the whale, people like me who
make money from living resources. These people who are against whaling,
they come here every year waving the green flag, but it's cheap, it doesn't cost
anything. And they're after their own profits, you know. They're just a business, just an industry, and every industry has to grow and expand. After the
whale, they'll turn to something else. But they're just pretending to care for
the whale. It's all just propaganda to appeal to people's emotions. The whole
whaling issue is a good issue to make money off of. And these people who
react so emotionally to such films, they're just misguided. They're useful
idiots. They think they're doing the right thing."

His theory is that Western politicians view the whale issue as an easy
crowd pleaser, a sop to environmentalists in their own countries whom they
otherwise ignore in matters such as logging, development, and industrial pollution, where there is actually money at stake. There's probably some truth to
this, I tell Steinar, though surely it does not mean anyone's actually getting
rich trying to protect the whale. Maybe he is just ascribing his own motives to
them.

"No, for us it is not just about money. Whaling doesn't mean that much
to the Norwegian economy anymore. But it's the principle of it. Do you see
this vest? It is made of sealskin. This might offend some people, but that is
their opinion and I'll wear what I please. It's a question of principle. People
should be allowed to wear what they want, and why should the seal be
restricted? What's so special about the seal, that they should be protected
while we wear the skins of other animals?"

The vest is not some white, fluffy number you could mistake for something else, but rough and silvery and spotted, as if peeled from the seal an

hour ago. It's a big hit here, at least if the idea is to draw as many gasps as possible. His comings and goings at the Adelaide Convention Centre bring taunts from the protesters outside, which Steinar seems to thoroughly enjoy. He wears it every year, I am told, and once ran into trouble when U.S. authorities briefly confiscated his prize possession as a marine-mammal import and therefore contraband.

"It's the same with whaling," Bastesen continues. "What is so special about the whale? Should our decisions be based on feeling, on emotion, on some notion of ethics, or on reason and science? The question answers itself. If you give in—'Okay, let's stop whaling because people feel bad about it'—then where does it end? Now it's 'Save the Whale,' 'Save the Elephant,' save this, save that, save the sea turtle, save the shrimp. There is no end to it."

The sealers are here too, represented by the Union of Marine Hunters. Their motto is "In Harmony with Nature." They are "a living link to the past," and have come to tell their own story of hardship and "years of scorn" at the hands of the protest industry. "Their struggle began in the 1970s," says Marine Hunters, "when images of battered whitecoats"—baby seals—"first splashed into the international stage. By the mid-1980s, the outrage had peaked, markets were drying up, and the sealers had been all but driven out of business. Indeed, just the word 'sealer' became a pejorative term in an increasingly urbanized world."[4]

There's been a comeback, however, and about half a million seals are once again "harvested" annually just in Newfoundland, using precisely the methods that once brought such scorn. In that "timeless rhythm of man and nature," as the Marine Hunters describe it, they take helicopters from the ship to where the seals are. Then by the hundreds the "pups are killed either with a spiked club, or *hakapik*, or a rifle. For adult seals the use of a rifle is compulsory, and then afterwards the animal's skull must be smashed with a *hakapik* to ensure that it is dead."[5]

What saved the sealers was a new market, along with government subsidies. The United States and most European Union nations prohibit the import of marine-mammal products, so sealers in Canada, Norway, and Russia have turned to Asian buyers. The finer pelts, says Marine Hunters, are "sold to international furriers, with the remainder being used for goods such as gloves, briefcases and wallets. Seal meat is either eaten by the sealers (a particular delicacy is flipper pie) or canned. The penises of adult seals are sold to Asian markets, where they are powdered and used as aphrodisiacs."[6]

So reason has prevailed over silly emotionalism. By helicopter and *hakapik* harmony has been restored. And it all serves such a vital purpose. The sealers get their flipper pie, Asia's aspiring lotharios get their "aphrodisiacs," and Steinar gets his vest.

The five or six Japanese delegates nearby are gathering up some papers, ready to go back into battle in the grand hall. Confirming Steinar's suspicion that if you give an inch on whales there will always be something else, this year's IWC meeting has begun with charges of cruelty to dolphins. Delegates from the United Kingdom and Australia arrived with a bootlegged film of the latest dolphin "drive hunt" by Japanese fishermen, seeking an explanation and reminding Japan that "regulations prohibiting cruelty to animals . . . are now accepted as hallmarks of a civilized, ethical and moral community." The same footage fell into the hands of CNN, which has been airing highlights all week in its coverage of the conference. We all head back into the grand hall to see how this affront will be answered by the government of Japan.

"These people," says Steinar as we part, "they are opposed to any utilization whatsoever. They would have us kill nothing, no whales, no animals, nothing. And what should we eat in this new paradise?"

COLLECTIVE GUILT

The film, taken eight months earlier in Futo Harbor off the Pacific coast, records the last moments of some 175 of the thirty thousand or so dolphins and porpoises killed in Japanese waters every year. As it begins, a school of dolphins has just entered the mouth of the harbor. The welcoming committee consists of one large boat, two small ones, and a crowd of villagers sitting on shore to take in the show.

The large boat slides up behind the school. It begins swaying back and forth, like a giant push broom, stirring the waters to drive the dolphins toward land. The skiffs fan out on both sides of the larger vessel to seal them off with netting—the "wall of death."

As the net closes in, the men shout and clang on metal shafts attached to their boats, frightening the dolphins until at last they are herded into the shallows, caught between the ship, the net, and the quay. A dozen men step in and turn the water red with their clubs and knives and hooks. Dolphins have been observed aiding one another and actually staying in nets to drown with their companions rather than escape. Here, there is no chance for any of them as one by one the frantic victims are lassoed by the flukes and, half dead, hoisted by crane onto the dock.

Some are still struggling. Others thrash as they lie on the concrete or hang by hooks awaiting slaughter. One creature lying on the quay has been slaughtered already, and yet moves. His throat slashed, he turns over on his stomach, and vomits. Six are spared the knife and lifted by cradle onto flatbed trucks, two expiring in the process, the other four off to live out their days at a place called Izumito Sea Paradise, delighting crowds with their tricks and play.

The IWC has a Working Group on Whale Killing Methods and Associated Welfare Issues, and Australia and the United Kingdom last week proposed to show this footage there to Japanese delegates. Japan, however, knows something about springing traps and declared it would have nothing to do with such "propaganda." The film lacked "scientific and technical merit." Besides, said Masayuki Komatsu, a senior official in his country's Department of Agriculture and Fisheries, the IWC is charged with responsibility for whales and only whales.

The other countries replied that like whales, dolphins and porpoises are cetaceans, warm-blooded, air-breathing marine mammals. And, like whales, many dolphin and porpoise populations are in trouble. Since 1970 some five or six million of the creatures have perished by fishing nets and pollution, and even now, despite international laws protecting them, tens of thousands die every year as "bycatch" or are hunted deliberately for the crime of competing with trawlers for fish. Negotiations followed, a majority finally agreeing that the film could be shown, but in another room, outside the meeting so as not to give offense. Japan walked out in protest, marching back to the Hyatt next door and leaving us to deal with the dolphins this morning in plenary session.

To give you just the executive briefing, committees here operate by simple majority. To get anything passed in plenary you need a three-fourths majority, thirty of the forty total votes. Japan in recent years has been cultivating delegates from the Caribbean with lavish gifts of foreign aid, lining up the Lower Antilles on the side of whaling. Since it is one nation, one vote, Antigua with its 60,000 inhabitants carries precisely the weight of Australia or America.

With Norway, the Caribbean bloc, and usually reliable allies like South Korea and the Russian Federation, the Japanese government thus commands the requisite eleven votes to bar any action it deems unacceptable, and all of this unpleasantness over dolphins will come to nothing. The worst that can happen this morning has happened already: Twenty or so cameras aimed its way, Japan must now publicly defend its taste for *iruka*, dolphins, once again answering to the world for matters Japan regards as none of the world's business.

Presiding are Michael Canny of Ireland and Ray Gambell of England, a pair of amiable academics who are leaving their posts after this conference and who this week have upset the anti-whaling side by urging more accommodation with Japan and a measured resumption of commercial whaling. "I think it's inevitable that there will be commercial whaling at some point," said Mr. Canny.[7] If whaling must occur, reasons Mr. Gambell, better that it should occur under IWC supervision. "Some people," he told the BBC, "think whales are such special animals that they shouldn't be hunted at all, but that's very much a question of different cultures."[8]

Neither man could be more civil, treating Japan with extravagant deference and the Western delegates with cheerful little proddings to split every difference, avoid contention, and keep the coffee breaks coming on time. Just now, however, all of this collegiality only heightens tension in the chamber as Mr. Komatsu turns to Australia's delegation, these Westerners who themselves have protected marine mammals since only 1980 and have dared to lecture his country on the "hallmarks of a civilized, ethical and moral community."

"It is a matter of common sense," he begins, pausing every few sentences while his words are translated, "that when animals are slaughtered they are not shown to the public. When I think of the situation of the driving hunt of dolphins, I felt that the situation was identical to the slaughterhouse, which may be why the gentlemen from the UK wanted to show it. If people felt that the videotape showed a cruel image, I think it is inappropriate to show it."

Watching from the gallery, you see the backs of everybody, about two hundred delegates, who in turn are looking up at a movie screen now featuring a giant Mr. Komatsu. By far the most animated member of the Japanese delegation, and the only one who ever removes his jacket, he is a man of fifty or so with gray hair receding up a wide forehead, round steel-rimmed glasses, a sharp, impatient air, and sad eyes. The scene could be a snapshot of any debate in any conference anywhere in international officialdom, except that here the Japanese occupy a quarter of the picture. Most delegations have four or five people. The United States has the second largest with twenty. Japan is here with a force of fifty-nine, including a team of public relations advisers from New York, all of them at this moment busy doing something with laptops, recorders, cell phones, the works.

As long as we have strayed beyond the subject of whales, Mr. Komatsu continues, then, okay, let's talk about kangaroos. Here in our host country, four or five million kangaroos are slaughtered every year for meat consumed domestically, for leather products exported to Europe and America, and for the diversion of the country's famed "weekend hunters" firing from careening trucks. Surely these scenes are no prettier than anything one might witness in Futo Harbor. The joeys, says Mr. Komatsu, are yanked from their mothers' pouches and impaled or bludgeoned, if not simply discarded as not worth a bullet and left to die by starvation or be devoured by predators. How, he wonders, would the Australian delegates care to see that on film, or the British delegates some footage of their own abattoirs, or the New Zealanders their lambs at slaughter, or the Americans their industrial hog farms? "If such a discussion were to escalate, then there would be no end."

Japan, in short, is being held to a double standard, says Mr. Komatsu. Perhaps it is out of a sense of "collective guilt" that others presume to instruct his country on the proper treatment of animals. The Western world has developed a soft spot for marine mammals. Westerners do not eat whale or dolphin meat and simply cannot understand why others do so. And that's fine, but each society must choose its own way according to its own standards and its own traditions. Japan, a sovereign nation, needs no advice from outsiders who know nothing of its culture and care nothing for the needs of its fishermen and consumers.

British delegate Elliot Morley, the minister of fisheries and agriculture, and a great friend to animals, ventures that these are "advanced mammals" we are talking about. Unlike slaughtered livestock, the dolphins "suffer unacceptable cruelty." The commissioner from Norway, a fellow named Odd Gunnar Skagestad seated next to Steinar, appeals for a "pragmatic position," meaning the dolphins are dead, we are here to talk about whales, so can we please just move on to something else.

There follows a parliamentary ritual in which each nation in turn declares which other country it "would like to associate itself with" in the matter at hand, a solemn, officious, and completely meaningless exercise since everyone knows that no action can or will be taken. Finally someone suggests that the appropriate committee be charged with further research on the matter and report back next year. The motion is seconded, and so ordered by Michael Canny, as to general relief agenda item 8.1 is disposed of and we turn to the next order of business, a report from the Infractions Sub-committee involving a humpback whale and her calf killed this past year in Caribbean waters.

It's about as close as they ever come here to confrontation, and despite gallant appeals from Mr. Morley and Jim McLay, New Zealand's commissioner and former deputy prime minister, the Japanese have prevailed—not only with sufficient votes, but with a perfectly valid line of defense. This is the most galling thing about their performance here: In a way, they are right. Mankind makes free use of other animals, hunting, capturing, and killing terrestrial mammals that feel and struggle and whimper every bit as much as marine mammals. Why do the latter deserve some unique protected status? As Bastesen, Mr. Komatsu, Mr. Gambell, and just about everyone else here keeps asking, what exactly is so special about whales?

TIME TO DEATH

You don't actually hear the word *kill* very much around here, at least not in official proceedings. The preferred terms are "non-natural mortality," "anthropogenic mortality," "human-induced mortality," "biological removal," "termination," and "lethal sustainable use." Everything must be made to sound as detached and scientific as possible, lest the speaker be accused of emotionalism or, worse, "anthropomorphism." The whales and dolphins themselves are termed, by pro-whaling delegates, "living marine resources," and even a simple thing like watching whales for the sheer pleasure of it is known as "non-consumptive utilization." When they're killed by accident, that's called "unintended stock depletion," and this is what the commissioner from Saint Vincent and the Grenadines, a sprinkling of islets a hundred miles north of Trinidad, claims happened last year in the case of agenda item 9.1, this mother slain while nursing her calf. We know the calf was terminated before his first year, too, because when they cut him open there was only milk in his stomach.

Why is a single case of unintended stock depletion of concern to the International Whaling Commission? Well, because there used to be so much intended stock depletion, and now every whale matters. This is why we are all here. An estimated 95 or so percent of the world's "whale resources" are gone, utilized. Now mankind must decide what to do with the survivors.

That humpback and her calf wintering in the Caribbean were among five or six thousand of their kind left on earth, compared to roughly twenty times that number a few generations ago. The IWC Scientific Committee employs intricate mathematical models and some sort of grid system to calculate populations ("a dispersal rate of 0.002 had the highest probability of obtaining the observed value, which corresponded to a power of 0.90 using the criterion of $a = b$, and a power of 0.81 using $a = 0.05$. . . ."), but even these are just educated guesses. And the only reason it gets so complicated is that Japan has its own models invariably showing more whale "stocks" there for the taking than others are able to find. Truth is, no one really knows how many are left. Whales are hard to count.

A striking fact for the lay reader is how little we know for certain about leviathans compared with other animals. Even now, it turns out, cetologists are not entirely sure from what kind of land mammal they might have evolved, how some whales live and in what kind of social groups, what they eat besides plankton and suchlike (a big issue here), how they swim underwater for as long as two hours without breathing, where they go over a lifetime (most following regular pathways to and from polar feeding grounds, others seeming to travel where they please), their natural life spans (anywhere from eighty to an incredible 150 years[9]), or why, as often happens, they swim right up to their killers in what the tribal whalers here will tell you is "an offering" of themselves to man. "Some you have to chase for hours," as Eugene Brower, an Eskimo from Barrow, Alaska, here on behalf of the Indigenous Whaling Association, explains to me. "Others, it's like they just wait there to be harpooned. That's why we say that they have offered themselves to us. We receive the whale who feeds us."

Bastesen, when I run this by him, takes a less theological view: "Yes, you see, if they were so intelligent they would escape! And of course some do. But the ones we catch, sometimes they actually come up to the boat, out of curiosity to see us. Most whales are no smarter than cows. They can be very stupid creatures."

The most urgent question still under investigation is whether whales, however stupid they might be, experience shock and unconsciousness as land mammals do, and therefore whether some, even after the thrashing and convulsions have ceased, might still be alive and aware as they are being shot and lanced and hauled aboard to be stripped of their blubber and meat. Japan and Norway report that there have been great advances lately in minimizing this "time to death," as the issue is termed. Japan is on the cutting edge with lances that kill by electrocution, and both countries have been experimenting with an explosive known as penthrite placed on the tips of cannon-fired harpoons, though even these, as Steinar tells it, are imperfect: "About sixty-five percent die immediately. The grenade explodes close to the brain, and he's gone, just like that"—a snap of the fingers. "Sometimes you don't hit exactly, and then it can take awhile. You have to winch him in, pull him back and shoot him. I use a .458-magnum rifle, full-metal jack, and a few shots will take care of him. Today's methods, I must admit, are more efficient than in the past, and I give credit to groups which have insisted on more humane killing methods. I started off in 1953, and back then we just used a cold harpoon."

On average, we are informed, whales take about five minutes to die from these grenade shots to their brains, though by Japan's own admission the job can take much longer, as in the case of one whale this year who took 96 minutes to expire and another who took 130 minutes. Whales taken by indigenous hunters like Mr. Brower, who still use "the cold harpoon" for tradition's sake, would be lucky to go that quickly. Norway's official statistics boast an average time to death of three and a half minutes.

Given Norway's other official claim of 63 percent killed "instantaneously," a word loosely defined in whaling circles, that still means a fair number take ten, twenty, thirty minutes or more to die. These figures do not include the chase, either, which in the case of "fast whales"—the term of art for a creature struck but still trying to escape—can stretch on through an afternoon. Nor do they average in the many whales "struck and lost," who are not really "lost" but doomed to linger for days or weeks unless the sharks or a pack of orcas should find them, in which case they will be eaten alive. The Working Group on Environmental Concerns reports of a young gray whale who washed ashore in southern California in 1999 with a Russian-made harpoon—the kind used by Eskimos—in his body, meaning he had swum at least from the Bering Sea before death came, and what was that journey like? Nor, again, is anyone quite certain that kills carried out by even the most advanced methods and recorded as "instantaneous" are really instantaneous. There is an awful possibility under discussion by cetologists today: Could it be that all of these time-to-death calculations are gravely in error, failing to take into account the unique physiology of the whale?

Here are animals, as this argument runs, with no predators to speak of. Healthy whales may be set upon by sharks or killer whales, and like all advanced mammals they clearly have the mechanisms of pain that make them convulse and flee when attacked. But such attacks are known to be rare, the exception and not a part and pattern of their natural existence. Whales, and certainly the largest among them like the blue, humpback and fin, are simply invincible. This may explain why so many whales, as Mr. Brower sees it, "just wait there to be harpooned." In reality, they are not waiting for anything. They do not fear anything. Their world, until that moment, has not been a place of fear and flight. When whalers first appeared with their spears and magnum rifles and electric lances, all just an instant ago on the whales' evolutionary clock, they were the first real killers, the first systematic predators, these creatures had ever encountered.

Here also are mammals who live in water yet need to breathe. How then do they sleep? It can't be fully unconscious sleep as we know it, for the simple reason that, like dolphins, whales must at the same time be able to swim and to surface for air. We assume it's a kind of semiconscious state, allowing them to rejuvenate while retaining some level of awareness. This could explain the oddly frequent collisions whales have with tankers and other ships one would think they could hear at a distance and easily elude.

We are left, then, to wonder how a creature with no natural predator, and designed never to lose consciousness, would experience a grenade, round of gunfire, or electrocution. For us and other mammals, there can at least be a buffer, a loss of feeling and awareness. Maybe for them there is none. Maybe for them there is no merciful unconsciousness to soften the trauma of attack, the pain and horror ceasing, if this is true, only when the brain itself is dead.

It is speculation, but so is much else in our still very limited understanding of marine life. We are endlessly reminded here that science, and only science, must guide us in our treatment of the whale. All the more amazing to reflect on how late science has been in understanding the whale. Though identified as mammals more than two millennia ago, it was not until the seventeenth century that the first accurate prints appeared showing whales as they really are. Before then we find them depicted as giant fish terrorizing mariners or scaly sea monsters of the cartographer's imagination. And it was only in our own time, in the early 1970s, that we humans got our first glimpse of live whales underwater, through the photography of Jim Hudnall. In the late 1960s hydrophonic technology broke the whale's "pyramidical silence," as Herman Melville called it, allowing the first whale sounds to reach the first human ear. (The first sounds of life, at any rate, for "they give a cry" when the harpoon has struck, as one Yamada Yosei described it in 1829, and when the lancing comes their "moaning is heard like thunder."[10]) Before the good work of Hudnall, zoologists Roger and Katy Payne, Jacques Cousteau, and others, most everything that humanity knew of whales we knew from the accounts of whalers themselves or from the occasional sick whale to drift ashore and die. Among their many misfortunes, the largest creatures on earth have been for us the least visible and least audible, our only knowledge of their ways supplied by their only enemies on earth.

We had never seen a whale "whaled," either, until to its eternal credit Greenpeace in 1976 filmed the Soviet catcher boat *Vlastny* launching one of these grenade-tipped harpoons at a sperm whale swimming with her mate. Still available on National Geographic's video *The Great Whales,* it's an incredible thing to watch. As the stricken creature heaves in a bloody convulsion, her companion turns violently toward the Greenpeace raft, at the last moment sweeping around to charge the *Vlastny.* He lunges upward, clapping his jaw as if to get at the harpooner, as the gun is aimed down and fired into his face.

Since then our cameras have captured other images of whales giving birth, caring for and even caressing their young, aiding the calves of other females, trying to keep sick companions afloat, refusing to leave when their fellows have been captured, beached, or ensnared in nets, communicating with one another, even allowing human divers to swim beside them. This is the kind of "propaganda" that Norway and Japan still complain about, which may be defined as simple pictures or video images of whalers doing what they do, or of whales doing what they do—the utter harmlessness of these creatures an unanswerable rebuke to their slayers.

Mention these whale films and "songs" around here, and you are immediately marked as one of those romantic types who has swallowed all that save-the-whales sentimentality. One would think that direct sounds and images of the creatures themselves, never available until our own day, were of immense scientific import. But it seems to be a case of people using the same word to mean entirely different things. There is the science of hydrophones and underwater cameras and communication with fellow creatures. And then there is the science of penthrite and precision brain shots and time to death for "stupid creatures." About the former—what whales do when they are not being chased or killed—the whalers here could not be less curious.

WISE USE

Melville's "high and mighty business of whaling" also left us with an abundance of records still used in trying to piece together estimates of current whale populations. We don't know exactly how many remain. We do have a pretty good idea how many were terminated. Subtracting total depletion from preexisting estimates of the number of whales that once filled the seas, you get our current "stocks."

Take just the past century's worth of stock depletion. The principle of sustainable use, advocated here by the Japanese and Norwegians for the management of current "stocks," holds that all resources of the earth, including "living resources" like the whale, not only can but must be exploited by man. We keep things in balance, culling here and there to avert overpopulation in the wilds and other catastrophes that would occur in the absence of our steadying influence. Indeed, this principle asserts, it is in our interest to take what we need, and only what we need, from nature. Overexploitation will only deplete the stock to dangerous levels, putting one's own resources and livelihood at risk.

Therefore, when left free to work his will on nature, rational man will tend to take no more than nature can bear. Hence the theory's latest name, "wise use." Whales, as the IWMC—World Conservation Trust reminds us, really aren't so different from elephants. Each must be seen as "a natural resource that lends itself to assignable ownership, and that ownership, coupled with benefits produced from hunting, provides an incentive for conservation."[11] Whales must be used, owned, appropriated, privatized, and "incentivized" just like other wildlife. Whales need economic value. What other motive could we possibly have to protect them?

Mankind's thousand-year dominion over this very first creature named in Genesis does not afford the best evidence of "wise use" in action. Comparing, perhaps, only to the fate of the elephant, it is one of the greatest human onslaughts ever visited upon any animal.

The story is summed up today in the humble form of the minke whale (pronounced "minky"), at six to eight tons and thirty or so feet in length among the smallest of whales. They are now the mainstay of Japan's *kujira* market, supplemented by that irresistible *iruka* to which Japanese gourmands have turned as whale meat grows more scarce and thus more expensive. Their size has always made them the least economical to hunt. From the day that the Basques of Spain, the first to whale in open seas, set sail in the Bay of Biscay in the tenth or eleventh century, until the mid-1970s, minkes were largely spared in favor of the bigger ones we think of when we think of whales: the sperm whale immortalized in *Moby-Dick,* the gray, blue, fin, sei, bowhead, humpback, right whale, and Bryde's whale.

Many whale names still attest to the mix of ignorance and arrogance man has directed at them. The sperm, for example, is named for the amber fluids in its head that its first killers assumed was just that, and whose actual purpose (perhaps buoyancy or temperature control) we still don't know. Minkes are named after a German whaler, one Meineke whose own first name is lost to history. Bryde's ("Bru-dahs") are named for Johan Bryde, a South African whaler who mistakenly believed he'd found a new species and triumphantly pronounced the carcass *Balaenoptera brydei*. But among them all, none bears a sadder name or has known more tribulation than the "right whale," of which at most a few thousand are still with us.

Until the late 1800s even the great whales stood a chance, all except these doomed rights who once could be seen off the coasts of every continent, and nowhere more than in North America. There is even a legend, which somehow has the ring of truth, that the very first shot fired in the New World was aimed at a right whale swimming by the *Mayflower*. Recognizable by their "beard" of barnacle-like callosities, the name captures their fate: Sixty to eighty tons and rich in oil, buoyant when killed, predictable in migration, slow swimmers, dwelling in harbors at calving season and thus easily taken inshore, for ages, from Nantucket to Victor Harbor just south of Adelaide, they were the "right" whale for killing.

They were the first to go, for centuries, as Melville wrote, "submitting to the harpoon like half-stunned bullocks to the Knife."[12] Then, in the late nineteenth century, the killing reached industrial scale with cannon-fired harpoons, primitive versions of the "electric lance," steam-powered catcher boats, radios, sonar, factory ships, compressed air pumps to keep the dead or dying victims from sinking. No longer could even the speedier of the large whales, known as rorquals, escape, or the mightier ones survive the first blow. Now they were all "right" whales. Now they could all be killed, and very nearly were.

It seemed to Norway's Svend Foyn, the man who gave the world the forward-mounted harpoon cannon, a long-awaited act of providence that now his steam-powered, eighty-six ton ship, the *Spes et Fides*—Hope and Faith— could return to port from all points of the planet with the oil, blubber, and bones of every kind of whale, even the blues theretofore spared by their speed and the shielding arctic ice. A man of both science and piety, it was his "vocation," Foyn wrote, to extend the reach of harpoon and ship to all whales in all waters, for "God had let the whale inhabit these seas for the blessing and benefit of mankind."[13] Japan, too, had its visionaries. "I am firmly convinced," declared one Juro Oka in 1910, revered by Japanese whalers today as the father of modern whaling,

> that we shall become one of the greatest whaling nations in the
> world. The whaling grounds round Korea and Japan offer unlimited
> possibilities, and should stocks of whales, contrary to expectations,
> fail in these areas, we have the Sea of Okhotsk and the Bering Sea to
> the north and we are aware of the great treasure houses to the south.
> The day will come when we shall hear one morning that whales have
> been caught in the Arctic and in the evening that whales are being
> hunted in the Antarctic.[14]

Except for the part about unlimited possibilities, it happened just that way, all of the world's whalers converging with greater and greater fury on a smaller and smaller stock of younger and younger animals. By the 1920s, stocks in the Sea of Japan, the Yellow Sea, the Bering and Okhotsk seas off Russia did indeed disappoint expectations, "whaled out" like all the other virgin seas before them, until finally the factory ships of the world, now with ice-cutters to clear their path and planes and helicopters to spot their victims, descended like the hosts of hell upon the remotest waters of the south where the last great whale colonies were discovered—depositing, as long as they were in the neighborhood, platoons of fur hunters to wipe out the seals.

Peruse the literature of this time and you will find the same talk of "science" and how only the laws of economics and "resource management" must determine whaling practices. And that is exactly what came to pass—human

knowledge and resourcefulness completely unhinged from human conscience. Japan by the late 1930s had five factory ships emptying the treasure
houses of the south ("the Great Refrigerator of the South," as the Antarctic
was also known), accompanied by more than a hundred catcher boats. All
were owned by the Nippon Suisan Company, a state-run entity using the
profits to subsidize Japan's onslaught in China and Manchuria. Its rivals in
whaling were the Soviet Union, the United Kingdom, Norway, and Nazi Germany, in need of its own oil and cash reserves and eager to experiment in
"electric whaling." And for a time there was enough for all. In a typical season
they killed some 35,000 great whales just in Antarctic waters, as tens of thousands more were being slaughtered elsewhere. The year 1938, with forty-one
factory ships at work, saw a record take of 45,010 great whales just in the
Antarctic.

Of these, about a fourth were calves and juveniles, and a staggering
14,922 were blue whales—The Largest Animal That Ever Lived from our
childhood picture books, and perhaps soon to be the largest that ever vanished. Yielding more than a hundred tons of oil, an adult the size of a fully
fueled 737 with passengers, and two or three times heavier, blue whales a
century ago are believed to have numbered around 300,000. The record season for them was 1931, when more than 32,000 were killed. By 1966 all the
fleets of the world could find and kill just seventy, and Japanese whalers as
late as 1978 were observed still killing the females.[15] Today, three decades
after hunting blue whales was forbidden—thanks to a valiant campaign at the
IWC by Charles Lindbergh—three or four hundred are known to be at large
in the Southern Hemisphere. Informal studies of late suggest there might be
as many as two or three thousand blue whales in northern waters, higher than
previous estimates, but even with that happy news we are left with less than
2 percent of their total population before the inspired Mr. Foyn discovered his
calling.

Even if whales, like elephants, are able to communicate danger to one
another and alter their migrations accordingly, there was not enough time, nor
any place to flee. The final catastrophe came to pass, as Richard Ellis writes
in his 1991 *Men & Whales,* in "less than a single cetacean generation. . . . The
whales had lost the battle before they had a chance to learn what was happening to them."[16]

We don't know the exact figures because there were pirate whaling ships
whose take went unrecorded, and it is doubtful that even official reports by

Japan, Norway and Russia were accurate. A safe guess would put stock depletion during the 1940s, when the IWC was founded after it first occurred to whalers that some restraint might be in order, at 160,000—down during the war years and then up again as freighters and warships were hastily converted to whaling vessels, the American government of occupation actually subsidizing Japan's conversion in exchange for the oil. The 1950s, when young Steinar made the first of his 1,550-plus career kills, brought a yield of no fewer than 300,000 great whales. The sixties, when twenty nations were still hunting whales, some 380,000. The seventies, when Greenpeace and its *Rainbow Warrior* arrived on the scene to challenge Soviet and Japanese factory ships, more than a quarter million, with the IWC itself still setting quotas as high as 46,000 a year and other nations and pirate whalers observing no limits at all— only now, as old records are examined, the full devastation left by Soviet fleets becoming clear.

All of this for corsets and cosmetics, candles and perfumes, combs and stylish umbrella struts, industrial lubricants, printing inks, tanning leather, glycerin for dynamite, bone meal for livestock, fertilizer, margarine, gourmet specialties, and other products not a single one of which could be called irreplaceable or essential to human life. Grasping their stricken prey by the flukes with a giant iron claw, swallowing them whole through a gaping mouth in the stern, stripping, boiling, and disassembling an entire whale in under an hour, these floating factories are among the ugliest creations of the human mind, only more so because powered by diesel fuel from petroleum, the very product that had long before ended any claims of need we may have had upon the whale.

Add it all up—or rather, subtract it all away—and mankind's total stock depletion in the modern era comes to somewhere between 1.5 and 2.5 million great whales, and before that God knows how many million more. Our grand totals living today: 2,000 southern right whales, 300 northern rights, 5,500 humpbacks, 47,000 fins, 21,000 grays, 40,000 Bryde's, 7,500 bowheads, 10,300 sei whales, and at most 3,000 blue whales in all the seven seas.[17]

Sperm whales are variously fixed at between 500,000 and a million, a healthy population only in comparison. Hunted primarily for oil, and for byproducts such as ambergris and bones for scrimshaw, they absorbed terrible casualties—267,000 just between 1964 and 1974. But as a species sperm whales survived the worst of the industrial killing because they follow less predictable migration patterns than do other whales, and perhaps also because unlike other species the males are larger, richer targets, allowing more females to survive and bear more young. Apparently the meat of sperm whales isn't very agreeable, either, and this may explain why Japanese whalers have largely left them alone—though not for long, as we learned this year. Japan now has plans for them, too, on the general principle that, as Takahiro Naka-mae puts it, "If they are not endangered, why should hunting be prohibited?"[18]

The Japanese delegation is here trumpeting "an abundance of ten millions of whales today," as if there has been some miraculous recovery and we needn't worry anymore. The whale has been saved, they would have us believe, and we can all go home. This deeply dishonest claim is not only an exaggeration: It also includes pilot whales, beaked whales, and other cetaceans hardly bigger than dolphins. And it includes the six or seven hundred thousand minkes Japan has only lately deigned to pursue in earnest, these overlooked survivors of the cataclysm inflicted on their world. The fact is this: If you leave aside the sperms, in the way of great whales we are really talking about maybe a hundred thousand left on the planet.

Japan, Norway, the IWMC—World Conservation Trust, everyone here who advocates whaling admits to these sins of the past. But their sense of entitlement has not diminished with the "resource." Still they do not grasp the enormity of what happened. From it all they have drawn only the lesson of "overexploitation." Modern industrial whaling, we are told, was a textbook case of poor stock management, the economist's classic "tragedy of the commons" in which the long-term interests of all are sacrificed to the short-term interests of the few. But now we know better. Now, with Science as our guide, and just the right mix of incentives and disincentives, mankind has learned to hunt whales sustainably, wisely, perpetually, conserving our stocks year after year and century after century, so that we can go on chasing and slaying and using them forever.

There are no real sins in this outlook, only economic miscalculations, and the only tragedies are shortfalls in supply. There is no such thing as remorse, or shame, or penance, no sense of guilt over the fact that the great whales are all but annihilated—gone, in one eye blink of geologic time, after fifty, sixty, who knows how many million years upon the earth. The relative survival of the little minkes seems for the modern whaler and his apologists only the most obvious reason to turn our weapons at last upon them, and indeed the most ominous argument one hears in Adelaide is that the whales of the world are suddenly a "threat" to our own global fish stocks, a menace to man who for that reason alone must never find refuge. An early friend of the whale, a French naturalist named Bernard-Germain de la Cépède, discerned their fate long before the worst had even come:

> Man, attracted by the treasure that the victory over the whales might afford him, has troubled the peace of their immense solitary abodes, violated their refuges, sacrificed all those which the icy, unapproachable polar deserts could not screen from his blows; and the war he has made on them has been especially cruel because he has seen that it is large catches that make his commerce prosperous, his industry vital, his sailors numerous, his navigators daring, his pilots experienced, his navies strong and his power great.
>
> Thus it is that these giants among giants have fallen beneath his arms; and because his genius is immortal and his science now imperishable, because he has been able to multiply without limit the imaginings of his mind, they will not cease to be the victims of his interest until they have ceased to exist. In vain do they flee before him; his art will transport him to the ends of the earth; they will find no sanctuary except in nothingness.[19]

SCIENTIFIC RESEARCH

So here we are today arguing over agenda item 9.1, one whale and her calf in the Caribbean, their death, for all anyone knows, the last push the humpback can take, the kill that will kill the species.

Humpbacks are the ones with the long flippers, grooved throats, and down-curving mouth that makes them look inconsolable despite having been praised by Melville as the "most gamesome and lighthearted of all whales." They are renowned today for their hit CDs, an eerie chorus of bellows and groans called "songs" because of a discrete, sequential phrasing changing from place to place and year to year, and included on a platinum disk carried by the *Voyager* spacecraft for an audience somewhere, sometime, when all of us have vanished. They're popular with whale-watchers—"non-consumptive utilizers"—because if you approach very slowly sometimes humpbacks will let you come close even when calves and yearlings are in tow. Now and then they might venture up to the boat for a look at you, or even allow you to touch them, which seems to be how these two came to grief off the coast of Saint Vincent and the Grenadines.

The "aboriginal whalers" who terminated them have violated a fairly clear IWC rule—"It is forbidden to strike, take or kill calves or any humpback whale accompanied by a calf."[20] They also forgot the very first tenet of sustainable use, since when you kill a lactating female and her young you are killing your own future stock. One would think, then, that Japan and Norway would be the first to condemn the deed. But it doesn't work quite that way. No debate here is ever about the specific question at hand, to be decided on its own merits, but always just one more clash in the media war, where solidarity is everything. Concede even a single point, admit to even one wrong, and we all know what happens then: There will be no end to it.

"It seems to me we are striking at gnats, wasting time on small matters," says Kerwyn Morris, chief fisheries officer for Saint Vincent and the Grenadines. "My country is a sovereign state and we are not going to be coerced." They did a survey in his sovereign nation of 120,000 inhabitants: "Sixty-one percent of over 1,000 people questioned consume whale meat. Eleven percent did so because of health reasons. Sixteen percent did so because of food. And 71 percent did so because of the taste. This is the environment in which the whole question has to be seen."

It's been polled. People like the taste. And, says Mr. Morris, "No one can convince me that we should give special consideration to the whale simply because people find it cute or emotionally appealing or what have you." If anything, his country needs "the taking of more calves, not less." Stuart Nanton, Saint Vincent's commissioner, is even more defiant: "We will be continuing our little whaling operation. Nothing they do in this meeting can stop that. . . . I'm not compromising because we've done nothing wrong."[21]

Antigua associates itself with the views of Saint Vincent, while reminding us that aboriginal peoples do not have the large ships and technology of more developed nations. "We are pleading for understanding." Dominica associates itself with Antigua. "Whaling," explains Dominica's Lloyd Pascal, "is conducted on a small boat. And when you are on a small boat it is very difficult to see things which are small"—a howler which leaves even the delegates from Japan laughing. Norway associates itself with Dominica, Mr. Skagestad with his familiar refrain that precious time is again being wasted, and "we really don't feel the need for further debate." Japan associates itself with Norway: "Total calf production" is still looking strong, and one slaughtered calf "will not adversely affect the stock."

With that, at the suggestion of Mr. Morris, the matter is tabled until next year when he promises a full report, and it's time for another coffee break. It seems there's been an identical incident off the coast of Saint Vincent during the 2000 season. So, as he reasons, we now have two infractions under review, and of course it only makes sense to deal with them both at once at the 2001 meeting.

They talk about "next year" around here the way we speak, in ordinary life, of "tomorrow" or "next week." There is always time to put things off, always more research to be done, always more working groups and committees and subcommittees to be heard from—even though, in this case, there were eyewitnesses to the hunt and everyone in the room knows exactly what happened. They baited the mother with her own dead calf.[22] In an ancient ploy of whalers, they killed the calf first because he could not get away, and they knew the mother would stay near him until she, too, had made her "offering" to man.

How do these things get reported at all? One useful function of the International Whaling Commission is to serve as a court of public opinion, hearing and weighing evidence of wrongdoing. The commission has no observers posted in ports or on ships, though Western delegates would favor that, and whaling nations are left to report their own violations. But environmental groups, along with independent news reporters, turn up a constant supply of damning evidence, and with the IWC at least they have a forum in which to present it. Without these groups and this forum, we might never know about that calf and others who meet the same fate. Or about the many whales struck and lost, or left for dead in ship collisions, or deafened, disoriented, and killed by high-frequency military sonar. Or about the ones who take days to die entangled in lobster nets or suffocated by buoy lines or debris caught in their throats. Or about an annual festivity in the Faroe Islands, a Danish territory 200 miles north of Scotland, in which hundreds of pilot whales are herded into bays and hacked to death in a scene of unbelievable mayhem.

That's the case for the IWC. Everyone's worst fear in Adelaide is that the whole thing might unravel, loosing the anarchy of former times—a threat always in the air when Japan and Norway get upset. Yet even they would pre-

fer to keep some structure of international order—quotas, stock mainte-
nance, and the like. They are sovereign nations here of their own accord, after
all. The whole thing is voluntary.

The case against the IWC is that everything is just a little too voluntary,
and that lacking any kind of enforcement apparatus it merely lends a civilized
veneer to the conduct of Norway, Japan, and their confederates. The 1982
United Nations Convention on the Law of the Sea requires all governments
to cooperate with the IWC, but the rules of the IWC itself are nonbinding, so
it all comes to nothing.

Norway, for example, announced in 1993 that it no longer considered
itself bound by the ban, and just like that started whaling again in the North
Atlantic. Norwegian whalers have since stored up some 800,000 tons of
frozen blubber against the day when the ban is lifted and they may legally
export it to Japan as in days of old. There are suspicions some of the stuff
already finds its way into Japan's black market. On the books, however, it's all
saved while the meat is consumed within Norway, where, we are informed by
some promotion materials,

> people eat whale meat in all kinds of ways, as a joint, a casserole, as
> whaleburgers and in pizza. The most recent addition is barbecued
> whale meat. "Absolutely delicious!" is what Bjorn Hugo thinks of
> whale meat, and his view was recently echoed by a tourist from
> America—land of the steak—who told an Oslo radio station after
> tasting a sample: "Meat can't get closer to heaven."[23]

The rules actually permit Norwegian commercial whaling. Any member
nation may, within ninety days of any given decision, simply file an objection
to that decision and no longer be obligated by it. So Norway still gets to come
here ever year, debating and voting just like everyone else, and we all have to
listen to Odd Gunnar Skagestad, this man who can hardly say "present" without sounding indignant and put upon, holding forth on IWC goals his own
country does not share, rules it selectively observes, and sanctuaries its ally
routinely violates.

Japan kills its six or seven hundred whales a year (that we know of) under
the rubric of "scientific research." Here again there's an IWC rule to give
them cover. Article VIII of its charter, the 1946 Convention on International
Whaling, reads as follows:

Notwithstanding anything contained in this Convention, any Contracting Government may grant to any of its nationals a special permit authorizing that national to kill, take, and treat whales for
purposes of scientific research subject to such other conditions as
the Contracting Government thinks fit, and the killing, taking, and
treating of whales in accordance with the provisions of this article
shall be exempt from the operation of this Convention.

The government of Japan every year simply issues itself these special permits under a program of "lethal scientific research" called JARPN. When did
this ambitious scientific venture begin? Oh, around 1986, when the ban went
into effect. How often did Japan use article VIII before then? Never. What is
being researched, exactly? It has something to do with "the role of whales in
the ecosystem," as the Japanese Whaling Association explains. The Japanese
Fisheries Agency is more detailed, telling the *Nikkei Weekly* it wants to "study
their earplugs, ovaries, muscle tissue, and stomach contents" and so better
calculate whale recovery rates.[24] One earplug won't do, apparently. They
need hundreds and hundreds a year for the "major scientific papers" of which
the agency boasts.

And what happens to the whales after they have been brought home by
the "research vessels," as Masayuki Komatsu calls them? Genetic testing of
meat recently for sale in one Japanese department store found that it
belonged to a blue whale, suggesting some major scientific breakthroughs
Japan has not even shared with us. The government denies this, but we do
know that all of the "by-products" from these scientific expeditions go straight
from ecosystem to eatery, the flesh of minkes fetching tens of millions in
sales to the stores and restaurants of Osaka and Tokyo, where it is served as
steak or in *miso* soup or as bits dipped in soy sauce. Some of the profits go, in
turn, to fund what else but more "research," with a view, says Mr. Komatsu,
to expanding the research to as many as four thousand minkes a year.[25]

To complete the illusion, Japan has set up something called the Institute
of Cetacean Research. Subsidized by the government at $5 million a year, on
top of the $35 million it nets from its own little meat business, the institute's
function is to set Japan's annual quotas and then to translate commercial
demand into the language of urgent scientific imperative. This year, for example, Japan announced that it would need a hundred more minkes per year,
and would also broaden its research beyond minkes to the study of sperm and

Bryde's whales. Sixty of these whales would have to be lethally "sampled" for science (just for starters) before the by-products are sold for food, a Bryde's going at five or six times the value of one minke. When Japan's team of scientists were done with it, this scheme of reckless slaughter came out as "A Research Plan for Cetacean Studies in the Western North Pacific under Special Permit (JARPN-II): Feasibility Study Plan 2000–2002."

Over Japanese objections, Australian delegate David Mason was given the floor and permitted to explain the common-law doctrine of "abuse of rights," summarizing the work of Melbourne law professor Gillian Triggs: Any right must be exercised by reference to common standards of reasonability and good faith and in keeping with the purpose for which that right exists—in this case, actual scientific research. This got brushed off as Western logic, with a bit of swagger from Mr. Komatsu: "I observe that since you people have found that your own scientific endeavor is not on equal footing with Japan, and maybe that's why you're denying it on another level. . . . So-called legal experts do not really understand the situation."

Marine biologists from the United Kingdom showed up with a long, painstaking monograph explaining various techniques by which biopsies may be taken from whales without the need to kill each one. The thing probably took months to prepare, all to elicit this official response: "The Government of Japan appreciates the comments on the usefulness of biopsy sampling techniques. However, OUR VIEW HAS NOT CHANGED. In other words, OUR RESEARCH NEED THE LETHAL METHOD."[26]

Year after year the anti-whaling nations propose some resolution urging, advising, or "calling upon" Japan to reconsider its scientific program and adopt non-lethal research practices, everybody politely playing along with the fiction that science has anything to do with it. "There was considerable discussion of methodological issues," reports the Scientific Committee. "These can be roughly grouped under two headings: Is the methodology described likely to meet the program's objectives; and can the research be carried out using non-lethal methods."[27] They talked about it for days in committee, and will have another go next year, but to no avail because the IWC is powerless and Japan's "methodology" is deceit.

Japanese scientists also keep busy trying to prove, as the Japanese Whalers Association (JWA) puts it, that "Whales Consume Much Fish." I had never heard this one before. All of a sudden, it turns out that whales are not only a very important resource for us, but a very grave threat to us.

"A threat to man and to our fish stocks," says the JWA. "A threat to world food security," says the commissioner from Saint Kitts, raising the specter of "world starvation." As the World Conservation Trust Foundation, an American wise-use outfit, warns in a full-page ad in *USA Today*: "WHALES EAT FISH TOO! The faces of hunger are multiplying. Today, there is not enough food on the planet to feed the world's population. And the situation is worsening. . . . Whales must be managed in the same way as other marine resources—based on science."

Even the little minkes are apparently devouring more than their share. "The sustainable use of whales as a food resource through the controlled harvesting of minke whales," explains the JWA, "would greatly help the recovery of other marine resources. Moreover, in the face of an ever-increasing human population and dwindling world fishery supply, there is further reason to reconsider the ban on whaling."[28] Driving the point home, the Japanese delegation this year treated us to a little slide show on the stomach contents of a gutted minke whale, revealing that the accused had indeed consumed "much fish," in this case much anchovies. *Our* anchovies.

In its own literature the Institute of Cetacean Research runs urgent commentaries on the theme, along with crude little cartoons like one showing a whale and a man seated opposite one another at dinner, the man looking faint and famished over his empty plate as the greedy whale, in evening clothes and a bib, gorges himself on a great big mound of fish.

If mankind's violence to whales is the most ruthless ever directed at any wild animal, this new line of propaganda is surely the most ungracious. The idea, of course, is to turn our hearts against them by appealing to our bellies, and especially to stir up alarm in the developing coastal nations whose support for whaling Japan and Norway seek.

There is a certain sinister logic to it. Yes, some whales have been known to eat fish, though baleen whales like the blue and bowhead content themselves almost exclusively with plankton and krill—the shrimp-like crustaceans they strain from the waters with bristly, comb-like plates from which baleens get their name. As a general rule, the bigger the whale the lower on the food chain it feeds, so that the largest mammals on earth, those two thousand or so blue whales still with us, each subsist on tons of tiny organisms. Nor is there any shortage of these that might have tempted baleen whales to compete for our fish. About a trillion krill inhabit just the Southern Ocean, so many that vast swarms of them can be seen from satellites—testimony to the sudden disappearance of their primary predators the great whales.

So baleen whales are in the clear, leaving the toothed whales to answer for the fish they do indeed consume. What fish they eat, however, in addition to their own diet of krill, copepods, and other crustaceans, are deep-sea and polar fish either inaccessible to us or inedible, except for the squid that sperm whales are known to favor and those anchovies held out as exhibit A in the case against the minke. Most whales migrate to the icy waters of the north and south, far away from our commercial fisheries, precisely to feed. They do not even eat year-round but for the most part only seasonally, some seven or eight months out of the year, storing up enough energy in those thick layers of blubber to carry them through the calving season.

In short, think of any primary seafood on your menu, and unless you have been feasting on plankton and small seabed crustaceans then no whale of any species presents the least competition. At the same time, we do know that the seas are indeed severely depleted of healthy, adult fish populations. And who might have caused that, if not the whales?

Well, let's think. Our own worldwide take has reached 95 million tons of marine life every year, according to a United Nations study. That's not quite five times what mankind hauled from the oceans just half a century ago. And it doesn't even include the 60 or so million tons of "by-catch" our industrial fleets throw overboard every year[29]—the hundreds of millions of juveniles, "non-target" fish, sea turtles, and cetaceans swept up by our trawlers in "unintended stock depletion" and discarded like refuse. Nor does it include the 30 million tons of fish raised in cages in our new "aqua-culture" farms. Whales, moreover, when they are not consuming enormous quantities of marine life, are returning that same biomass into the marine ecosystem as fertilizer. Man, on the other hand, only removes biomass, thus constantly depleting the nutrient base of the sea.

Somebody is taking too much, all right, but it isn't the whales. And even if they *were* found to be consuming more fish than suspected, who are all these officious "resource managers" to complain? These are the same folks who, for all of their insufferable sermonizing about the "riches" and "bless-ings" of the sea, have nearly destroyed the sea's most majestic and peaceable inhabitants, and would finish the job if they had their way. Yes, as mankind now spares more whales from hunting, there will be more whales alive and swimming around the earth and eating more of whatever nature has designed them to eat. Good. That is what happens when you decimate a species of giant animals down to 4 or 5 percent of what their population would otherwise have been, and then finally, mercifully, allow those survivors to live and repopulate. They will need more food.

What's really behind all this chatter about some worldwide anchovy crisis is the growing need for self-restraint by our own fishing industries, for the "wise users" here an unthinkable alternative. What it means is that if whales and other marine mammals are to flourish (and it is only a matter of time before we hear warnings that DOLPHINS EAT FISH TOO!), then mankind cannot go on as we are plundering to no end the 70 percent of earth that is ocean—and especially the fleets of Japan, Taiwan, China, North Korea, and Russia with their history of using illegal drift nets, and their now standard use of longline fishing methods just as reckless and indiscriminate. It means that other creatures have a place here too, that we must keep our nets, buoys, pollutants, and oil spillage out of their path, that we must actually share and, yes, if need be, leave enough of "our fish" for them.

Cultural Imperialism

Then there is this business of whaling as a "cultural right," indeed a kind of religious duty, regardless of how "stocks" are holding up or of what science requires. This gets confusing. On the one hand we are told by the government of Japan that whaling must continue because research demands it—studying whale earplugs and all the rest. On the other, we are told that whaling must continue because in certain cultures tradition and cuisine demand it—*miso* soup and all of that. It doesn't seem to matter that these claims are at times entirely contradictory. When it comes to the customs and cuisine attached to whaling, suddenly we enter sacred ground, and reason and objectivity are to be left at the door like shoes. It's okay if we get emotional about whales, provided it is on Japan's terms and in Japan's way. And then there is no limit to the depth of sympathy and feeling permitted to us.

Westerners, as the Japanese Whaling Association put it, "have elevated whales to the status of sacrosanct—almost religious—icons." Now, with the Australian proposal, they seek "to build a sanctuary for their adoration. They know, and we know, that their proposal is a sham."[30] What we Westerners fail to appreciate, say the whalers, is that for them

whales are associated with a widespread sense of security and prosperity. . . . Whale as a customary food involves a variety of very positive associations in people's minds, so that contemplating a future
without these foods brings worried, indeed depressing thoughts. . . .
The uncertainty of the moratorium led to *stresses far greater than just
economic*. Families, as well as individuals, suffered from a variety of
social and psychological stresses, and, as a consequence, individuals'
and families' health and well being suffered too.[31]

According to this very group, "the total workforce engaged in Japanese
small-type whaling was about 100 people in 1987, of which 75 were full-time
employees."[32] Another thousand or so are employed on or for Japan's entire
five-ship whaling fleet,[33] as against the 10,000 workers the JWA tells us were
laid off in the early 1980s. And since most whalers fish throughout the year
and hunt part-time, very few if any of those 10,000 actually faced full unem-
ployment. In a survey by the independent MORI organization, moreover, as a
Japanese animal-welfare group called the Iruka & Kujira Action Network
reports, 60 percent of Japanese people say they have not eaten whale meat
since childhood. All of 1 percent report eating it regularly. And just 11 percent express support for Japan's whaling industry.[34]

So whatever the economic stresses here, they are not really so "widespread" at all. Maybe once, but not now. We are talking about a very small
number of whalers serving a small, affluent, and aging minority—consumers
like Naoshi Goto, a sixty-six-year-old gentleman interviewed by a *New York
Times* reporter over a bowl of whale soup at Taruichi restaurant in Tokyo: "As
a child, we ate *miso* soup with whale meat every New Year's Eve. It was a
centuries-old tradition in my village. You can't imagine how precious this
soup is to me right now."[35]

For such consumers and for the whalers, we are told, it is not just the loss
of a trade or tradition but of the flesh itself, this precious flesh, that brings on
these depressing thoughts. As the Japan Small-Type Whaling Association
explains in its brochure:

The importance of *kujira* relates to its *symbolic associations* with a
number of positive aspects in people's lives (e.g., health, longevity,
vitality); the social and cultural importance of gifts of whale meat;
the use of edible whale products in local/regional cuisines; the

important role these cuisines play in maintaining cultural identity; the cultural value placed on maintaining and transmitting *traditional skills and occupations*; and the fostering of *traditional spiritual values* that connect whalers and their families with their past and with whales.[36]

Whale meat "relates," in other words, to just about everything. Covering all the bases, killing whales is also a means to "court divine favor." There are deep spiritual values at play:

> Members of the whaling communities also participate in Buddhist ceremonies, two of which are particularly important: first, memorial services for the souls of the whales killed; and second, for the souls of whalers who, having taken a life, seek forgiveness for the loss of merit for having done so. In some whaling villages, virtually the whole community participates in these services.[37]

Something of this spiritual element is lost in color pictures to be found in this very same brochure, which capture scenes of bustling butchers in construction hats and blood-soaked overalls wielding industrial tools aboard the factory ships that only Japan still uses, none of the workers in apparent devotion.

If any actual reverence still inspires Japan's whalers, it seems to be of the self-directed variety. Thus, we may "adore" whales all we want, provided we have killed them first. We may indulge sentimentality, but only if it is showered upon the butchers themselves and their cherished ways. One may demand again and again to know just what is so "special" about whales, only one must never, ever ask just what is so special about whale meat. One may even acknowledge the "loss of merit" in a man who would kill a whale or dolphin, but only if the reproof is confined to empty, self-serving ritual. And one is permitted to feel pity, even to wallow in it, just so long as it is self-pity.

It is galling, moreover, to see Japan's quite prosperous-looking Western PR team walking around here posing as altruistic defenders of science and cultural understanding and all of these poor, struggling Japanese whalers, while daring, repeatedly, to accuse others of cupidity. To hear them talk, you'd think that everyone else is in it for money, money, money—everyone except for them and the businesses they represent. "Whales are not endangered and [Japan's] research program is a valid scientific program," as Dan Goodman puts it. "They [Greenpeace] make millions of dollars every year from misleading the public."[38] Mr. Goodman, who used to represent Canada at the IWC, is now employed to mouth this propaganda by the $40-million-a-year Institute of Cetacean Research. And just what do they pay him with? Sacred offerings of *kujira*?

Whaling, and with it this same sanctimony and sense of grievance, survives today largely because Japan has been supporting it in an effort to divert attention from itself. If all of this were just about money, after all, or about a certain food favored by a Japanese elite, world opinion will weigh on the side of the whale. The Japanese whaling interests would look arrogant and greedy and even a little silly. So it has to be about something else, something higher and nobler and universal. There's science, but nobody believes that—it's just for legal cover—so they needed a moral angle to go with it. With help from Tele-Press Associates of New York, they came up with Japanese whalers as victims of intolerance, as champions of less developed peoples, and their industry as a proud symbol of cultural diversity in a world falling ever more under the sway of "Western cultural imperialism."

When the moratorium was enacted in 1982, for instance, Saint Vincent and all other Caribbean nations then belonging to the IWC voted for it. The six delegations now in Japan's control were then newly sovereign countries, having a few years earlier shaken off formal rule by the British and the French. They favored the ban doubtless in part because of influence from the United States, which was then sending some $225 million in foreign aid to their countries, but also because they are largely fishing, agricultural, and tourist economies, and tourists tend to enjoy the sight of whales more than the sight of whales being baited and butchered.

With humpbacks dropping by every year, these countries are prime locales for "eco-tourism" and especially for whale-watching businesses of the kind today earning some half a billion dollars in profits in seventy different countries.[39] What whaling traditions these islands had, they got from Europeans and Americans who built whaling stations on Saint Vincent, and for many years trained and employed the locals in hunting and processing. When the Americans and Europeans withdrew around the beginning of the last century, organized whaling ceased in the Caribbean.

The Japanese government has coaxed them all into its pro-whaling bloc with untold millions of dollars in new boats, fisheries, and public works projects, and even picks up their $340,000 annual tab at the IWC. And, in a way, the U.S. government can blame itself for the loss of allies: Vulnerable to hurricanes and constant natural disasters, these islands still depend on foreign aid and investment, and American aid from 1985 to 1995 fell by some 90 percent. Japan saw its opening, and the governments of these nations have understandably welcomed the help.

How the people themselves view Japan's whaling agenda isn't clear, though we got one sign at this meeting when the fisheries minister for Dominica, Atherton Martin, resigned in protest, revealing that Japan had given his country $7 million in exchange for pro-whaling votes. "If Japan didn't have this influence," said Mr. Martin, "Dominica wouldn't have any business as a member of this political organization. We're not a whaling nation, we are a whale-watching nation."[40] Mr. Martin, Mr. Komatsu told the *Advertiser,* was "a plant" by enemies of Japan.[41]

It was also revealed this week that the FBI and U.S. Treasury Department have identified these very same sovereign countries, and Dominica and Saint Vincent in particular, as havens for tax evaders, drug cartels, and other unsavories.[42] One cannot drag any of these particular officials into all that, but I will tell you this much. They display an unnatural deference to their Japanese and Norwegian benefactors, and one feels embarrassed for some of the Caribbean delegates who hover around Mr. Komatsu and Mr. Skagestad like valets. During breaks you can see them come up to Mr. Komatsu and to Eugene Lapointe, president of the IWMC—World Conservation Trust, with their proposals and speech texts for correction, like children with their homework. Nor is it clear that all of this money from Japan goes to fisheries and the like. On the coffee line I overheard what sure sounded like the tail end of a bribe between one delegate and a gentleman from the Caribbean: "Look, it doesn't matter how it gets laundered. The point is we send you twenty thousand U.S. dollars." Is there, I later ask Steinar, a quid pro quo with the Caribbean delegates and their new benefactors? "Of course there is. We're organized. We want to win."

Thus have the votes of six financially coerced pro-whaling nations (Saint Vincent, Grenada, Dominica, Saint Kitts, Antigua, and Saint Lucia) representing half a million people canceled out the votes of six anti-whaling nations (the United States, Britain, New Zealand, Australia, Spain, and Brazil) representing a billion people.

✤

It was a similar story with the Makah Indians of northwest Washington State a few years ago, when out of nowhere, seventy years after the last Makah had hunted the last gray whale in the North Pacific, the tribal council decided to resume the tradition, gaining permission from the U.S. to whale under the "ceremonial whaling" exception to the IWC ban.

Whaling is a Makah tradition in exactly the same sense that buffalo hunting is the tradition of modern Native Americans: It stopped long ago when Europeans and Americans came along and annihilated the herds of animals upon which they had depended—in this case, the California fisheries of the 1800s which had just about finished off the gray whales by century's end. Now all of a sudden the Makah wanted to whale again. This reversion to old ways was welcomed as an exquisite PC dilemma for environmentalists, torn between their solicitude for whales and their concern for the rights of native peoples. "The harassment of the Makah by animal-rights activists," declared Mr. Lapointe's IWMC *Conservation Tribune*, "is reminiscent of equally vehement harassment of African Americans by other self-righteous racists/supremacists during the Civil Rights era of the 1960s." Here was the *Wall Street Journal's* take on the first Makah hunt in May 1999:

> "Thou shalt not kill whales" ranks among the top commandments in the canon of political correctness. So when the Makah Indian nation speared a whale off America's Northwest coast on Monday, the environmentalists practically choked on their granola bars. But pity the animal lovers, for this is no clear-cut call. To the average activist, interfering in native American cultures is almost as taboo as chopping down redwood trees. . . . Surely by prevailing over enormous bureaucratic obstacles, the Makah have more than earned their traditional supper.[43]

What actually happened was that the Makah were all going about their business when, one day in 1991, someone in Tokyo dreamed up the idea that maybe it was time the Makah Nation reclaimed their ancient right. Before long the World Council of Whalers, a joint operation of Japan and Norway, had set up an office in nearby Port Alberni, British Columbia. They provided some start-up money for a "cultural exchange program," teaching the tribe to whale and helping with an intricate series of agreements by which various U.S. agencies (as we later learned in a federal lawsuit filed by Washington Representative Jack Metcalf) removed the Eastern Pacific gray whale from our endangered species list and gained permission for the Makah to take whales from the quota allowed to Russia for its Chukotka tribe. After a vote in the tribal council (200 of 600 members present), finally a new generation of Makah went forth to subdue leviathan. To great fanfare, and under the protection of the U.S. Coast Guard, eight of the men embarked on their canoe into Neah Bay, bearing their cold harpoons and an assault rifle that had to be fired four times at a juvenile gray whale who swam right up to them.

Alberta Thompson, a Makah woman who opposed the hunt, tells me she was harassed and fired from her job by Japan's supporters in the tribe, whom, she believes, also harassed her grandson and killed her dog. The whole extravaganza was seen from the start as a "symbolic victory" for Japan, which had now engineered a return to whaling sanctioned by American law and occurring in American waters.

Mrs. Thompson didn't think much of the Makah men, either. A videotape was taken of the sacred ceremony, which consisted of the men jumping up and down on the slain whale in idiot euphoria, the creature still moving her flippers, before carving her up with chainsaws and then, as night fell, leaving half the carcass to rot. "For hunters long ago," she says, "it was very important that you live a clean life a year before the hunt. Men were dancing on the whale after the hunt. The men of another time would never have done that. It took a young lady from the tribe to tell them to stop. A young lady, and she was pro-whaler. The men of another time would never have done that. They would have had more reverence for the life they had taken."

Selling the whole thing as a kind of Makah self-esteem program, Japan in this way has found its own "empowered peasants." And doubtless one day it will dawn on both the Makah and Caribbean leaders that "imperialist" manipulation may come from the East, too. For now, they make excellent props in the media war, evoking the sympathy long denied to Japanese whalers themselves, just like the African people on whose behalf the trophy-hunting industry and Japan's own "aphrodisiac" and ivory industries are working to expand tiger and elephant hunting. Having twisted the meaning of "science," Japan's whaling interests now pervert the meaning of "culture" by stirring up phony indigenous movements to revive long-gone traditions decades after the whaling industry should have died its natural death—as the "resource" itself was dying off and new substitutes were found for its flesh and oil.

The closest people at the IWC to real-life aboriginal whalers are the Inuit, who have come all the way to Adelaide from their coastal villages in the far corners of Alaska, Canada, and Russia and kill a combined four or five hundred whales a year. Their argument is that they have been whaling in bays for at least four or five thousand years, and who is anyone to come along and tell them it's time to stop? In theory, international law and various treaties bar the Eskimos from selling whale products. So it is for the meat alone that they hunt, we are assured, and for sacred tradition.

But when is "sacred tradition" just sport? Like the Faroese with their annual pilot whale slaughter—45,000 people enjoying one of Europe's highest standards of living, with no need for the meat but merely a taste for it—most Eskimos who hunt whales today are not primitives struggling to subsist in the harsh fringes of civilization. They are young men for whom whaling is a passion and, as we are told, an act of cultural self-affirmation. They whale, not because they must, but because they want to, otherwise living quite civilized lives in heated houses, driving cars and trucks and snowmobiles, working on oil rigs and in stores and factories and offices, and in northern Alaska generally prospering thanks to, of all things, the petroleum industry. Mr. Brower, the Eskimo "aboriginal subsistence whaler," gave me his card and e-mail address, and I doubt the computer is set up in an igloo.

Whaling was dying off in these communities until the early 1970s, when the Alaskan pipeline had the perverse effect of reviving it with new wealth and free time for recreation. Today, one is hard put to distinguish the practice from trophy hunting, and especially our modern bow-hunting craze with its same self-conscious acting-out of primitive passions, the same parody of heroic exploit, and the same selective reverence for custom. Thus, the cold harpoon must be used, regardless of the whales who will suffer more or be struck and "lost," because, well, that is how great-grandfather did it and his father before him. For every thousand whales the Eskimos kill, the IWC estimates, more than a hundred escape with harpoons still in their brains or backs, and more than one in four of those are pregnant females. But as to the speedboats, chainsaws, CB radios, spotter planes, and sixteen-wheel rigs your typical "aboriginal" whalers now use to drag their quarry from the waters, somehow sacred tradition is silent.

Brave Fish

Entering the convention center on the morning of the sanctuary vote, Masa-yuki Komatsu receives the plaudits of cheering men in suits and women in kimonos shipped here to stage Japan's idea of a spontaneous protest. Things are going Japan's way, and it looks like they'll be leaving Adelaide with an even greater rout of the West than had been expected.

It's not much of a protest either way—maybe seventy or eighty demonstrators in all, and then only when cameras are present. On one side we have the JWA and groups with names like the Whale Cuisine Preservation Association with signs like "Mutual Understanding of Cultures, Sustainable Use of Resources" and "Cuisine is Culture." And, the whalers' trump card: "Leave Us to Our Whale and We Will Leave You to Your McDonald's and Pork Chops." On the other side are Greenpeace, Kids for Whales—a delegation of thirteen children who have come all the way from Europe with a life-size inflatable whale—and various solitary protesters with signs declaring "Stop the Slaughter" and "The IWC is a Corrupt Farce."

Among Kids for Whales is a very sweet fifteen-year-old named Simone Lemmes of Cologne, who yesterday planted herself in the path of Mr. Komatsu and his entourage, pleading with him to allow the sanctuary and "just stop killing whales." Though I didn't catch the entire exchange—the cameramen had immediately moved in—she seemed to be holding her own and it took everything he had just to break away, telling the girl to study science. When the Japanese were gone, Simone, the new star in her group, was surrounded by admiring friends a-twitter at this blow struck by Kids for Whales.

Among the other protesters is a scraggly fellow of forty or so named Howie Cook, a genuine hippie who hitchhiked here from Melbourne with his girlfriend, a scraggly beauty named Trudi. They stand out here all day long, even in the rain. They have swum with whales and studied whales—*waaals*, in Australian—and speak with great feeling about whales and dolphins alike, especially this possibility, as Howie puts it, that "marine mammals don't have the gift of unconsciousness. They suffer until the very end." Of the Japanese and Norwegian delegates who come and go throughout the day, he says, "They laugh at us. But they are hard of heart"—*haaad of haaat*. "They create these systems of cruelty, destroying these beautiful creatures, and then they laugh at anyone who questions them."

Inside, it could be any IWC debate on any given agenda item at any given hour in any given year: ". . . . Whaling is part of our cultural heritage and we will not surrender it! . . . The United States urges Japan to cancel this imprudent project! . . . We must harvest these blessings of the sea! . . . Foolish and greedy exploitation! . . . Scientifically based global ocean governance for optimum utilization of whale resources! . . ."

I am struck by Masayuki Komatsu, this obviously smart and serious man whose life's work has become the defense of a delicacy. Insisting as they do on using translators even though most or all speak impeccable English, arriving and departing in packs with little mingling among us Western cultural imperialists, the Japanese seem harsh and unapproachable, a little like Soviet delegations in Cold War days. With Mr. Komatsu, among others I met in his delegation, this turns out to be an entirely false impression. I ask to speak to him when he has a moment, and a few hours later he actually seeks me out, cordial as can be and eager to make his case.

It is true, of course, that an island nation with 13,000 miles of coastland was bound over the ages to view marine mammals differently from societies less reliant upon the seas. Then again, America, Australia, New Zealand, Spain, Brazil, Holland, Germany, South Africa, Britain, and just about everyone else were once whaling nations—the Dutch long before and more so than the Japanese ever were. All of these countries gave it up, and many old whaling ports have today become profitable centers for whale-watching. So why can't Japan give it up? When did a single food type become the be-all and end-all of Japanese life?

"Our view," explains Mr. Komatsu in his clipped, precise manner, "is that we should utilize any wild animal—wildlife—under appropriate management based upon scientific grounds and based upon sustainable use, whereas the other side—Western side—says in no circumstances, since whale is special, therefore whale should not be utilized, regardless of conservation status. That is one fundamental difference. And secondly, we have [a] whale-eating culture. And we consider whale as simply one of the living marine resources. Whether it's fish, whether it's whale, whether it's dolphins, we don't see any difference. Of course, taste is different, and appreciation—depending on the locality—is different. But it's just one of the marine living species, whereas they think that [the whale] is an adorable or sacred animal and could be treated as equal to human beings. Sometimes they consider that whales are more intelligent than Asian and black people, lower than white Caucasian, and therefore that this creature should not be killed or even never harassed."

Leaving aside that last observation, what about the problem that whales and dolphins are, in reality, not fish?

"Japan believes that difference of view, in particular culture, should be respected. Culture is unique. Culture is local, at most national. However, [the] other side's view is that their judgment should prevail all over the globe, and they try to impose their judgment, their views, over us. . . . You see, we [do] not judge different cultures. Killing whale is not different from killing fish in Japanese culture, because whale is a kind of fish. So the Japanese fisherman does not care."

The Japanese government, in its extensive research, has discovered that if a particular culture believes that whales and dolphins are fish, then for that culture whales and dolphins are fish. Still, beyond the Sacred Isles, there is an awful lot of evidence that the creatures are not only mammals but advanced mammals, and on this score even Steinar has some doubts about his Japanese comrades: "They treat them like fish. That is wrong. You don't treat mammals like fish. Fish you kill as quickly as possible too." Through real research, I remind Mr. Komatsu, conducted by real scientists, we now know things that we simply did not know centuries ago—about their minds and lives and emotions and how they must feel being harpooned or trapped and hacked and knifed. Doesn't tradition at some point have to accommodate that new information, especially in the case of marine mammals needing years to grow and breed, and so thoroughly decimated precisely because they have been treated like fish?

"Yes and no," he replies. "I think your question is to some extent relevant. But you see, the depiction we are now finding as evidence is a part of the accumulation of knowledge. For many years when fishermen were dealing with those creatures—whether it's the fish or the cetaceans—[they gained direct knowledge]. They know by direct contact such knowledge as direct contact [has] accumulated through several hundred or up to thousands of years, [and this] may supersede our modern knowledge. So, I think what we have to do is accumulate all information and decide. And we should not say that long experience of fishermen is inferior to those depicted in recent years. We shouldn't be so arrogant to quickly decide to do so."

Funny how the moment we turn the light of science upon the whales and dolphins themselves, all Mr. Science wants to talk about is the ancient, intuitive wisdom of fishermen and whalers—because "sometimes direct experience really tells us more." He likens it to the "direct experience" of communicating with someone in person versus communication by telephone, e-mail, or some other impersonal means. When you aim a camera or hydrophone at a whale, in this analogy, or simply observe the creature, somehow that is an indirect experience, removed from immediate realities. Aim a harpoon at a whale, or a spear or rifle at a dolphin, and then you're gaining *real* knowledge of the creature. And how "arrogant" of us to brush off such first-hand experience.

Is there any conceivable information that might lead Mr. Komatsu to different conclusions? If, hypothetically, it were demonstrated to his satisfaction that whales and dolphins really do experience thoughts and emotions and conscious suffering, would that change his mind?

"We conducted a study on this, and we know that dolphins and whales are to some extent intelligent. But they are not as intelligent as—at least not more intelligent than—horses or cows. They have no kind of exceeding or superseding capacities. So, since we are utilizing horses and cows, we must also utilize whale and dolphin. We have to treat all animals by the same standards."

Such . . . *evenhandedness.* If we are exploiting one kind of animal, by this standard, why then it is only fair to exploit all others of comparable capacities. From there Mr. Komatsu returns to his "collective guilt" theme: Who are we to judge X when we ourselves are doing the same thing, and where do Westerners get off judging Japan or any other culture, and just what is so special about whales?

Aristotle, twenty-three centuries ago, classified the whale and dolphin as "cetacea—that is to say, they are provided with a blow-hole instead of gills, and are viviparous . . . just as in the case of mankind and the viviparous quadrupeds."[44] Probably even earlier, Japanese scientists discovered this for themselves. Richard Ellis, in *Men & Whales,* gives us this interesting tidbit:

"One reason that whales do not figure in the social or culinary history of early Japan is that the Buddhist emperors of the sixth and seventh centuries prohibited their subjects from eating meat of any kind. Even so, certain segments of the population managed to circumvent the imperial ordinances by deciding that a whale was not a mammal at all, but rather *isana*, a 'large fish' or a 'brave fish.'"[45]

Sounds familiar, only instead of imperial ordinances to evade we now have Western "cultural imperialism." Yet it's not really the existence of shared standards that Japanese officials deny—their whole "collective guilt" argument assumes we're all guilty of *something*. It's the particular application of those standards to marine mammals, and here they offer not a single rational argument but only a spray of scientific verbiage, multicultural clichés, and diffuse accusations. "To say whales are loveable, dignified, intelligent and not domesticated is nothing but an arbitrary assessment from the point of view of one set of human standards," as Sho Shibata writes in the journal of Japan's fisheries association, fittingly enough called *Isana*. "If someone asserts that a culture which has affection for whales is the only excellent and righteous culture, then he is propounding cultural imperialism and intolerance."[46]

Shigeko Misako of the Japanese delegation describes whaling almost as a matter of national security. "Whaling," she told the *Australian*, "is a national symbol against the cultural imperialism of Western nations. If we succumb to the moral standards of the Western world, we would lose control over our own people."[47] When anyone dares criticize whaling, as Japan's ambassador to the UN puts it, they are trying to "impose their particular Western view of whales on the rest of the world."[48]

All of this is a diversion. And frankly it is just a little much hearing the government of Japan incessantly warning about the dreaded Western influence. We don't hear such warnings about Western capitalism, which has made Japan so prosperous. Or about Western democracy, which gave Japan its own constitution as well as democratic forums like the UN and IWC in which to rail against Western imperialism. Or about the Western sciences and technologies Japan has turned to advantage, from this Toshiba laptop in front of me to the very machinery of modern whaling. Or about the Western military influence that today safeguards Japan's very existence as a nation. Or indeed about these quite Western ideas of tolerance and pluralism packaged for the Japanese government by a Western PR outfit to manipulate Western public opinion.

The difference is that this particular Western influence requires a modicum of self-restraint and a sacrifice of profit and accustomed treats, which Japan is resolutely unwilling to make. And the basic problem is that while all the Western imperialists at the IWC are engaged in diplomacy, moral suasion, and earnest scientific inquiry, the governments of Norway and Japan (as distinguished from the Japanese and Norwegian people, who one doubts are even following much of this) are engaged in power politics. Mr. Komatsu describes the whole thing to me as "a game," and for his government it has become a game of waiting. Whatever outrage their conduct provokes in the West, Japan has discovered that it will pass if only they are patient, and it certainly will not bring any actual consequences, least of all in the form of trade sanctions.

When the ships returned from killing their forty-six Bryde's and five sperm whales in August 2000, a delegation of government officials stood at portside with raised glasses, literally toasting this triumph for Japan.[49] The *New York Times* called it "a reprehensible hunt," urging the U.S. to invoke a law known as the Pelly amendment to apply trade sanctions. "The rest of the international community should follow suit," said the *Times*.[50] There were reports that President Bill Clinton was considering this step. Responding to the threat, a spokesman for Japan leveled one of his own threats: "If the United States takes unilateral action, it is almost certain that Japan will win in the World Trade Organization."[51] The president sent a personal appeal to then–prime minister Yoshiro Mori, and, when that failed, to his credit finally barred Japanese fishing boats from American waters and proposed that Congress lay sanctions on companies producing whaling equipment. No sanctions ever materialized, however, and with that went the only threat ever to give Japan or Norway a moment's hesitation.

Without venturing too far into the legal bramble patch, the Pelly amendment was adopted in 1967 and is today urged by environmentalists and animal-welfare groups as a means of deterring or punishing Japan, Norway, and other whaling nations. Our Marine Mammal Protection Act, signed in 1972 by President Richard Nixon, forbids the harming of any whale or other marine mammal within American waters, and authorizes sanctions against nations that do harm them. The Pelly amendment gives force to this authority, instructing the U.S. Department of Commerce to certify to the president whether members of the IWC are complying with our standards and with international conservation regimes. The president then has the option of imposing sanctions on any offending nation. This is why Norway is still stuck with all that blubber. They fear sanctions if they try to export it. And this is why Norway suspended whaling operations back in 1986 when there were indications President Ronald Reagan might act against them.

Seven years later, informed that Norway had resumed whaling, Mr. Clinton let it pass. "The United States is deeply opposed to commercial whaling," the president told Congress, "but has an equally strong commitment to science-based solutions to global conservation problems," and "not every country agrees with our position against commercial whaling. . . . Our objectives can best be achieved by delaying the implementation of sanctions until we have exhausted all good faith efforts to persuade Norway to follow agreed conservation measures."[52]

The upshot was a "resolution" by Congress to condemn commercial whaling in general while doing nothing in particular, a Nobel Prize nomination for President Clinton from Steinar himself on the floor of the Norwegian parliament, and another seven years of waiting until all good-faith efforts have been exhausted and Norway has finally come around to see the wisdom of our ways.

Of course what Norway and Japan see is weakness, moralistic huffing and puffing with little intention of backing it up. The Pelly amendment has been used just once in all these years, against Taiwan in 1994 for its imports of "aphrodisiacs" and other products taken from endangered tigers and rhinos. And today, even if the U.S. or any other nation tried to lay sanctions on Japan or Norway or, for that matter, Taiwan again, these sanctions would be challenged at the World Trade Organization (WTO), which, unlike the IWC, actually has power.

Free trade is a fundamental principle of economics, encouraging competition, lower prices, and material uplift to developing nations. Where animal welfare is concerned, to say nothing of human welfare, the problem is that in our dealings with sovereign countries trade and import policies are just about the only means we have of asserting moral standards where we find things that are cruel, corrupt, or unconscionable. They can be a highly effective means, as the sealers will attest. Sanctions are a way of saying, "We can't stop you from doing such and such, but if you insist on continuing then we want no part in it, and we cannot in good conscience support you with our markets." As more responsibility shifts to the WTO, we lose these standards and the sovereign freedom to assert them. Free trade under the WTO has become not just a principle but a kind of mania, not just a good but the highest good, leveling standards in both human rights and animal welfare to the lowest common denominator and reducing all moral problems to questions of economic advantage.

When the U.S. applied its own laws in the early 1990s and barred the import of tuna caught by Latin American fishermen using the purse-seine method, drowning tens of thousands of dolphins in the eastern Pacific, Mexico filed a complaint. The WTO a few years later compelled Congress to alter the law. We're not even allowed to require labels on tuna cans informing consumers how the goods were obtained, because that, too, is considered an unfair barrier to free trade.

When the European Union in 1996 barred the import of furs from the U.S. obtained by use of steel-jawed, leg-hold traps, the American trappers and furriers' lobby prevailed on the Clinton administration to sue at the WTO, forcing the EU to back down. The EU in 2000 proposed offering subsidies to help European farmers meet labor and animal-welfare standards. Now it was New Zealand, noble defender of marine mammals, that objected on the grounds that this was nothing more than a hidden trade barrier placing foreign producers at a disadvantage. As James Sutton, New Zealand's agricultural minister, put it in a poke at the French, "We do not need lectures on animal welfare from people who force-feed geese."[53]

Everybody has some product or practice they view as no one else's business. And harsher methods of producing animal commodities are always more cost-efficient than kinder ones—in the space and type of food and degree of human care afforded to them—just as harsher labor conditions are often the most economical. When no country is willing to make concessions, and thereby risk losing a market, the only alternative is to drop the subject of animal welfare entirely, and exactly this is happening. The WTO makes it easy, permitting even prosperous interests like furriers and factory farmers and Japan's government-subsidized whaling industry to present themselves as aggrieved victims of unfair trade barriers. Undoing decades of progress in more developed nations, the WTO treats animal welfare as an illegitimate question, a purely commercial consideration relevant only as it helps or hinders trade. In the global economy, even minimal consideration for animal suffering can be a competitive disadvantage.

Confronted with each nation's own questionable products and practices, we have two choices. We can say, as Mr. Komatsu hopes, "Well, they do X but we do Y, so who are we to judge?" We then end up with no standard at all, instead using other people's cruelties as an excuse for our own. Or, in each country, we can take animal welfare seriously enough to examine X and Y on their own merits, by reference to clear and fixed standards we apply to ourselves and our own industries and all who enjoy the privilege of trading with us.

Without that kind of seriousness, the world's guardian of whales is a useless academic bureaucracy, with no power but plenty of the "moral authority" it directs at Japan and Norway in volumes full of resolutions, remonstrances, and appeals to the opinion of mankind. Here's one addressing Japan's repeated invasions of the Southern Ocean Sanctuary—from the Indian Ocean to the west coast of New Zealand—in theory a haven for whales:

> NOTING that since the 51st meeting in May 1999, the Government of Japan has issued special permits for lethal scientific research on minke whales in the Southern Ocean Sanctuary. . . .
> NOW THEREFORE THE COMMISSION:
> REQUESTS that the Government of Japan refrain from issuing any Special Permits for the 2000/2001 season for the take of minke whales from the Southern Ocean Sanctuary.[54]

Japan, of course, will continue to do as it pleases, and most of its killing in the weeks after this conference took place in the Southern Ocean Sanctuary.

The Scientific Committee notes that Japan's lethal research is unwarranted: "The Committee therefore endorses the recommendation that a steering committee be established to develop protocols, review results and progress, and recommend revisions to the research programme recommended in the report."[55] Now there's a stirring call to action: A committee must be formed to recommend revisions of other recommendations for a program previously recommended.

Canada, another noncompliant government that still gets to send people here to harangue everyone else, last year authorized the killing of an endangered bowhead whale in the eastern Canadian Arctic despite emphatic requests from the IWC not to do so. But now comes the day of reckoning for

Canada. Here, in agenda item 10.3.2, is how they are to be dealt with. Sternly "noting" this, that, and the other thing:

> NOW THEREFORE THE COMMISSION:
>   REAFFIRMS its opposition to whaling conducted on highly endangered stocks of whales;
>   EXPRESSES particular concern that whaling activities in the Eastern Canadian Arctic are ongoing outside the control of the IWC;
>   URGES the Government of Canada to refrain from issuing licenses;
>   INVITES the Government of Canada to rejoin the IWC and, in the meantime, not to issue further whaling permits;
>   REQUESTS THAT the Secretariat transmit the text of this Resolution to the Government of Canada.[56]

We hoped it wouldn't come to this, but Canada has left us no choice and now we must, well, send them a letter. That's the Resolution, to mail the Canadians a copy of the Resolution itself—by Federal Express, one hopes, just to show them how RESOLVED we are.

SANCTUARY

The day after the sanctuary debate I went off do some nonconsumptive utilizing down in Victor Harbor, one of those hundreds of old whaling towns across the world where whale-watching services have recently opened for business. By midmorning in the debate it was pretty clear who had the votes, the Caribbean nations effusively "associating" themselves with the views of Japan and Norway. The final tally was 18 for, 11 against, and 4 abstentions including a last-minute waffle from Spain.

Outside in the rain Simone and some of her companions were crying and hugging. Howie and Trudi were still there, faithfully at their post. Inside Mr. Komatsu was exuberant, going from one camera crew to the next explaining all that whaling means for science and culture, and receiving congratulations from one and all—his fellow delegates, Dan Goodman, Alan Macnow of Tele-Press, Bastesen and Skagestad, Eugene Lapointe, the Caribbean delegates coming up for hugs of their own. My last glimpse of the scene, from across the Hyatt bar, had Steinar, Mr. Komatsu, and Mr. Lapointe among others all seated together in a little nook raising their glasses in victory, presumably *"To wise use!"*

Mr. Lapointe had apparently noticed Simone too, and no report would be complete without a few words from him.

"Yes," he told me after the vote, "we are pleased with the outcome, but the vote for us was far too close. The debate was far too emotional. I found it almost pitiful to see young kids with tears in their eyes after the vote, because they view the whale as some kind of god. We heard only these emotional and unscientific arguments, especially this suggestion that whale-watching could be a substitute for whaling. The Australian proposal was not supported by science and by legality."

I never did get a fix on his role in all this. Mr. Lapointe used to be general secretary of the Convention on International Trade in Endangered Species (CITES), where he turned the organization into a brisk ivory concession, campaigning against legal and trade protections for elephants, easing the sale of hundreds of tons of tusks to Asian carving and "aphrodisiac" industries, and actually accepting donations to CITES, as *Time* revealed, from the ivory traders themselves including the Japanese Ivory Association.[57] This would "incentivize" elephants and, well, you know the rest. As it turned out he never saw his elephant privatization scheme come to full fruition. During his nine-year tenure, from 1982 until Mr. Lapointe was removed in 1990 at the insistence of the U.S., Africa's elephant population was cut in half, from some 1.3 million to 635,000.

How comforting, then, to learn from Mr. Lapointe that he is here with an equally ambitious plan for "a universal cetacean strategy." A Canadian who now lives in Florida and Lausanne, where CITES is headquartered, the son of a gamekeeper, as he tells me, who learned early in life to hunt and kill and never lost the taste for it, his name turns up quite a bit among animal-welfare people here, who have come to view him as a sort of Professor Moriarty figure, out of the Sherlock Holmes novels, whose lawful yet perfidious hand may be detected the world over.

Japan, Norway, and their new Caribbean allies, for instance—including many of these very same delegates here at the IWC—have conspired at CITES to "downlist" from endangered status not only whales but elephants, too. This would allow international trade in whale products, so that Norway and Japan can start exporting. And it would allow the killing of more elephants, with a quota of 30 tons of ivory sold annually to Japan and other Asian buyers. Given his solicitude for the ivory interests as secretary general and his service as their consultant to this day, it is surmised that Mr. Lapointe is somewhere involved in that.

Japan has also managed to recruit Zimbabwe into the IWC, and is working on Namibia and other African nations in what Hiroaki Kameya, vice minister for fisheries, frankly describes as an effort to form a pro-whaling majority.[58] Since neither Zimbabwe nor Namibia figures prominently in maritime history, and until now have never displayed the least interest in whaling, we all know who might be helping with that, too.

From what I have been told, it would take an entire book just to lift the rock on all of these networks and connections, which in the end are probably not so conspiratorial but just a very extensive and shrewd political organization. Enough to observe that in all of these matters Eugene Lapointe is a man of some influence, and when it comes to the demands of sustainable use he means business, especially for whales and elephants. A woman from the Humane Society of the United States tells me she believes that these two creatures have been singled out by hunting interests precisely because of the special affection people bear them. They have become the symbols over which the battle will be won or lost, martyr figures in the public mind who must never, ever be given protection. After meeting Mr. Lapointe, I do not doubt it.

"Our main purpose is sustainable use," he explained over a cup of tea. "For us, the principle of sustainable use will suffer no exceptions, except for science. The worst crime against nature is waste, not to use resources. Whether it is the elephant, the whale, deer, elk, bear, it must apply to all animals. No exceptions or emotional considerations must be allowed—only science."

"There's been this tendency to humanize the whale," he continued, after a brief interruption from Kerwyn Morris of sovereign Saint Vincent, who was quickly dispatched with some whispered instructions and papers from Mr. Lapointe's briefcase. "But it's all based on a misconception. You know, they're 'special,' like humans and such. They 'sing,' they're so smart, and all this nonsense. The idea that we must 'save' whales has become a dogma, but when the facts are explained, people understand. There have been surveys proving this. People know very little about whales, and what they know is wrong. As far as dolphins are concerned, most scientific studies would call them dumb animals. Intelligence slightly lower than a cow."

You had to hear the pure contempt with which "*special*" and "*sing*" and "slightly lower than *a cow*" all came out.

"Asia, in particular China and Japan, are the main target of those who would impose their Anglo-Saxon cultural values on the rest of the world. So we see these films of whales being harpooned and flounced, or dolphins being caught in fishing nets, and everyone becomes so emotional about it. You see the same kind of thing in the propaganda about elephants—elephants being shot and the calf nearby making noises and so forth. You see, you need a villain. To run these campaigns and raise money, they have to create a villain. . . ."

"These people trying to stop hunting don't understand elephants. A hunter's bullet spares the elephant from the suffering of natural mortality. It's for their own good, to be hunted and used. The problem is misinformation [about elephants]. The reality isn't what we see on television. The reality is that's an animal that has to be contained. That's an animal that has to be controlled. That's an animal that tramples people. That's an animal that threatens people. You have to give it economic value. You have to use them."

He certainly has *his* villain. And how incredible to think that here sits the man who once had more power than anyone over the fate of the elephant. A young Japanese aide to Mr. Lapointe, running one of the many groups in his network called Riches of the Sea, had told him I was a contributing editor of a conservative magazine, which seems to have led him to assume we were all *compadre* here, and he looked at me as if surely I agreed with this, all of it so sensible and rational and scientific. But I was thinking only, God spare the creatures from this grim little tyrant and his kind. Grant them this sanctuary, and many more across the world, from cruelty and avarice and the pride of man that knoweth no bounds.

He talks like a man who will never die, who is here on earth only to mete out death. He is a dealer in death, with a wave of the hand declaring herds of whales and elephants unfit to live, and "suffering no exceptions." He looks with pity upon others like Simone and her friends for making a "god" of the whale—this man with all his lucrative schemes for selling ivory and blubber and now this Lilliputian dream of a "universal cetacean strategy" to control, contain, and cull the whales. And what god inspires those? Whatever whales with their groanings communicate, or elephant calves with their "noises and so forth," there is more truth and goodness in those sounds than in anything he has to say, and of all the contending interests here I think I'll associate myself with the hippie and the girl in tears.

What a relief to get away and spend some time with the "resources" themselves. I only got to utilize from far away, which is just as it should be. They'll take you within a hundred meters of the whales in Victor Harbor, 300 meters when newborns are present. Our boat stopped and everybody, some twenty fellow gawkers and I, just waited. From there we could see only the "black, treeless island" Saint Brendan described on his voyage, and beside it a black speck of a calf still being nursed. One of those few thousand right whales still among us, and this calf among the first of his or her kind in centuries who may actually grow to full maturity, today they were not even the "right" whales for watching. I wish I could report some spectacular breaching or moving mystical encounter worthy of the Discovery Channel. This time, after hours in the cold, all we got for our $30 were a few dives and flips of her great tail, and some foamy stirring of the little tail, and then it was time to make for shore.

But that is enough. Whales have bent enough to our wishes. Now it is time to leave them be, to merely look and learn and love what is so special about whales as we go our way and they go theirs.

‑e‑

THE LAWS

God sat at the organ of possibilities and improvised the world. Poor creatures that we are, we men can only hear the vox humana. *If that is so beautiful, how glorious the Whole must be.*[1]

CARL LUDWIG SCHLEICH

Back from the sea, we must repair to the study to examine the current literature on animal intelligence and emotion. It is an ethereal world, difficult at times to make sense of, but there is no avoiding a thorough inquiry. These are the theories that today define what is permissible in our treatment of animals and what is not. In our moral conduct, they prevent any final definitions at all.

Is there, ask the modern theorists, "something that it feels like to be an animal"? Can it be scientifically established that animals feel anything? Can an animal "think thoughts about thoughts"? Do animals act with "intentionality," conscious and deliberate in their actions, or are they merely "purposeful," driven hither and yon by the blind instinct, impulse, or appetite of the moment? Can any animal be "an appropriate object of sympathy"?

As a practical matter it comes down to this: Do animals suffer and, if they do, what duties do we bear them?

Our laws today, here in America and throughout the world, leave it for each person to decide the question for himself or herself. Some animals are covered by cruelty statutes, some are not. This creature you may use as you will, this identical one you may not. To the butcher shop with these dolphins for our consumption, declare the lords of the earth, to Izumito Sea Paradise with the rest for our entertainment. The pain and well-being of our own dogs and cats is real enough to warrant, in America, $8 billion a year in veterinary bills. The pain of dogs and cats bred or rounded up from shelters for experimentation doesn't count. The small farmer may be kindly toward his livestock, the corporate farmer ruthless, and the law is silent about the difference. A California dairy farmer describes the change in outlook required by the industry's recent shift to mass-confinement operations: "On a lot of those farms in the Midwest and back east, every cow has a name. They're sort of pets. It's not like that here. A cow's a piece of machinery. If it's broke, we try to fix it, and if we can't, it gets replaced."[2]

Just like that, from mammals to machines, here rating names and decent treatment, there regarded as so many pieces of equipment, milked and monitored by other equipment, and easily replaceable by still more equipment. No absolute right and no absolute wrong obtain in our treatment of animals. Our very language in referring to animals, shifting at random from "it" to "him" or "her" and back to "it," reflects the same incoherence.[3]

The creatures under our dominion thus inhabit a moral void of subjective human desires and situational ethics. The value of any animal is determined by the circumstances, designs, occupation, and personal code of whatever human it happens to encounter—or as Masayuki Komatsu would have it, by cultural perception, so that as tens of thousands of dolphins are mercilessly trapped and slaughtered each year, we are all supposed to avert our eyes and accept it as an honest philosophical difference.

I notice on this score that critics of animal-welfare causes have lately adopted the vernacular of privacy and choice, so that even a traditional-minded fellow like Steinar Bastesen speaks of his right to wear sealskin as a matter of the highest principle. "The fur industry," declares the Fur Information Council of America, "believes that the decision to wear fur is a matter of individual choice. Freedom of Choice is one of the fundamental rights on which this country was founded. It is up to the individual to decide what he or she will or will not wear."[4] Nature, writes libertarian Virginia Postrel in her 1998 book *The Future and its Enemies,* "does not provide the moral imperatives [that environmentalists] and other reactionaries would like, the arguments that would silence the claims of freedom, exploration, and material progress." Human beings "do indeed have to choose, and, in that choice, human wants and desires will be what matters. That is the way the world is."[5] Autonomous Man versus The System. Choice under attack by Reactionaries. James Swan in his *In Defense of Hunting* makes the inevitable comparison:

The goal of many anti-hunting moralists is to get people to conform to anti-hunting standards, regardless of whether these standards are compatible with the inner nature of other people. The anti-abortion protester who throws blood on a pregnant woman wanting an abortion, sets fire to an abortion clinic, or shoots an abortion doctor is a kindred spirit to the anti-hunter protester who slashes tires, burns a taxidermy shop, poisons a hunting dog, or even shoots and kills a hunter—and all in the name of preventing cruelty and suffering. Psychologically speaking, freedom of choice to be who you are and to follow the guidance of your conscience is the most humane ethical position for conservation of the human soul.[6]

You like watching elephants through the lens of a Polaroid, I prefer to use my Nitro Express, you like dolphins, I like clubbing dolphins—and we're *both* right. Saint Francis for you, Safari Club for me, one man's horror another man's hobby. What matters is that we each follow our own "inner nature." And each person's choice is equally valid.

Even in our dealings with the lowly animals, this sort of relativism works its evils. What makes Mr. Komatsu's argument so insidious is its denial that there are realities about animals, that these realities are in crucial respects knowable, and that once known we are morally obliged to accept and to act upon them regardless of culture or personal preference.

Just as in the case of fetal pain—as long as Mr. Swan has brought it up—conscience must be informed conscience or else it is just caprice, a tyranny of self that shrugs off inconvenient facts or the suffering of other beings. Informed by what? Informed by the objective facts of animal consciousness and animal pain. We cannot imperiously declare "the way the world is," as Ms. Postrel puts it, until we know what the world is like for the creatures with whom we share it.

The scientific proposition "animals suffer" is either true or false. It is not an opinion, but one way or the other an objective reality. If one elephant thinks, and feels, and suffers, then all elephants think, and feel, and suffer. Any moral obligations we have to one, we have to all.

It is a fundamental principle of moral reasoning that natural equals must be treated equally. The same kind of beings require the same kind of treatment. We need not suppose some kind of equality between human beings and animals to establish a standard of animal welfare. We just need a fixed standard of equal consideration among various kinds of animals themselves. And that standard must arise from the facts of science and veterinary medicine, applied to our treatment of animals not by personal whim or convenience or custom or economic calculation, but by human reason.

The moral and rights questions we will come to shortly. Here we'll examine that evidence. Do animals think? Are they really conscious? Do they really suffer?

UNKNOWABLE TERRITORY

Jack London in *White Fang* describes how in the first months of life the wolf cub perceives step by step "the laws" that regulate his existence. "The hard obstruction of the cave-wall," he writes, "the sharp nudge of his mother's nose, the smashing stroke of her paw, the hunger unappeased of several famines, had borne in upon him that all was not freedom in the world, that to life there were limitations and restraints. These limitations and restraints were laws. To be obedient to them was to escape hurt and make for happiness."[7]

How different from our own life this is, with our ability to see the world more broadly and to reason things out, and yet how much alike in the blunt facts of reward and punishment—of pain and want and appetite, the stirrings of instinct and desire, the quest for comfort and security. It is easy to look down upon the animals as utterly alien to us, driven on by need and instinct in their grubbier, less rational way, slavering for food and attention like our pets, jostling at the trough on our farms, battling one another in the wild over mates and territory and status in the group. But the person who thinks himself entirely above and apart from this world need only take a closer look at his or her own daily existence, at the struggles and hurts and yearnings of body that still mark each and every human life. We do our share of grubbing and jostling and competing for mates, too, and for good reason do we say of people hurt or humiliated that they are "licking their wounds." There is a kinship in this, for all of our loftier capacities, a fellowship with the creatures one feels especially in moments of desperation and dependence, when the padding and refinements of civilization fall away and we plummet back into stark need, when we are hungry or outcast or defeated or lonely. Had the wolf reasoned things out "in man-fashion," London continues, he might have epitomized life as a voracious appetite, and the world as a place wherein ranged a multitude of appetites, pursuing and being pursued, hunting and being hunted, eating and being eaten, all in blindness and confusion, with violence and disorder, a chaos of gluttony and slaughter, ruled over by chance, merciless, planless, endless.

But the cub did not think in man-fashion. He did not look at things with wide vision. He was single-purposed, and entertained but one thought or desire at a time. . . . The world was filled with surprise. The stir of life that was in him, the play of his muscles, was an unending happiness. . . .

And there were easements and satisfactions. To have a full stomach, to doze lazily in the sunshine—such things were remuneration in full for his ardors and toils, while his ardors and toils were in themselves self-remunerative. They were expressions of life, and life is always happy when it is expressing itself. So the cub had no quarrel with his hostile environment. He was very much alive, very happy, and very proud of himself.[8]

This strikes me as a pretty plausible account of life as a wolf. London in *White Fang* managed to compose an entire biography of an animal's wordless life with few, if any, anthropomorphic imaginings. For prey animals like deer and moose we might suppose an existence at once gentler and more terrifying, lived on that same plain of hard laws and satisfactions and afflictions and easements. Theodore Roosevelt, not exactly the anthropomorphic type, noted in his safari journal "the intensity and evanescence of their emotions," the shadow of death and violence following in their path "every hour of the day or night." With lions never far away, he wrote, the zebra and eland and giraffe are "ever on alert against this greatest of foes, and every herd, almost every individual, is in imminent and deadly peril every few days or nights, and of course suffers in addition from countless false alarms."[9]

In this way, intuitively, do most people perceive the creatures, rarely doubting that however far beneath us they may be in mental capacity, they are still quite conscious beings, aware of their own existence and presence in the world, with some measure of emotion and certainly of raw fear, physical pain, and physical longings.

Some modest measure of reason, too. The philosopher David Hume called it "experimental reasoning." Like us, animals are subject to the operations of instinct and appetite. Like us, too, they must learn individually to apply these drives and appetites and fears to their world. In their cruder way they must also form basic concepts and beliefs with which to make sense of their surroundings, grasping categories and patterns and sequential laws. It is not blind instinct but "custom alone," Hume wrote in 1740, "which engages animals from every object that strikes their senses, to infer its usual attendant, and carries their imagination, from the appearance of the one, to conceive of the other, in that particular manner which we denominate *belief*."[10]

This was a controversial argument at the time, and among today's theorists there is still no more dreaded accusation than "anthropomorphism," or ascribing any trace of conscious thought or feeling to any animal. We are prohibited by the terms of modern behavioral science, the reigning school of animal research, from saying that animals can *believe, think, desire, want, intend, try, hope, feel,* or *suffer* anything.

Many readers will be surprised to hear this, but it remains the working assumption of many if not most animal researchers that their subjects do not experience conscious pain, or, for that matter, conscious anything else. Best known to the public are researchers like Jane Goodall, Dian Fossey, Roger Fouts, Frans de Waal, and Marion Stamp Dawkins, who in their various studies offer compelling evidence that primates, among other mammals, possess the rudiments of conscious communication. But for every one of them we find a dozen other scientists all the more intent on keeping the creatures in their place. "They eat without pleasure," as the French scientist Nicholas de Malebranche believed, "they cry without sorrow, they desire nothing, they fear nothing, they know nothing."[11] Three hundred years later, this claim is still quite seriously advanced, and it would be hard to overstate the intensity of the debate at laboratories and universities the world over.

Even fear, the conscious apprehension of danger that animals display, has not been proven to everyone's satisfaction. "[I]t may be," writes British philosopher David S. Oderberg in an otherwise thoughtful treatment of the subject, "that some animals have a sense of *their own future,* as is at least suggested by the behavior of animals in abattoirs, where cows and pigs, for instance, act as if they know what is in store for them." However, he adds, "I cannot see that such an interpretation is forced upon us by the facts."[12] What looks for all the world like an awareness of danger and a desperate desire to live could be "mere defensive behavior"[13] arising from "mere sentience."[14]

Academic debates have a special ferocity and bitterness, usually, as someone has observed, because the stakes are so insignificant. Here the stakes could hardly be greater, affecting our whole understanding of ourselves, our place and purpose in the world and our duties to our fellow creatures. Stephen Budiansky, whose theory of "mere pain" in animals I noted in Chapter 1, once again frames the matter for us. He has become a leading voice in recent years for "sustainable use," carrying the idea into the popular press with widely read books and with articles in such publications as the *Washington Post*, the *New York Times,* the *Atlantic Monthly,* and for that reason merits our close attention. "Tales of elephants grieving for their dead," Mr. Budiansky writes, "of red foxes as doting fathers full of parental love for their cubs, of chimpanzees that silently watch sunsets—such are the stories that animal rightists invoke in their effort to knock man off his anthropocentric pedestal at the top of creation."[15] Rational argument is of no use against such people, he adds, for their "commitment is both emotional and political; these are people out to knock man off his anthropocentric pedestal, after all, and what better way to do it than by setting up animals as our spiritual equals—or betters."[16]

Mr. Budiansky shows a little emotional commitment there himself. But no one is saying animals are our intellectual equals, much less "our betters." Until chimps and dogs and elephants can write books in their own defense, we are all quite safe atop creation's pedestal. Nor would anyone quarrel with Mr. Budiansky's point that human beings alone can "develop physics and astronomy and philosophy and ethics and electronic engineering and linguistics and history and education and justice and neurophysiology."[17] That's raising the bar a tad high. An animal to rate decent consideration in our hands doesn't need to philosophize or orate or compose an *Ode to Joy*. If the creatures experience some humbler degree of thought or emotion, then that's enough and the burden is thrown back upon us.

The theorists admit as much themselves by insisting that animals think and feel absolutely nothing, for if it turns out the creatures think and feel *anything,* consciously, then all of these theories would all be left in ruins. "[I]t seems likely," concludes Professor John S. Kennedy, an eminent behavioral scientist at the University of London, that consciousness, feelings, thoughts, purposes, etc. are unique to our species and it is unlikely that animals are conscious. If we were entirely logical about it these probabilities would be enough to make us try to avoid descriptions of animal behavior. But we are not entirely logical about it, and we have to ask why scientists as well as laymen should be so addicted to anthropomorphic expression.[18]

Animals, argues Mr. Budiansky, lack language: Therefore they must lack the ability to form concepts: Therefore they must lack consciousness: Therefore they cannot suffer. A student of evolutionary ecology, Mr. Budiansky believes that all animals act by a kind of "unthinking intelligence" arising from their genetic coding or "hardwiring." Their uncanny "mimicry" of thought and feeling deceives us into ascribing conscious life to them.[19] "This is the curse of anthropomorphism," he cautions in *If a Lion Could Talk: Animal Intelligence and the Evolution of Consciousness*, "and it is by all appearances an incurable disease."[20] His final conclusion is worth examining again. Animals are sentient beings, he allows, but

> sentience is not sentience, and pain isn't even pain. Or perhaps, following Daniel Dennett's distinction, we should say that pain is not the same as suffering. . . . Sadness, pity, sympathy, condolence, self-pity, ennui, woe, heartbreak, distress, worry, apprehension, dejection, grief, wistfulness, pensiveness, mournfulness, brooding, rue, regret, misery, despair—all express shades of the pain of sadness whose full meaning comes only from our ability to reflect on their meaning, not just their feelings. The horror of breaking a limb that we experience is not merely the pain; the pain is but the beginning of the suffering we feel as we worry and anticipate the consequences. . . . Consciousness is a wonderful gift and a wonderful curse that, all the evidence suggests, is not in the realm of the sentient experiences of other creatures.[21]

Breaking a limb seems to be a much deeper experience for Mr. Budiansky than it is for me. People do a lot of "reflecting" in his theories of pain, as if with every break, bruise, or scrape we all undergo some sort of Socratic self-examination or burst into verse to express the profound tragedy of it all. One wonders, too, where babies fit into this notion of language as the threshold of consciousness and meaningful pain. Human infants do not spend much time "thinking about thoughts." A burbling infant, by Mr. Budiansky's language criterion, is an unconscious being, and indeed until modern times medical dogma held that infants could not feel pain, just as many people still deny fetal pain.

There is the further problem that conscious thought must logically have preceded language, since otherwise there would have been no thought to express, just as infants, before they can say "Mama," presumably have some preverbal concept of their mothers. A still more glaring flaw in the argument is that when we human beings, with all of our linguistic and conceptual endowments, really are in grave physical pain, trauma, or danger, we do *not* use language to express it. We just cry and scream and convulse and writhe and moan like animals. Reflections on the "full meaning" of a broken limb— whatever that might be—come later if they come at all. Our worst sorrows are even harder to put into words—"groanings which cannot be uttered," as Saint Paul calls them.[22]

How often, come to think of it, do people who have been subjected to the worst torment or privation describe having "felt like an animal," the degradation lying precisely in the brutal cruelty directed at them and their own brutish helplessness against it. Recall your own moments of terror—the chill of sensing an intruder in the house, the reflexive flinch from a blow or attack. How much thinking about thoughts did you do at such moments? Recall your purest moments of delight and joy, too, and there is often something of the animal experience in those. Euphoria, deliverance, reunion, deep rest after great exertion—these are pre-rational experiences, as we often admit in calling them "beyond words." If anything, there is no surer way to dispel the joy of such experiences than to start intellectualizing them.

Daniel Dennett himself, in any case, is subtler on the point, leaning toward the idea of "mock anthropomorphism" at least as a method of research. Mock anthropomorphism acknowledges that an assumption of animals as rational, conscious agents—that is, as creatures with mental states, beliefs, and desires—will usually prove the best predictor of animal behavior. As to whether these states of mind in fact exist, Professor Dennett, a noted cognitive theorist at Tufts University, is uncertain. "So yes, animals have beliefs," he concludes in his 1998 *Brainchildren: Essays on Designing Minds.* Then again, "even amoebas—like thermostats—have beliefs":

What structural and processing differences make different animals capable of having more sophisticated beliefs? We find that there are many, many differences, almost all of them theoretically interesting, but none of them, in my opinion, marking a well-motivated chasm between the mere mindless behaviors and the genuine rational agents.[23]

Throughout the literature, one encounters again and again this basic theoretical barrier between the observable and the knowable, what animals display and what they actually experience. The creatures, these theories concede, give every appearance of conscious experience. But proving it is something else again. For all we know they might experience nothing, even mammals being just so many big furry amoebas traipsing around without a glimmer of consciousness. "Throughout its waking life," writes Tim Ingold, a professor of anthropology at the University of Manchester,

the animal continually emits a veritable profusion of signals, but without a reflexive linguistic facility it cannot isolate thoughts as objects of attention. That is, rather than thinking without communication, the animal *communicates without thinking*; so that the signals it transmits correspond to bodily states and not to concepts.[24]

And so on, the general idea being that language is necessary for any kind of inner life or conscious experience. Animal life, we are told, is a stream of unconsciousness, any thoughts they have but the blind operations of stimulus and response, their very existence as individual beings unknown even to themselves—an assumption applied even to primates. "Though a monkey," explains one researcher, "may make use of abstract concepts and have motives, beliefs, and desires, her mental states are not accessible to her: she does not know what she knows."[25]

THE MASQUERADE

To make matters more complicated, these very same thinkers often pause to remind us that even if animals are conscious beings, it would be impossible to demonstrate, and so we must assume they aren't. We find the scholars asserting at one and the same time that the creatures think and feel nothing and that, ultimately, we know nothing about what the creatures think and feel.

"If the study of animal behavior is to mature as a science," declares Professor Kennedy, "the process of liberation from the delusions of anthropomorphism must go on."[26] Elsewhere in his 1995 book *The New Anthropomorphism,* he calls the tendency "a drag" and "a throwback to primitive animism."[27] Science, declares the professor, must once and for all "free itself from this incubus,"[28] admitting once and for all that "we cannot hope to tell from their behavior whether [animals] suffer or not."[29]

An incubus is a male demon believed in medieval times to disturb sleepers. So these are strong words. Why do so many people, against all scientific data, persist in believing animals have thoughts and feelings? Professor Kennedy has a theory, drawn from the same doctrine of genetic and evolutionary determinism he applies to animals: "[A]nthropomorphic thinking about animal behavior is built into us. We could not abandon it even if we wished to. Besides, we do not wish to. It has presumably also been 'pre-programmed' into our hereditary makeup by natural selection, perhaps because it proved to be useful for predicting and controlling animal behavior."[30]

So not only is everything that animals do preprogrammed into them: Any notion we have that they have feelings is preprogrammed into us. (The question of whether Professor Kennedy's own ideas might be "preprogrammed" into him never comes up.) Mr. Budiansky offers the similar theory that "our tendency to anthropomorphize the animals we hunt may have given us a huge advantage in anticipating their habits and their evasions." The same tendency, he adds, "has made us very bad at being objective about the true nature of the things in the world that actually are not like us."[31]

Actually, one would assume the opposite, that "anthropomorphism" would tend to evoke empathy and thus hinder the hunt. I didn't detect much anthropomorphic sentimentality among the Nimrods of our own day back in Reno. Mr. Budiansky's larger point, however, seems to be that the more we agree with him, the more "objective" and highly evolved we are.

Apparently Professor Kennedy is the high arbiter of scientific objectivity in his field. Mr. Budiansky often invokes his authority, and the professor himself tells us that "anthropomorphism in the study of animal behavior has been a hobby-horse of mine for more than fifty years." In all that time, never once has he encountered evidence of consciousness or pain that could not be adequately explained by the unconscious mechanisms of stimulus and response. "To sum up," writes the professor,

> although we cannot be certain that no animals are conscious, we can say that it is most unlikely that any of them are. Science does not deal in certainties, but in order to keep going it must adopt working hypotheses, the most plausible at the time. These are by common consent "true" until replaced by more plausible ones. It is in that spirit that anthropomorphism is treated here as a definite mistake. In point of fact, the hypothesis that animals are conscious is not a scientific one, since it cannot be tested.[32]

The logic of this argument may be broken down as follows: (1) We cannot be certain animals are conscious. (2) We cannot be certain animals are not conscious. (3) The evidence available suggests that they are not. (4) Any evidence to the contrary is untestable and therefore unscientific.

Of course, if animal consciousness can never be tested, it can never be proven. Hence Professor Kennedy's view can never be disproved. So, even while "science does not deal in certainties," it looks like we're stuck with our "working hypothesis" forever.

No wonder that in fifty years he never found cause for doubting his own assumptions. By definition, he's right, everybody else is wrong, and that's the end of it. Any evidence contradicting him is *a priori* inadmissible. Merely to question Professor Kennedy is "unscientific," an intellectual error, a mark of the incubus, just as to question Mr. Budiansky is a sign of folly if not some incurable disease.

A kind of "romantic pessimism," as philosopher Stephen R. L. Clark describes it in his 1997 book *Animals and Their Moral Standing,* pervades the literature of behaviorism, ethology, cognitive theory and other fields devoted to studying animal consciousness: Oh, if only we could know how animals experience the world! If only we could be *sure* that they think and feel at all. "If a lion could talk," observed the German philosopher Ludwig Wittgenstein, inspiring Mr. Budiansky's book title, "we would not understand him." We are to believe that the inner experience of a lion or of any animal is so far removed from ours, so alien to human experience, that even if one of them were miraculously endowed with words the creature would have nothing to say that we could possibly grasp, as if we were dealing with beings from another planet. "To literally see inside a horse's brain," adds Mr. Budiansky, "would be to enter a world that is without the words to describe it—and so is meaningless to us."[33]

Both of these strike me as the kind of observations that sound profound on first hearing and preposterous on the second. Observing a lion or lioness, prior to any theories we might bring to leonine reality, you or I might match the creature's behavior with simple words like: *I'm hungry—time to go run down a zebra. . . . I'm tired—time for a long nap. . . . The cubs are driving me to distraction. . . . Don't come any closer—this is my territory!* Lions don't live in the world of conceptual language. But the words do objectively describe their behavior and the thoughts and desires that would seem to accompany that behavior, even if we shall never quite know the full dimensions of lionhood.

Horses, as more social animals, admit of even readier translation from behavior into words: *Footsteps—he's coming to feed me. . . . I'm tired—I want to go back to the barn. . . . I wish my stablemate were here.* Simply because horses experience these things non-verbally hardly proves that they do not, in fact, experience some conscious equine equivalent of such desires and intentions, and caring for horses involves acting on precisely the assumption that they do. Horses, cows, pigs and other livestock, after little training, learn to line up at the appointed feeding hour even before the feeder arrives. To call that "expectation" would seem a modest leap of speculation, similar to the assumptions we make about our dogs and cats whose desires and intentions we usually have little trouble deciphering: *Feed me. . . . Take me out. . . . Let's play. . . . Don't go!* The same for the mistreated pet or lab animal shaking and whimpering at the approach of the malefactor: *Leave me alone! . . . No, not again!*

Even when animals do speak in their way, the theorists dismiss it as more exterior behavior about which we are barred from drawing final conclusions as to interior states and motives. Chimps in various experiments have been trained to communicate in American Sign Language, possessing vocabularies of about 250 words employed usually in simple, childlike requests for food and care. They sign things like "Please machine give apple," or "You me go out," or "Where cat?" They identify themselves and their human interlocutors by name. Occasionally they form their own word combinations, as when a chimp named Dar trained by Roger Fouts signed "rice drink" when his bowl of rice arrived without the soy sauce to which he was accustomed.[34]

Examining these studies of word use by primates, the linguist Steven Pinker writes that "this preposterous claim is based on the myth that ASL is a crude system of pantomimes and gestures rather than a full language with complex phonology, morphology and syntax."[35] Another skeptic writes that "no chimpanzee has mastered the phenomenon of tense. . . . Nor have they mastered the concepts necessary for representing causality,"[36] which again is setting the bar mighty high. Nobody has ever claimed that chimps have *mastered* sign language, but only that they are able to use it in a very elementary way, which for most of us is a surprising thing to learn. For his part, Mr. Budiansky's idea of a rebuttal is likewise to note the chimps' faulty grammar and syntax, and to observe that "96 percent of their demands [are] for food, toys, or tickling,"[37] as if the chimps have to engage in polished repartee before we concede they are consciously communicating. Never mind, too, that *other* 4 percent of communication (he never does tell us what it was), and never mind that at the end of the day we still have apes using sign language, to their trainers and sometimes even among one another—facts which thirty years ago no one, least of all Mr. Pinker or Mr. Budiansky, would have imagined possible.

Mr. Budiansky cites researcher Herbert Terrace, who studied Nim Chimpsky, as having proved the chimps were "usually" just imitating trainers' signs. Here, too, what *unusual* signs they made we never learn. The trainers themselves describe the renowned Washoe, for example, hiding in a tree signing "quiet quiet" to herself, and at one point the chimps signing to each other. Nor does Mr. Budiansky mention Professor Terrace's finding that "Nim's vocabulary included signs that seemed to serve as substitutes for aggressive behavior (*bite* and *angry*)," which in our own case we would call an expression of emotion; or that Nim came to understand, "with no help from his teachers, that signs were powerful tools and that he could manipulate the behavior of his teachers by misrepresenting the meaning of certain signs," which in our case we would call conscious deception; or that "Nim often signed spontaneously, without food or drink rewards, about pictures in order to identify what he saw," which in our case we would call being mentally alert or even being a show-off.[38] In another "anecdote" Mr. Budiansky dismisses, Washoe is taken to a lake where she sees a swan. Combining two words in her vocabulary, and without prompting by trainers Allen and Beatrice Gardner, Washoe points to the swan, signing "waterbird." This, Mr. Budiansky concedes, "was a novel combination and seemed to show a creative insight."

Maybe it did, but given the number of inane and meaningless (or excruciatingly repetitive) signs Washoe made, it is hardly surprising that one or two novel combinations should appear to make sense. . . . As others have pointed out, too, there was both water and a bird present in Washoe's environment when she signed *water bird*, so there may be an even simpler explanation.[39]

One can be too eager to find evidence of conscious communication in animals, as Mr. Budiansky often reminds us. One can also remain obdurate and willfully ignorant when evidence appears. Clear in his tone is a straining to put any sign of conscious life in the worst possible light and thereby, as it seems, to kill any sense of kinship we feel even with primates. We have a chimpanzee here, not only able but apparently *wanting* to communicate knowledge of her surroundings, and it gets shrugged off on the grounds that most of what she says is "inane." For all we know tedious, repetitive old Washoe was merely saying "water" and "bird" separately—as if that's not pretty impressive all by itself.

In the world of theory, everything animals do is "merely" something. Mr. Budiansky lets it slip that when the chimps, after correctly identifying certain objects, didn't get the usual reward—tickling, treats, their pet kitten and the like—they "would point, now deliberately and with a more expressive gesture, at the object they just named. . . . [They] clearly expected some sort of reward (either food, tickling, or praise) for having named and pointed to an object."[40] That's merely "instrumental" communication since the apes in previous experiments always got a food reward.

But wait a minute. Let's think here. A hand-pointing, praise-hungry, bipedal, ticklish attention-hound of reputed simian origin. Who does *that* bring to mind? Moreover, if apes have no sense of self or "other"—a claim refuted by, if nothing else, their unmistakable capacity for jealousy and loneliness—just whom did these apes mean by "You me go out"? If they cannot grasp, as Mr. Budiansky contends, the "if-then" construction of conceptual communication, why do they *ask* for things at all? Obviously they perceive at least that *if* they point or sign *then* they will get a treat. And what is this business of pets, a matter Mr. Budiansky glides right over without comment? If everything they do is preprogrammed instinct, what on earth are chimps doing with a pet kitten?

Mr. Budiansky dismisses all animal communication as unconscious "informative signaling," always explicable by their evolutionary programming. Yet dolphins in repeated experiments over twenty years have been given hand signals not only instructing them to perform tricks, but to perform tricks of their own devising. The trainer simply tells them to do a trick, any trick. The *iruka* dive below, squeak among one another, and then emerge to perform exactly the same stunt simultaneously—an act of creative collaboration.[41]

Dolphins in other tests have taught one another tricks they learned from their human trainers.[42] And we now know from hydrophonic studies that the sounds made by dolphins are unique to each individual, with a frequency and amplitude identifying a specific creature to its fellows.[43] Not only is communication among dolphins conscious, in other words—it is personal. So are their relationships, as witness the way they help one another in sickness and distress, and not only their own young but other adults and indeed many a human over the ages from the Greek mariners to the Cuban refugee Elian Gonzalez in 1999. Elian, we are told, after his rescue off the coast of Florida couldn't "stop talking about the fact that his best friends were dolphins. Do you realize that when his mom died, the dolphins started surrounding him, entertaining him, protecting him from the sharks. And for almost two days, the dolphins kept him alive and away from harm?"[44] Associated Press reported some years ago the similar case of a ten-year-old boy swept away in the currents of San Francisco Harbor who, for two hours, was circled by a dolphin fending off the sharks until help came.

Behaviorists dismiss such stories as not only anecdotal but as "selective aiding behavior," inadmissible because dolphins don't *always* aid others in distress. Well, neither do we. A 1999 study discovered "an unexplained darker side" of dolphins, noting that while some fit our impression of benign and personable creatures, others can be aggressive and violent even toward other dolphins.[45] It was my friend Joe Sobran again who seized upon this as further evidence that our view of wild animals is romantic and that "we owe them no apologies. Besides, many of them taste good."[46] I would think it proves just the opposite—that dolphins are not all exactly identical but are surprisingly complicated creatures, with varying experiences, dispositions, and personality traits not always charming. What has probably happened here, in fact, is the same experience that's given Africa its rampaging juvenile elephant calves— these violent male dolphins are the young of mothers killed in nets before their rearing was complete.

In other tests, we learn from Professor Kennedy, chimps in the wild also seem to aid one another. They shake branches at the approach of danger. One assumes this is some sort of warning to the other chimps, who usually confirm this suspicion by scattering. But this, too, would be a case of anthropomorphism. "Describing an animal's actions (shaking branches, etc.) as a warning to its fellows effectively takes it for granted that those actions were intentional on the part of the animal. Intentions are proximate causes of behavior, so again we have an ultimate, functional cause masquerading as a proximate one in an animal."[47]

Animals do a lot of "masquerading" in behavioral theory, inside the lab and outside. "The plural of 'anecdote,'" as Mr. Budiansky often reminds us, "is not 'data.'"[48] And data can come only from expert opinion drawn from clinical experimentation on animals. (This works the other way around, too, as when Mr. Budiansky notes that even if apes and parrots display speech in lab experiments, "none of these animals displays such abilities in the wild." So we have but "a few trivial examples."[49]) One of the signs of consciousness is a creature's understanding of itself as a particular being. A way of measuring this is to use a mirror and observe whether the animal displays some sense of seeing his or her own body, "me," in the reflection. In one such experiment, a mirror was so arranged that to reach some food placed around a corner the elephant had to manipulate his trunk by using the mirror. "Elephants," explains Mr. Budiansky,

> were able to find hidden food by looking in a mirror, and chimpanzees could maneuver their hands to hidden targets using a television image that reversed the chimpanzees' hand movements. The common feature in all these performances is that the animals had to adjust their hand (or trunk) motions according to some displaced and unfamiliar visual feedback. But the elephant did not need to know that it was *his* trunk in the mirror; all he had to learn was that when the trunk in the mirror touched the food in the mirror, his real trunk touched the real food.[50]

Reading carefully here, we see that the elephant actually passed this particular test. He watched his trunk in the mirror and got the food. But, no, says Mr. Budiansky, this conclusion would be hasty. For how can we be sure the creature knew that it was *his* trunk passing the food up to *his* mouth? Probably another case of mere "self-directed" behavior, the scientific term used to describe animals feeding, licking, grooming, scratching and the like. Or it could be mere "lower-order intentionality."[51] Or mere "unthinking intelligence." Gosh, who knows, maybe in some dumb, preprogrammed way the elephant merely figured there was some *other* elephant over there generously passing him food around the corner.

Cicero, after a day at the coliseum in 55 B.C., described how the slaughter of eighteen elephants ended in the crowd "pitying the beasts and in their feeling that a certain affinity exists between men and elephants."[52] Theodore Roosevelt, in the course of slaying eight of them, extolled the elephant's "great intelligence, in which it is only matched, if at all, by the highest apes."[53] In his journals, T.R. relates his son Kermit's account of seeing "an elephant, while feeding greedily on the young top of a thorn-tree, prick its trunk until it uttered a little scream or whine of pain; and it then in a fit of pettishness revenged itself by wrecking the thorn-tree."[54] We have it from John Sharp, Pieter Stofberg, and others who spend their lives tracking and killing elephants that the creatures are smart and alert. But neither Cicero, T.R., nor the professional elephant hunters of our own day ever spent much time theorizing about elephants. It never even occurs to those who work with elephants for a living, or those who kill them for a living, to question whether or not the creatures are aware of their own trunks.

Chimps, we learn, have also been run through the mirror test. The creatures were put under anesthesia while mirrors were installed. Bright, odorless red dots were then painted on the foreheads of the sedated simians. If they used the mirrors to examine and wipe away the dots, this would establish self-awareness. And, coming to, the chimps did just that. "On recovering from the anaesthetic," writes Professor Kennedy (a nice little finesse around *"on recovering consciousness"*), the chimps "repeatedly touched the dye-marks while watching their reflections, and looked and sniffed at their fingertips after touching the mark."[55] The chimps then proceeded to groom themselves before their mirrors, while also availing themselves of the chance to explore and scratch normally inaccessible parts of their bodies. This, and the fact that chimps will also use combs when researchers provide them, would seem to confirm not only self-recognition but also tool use (the mirror). So they passed too, right? Not quite:

> When grooming itself, "the organism is ostensibly directing its attention to parts of itself but this does not presuppose that it is able to conceive of itself as a separate, independent entity with an identity of its own. When a monkey grooms its own arm, the monkey is not

the subject of its own attention; the arm is. Indeed, I would argue that because of proprioceptive feedback and kinesthetic cues, coupled with response-contingent stimulation, the appropriate use of your arm *does not require that you know it is yours.*"[56]

This masquerade of self-awareness, writes Professor Kennedy, may thus be dismissed as an "associationist mechanism," a "synchronous concurrence," mere "self-reinforcement, producing positive feedback."[57] Mr. Budiansky, reviewing the same experiment, speculates that "Evidence of mirror recognition may have been nothing more than an artifact of the way the experiments were carried out."[58] These particular organisms regularly display grooming behavior, after all, and how do we really know that the mirrors caused this particular display of grooming behavior? Just as elephants cannot scientifically be said to know their own trunks, so chimpanzees—creatures with 98.4 percent of our own DNA, observed in the wild using sticks to catch ants, stones to crack nuts, and leaves to dab at bleeding wounds[59]—cannot be said to know their own arm when they scratch it. The fact that these chimps, after "coming out of the anesthesia," were facing the mirrors on this particular day, in this particular experiment, Mr. Budiansky speculates, may well have been "pure chance."[60]

WANT NUT

I leave it to mathematicians to figure out the odds here that all the chimps just happened, by pure chance, to be facing the mirrors during their daily coiffure. It reminds me of the old statistical proposition that if you sat a million monkeys down at typewriters, eventually one of them would produce *Hamlet*. Which is about what it would take to convince the modern behavioral scientists and cognitive theorists that animals are conscious beings. In 2001 the mirror test was conducted on dolphins at the New York Aquarium, and they responded in just the same way, clearly angling themselves to see the marks on their bodies.[61] So now, along with elephants, we have another non-primate species displaying self-recognition, though doubtless the papers are being written even now that will explain all this away too. We are dealing here with the sort of human minds that can prove anything they believe, and believe anything they can prove. The trick is to demystify everything that any animal does, stripping it down to the language of functionality, and then with an air of finality declare that the animal's inner experience is a hopeless mystery.

A classic example of the method comes in criticism directed at Professor Donald R. Griffin of Harvard University, the venerable zoologist who first discovered bat sonar and who in books like *Animal Minds* has been arguing for years that animals not only seem to have conscious thoughts, intentions, beliefs, and desires: They really are conscious. This view has made him a reviled figure among animal scientists, who, like Mr. Budiansky and Professor Kennedy, fault him for his exasperating "anthropomorphism."

Beavers, notes Professor Griffin, pose a particular problem to behavioral theory because of their noted gifts of planning and ingenuity. In "novel challenge" experiments, researchers waited for beavers to venture off and then smashed holes in the beavers' dams and lodges. Upon their return, the bewildered beavers were observed surveying the damage. They swam off and then came back hours later with just the right materials needed to patch each particular leak. In one test, the beavers returned the next day with the requisite materials, having gnawed pieces of wood into shapes precisely fitting the holes in the dam. Since the dam and lodge were out of view when the beavers fashioned these pieces, this would suggest memory, versatility, and a capacity for deliberate action. In short, the elements of consciousness. Alas for the beavers, explains Professor L. Wilsson, a Swedish ethologist, this behavior

> can just as well be interpreted as stereotyped phylogenetically adapted reactions. For example, the fact that a beaver often thoroughly investigates a leak in the dam, then leaves it for some hours and later brings different kinds of material with it when it returns to repair it, does not necessarily mean that it is able "to forecast in the choice he makes of building materials which depends on the use made of them as well as the shape his construction will take." . . . Dam building behavior is activated when the animal has received stimuli from the dam for a certain time and a delayed response is not unusual in phylogenetically adapted behavior.[62]

Alas for Professor Wilsson, all he has done here is rename things, much like the beavers themselves fashioning new material to patch the leaks. The damaged dam is now "stimuli." The beaver's response to the leaks is now "activation." Evidence of memory is now a "delayed response." These have a more objective and scientific ring to them, but get us exactly nowhere in explaining how the beavers did what they did. The new "phylogenetic" jargon simply recasts the terms of debate, narrowing the range of available explanations to external and biological causes while barring any consideration of internal states or conscious action—never mind that to examine internal states was the whole point of the inquiry.

My favorite example is Mr. Budiansky's unmasking of the ground squirrel. The creatures, he notes, have two separate calls at first sight of danger, one for hawks and one for badgers. Straightaway this suggests conscious action, because the squirrels must immediately distinguish one kind of predator from another. When either call is heard, they react just the same by scattering. One call is a shrill whistle, to all appearances signifying crude yet effective communication ("*Run!*"), alarm, fear, maybe even some sort of basic ground squirrel solidarity. Hawk-like, Mr. Budiansky then picks the ground squirrel apart to expose its preprogrammed evolutionary "hardwiring." Here, it turns out the caller was merely using an unconscious "diversionary tactic" to turn the predator's attention to the other squirrels by creating a general panic. Another case of unthinking intelligence, lower-order intentionality, the "mutual exploitation of two self-interested parties," and thus not evidence of either conscious communication or even of conscious physical distress:

> This evolutionary perspective underscores the important fact that signals don't evolve because they "mean" something; they evolve because they work. Again, the unwitting feedback between sender and receiver works to create a signal that is informative without any conscious intent for it to be so. Sender and receiver continually exploit one another. . . . Evolved signaling can be intricate, effective, even "devious" or "Machiavellian"—without being either conscious or possessing semantic meaning.[63]

Just a few questions: When the ground squirrel continues shrieking after it's too late, when the others are safely back in the burrow and he is all alone being devoured by the hawk, what's the diversionary tactic there? Why do any animals scream when they are wounded or killed, even when those screams can have no possible utility? Why do we scream, and why has evolution designed us to consciously experience *our* physical pain, but not them? Why are some animals when they are in extreme danger, like lab mice being fed to snakes, unable to make *any sounds at all*, paralyzed, as we say of ourselves at such moments, by the horror of it? Why are the central nervous systems of mammals so much alike, and wouldn't it stand to reason that they serve precisely the same evolutionary purpose, motivating each creature to flee bodily harm and thereby perpetuate the species? If the purpose of pain is the same for us as for other animals, if the internal mechanisms of pain are the same, if the outward expressions of pain are the same, and if the medical treatments for pain are the same, why wouldn't the physical experience of pain be the same—and for that matter, the psychological experience of it as well?

Throughout *If a Lion Could Talk*, Mr. Budiansky shows some pretty good diversionary instincts himself. He spends pages going over the chimp data, pages analyzing the "unthinking intelligence" of dogs and cats and horses and elephants, never once touching on the pain question. Probably the ground squirrel was selected for this exercise because it would have been a lot harder to convince us that some more familiar mammals, like our own cats or dogs, do not feel pain when they cry. On the matter of suffering—the center of Mr. Budiansky's argument—we're just left to assume that what he claims is true of the squirrel is true throughout the animal kingdom. A ground squirrel, if he could talk, might call this the fallacy of composition.

Finally there is the famed Alex, a twenty-five-year-old African gray parrot trained by Irene Pepperberg, a psychologist at the Massachusetts Institute of Technology. Alex can form simple sentences, drawing from a vocabulary of a hundred or so words. He can recognize quantities of up to six, identify colors, shapes, toys, materials, and food types. Shown identical objects of different colors and asked, "What's the same?" Alex replies, "Shape." Ask "What's different?" and he replies, "Color." Shown entirely different objects and asked, "What's the same?" he answers, "None." Alex can decline requests ("No"), make requests ("Go away," "Come here"), suggest favorite activities ("Go see tree"), ask questions ("What's this?" "You tell me"), give orders ("Talk clearly!"), and even apologize when he answers incorrectly. And he does all this regardless of who's asking the questions, so we can rule out the unconscious physical cues that have marred similar experiments in the past. The creature was actually a guest on National Public Radio a few years ago:

IRENE PEPPERBERG: OK, Alex. I'm going to give you a tray of different objects. We got red and blue balls and blocks. OK? Now, look at the tray. Can you tell me how many blue block? How many blue block?

ALEX: Two.

IRENE: OK. You're a good boy. Can you tell me how many rose block?

ALEX: Four.

IRENE: Four. Good boy.

ALEX: Want nut.

IRENE: That's a good birdie. OK. You can have a nut.[64]

This was a particular triumph for Alex because the exchange occurred in the presence of fellow NPR guest Professor Daniel Dennett, the very author from whom Mr. Budiansky got his theories of unthinking intelligence and mere pain in animals. For a moment at least, Professor Dennett seemed to cast theory aside, apparently convinced that Alex really is conscious and not at all like an amoeba or thermometer:

DENNETT: Alex is a remarkable and important individual in this world. I have seen enough of what Alex, the parrot, can do to realize that he is not just a well-trained circus animal. He is not just doing this by rote memorization. It hasn't just been dinned into him. He makes remarkable transfers of knowledge and inferences. Alex is a pretty amazing parrot.

IRENE: What's here?

ALEX: Truck.

IRENE: That's a good boy. Truck. Good parrot. How many?

ALEX: Two.

IRENE: That's right. Good boy.

ALEX: Want a nut.[65]

I'm going to go out on a limb here and assert as an empirical fact that this particular organism *thought* about, *wanted, intended,* and *desired* nuts. Nor does it sound to me like Alex threatens to knock us all off our "pedestal at the top of creation." A few treats and Dr. Pepperberg's kindness seem to satisfy him.

But he does pose mortal danger to Mr. Budiansky's contention that no animal can think and feel, to Professor Kennedy's assertion that any attribution of thought to an animal is "anthropomorphism," and to Professor Tim Ingold's belief that animals "communicate without thinking." It is not really our own uniqueness as rational beings that is in the balance here: It is the

presumption that all creatures but us are excluded from the world of conscious thought and feeling, that their suffering is meaningless, and that our
rule, therefore, is absolute.

Mr. Budiansky and other theorists still wave off such examples with vague
conjectures about associationist mechanisms and proprioceptive something or
other. Alex would have to host the show before any of them would admit that
any animal is capable of any kind of conscious thought or feeling. Some conclusions by an assortment of eminent behaviorists and cognitive philosophers:

- [W]e are not able in any manner to prove that there is in the animals a soul which thinks. . . . I regard it as a thing demonstrated
  that it cannot be proved that the animals have thought.[66]
- Conscious awareness in other animals is a closed world about
  which we can do little more than speculate. Sadly . . . there is no
  evidence that it is anything but unattainable.[67]
- None of [the evidence] proves that animals do not suffer, of
  course. What it does show is that we cannot hope to tell from their
  behavior whether they suffer or not.[68]
- No statement concerning consciousness in animals is open to ver-
  ification and experimentation. Isn't it time we set aside such tan-
  talizing, but unanswerable, questions and direct our energies to
  more productive pursuits?[69]
- The question of whether animals suffer must remain unresolved.[70]
- To understand what we truly can about how animal minds work
  inescapably means to abandon any real hope of penetrating their
  thoughts, of translating their thoughts into human terms.[71]
- [Studies] of an animal's mind can tell us volumes about its mental
  capabilities, and even give us insight into how an animal perceives
  its world—at least as a practical, functional matter—without drift-
  ing into the unknowable territory of what it *experiences* as it does
  so.[72]

These last two come from Mr. Budiansky, raising yet again the question of
how he keeps getting from "unknowable territory" to the confident assertion
that animals think and feel nothing. The first of the above quotations comes

from René Descartes, asserting in 1649 exactly the same conclusion that our modern behaviorists and evolutionary ecologists now hold out as fresh, cutting-edge science. Notice that none of the statements are even conclusions at all, subject to the rules of rational debate and empirical demonstration. They are prohibitions on the assumption that any final conclusions are possible. They're not saying we don't know. They're saying we can't know. Ever.

In the case of pain experiments, this circularity of reasoning becomes a maniacal quest for more and more data. *The Oxford Companion Encyclopedia to Animal Behavior* defines pain as "a state of motivation which is aroused by certain stimuli and normally gives rise to defensive behavior or escape," a tautology telling us only that pain is escape behavior and escape behavior is pain. Again and again, in endless dense reports and studies—the currency of credentials and grants and department budgets—we find the researchers arriving lemming-like back at this same predestined nonconclusion. One hesitates even to call them scientific investigations, since the experimenters assume from the outset that animal pain is negligible, somehow unreal, and they are often to be found on the payroll of one or another enterprise whose whole existence presupposes the same, as in this 1996 study of pain at a slaughterhouse:

> Research conducted in commercial pork slaughter plants indicated that the intensity with which the pigs squealed (measured with a sound meter) in the stunning chute area was correlated with physiological measures of stress and with poorer meat quality (Warriss et al., 1994). Professor R. G. White et al. (1995) also found that the intensity of pig squeals is correlated with pig discomfort.[73]

Glad we finally solved that mystery. Thanks to the pathbreaking research of one R. G. White, we may now posit as an empirical fact that when pigs are uncomfortable, they squeal. And when they're really uncomfortable, they squeal a lot. We can't go any further than that, however. It's all unconscious pain, all these shrill squeals on the sound meter only so much muffled, indecipherable data admitting of no final conclusions. (The title of Professor White's own study captures the scene: "Vocalizations and Physiological Response of Pigs during Castration with and without Anesthetic.")

Not even primates are spared. Mr. Budiansky, by way of proving his thesis that all animals are unconscious beings and therefore incapable of experiencing any kind of suffering comparable to human suffering, shares this datum with us:

> Neurophysiological experiments in monkeys have shown that cells in the temporal lobe of the brain are sensitive to an object's shape or color, while cells in the parietal lobe react to an object's location. Destroying the temporal lobes renders monkeys incapable of discriminating patterns, but leaves them with the ability to distinguish locations; destroying the parietal lobes has exactly the opposite effect.[74]

Given that these researchers have just carved out a portion of the chimps' brains to conduct this inquiry, what are the chances they are going to report back that, by golly, it turns out chimpanzees *do* feel conscious pain after all? The whole exercise is carried out on the premise that the subjects—these same creatures capable of learning basic sign language and asking for treats and tickling and kittens—are unfeeling organisms whose cries may be serenely ignored and whose lives may be disposed of at will to satisfy the experimenters' curiosity or quest for credentials. They're not a "who" at all, they're a "what." Any other conclusion, when the dissecting is done and the operation table tidied up, would amount to a confession of gross professional misconduct and personal cruelty. We may assume that the chimps displayed defensive behavior in response to such aversive stimuli. But not to worry. Happily for them, there is no "me" to suffer.

The very chimps who taught us so much about language, cognition, and emotion were similarly dealt with when their usefulness had passed. I actually saw the celebrated Nim Chimpsky himself at the Black Beauty Ranch, a sanctuary in Murchison, Texas. He was sitting there, when I found him in late 1999, thumbing through a picture magazine while drinking from a plastic cup. I saw him sign, too, making requests for things and giving the "hug" sign to ranch director Chris Byrne, who told me that the actress Marlee Matlin came by once and was able to communicate with Nim.

Whatever one makes of this chimp's cognitive skills, however, you might have thought that when they were done with him Nim was at least entitled to peaceful retirement. Yet after all the fanfare had passed, he was about to be carted off to a laboratory specializing in dentistry experiments until the Fund for Animals stepped in to buy him. Other signing chimps have been less fortunate, as in the case of one Booee trained by Roger Fouts. A film of their reunion was shown by Dr. Fouts to Justice Faith Ireland of the Washington State Supreme Court, in an attempt to persuade her that primates are due special legal protection:

> Justice Ireland's mind was not opened by legal arguments or philosophical treatises. Her view shifted after watching a videotape of a meeting between Dr. Fouts of Central Washington University and a 27-year-old chimpanzee named Booee.
>
> Fouts had been Booee's sign-language teacher. When that project ended, Booee was sold off to a biomedical lab, where he was kept in a windowless cage and deliberately infected with Hepatitis C and other viruses. Thirteen years passed without contact between teacher and pupil. Then Fouts decided to pay a surprise visit and brought a film crew.
>
> The recognition was instant. Despite years of being subjected to experimentation, Booee remembered his teacher and immediately signed both their names: a finger drawn down the middle of the head for Booee and a finger-flick of an ear lobe for Fouts. The two signed back and forth and played games between the bars. When Fouts finally signed that he had to leave, Booee visibly slumped and shrunk to the back of the cage.
>
> "It was so obvious that chimpanzee retained memories and had feelings and could communicate," Ireland says. "For me it was, 'Insert key; unlock mind.' All of a sudden there was this 'Aha. Now I understand.'"[75]

THINKING ABOUT THOUGHTS

The particular human behavior at work in behaviorist theories is known as false humility, for of course there could be no more sweeping or brazen assertion than to say that the question of animal consciousness is closed, the matter eternally inconclusive, and no further evidence will be admitted. What an animal like Booee feels when treated this way, abandoned to a life of loneliness and pain in a laboratory, is not entirely unknowable territory. It is just forbidden territory to anyone who ventures the conclusion that our fellow creatures really do think, feel, and suffer.

Rational debate requires that there be at least some hypothetical evidence that, if produced, would settle the matter one way or the other. If I say, "There is no such thing as the Sasquatch," and one day this beast of lore is caught and hauled before my eyes, after due confirmation by zoologists that this is indeed Sasquatch I must admit to being wrong. I am at this moment prepared to assert that no such being exists. But I admit at least to the remote possibility of its existence. Enough so that I'll look at the evidence. I do not say it could *never* be proved. I just say find me the Sasquatch and then I'll believe it.

A theory by definition admits the possibility of error, depending on what evidence can be produced to disprove it. In science a proposition must be drawn inductively, by a process of arriving at general conclusions from the particular set of available facts. "Animals experience pain" is a conclusion drawn inductively from some basic facts of biology and veterinary medicine. Most vertebrates and all of our fellow mammals have similar chemical and neurological mechanisms that transmit and control pain. Under stress or trauma, they display physiological reactions identical to ours—increased heartbeat and perspiration, higher cortisone levels in the blood, a release of endorphins, serotonin, and other natural opiates. Their bodies respond to anesthesia just as our bodies do, and of course they display vocalizations, defensive behavior, and bodily contortions similar to ours. We may add to this physical evidence the fact that veterinarians today routinely prescribe exactly the same antidepressant drugs to dogs, cats, pigs, horses and other animals, including Prozac, Ritalin, Xanax, and beta-blockers, and these drugs have exactly the same soothing effects on them as on us. All mammals and birds sleep, too, their slumber (including REM sleep) diminishing as they get older just like ours, serving presumably the same restorative function for the brain as ours, and involving the same suspension of what in our own brains we call mental awareness.

What, then, *would* prove to Mr. Budiansky, Professor Kennedy, et al., that the creatures really feel and suffer and that our empathy is not just silly anthropomorphism? One searches in vain. Their argument suffers from the problem of circularity, arrived at deductively—applying a general proposition to particular facts—and admitting of no counter evidence. Their case concedes some degree of sentience in animals, but then cuts the creatures off at the pass with language, erecting this elaborate "thinking-about-thoughts" construct that, upon closer inspection, *requires speech*. Only with language, writes Mr. Budiansky, can "ideas be represented ad infinitum: language automatically offers the means to represent ideas about ideas about ideas about ideas," making possible "the all-important leap from merely having intentions and beliefs to having intentions and beliefs about having intentions and beliefs."[76] Roger Scruton, in *Animal Rights and Wrongs*, relies on the same argument, telling us on the one hand "it is obvious that animals *are* conscious,"[77] and on the other that, lacking language, they cannot be conscious *of themselves* as individual beings and thus cannot rate our direct moral concern.

Another determined skeptic of animal awareness writes that "the definition of consciousness has eluded us for over a century."[78] But this isn't the problem at all. The problem is that as animals meet the old definitions, like conscious pain and deliberate communication, the experts keep making up new definitions, until now they would have to tell us—with flawless syntax— that they are conscious beings before many scientists and philosophers are convinced. Naturally if one assumes from the outset that the animals' inner experience is by definition inaccessible to inquiry, and that only with language is consciousness possible, we're not going to get very far. The conclusion ("animals cannot think and feel") is contained in the premise ("thought and feeling are exclusive to verbal beings"). Begged is the question with which the inquiry began: whether thought and feeling are, in fact, exclusive to us, whether animals might still be conscious without the words and abstract concepts only we possess.

It would come as some consolation to the creatures, in any case, if they could read and grasp our theories about them, to find that Mr. Budiansky and similar thinkers still aren't so sure about human consciousness, either. This requires some explaining.

Mr. Budiansky counts himself a student of "evolutionary ecology," an offshoot of behaviorism that takes account of recent discoveries in genetics. Traditional behaviorism holds that the actions of any creature can be interpreted only by reference to observable stimulus and response, and to the internal mechanisms of that creature. This is now called the school of "radical behaviorism," he tells us. Today we take a subtler view. Today we know so much more:

> The so-called cognitive revolution in psychology in the 1970s proposed that there is a great deal that animals can *do* that perforce requires them to hold mental representations of information and to manipulate those representations, and that appropriately designed

experiments can reveal something about what sort of mental *events* may be taking place in an animal's head—even if we can never get at mental *experiences*. This view was a mighty leap from the strict behaviorist position championed by psychologists like B. F. Skinner, who insisted that all behavior was a simple, learned stimulus-response link that told nothing about the inner workings of the mind—a position that has been much vilified for reducing animals to automatons.[79]

Note, however, that even after this great cognitive revolution we can still "never" get at the inner experience of any animal. Why? Because legitimate inquiry is still confined to outward behavior. What they *do* we may study and measure. What they *feel* remains unknowable territory. Indeed, Mr. Budiansky continues, how do we know that our fellow humans experience thoughts and feelings as we do? "For all that any of us know, we are each the only beings in the universe capable of thinking thoughts. . . . [M]aybe even *our* own consciousness is an illusion, too; maybe everything we seem to be experiencing and thinking is not real at all. . . . This is not as fanciful a point as it seems."[80]

This is an echo of B. F. Skinner, who started all this with his 1938 book *The Behavior of Animals: An Experimental Analysis*. "As far as our own feelings are concerned," he observed, "we are locked within our own skins."[81] Apparently there has been little progress on the matter since. Professor Kennedy gives us this summary of the current consensus:

> It has again become a matter of serious discussion that human beings as well as animals may be machines. . . . Although nowadays, of course, no one is thinking of machines as simple as the ones that [Descartes] envisaged, nor for that matter of machines that anyone yet knows how to construct. Animals as envisaged now are not the stimulus-response automata which anthropomorphists seem to think are the only alternative that anti-anthropomorphists can offer to animals with minds.[82]

So animals are still stimulus-response machines, but far more intricate machines than previously suspected. It may be that human beings, too, are highly complicated stimulus-response machines. We don't know yet. It's under serious discussion, and they'll report back when more data come in.

⚘

We will not linger long on the consciousness question except to note the incoherence to which it reduces those who contend that animals are unconscious beings. Pouring over the literature, one still finds long, earnest essays with titles like "The Concept of 'Consciousness,'" "Does 'Consciousness' Exist?" "What Is 'Self-Awareness'?" and "The Problem of 'Other Minds.'" And this is human consciousness they're wrestling with. A sample from this literature, questioning whether the physical world exists as we perceive it, could be a "Deep Thoughts" segment on *Saturday Night Live*:

> Far from being a physical property of objects, colour is a mental property—a useful invention that specialized circuitry computes in our minds and "projects onto" our percepts of physically colourless objects. . . . What is true for colour is true for everything in our experienced worlds: the warmth of a smile, the meaning of a glance, the heft of a book, the force of a glare. . . . We inhabit mental worlds populated by the computational outputs of battalions of evolved, specialized, neural automata. They segment words out of a continual auditory flow, they construct a world of local objects from edges and gradients in our two-dimensional retinal arrays. . . . Oblivious to their existence, we mistake the representations they construct (the colour of a leaf, the irony in a tone of voice, the approval of our friends, and so on) for the world itself.[83]

Is there really such a thing as a "leaf" as we know it, or do "leaves" just exist as subjective retinal phenomena? Does anything at all objectively exist apart from our perception of it? Last night I dreamed I was a butterfly: Was I Matthew dreaming I was a butterfly, or am I really a butterfly dreaming I am "Matthew"?

Such metaphysical speculations have their place, and one has to admire the brainpower that goes into them. The problem is that when you're done with all the theorizing and speculating, you don't have a whole lot to show for it, especially when the object of inquiry is the human mind itself and the purpose to inform our own moral conduct, toward one another and toward the creatures.

Obviously we each have the evidence of our own direct experience, and from that we infer that other people have it too: I infer from the fact of my own conscious thoughts and feelings that you, too, have feelings. You, the reader, and all the rest of humanity are not just non-Me, so many humanoid-like machines "mimicking" conscious feeling to fool me into thinking that you have conscious feelings too, while in reality only *I* have feelings. People who think that way we call solipsists. People who act upon it we call psychopaths.

Consciousness, in our own case, is one of those primary facts beyond which the mind cannot go, any more than an eye can see itself. If our own minds cannot perceive objective reality, but merely construct "reality" and its properties, then any theories of consciousness we might devise would likewise be subjective constructs without any claim to objective validity, and so we're right back in the same epistemological cul de sac—as witness Mr. Budiansky's next theory.

Having explained all animal behavior by the terms of unconscious evolutionary forces, he has to explain how, unique in all the world, the naked ape acquired consciousness. "Language," he speculates, "is the rocket that has escaped the gravitational pull of biological adaptation." Language is "a discontinuous leap that took us, uniquely among all species, into a realm where ethical thought becomes possible."[84] Unlike animals, "we soar above whatever evolutionary purpose (or accident) drove its creation."[85] This theory also explains religion:

> To imagine a god is the ultimate attribution of mental states: we attribute nothing short of omniscience to a being outside our own minds. This is the ultimate expression of Darwin's "utopian animal," for, in so doing, man has created the ultimate moral conscience. . . . A literal "god" is the ultimate container of this concept.[86]

So now we have created God, too. He's a concept contained within our own minds. Mr. Budiansky makes light of the "deep ecology" movement with its airy spirituality, but it would be hard to find anything in environmentalist literature flimsier than this "rocket" theory of human conscience. The whole construct is based, by his own admission, upon an audacious act of anthropomorphism running the other way, projecting onto God the thoughts and designs of man.

The problem, of course, is that however far we might "soar," "God" and "truth" and "ethics" all remain subjective mental states in the human mind.

They're conventions, things we just made up over the ages, not things true in themselves which, using reason, we are able to perceive and assert as True. The argument declares all human thought to be a product of biological processes, with no claim to objective validity, but then exempts itself from its own verdict about human thought. It may have all happened just that way—no God, no truth, only us—but that still leaves us, in Skinner's apt phrase, "locked within our own skins." It is a self-refuting argument, denying our capacity to perceive objective reality at all.

Having "created" ethical truth ourselves, moreover, it would not be surprising if man over the ages had skewed things unduly in his favor. We are left, in other words, as in all philosophies of moral relativism, with a doctrine of power. Things are true and ethical, not in themselves, but because we, the lords and masters of the earth, have declared them to be so.

Peter Carruthers, a professor of philosophy at the University of Sheffield, offers a similar theory in his 1992 book *The Animals Issue: Moral Theory and Practice*. With Professor Kennedy and Mr. Budiansky, he is among the authorities one is most likely to find cited in defense of the claim that animals can neither think nor feel in any conscious or morally relevant way. "It is an open question," he writes, "whether there is anything it feels like to be a bat, or a dog, or a monkey. If consciousness is like the turning on of a light, then it may be that their lives are nothing but darkness."[87] Regarding animals as "inappropriate objects of sympathy," our concern for them as so much foolish modern sentimentality, the professor here gives us a demonstration of *recta ratio* in action:

> [A] conscious, as opposed to a nonconscious, mental state is one that is available to conscious thought—where a conscious act of thinking is itself an event that is available to be thought about similarly in turn. . . . Although there is a hint of circularity to this suggestion, it is not in fact so. Rather, the account is reflexive. It is the very same thing that makes thinking conscious as makes experience or belief conscious—namely, availability to thought that is, in turn, regularly made available to thought.[88]

The question is whether this argument itself is available to rational thought. It not only "appears circular," it is circular, winding round and round until consciousness has been redefined into the use of linguistic concepts. Like Mr. Budiansky, Professor Carruthers hasn't proved that animals are unconscious, but only that animals are not verbal and philosophical. Your dog can think about going for a walk; he just can't think thoughts about thoughts about thoughts about the concept—in all of its philosophical complexity—of A Walk. A cat in the lab can believe he or she is in pain and try to escape it; the creature just can't have beliefs and intentions about beliefs and intentions about . . . and so on.

When they're done theorizing, the animals are like machines and we like angels, pure consciousness, forever contemplating and reflecting. Yet both arguments tacitly concede that by the normal, everyday use of the words, animals *think* and are *conscious*. For Mr. Budiansky's "unthinking intelligence" we now have Professor Carruthers's unconscious consciousness. The former carries this logic a step further, allowing that animals do indeed *know* things, and they can *use* that information, but do not "know what they know." To put this parlor sophism as clearly as it can be put: Animals can use what they know, but they do not know what they use when they use what they know.

"Granted," Professor Carruthers continues, "that animals can be conscious *of* events. Our question is whether those states of awareness are, themselves, conscious ones. Our question is not, whether animals have mental states, but whether animals are subject to *conscious* mental states."[89]

Actually, that was not the question. The question was whether animals are conscious in the simple sense of experiencing events and feeling pain as we do, then and there, at the moment pain occurs and not in some subsequent stage of philosophical reflection. What he's really saying here is that animals have a less sophisticated state of consciousness. But, of course, consciousness is still consciousness.

Besides, how does *he* know they can't reflect on their pain? They can certainly anticipate pain, as mistreated animals cower and whimper at the mere appearance of their tormentor, a fact observed daily in many a laboratory. If they can anticipate pain, storing in their minds some image or feeling of past experience, why can't we suppose that the same faculty of memory allows them to reflect on past experiences? They dream, too, for heaven's sake. What does that tell us, and why do neither Professor Carruthers nor Mr. Budiansky, in all of their musings and speculations, ever once mention this fact?

Probably they would both concede that animals display a dreamlike state, the internal experience of which we can neither prove nor disprove. But science has already come awfully close to proving that animals dream just as we do. In early 2001, for example, researchers at the Massachusetts Institute of Technology published findings that rats dream. And not only that: They appear to dream of the very experiments to which they have been subjected. Professor Matthew Wilson and assistant Kenway Louie implanted electrodes in the same part of the rats' brains, the hippocampus behind the temples, believed to form and store memory in our own brains. As the rats were trained to navigate a maze, the electrodes fired a distinctive pattern, "a unique signature for that experience," as Dr. Wilson describes it. The same pattern was recorded during their REM sleep, with such precision that the researchers could locate where the rats were in the maze of their dreams. "The ability to recall, reflect and evaluate prior experience is something that goes on in animals at many levels," Dr. Wilson concludes. "They may be thinking more than we had previously considered." [90]

For his part Professor Carruthers goes on, after a few pages more of intellectual tail chasing, to liken animal unconsciousness to his own state of mind when, while mechanically engaged in household chores, "I was swept up in the Finale of Schubert's *Arpeggione Sonata*":

> Let us call such experiences *nonconscious* ones. What does it feel like to be the subject of a nonconscious experience? It feels like nothing. It does not feel like anything to have a nonconscious visual experience as of a vehicle parked at the side of the road, or as of two coffee mugs placed on a draining rack—precisely because to have such an experience is not to be conscious of it. Only conscious experiences have a distinctive phenomenology, a distinctive feel. Nonconscious experiences are ones that may help to control behavior without being felt by the conscious subject. [91]

For animals, however, the sonata never ends. They are, he argues, forever lost in this world off somewhere on the fringe of conscious life, a state he compares to human beings under morphine or anesthesia.

Suppose, however, that as Professor Carruthers was working away at his chores while swept up by the strains of Schubert, some prowler were to creep up on him in attack. That would snap him out of his nonconscious state, wouldn't it? Suppose that while nonconsciously listening to the *Arpeggione*

Sonata (nonconscious, and yet apparently *experiencing* and indeed *enjoying* the music), the professor suddenly heard a rustling by the window or the creaking of a door. That wouldn't "feel like nothing," would it? A chill of fear would pass over him. His mind and body would go from nonconsciousness to full alert. That is the whole purpose of fear and pain, to alert our defensive mechanisms. On what rational or scientific grounds are we to believe that the immediate experience of those physical responses is not precisely the same in animals as in us? How would fear and pain operate if they were not dramatically distinguishable from the creatures' normal state?

As to Professor Carruthers's morphine argument, we may ask as a logical matter what it is that animals lose when they are put under sedation. Their bodies under anesthesia or morphine react exactly as ours do. Something passes away even as the body experiences intrusion and pain. All the mechanical processes continue, but the brain doesn't register them as it does without the anesthesia. When it happens to us we call it a loss of consciousness. Both Professor Kennedy and Mr. Budiansky, in describing the chimp experiment, skirt this by saying the creatures "recovered from the anesthesia."[92] Recovered what? Their *un*consciousness?

Finally, none of these theories take into account the fact that animals have to make choices and decisions. It may well be, as Professor Carruthers speculates, that the creatures live out most of their lives in some state comparable to ours when we are on a long drive, somehow operating the car without really paying attention. We live out an awful lot of our lives that way, too, in reflexive motions and vagrant thoughts and feelings of which, submerged in the present, we are usually unaware. I did not pass the last few hours thinking, "Here I am reading the morning newspaper. . . . Now I am going up the stairs where I shall open the office door, sit down, and begin working. . . . It is 8:32 A.M. now, and here I am again, me, writing this sentence." Conscious life isn't experienced that way. Indeed, such self-consciousness is a paralyzing form of neurosis.

Typically, what snaps us out of this state is the need to decide something, something as simple as when to eat, whether to rest or come out of rest, and so on, or something dramatic and complicated. We have to concentrate, to collect ourselves, to do one thing or the other, and it stands to reason that animals have this same faculty.

Something my dog Lucky once did has always stuck with me. He always got very nervous when I climbed trees, particularly in his later years. All I had to do was reach up and grab hold of a branch and he'd get all edgy, growling and whimpering uncharacteristically. Whatever he was doing on our walks—sniffing around, wading into the stream or whatnot—the moment he spotted me climbing he'd trot over to intervene, often taking matters into his own mouth by pulling me down by the pant leg.

On one occasion I got a little way up the tree and then pretended to fall, tumbling with a yelp and then laying limp on the ground. He nudged me with his muzzle, circling me, looking nervously around. Across the lake, in view, was our house. He looked in that direction, then down to me, then over at the house, then at me, and so on for maybe twenty seconds. Suddenly he bolted, running back around the lake toward our house. And then, just as abruptly, he doubled back and returned for more pacing and nudging.

Doubtless there's some theory of canine behavior to explain all this. Lucky was preprogrammed to stop bipeds from climbing trees. My theory is that he was afraid I would fall and hurt myself, making a simple causal connection. (If it was instinct, somehow he caught on and the trick never worked again.) But let the point go. My point here is that he was faced with a decision. When he stood over me, looking here and there, he was trying to figure out how to handle the crisis. When he ran toward the house, then came back, he had a sudden change of mind (*No, I have to stay with him!*). Animals do this all the time, especially in our company when they are placed in novel situations, and it is no answer to say, as behavioral and genetic determinism explains everything, that whatever they did they *had* to do.

Between us and all other creatures, as David Oderberg observes, there is the great difference that "no matter how instinctive, every human activity can be brought within the sphere of choice and free will."[93] This is true, but does not justify his conclusion that while human beings "are governed *partly* by instinct," animals "are governed wholly by instinct," incapable of any conscious intention, action, or feeling whatever.[94] It will not do to simply declare, after the fact, that in every case the instinct that prevailed was the strongest instinct, and that therefore the action was predetermined from the start.

Skinnerian behaviorists apply the same logic to human action and it is equally fallacious. Like Lucky, the creatures sometimes have to abruptly change course, to recalculate things in the same flashes of deliberation that we experience. The broad "instinct" argument doesn't hold up because, like us, animals have different and at times conflicting instincts. In them, as in us, these impulses sometimes clash, demanding a choice—to defend their young or to flee the danger, to fight for dominance or to accept submission, to endure the harsh winter or to give up and die. *Something* has to choose, to mediate, to organize, which is why identical animals will often react differently to identical circumstances. And whatever that something is, it cannot itself be instinct. It must logically stand above instinct, presiding and selecting as it does in us. In our case we call it consciousness. What could it be in their case but a humbler version of the same thing?

We tend to assume, moreover, that instinct, even when it is clearly at work, means there can be no accompanying thought or feeling—as if a doe when she caresses her fawn, or lions when they hunt, or your cat when he or she kneads on you, can have no awareness or pleasure in that instinctive experience. We certainly don't assume that about ourselves when we feel the tug of instinct, in avoiding danger or safeguarding our young or seeking potential mates. On the contrary, the thoughts and emotions accompanying instinctive desires are usually the most vivid. The most earthy, ordinary human experiences—coupling, birthing, dying—are, in fact, the most deeply experienced. Instinctive desire and action in our own case does not always mean blind, unfeeling reflex, and there is no reason to suppose it is any different for them.

With "mock anthropomorphism," allowing us to assume "metaphorically" that animals are conscious, behavioral theory goes from pedantry to perversity. This new behavioral concept acknowledges, as Professor Kennedy puts it, that "natural selection has produced animals that act *as if* they had minds like us."[95] Professor Dennett calls it the "intentional stance," the "Sherlock Holmes method" of animal research, studying animal behavior by reference to what we ourselves, in a given predicament, might think, feel, desire, and decide.[96] Mr. Budiansky can hardly contain his excitement over this new breakthrough in animal research—so very new and innovative that you can find the Stoic philosopher Chrysippus maintaining, around 190 B.C., that animals do not think and feel, but only "as it were" think and feel.[97] Mock anthropomorphism, writes Mr. Budiansky, is the very "foundation of evolutionary ecology," this "burgeoning field of research that has produced wonderful insights into the adaptive value of otherwise inexplicable behaviors and physical forms that appear in nature."[98] The key, says Professor Kennedy, is to bear in mind that it's not for real, that "the beliefs and desires of animals remain purely metaphorical."[99]

A mighty handy thing, this "mock anthropomorphism," for now we get to use the assumption of animal consciousness as a research tool, yielding all these marvelous new insights, without having to admit the *reality* of animal consciousness. Indeed, all of the wonderful and "otherwise inexplicable" evidence of consciousness in animals now becomes evidence against them, only further proof of the validity of the "mock anthropomorphism" method, and so in turn of the assumption that the creatures think and feel nothing. Animals act *as if* they have conscious thoughts, react *as if* they have emotions, cry and wail *as if* it really hurt. But it's all metaphor, an elaborate game of "pretend," as Mr. Budiansky puts it.[100] Only in our moral conduct do we suddenly drop the pretense. Somehow, in our treatment of animals, we do not need to act *as if* they suffer.

PROFOUND RESPECT

None of these abstract theories would warrant such space and attention if they stayed where they belong—in the world of theory, mind puzzles to be debated in the faculty lounge. The problem lies in their practical application. They are what gives license to the vicious things that people actually do to animals. Here, piling conjecture upon conjecture, we have a smart fellow like Mr. Budiansky straining to prove that an elephant doesn't even know his or her own trunk. Somewhere in Africa, meanwhile, some unphilosophical lout is tormenting and killing an elephant, that elephant is trumpeting in fear and rage, the calves are crying and scattering, and the law does nothing to stop it because we're still not *quite* satisfied that the creatures suffer or that their suffering is meaningful or that they think or feel anything at all, and on and on. I am not sure which is the worse evil, the kill or the theory.

One tires especially of this posture among the theorists that they, and they alone, are guided by reason, while the rest of us wallow in our silly emotionalism. This is why we must press on a little further in examining their assumptions, inspecting here the bottom theoretical layer and finally, in the section below, the theories carried out in practice to their logical terminus.

Obviously, minds that have difficulty accepting the validity of human consciousness are going to need a lot of convincing in the case of animals. It seems to be Reality itself that they are struggling with. Obviously, too, Mr. Budiansky et al. do not as a practical matter doubt the validity of their own consciousness or of ours, else they would not be writing books on the subject of consciousness. The difference is that whereas they defer to common sense, empathy, and decency in the case of human consciousness, in the case of animals they do the opposite. The creatures are held to an impossible standard of evidence, an ever receding empirical horizon, allowing us to declare in theory that since we can never *really* know they think and feel, we may safely conclude that they do not and act accordingly.

Researchers and theorists who make this argument typically go to great lengths to soften the blow, assuring us, as Mr. Budiansky writes, that animals may still be appreciated "on their own terms." His own more "honest view of animal minds ought to lead us to a more profound respect for animals as unique beings in nature, worthy in their own right":

> The shallow and self-centered view that sees what is worthy in nature as that which resembles us seems vapid and petty by comparison. We try so hard to show that chimpanzees, or monkeys, or dogs, or cats, or rats, or chickens, or fish, or frogs are like us in their thoughts and feelings; in doing so we do nothing but denigrate what they really are. We define true intelligence and true feeling in human terms, and in so doing blind ourselves to the wonder of life's diversity that evolution has bequeathed earth.[101]

Leaving aside the anthropomorphism apparent in this very passage—evolution has "bequeathed" diversity to the earth, as if by conscious will—it all seems a lofty enough sentiment. We have to respect animals "in their own right." Glad to hear it. Doubtless, too, Mr. Budiansky's own study of animal minds is born of a sincere if somewhat abstract affection for them. A suburbanite, as Mr. Budiansky describes himself, who discovered the joys of agrarian life and rented a Maryland farm of his own, he has two basic theories. There's "thinking about thoughts." And then there's his "covenant of the wild" theory, explained in a 1992 book by that title, the short version of which runs as follows:

The more mankind uses a particular species of animal, the more that species flourishes. There are no rights and wrongs in nature, even where man is involved, but only "blindly amoral evolution," all of those unconscious, preprogrammed survival strategies with the single aim of species perpetuation.[102] The animals we use thus gain our "protection" under a kind of evolutionary "covenant," escaping the inevitable extinction now befalling other species as human mastery expands across the earth. These chosen ones become our "evolutionary co-partners," so that today, for example, no animals are flourishing more than the livestock crowded by the billions into our factory farms, or the research subjects abounding in our labs, or the inhabitants of our game parks. Far from being exploited, the theory runs, these animals are in a sense exploiting us, like so many parasites, their collective survival assured by their utility to the "dominant evolutionary partner." Indeed, factory farming becomes a kind of ultimate good in this scheme, a supreme act of fidelity to our evolutionary "covenant":

> If, rather than just another instance of man's arrogant exploitation of nature, domestication is instead a product of nature, then we will have to think more carefully about the interconnections between all species, and be less quick to apply the glib slogans of human politics, the language of "rights" and "exploitation" and "oppression," to relationships crafted by forces in many ways beyond our control. We cannot all be farmers but we can all be students of evolution. As more of the natural world comes under our control, we had better start understanding how the natural world really works, one way or the other.[103]

Notice how, in the space of two sentences, the natural world is both "beyond our control" and falling ever more "under our control," this even as he is advising others to "think more carefully." Like the "sustainable use" dogmas we have encountered, it is an argument perfectly tailored to our age—indeed, less an argument than a kind of secular absolution for all of mankind's excesses, for the cruelties we have committed and the worse ones we may yet contemplate: We are all-powerful over the animals, and yet powerless to alter our own ways. We are the evolutionary masters of the earth, and yet ourselves entirely at the mercy of evolution. How very convenient, too, that the creatures have "chosen" this horrible fate for themselves, for then the choice is not even ours to answer for. All responsibility, all guilt, is shifted back on "nature."

Combined—*mere pain* plus *unthinking intelligence* plus *blindly amoral evolution*—they form a kind of unified field theory for the hunters, whalers, factory farmers, and other "wise use" advocates among whom Mr. Budiansky has gained a wide following. The only question is this: If animals are unconscious beings, then exactly what rational grounds are left to restrain us in our conduct toward them? What's left for them "in their own right"?

Being appreciated as "wonderful" and lavished with all of this "profound respect" from humanity is, after all, thin gruel for the creatures unless there is some sort of moral component to either theory. In *If a Lion Could Talk,* Mr. Budiansky is uncharacteristically modest, utterly silent on the moral points. One would think that in a study devoted to proving that human beings are endowed with a distinctive capacity for ethical conduct—which few doubt anyway—he might somewhere pause to specify any kind of conduct toward any animal that would be considered unethical. But the subject of cruelty never comes up, leaving us to search his many writings in *U.S. News & World Report* to see how profound respect applies to each particular animal. "Make it pay," reads a typical piece. "Killing animals to save them sounds paradoxical, even cynical and perverse. Yet economics and history offer a strong brief for 'sustainable use.' In the United States, the market for sport hunting has been a spectacular success in saving targeted species. . . . The best hope for wildlife is to use it."[104]

Which theory came first, I wonder, mere pain or blindly amoral evolution? In any case what began as a scientific theory has now merged into economic dogma, a view of all creatures of the earth as so much cattle, and the most horrific abuse we can inflict on them as a kind of evolutionary favor, their well-being now equated with their utility to us. To feel moral concern for animals, by this logic, is to "denigrate" them. To respect them "in their own right" is to make them pay in pain and death at our hands. If we are to apply Mr. Budiansky's argument rigorously, then by his own terms there is no longer even any such thing as cruelty to animals because there is no longer any such thing as animal pain. To speak of cruelty to an animal would be as nonsensical as to speak of cruelty to a plant or mineral. If the worst an animal can feel is mere pain, the worst we can inflict is mere cruelty. As God and moral truth exist only in our minds, so His creatures exist only at our pleasure.

The same, of course, for "love," "compassion," "mercy," or any other such terms applied to an animal. Who says A must say B, and if animals are unconscious beings then they are *things,* living, breathing, animate things we may use as we will. Useful things, things that pay. Not only do they have no rights;

they have no claims to any sympathy whatever—a point made more explicitly by Professor Carruthers. "I regard the present popular concern with animal rights in our culture as a reflection of moral decadence," writes the professor, who traces his own "contractualist" theories back to the nineteenth-century German philosopher Immanuel Kant. "Just as Nero fiddled while Rome burned, many in the West agonize over the fate of seal pups and cormorants while human beings elsewhere starve or are enslaved."[105]

Nero's reign marked the height of the gladiatorial games and animal slaughter at the Colosseum, so this decadence argument will need some work. Like Mr. Budiansky, Professor Carruthers cautions us to respect and treasure animals. Indeed he counts himself an "animal lover."[106] But we must think straight about the matter. We must put mere emotion aside and "follow the course of a rational argument."[107] For, he explains, "it is one thing to love animals for their grace, beauty, and marvelous variety, and quite another to believe that they make any direct moral claims upon us."[108] Where animals are worth preserving at all, they "are worth preserving for their importance to *us*."[109] Here Professor Carruthers ponders the hypothetical case of a wounded dog:

> On my account, the disappointments caused to a dog through possession of a broken leg, as well as its immediate pains, are themselves non-conscious in their turn. In which case it follows that if they, too, are not appropriate objects of our sympathy, then neither the pain of the broken leg itself, nor its further effects on the life of the dog, will have any rational claim on our sympathy.[110]

Suppose we caused the broken leg? Would that affect the moral calculus? No.

> For if animal pains and dissatisfactions are not appropriate objects of sympathy, then no cruelty need be displayed in one who fails to take them seriously. In fact, the remarks made [previously] about children's supposedly cruel treatment of insects would extend to all animals. If insects are not genuinely sentient, then brutish cruelty need not be displayed in one who causes them damage. But then so, too, if the experiences of birds and mammals are non-conscious—those who discount their experiences, in consequences, need not be brutishly cruel.[111]

Suppose we love the dog?

Anyone who continues to believe that animal pains are relevant to our own will (in our culture, at least) display cruelty in causing an animal to suffer for no good reason. But if my views are widely accepted then all psychological connections between our attitudes to human and animal suffering would soon be decisively broken. . . . The truth may be that it is only our imperfect rationality that enables us to feel sympathy for animals at all.[112]

"Cruelty need not be displayed" means, in the parlance of armchair ethical theory, "*is* not cruel." It all depends on whether we *believe* animals feel pain or not. They don't, says Professor Carruthers, but if one is operating under the sentimental illusion that they do, then to inflict further harm on the dog would be cruel only because the motive was cruel. In either case the dog's own welfare is irrelevant.

Objectively, he believes, the little cur's pains and whimpers are morally meaningless, the pain not even consciously experienced. Subjectively, we may still care about the animal's well-being, but it is completely irrational nonsense. Once his own more enlightened view is accepted—presumably Professor Carruthers's aim, since he has written a book on the subject—all sympathy for animals passes away. The psychological connection is broken. To torture an elephant, by this logic, would be no worse an offense than to pull apart an insect. We could, if it suited us, break the dog's other three legs, and no cruelty need be displayed.

Ingrid Newkirk of PETA, a devoted friend of animals (whose book *You Can Save the Animals: 251 Simple Ways to Stop Thoughtless Cruelty* I recommend), has been criticized for her statement, "When it comes to feeling pain, hunger, and thirst, a rat is a pig is a dog is a boy." The remark has been misunderstood—she was speaking only about physical pain—but here in any case Professor Carruthers shows us the other side of the slippery slope, a mirror image of the same moral reductionism for which Ms. Newkirk has been faulted. In everything, the professor sees "nothing but" something else: An elephant is a dog is a bird is a flea. (That goes for Alex the parrot, too.) And in his way Professor Carruthers *is* thinking straight. To his credit, he does not shy from his own logic, for that is exactly where it leads.[113]

Nor is it any answer to Professor Carruthers to point to the ghastly implications of his theory. It could be both ghastly and true. If he, Mr. Budiansky, and like-minded thinkers are correct, if animals are unconscious of pain or any other feeling, then really it isn't ghastly at all. Our sympathy is misplaced, just as he says, our moral concern based on an irrational psychological connection that needs breaking once and for all before we plummet into further moral decadence. Our concern for animals is all so much anthropomorphic foolishness, and we'll just have to grow up and get over it. Professor Carruthers's book has an odd little dedication to his son, "whose animal days are almost done," meaning apparently that the boy will soon reach the age of reason and realize that animals do not rate his sympathy. Coming into full manhood, the child must learn that it's all about *us*, and only us.

Dispensing with the niceties, then, let us state their proposition without flinching: Animals "in their own right" are nothing. They feel nothing and we owe them nothing. Any pain that any animal exhibits, any happiness, any play, contentment, enjoyment, affection, loyalty, boredom, anger, fear, desire are all equally meaningless. When cats purr, they're not really feeling anything we might call contentment. When puppies roll around in play or when foals and lambs kick and frolic, they're not really feeling anything we may call glee or happiness. When dolphins burst free of the net and dive and splash, they're not feeling a thing. When dogs yelp from beatings or neglect, or when elephant calves cry in their sleep, it's mere pain and nothing more. No emotion. No feeling. No thought. No consciousness. Nothing—not even that primal, unknowing misery Jack London ascribes to the wolf cub, separated from his mother and now in the hands of a cruel master:

> That night, when all was still, White Fang remembered his mother and sorrowed for her. He sorrowed too loudly and woke up Gray Beaver, who beat him. After that he mourned gently when the gods were around. But sometimes, straying off to the edge of the woods by himself, he gave vent to his grief, and cried it out with loud whimperings and wailings.[114]

THE STRESS GENE

Which brings us finally to the creatures themselves, the living reality and, for many of them, the living nightmare as these very theories now embolden the gods of modern genetics. While behavioral scientists, ethologists, and cognitive philosophers debate thoughts about thoughts, unthinking intelligence, and all the rest, it turns out those with the clearest stake in the matter are far ahead of them all. We saw earlier how deer and other coveted prey are now sporting bigger, genetically improved "racks" to suit the tastes of the market. This was but one benefit to civilization accruing from experiments begun by agricultural researchers in the 1980s, when the first patented animal came into existence, and today giving the world better and better cows, sheep, fowl, and pigs.

Peruse the literature and you find endless agricultural studies, panels, and conferences abuzz with talk of the "stress gene." The precise "stress"-causing strand of DNA—the protein molecules present in chromosomes, carrying the hereditary information of all creatures—has been located. It is a big breakthrough, promising once and for all to bring order and efficiency to our farms. One agricultural scientist, in a study entitled "Handling Pigs for Optimum Performance," explains:

> Observations at packing plants indicate that some lines of hybrid pigs have a very nervous temperament and others are calm. Some pigs are easy to drive up chutes and others are nervous and constantly balk and back up. Certain lines of lean pigs, which contain the stress gene, tend to be more nervous and excitable than lean lines without the stress gene. . . . Within the last year some producers have moved away from lines which are extremely nervous and carry the stress gene. This also has the added benefit of improving pork quality.[115]

The trick is to eliminate that gene, known in the pork industry as "porcine stress syndrome," or PSS, by means of careful genetic selection so that the creatures might all reach "optimum performance," comporting themselves agreeably and then, on command, sauntering shoulder to shoulder down the chute to a clean, squealless kill. As D. E. Gerrard, a "meat scientist" at Purdue University, puts it in "Pork Quality: Beyond the Stress Gene": "The primary goal of the pork industry is to produce the greatest amount of high quality protein possible for the least amount of input"—"input" here including the time it takes to transport and herd the creatures to slaughter.[116] The U.S. Department of Agriculture offers a similar formula for the treatment of sows: "If the sow is considered a pig manufacturing unit, then improved management . . . will result in more pigs weaned per sow per year."[117]

The lower the "stress tolerance" in each unit, the longer production takes. Hence the costlier the operation and smaller the profit margin. Man has learned to engineer crops and plants to suit his designs, for example insect-resistant fruit and produce. To a certain cast of mind it was an obvious next step, an economic imperative, a wondrous new opportunity: Why not redesign the animals, too? Poultry producers, who gave us the first factory farms, have again led the way with gene-splicing schemes to make chickens less susceptible to the pain of being constantly pecked in mass confinement.

Complicating matters for America's $28 billion pork industry, an average packing plant turning out "1,000 units per hour,"[118] is another malady called "PSE," the acronym for "pale soft exudative" meat common to "production units" raised and slaughtered by intensive farming methods. Breeds of pig engineered to erase PSE turn out to have a higher incidence of PSS—stress—and both conditions are only aggravated by modern farming techniques. "PSS increases if pigs are handled roughly at the plant because excited pigs become overheated," causing "bloodsplash" and attendant cosmetic defects in the carcass.[119] Stress is also common among pigs already subjected to extensive genetic manipulation, affecting not only their comportment on the slaughter line but fertility rates in sows and even appetite. Such is the "stress" on our farms that even pigs are losing their appetites, displaying "the classic symptoms of anorexia."[120] "Genetics," we learn in "Methods to Reduce PSE and Bloodsplash," "is probably the single most important factor contributing to the prevalence of PSS pork today":

> Present pork grading systems motivate producers to breed pigs that carry the stress gene. Today those animals have maximum lean and weight gain (Aalhus et al., 1991). Unfortunately, they also have high levels of PSE. Some of the highest levels of PSE were reported in hybrid pigs, which had been selected for leanness and rapid growth. The breeding companies have recognized the problem and are taking steps to produce lines that will have lower levels of PSE. New DNA testing methods will enable the PSE gene to be eliminated (Sellers, 1993).[121]

How then to obtain optimal performance with minimal input? How to create pigs with high growth, acceptable bloodsplash, low stress, and little or no PSE—all at maximum efficiency and profit? Hundreds of millions of dollars each year go into solving this dilemma. At stake for American farmers are vast new markets abroad, especially in Europe, where genetically altered food is still viewed warily. Most every agricultural science school now has a specialty in stress studies, if not entire departments of stress physiology and management. At North Carolina State University, center of the state's ten-million-hog-per-year industry, there is a National Swine Improvement Federation working round the clock to crack the nut of "porcine stress."

Dr. Temple Grandin, the scientist whose findings on porcine temperament and slaughterhouse handling are quoted above, is a remarkable story all by herself. Her 1996 memoir, *Thinking in Pictures,* explains how, as an autistic child growing up on an Arizona cattle ranch, she discovered a gift for perceiving how animals experience things, above all their capacity for "stress." Being autistic, "I know how it feels to totally panic," as, she found, animals panic when treated roughly or confronted with death.[122] In the world of mass livestock production she is the closest thing the creatures have to an advocate, and was recently hired as an adviser to the McDonald's Corporation. Half of all livestock slaughtered in America now pass through her patented "highway to heaven," a curving chute exploiting the creatures' herding instincts and restricting vision until it's too late to balk. "I think in pictures," she explained to *Forbes* in 1998, "and I assume [the animal] does too. You've got to get down and look right up the chute to see what the animal is seeing."[123]

To be autistic, as Dr. Grandin describes it in *Thinking in Pictures,* is to live in a nonverbal world in which words, to have meaning, must be associated with some image. "Many people are totally baffled by autistic symbols, but to an autistic person they may provide the only tangible reality or understanding of the world." Autistic people in their reasoning "aren't logical, they're associational."[124] For example, "'French toast' may mean happy if the child was happy while eating it. When the child visualizes a piece of French toast, he becomes happy. A visual image or word becomes associated with an experience."[125] Even abstractions such as *over* and *under* require the recollection of some concrete image such as a bridge. For the word *peace,* she must summon the image of a dove. As a child, Dr. Grandin recalls, "The Lord's Prayer was incomprehensible to me until I broke it down into specific visual images. The power and the glory were represented by a semicircular rainbow and an electrical tower," and so on.[126]

Emotions for an autistic person are different, too, she writes: "My emotions are simpler than those of most people. I don't understand what complex emotion in a human relationship is. I only understand simple emotions, such as fear, anger, happiness, and sadness."[127] Happiness for her is more immediate, unreflective: "When I get this feeling, I just want to kick up my heels. I'm like a calf gamboling about on a spring day."[128] She has always felt a special identification with animals:

> My experience as a visual thinker with autism makes it clear to me that thought does not have to be verbal or sequential to be real. . . . I am not saying that animals and normal humans and autistics think alike. But I do believe that recognizing different capacities and kinds of thought and expression can lead to greater connectedness and understanding. Science is just beginning to prove what little old ladies in tennis shoes have always known: little Fifi really does think.[129]

Throughout her more clinical writings we find Dr. Grandin trying to balance this empathy for animals with her consistent support of intensive farming and its economic objectives. "I don't want to eliminate the meat industry," she told *Forbes*. "I just want to reform it."[130] Here she outlines techniques of avoiding porcine stress syndrome, advancing her case for "environmental enrichment" as a cost saver in large-scale livestock plants:

> Weekly weighing may have a detrimental effect on weight if the pigs see the "mean" man who shocked them with a prod. Most animals are smart enough to associate certain people with painful experiences. . . .
>
> Stimuli which may initially frighten a pig can often become pleasurable. During pen washing the animals squealed and became excited the first few times. By the third or fourth washing the animals appeared to eagerly anticipate pen washing. They approached and played in the water. Some turned broadside to get the full blast of water. . . .
>
> [B]aby piglets which receive frequent gentle handling are still tamer weeks later. They are more likely to approach strange people.
>
> The effect of toy, mingle and driving treatment on handling was

tested on Landrace sired crossbred pigs. In the first trial, the controls were slightly easier to drive. The mingled pigs had become so tame that driving was difficult. The pigs used in the second trial were tame and calm before Trial 2 started. The pigs used in Trial 1 were more excitable than Trial 2 pigs at the beginning of the experiment. The animals in Trial 2 also received more pen-washing. This provided additional environmental enrichment that commercial pigs do not receive. . . . There may be an optimal level of stimulation for animals that will be marketed for slaughter. You want a calm animal which will not panic and become excited. . . . Breeding stock benefit from lots of tender loving care.[131]

Pigs of identical breeding display different individual temperaments, Dr. Grandin has found, and should therefore be bred not only for their physical characteristics but for emotional ones, too.[132] There are even regional variations among breeds. Danish pigs tend to be calmer and more passive on approach to the stunner, while Irish pigs, I am proud to report, are more defiant and unruly.[133] Nor do all pigs within each breed react the same to external conditions. Different pigs react in different ways to different stimuli, and all have brains with marked similarities to ours. "When the brain was sliced down the middle," she writes, recounting her first class in human anatomy, "I was astounded to learn that the limbic system, which is the part of the brain associated with emotion, looked almost exactly like the limbic system of a pig's brain."[134]

Studies by the Institute for Animal Science and Health, a Dutch consulting firm to the EU and to private livestock companies, support her findings: "Farm animals show individual differences in stress responses that are consistent over time and across situations. This means that, depending on the individual characteristics of the animal, similar conditions may evoke different responses and in turn may have different consequences in terms of stress pathology."[135]

The Dutch group has an entire Department of Behavior, Stress Physiology and Management, which reports on other experiments revealing physical symptoms in ill-treated animals, such as an increased heartbeat, higher cortisone levels, and immunological failures resulting in "social defeat." "Furthermore these effects were long lasting when animals were housed individually after social defeat, whereas social defeat had only a mild effect when animals were group housed, probably due to social support."[136] It turns out the pigs are very particular even in their preference in toys and diversions, and like to be stroked on their bellies. A 1988 report by Dr. Grandin, "Environmental Enrichment for Confinement Pigs," today seems quaint in its solicitude for the creatures. Some farmers, she writes,

> have been giving pigs toys for many years to prevent boredom, reduce vices such as tail biting, and help prevent aggression when pigs are mixed. Providing pigs with additional stimulation will make them calmer and less excitable. Pigs raised in a barn with a radio playing are less likely to startle when they hear a sound such as a door slamming. Calmer pigs are more likely to have better meat quality because they will be less likely to become excited on the slaughter line. . . .
>
> Pigs have definite toy preferences. If a ball rolls into the manure they will no longer play with it. . . . Soft pliable objects were definitely preferred over the hard chain. There were two different behaviors the pigs performed with the toys. The behaviors were chewing or jerking or shaking. They shook the toy like a dog tugging on a towel. The pigs seldom jerked or shook the chain. It probably hurt their mouths.[137]

Knowledge Without Love

One has to admire Dr. Grandin, not only for her personal triumph over adversity but for at least trying to make industrial farming more humane. Every little bit helps, if only a ball tossed into the pen or a few nightmarish seconds spared in the killing.

But there is a problem here, and it doesn't seem to have occurred even to her what is happening. If all of this is just more "anecdotal evidence" for animal consciousness, it is quite a yarn, for here we have the livestock industry and its best minds admitting that the production units *suffer*.

They now concede, in theory and practice, that the animals are feeling pain, and not just physical pain either but emotional torment. Dr. Grandin herself, even in these otherwise dry and clinical reports, uses the words *stress, pain, fear,* and *suffering* interchangeably. The creatures she describes are sensitive, sociable, communicative, alert beings who form images in their minds, *think* in pictures, respond to gentleness, fear harsh treatment, act by conscious intention, anticipate danger, make choices, and dread slaughter so much that their emotional terror can trigger traumatic physiological reactions affecting meat quality. Most notable of all, they display individual differences in temperament and personality. As she describes the pig playing with the toy: "Like a dog."

This is almost as chilling as hearing the professional hunters at Safari Club describe the frightened elephants rushing back to the protected area ("You can see the relief. They know."). Yet were Dr. Grandin delivering her findings in any other setting, she would be dismissed by skeptics of the animal-welfare cause as a silly, meddlesome crackpot instead of as a savant and visionary in her field. "A bore," as columnist Auberon Waugh might have called her. The woman wants to give *toys* to livestock!

What exactly is the difference between "stress" and suffering? From the industry's standpoint, all the difference in the world. "Stress" is a scientific and economic problem. Stress is a defect in the product, a correctable "syndrome." Stress is holding things up at the packing plant. Stress is requiring too much input in the care of the production units. Stress is costing good money, and we've got to make 'em pay.

Talk to these same folks about the pain and suffering and terror and loneliness of the creatures raised in these squalid factories, never seeing the light of day, denied company or recreation, denied the least bit of human warmth for all of Dr. Grandin's touching advice—and, no, that just doesn't make sense to them. That's all a lot of moralistic, anthropomorphic nonsense. But talk about the "stress gene" and suddenly they're all ears. Explain to them in long reports and charts and gene maps how modern science can now eliminate this mysterious "profit robber," genetically redesign the animal itself, expunge the "stress" right out of it—and *now* you're talking a language they understand. Farm animals, it turns out, are not just unconscious, unfeeling automatons after all. Not yet. Just give the industry a few more years. They're working on it.

If only we could pinpoint the "hubris gene" in our own makeup and be rid of it once and for all. In such projects of genetic engineering we see the "Dr. Deer" school of veterinary medicine shining its light on the factory farm—not only an explicit acknowledgment of animal pain but, in effect, a conspiracy to destroy the evidence.

Here we have an industry dominated today by a few conglomerates like

ConAgra, Smithfield, IBP (Iowa Beef Packers), and Archer Daniels Midland, raising and slaughtering most livestock in America. For a generation they have been tampering with the genetic coding of livestock. A little leaner here, a little fatter there, this creature's flesh a bit more pale, this one's a bit more red. Hormones and antibiotics are added to the mix to bring growth up to maximum speed, so that your average pig today exists six months upon the earth from suckling to slaughter, and your chickens are hatched, tortured, and ready to serve inside two months. It was these very technologies (along with endless government subsidies to the industry) that concentrated agricultural production and rendered most smaller farms unable to compete with the agricultural monoliths.

But now it turns out all this genetic tampering has left the creatures more nervous and afraid than before. So it's back to the lab to figure that one out.

Then the "stress gene" is located, the source of this costly "syndrome" spreading like a contagion. But there is a cure! Yet more genetic manipulation. Splice and breed away that troublesome strand of DNA and you don't even have to bother with "environmental enrichment" anymore, all those costly and time-consuming methods of "tender loving care" Dr. Grandin advised back in the 1980s. Instead of redesigning the factory farm to suit the animal, they are redesigning the animal to suit the factory farm. One producer, Babcock Swine, Inc., of Minnesota, has already declared victory. As of 1994, the company boasts, "all Babcock breeding stock is certified 100% free of the stress gene."[138] No need for toys at Babcock.

European consumers alone seem to have qualms about all this, leaving their diplomatic and trade representatives to deal with truculent demands from the American cattlemen and hog farmers' lobby to open up their markets. As I write, this is the big issue before the European Community, involving not only genetically altered livestock but crops. I don't know about the crop issue, but I do hope that where animal products are concerned the Europeans will hold their ground. Their suspicions are correct. The whole sorry business is a case of corporate America at its worst, bringing that unique, bumptious audacity even into nature's greatest mysteries.

To rest our case, Mr. Budiansky, Professors Carruthers, Kennedy, and the others need not worry about sentimentality getting the best of us in our treatment of animals. The creatures are "paying," all right. Mankind is now taking away their natures, their capacity to feel and to suffer and to want to live—the very capacity these same theorists denied animals ever had.

The lure of cold theory can be seen even in Dr. Grandin, who, it turns out, is one of Mr. Budiansky's readers. His writings, she tells us in *Thinking in Pictures,* had "a profound effect" on her outlook. Previously she had been troubled by her involvement in livestock production, serving the industry even while knowing that animals think and suffer. After her first visit to a slaughterhouse, she thought, "This should not be happening in a civilized society." She wrote in her diary that night, "If hell exists, I am in it."[139] Then she came across Mr. Budiansky's writings, which seemed to present "a middle ground between supporters of animal rights, who believe that animals are equal to humans, and the Cartesian view, which treats animals as machines with no feelings."[140]

A high tribute to his powers of obfuscation, but a compliment Mr. Budiansky does not return by taking into account any of Dr. Grandin's insights. He denies any kind of conscious thought or feeling in animals, period—in pictures or anything else. Yet in a strange twist, her insights are being used to put his falsehoods into practice. His "mere pain" theories stand discredited even as the darkness of "blindly amoral evolution" descends upon our farms.

> DR. GRANDIN: "Animals have the ability to generalize, even though they do not use language. . . . Autistic people like myself . . . would be denied the ability to think by scientists who maintain that language is essential for thinking."[141]
>
> MR. BUDIANSKY: "[L]anguage is so intimately tied to consciousness that the two seem inseparable. The 'monitor' that runs through our brains all the time we are awake is one that runs in language. The continual sense that we are aware of what is going on in a deliberate fashion is a sense that depends on words to give it shape and substance."[142]
>
> DR. GRANDIN: "Studies by Jane Goodall, Dian Fossey, and many other researchers have shown very clearly that primates such as chimpanzees and gorillas can think, though few scientists would also concede that farm animals have thinking abilities. . . . My experience is that these animals think in discrete visual images.

They are able to make an association between a visual image
stored in their memory and what they are seeing in the present."[143]

MR. BUDIANSKY: "The huge difference in the sheer number of
symbols that humans use in human language versus the number
that apes can acquire in training . . . suggests that the difference
is not one of just degree (say memory capacity) but of fundamental underlying process."[144]

DR. GRANDIN: "When cows are weaned, both the cows and calves
bellow for about twenty-four hours. Some calves bellow until they
are hoarse. Cattle will also bellow for departed penmates. . . . I
have seen Holstein steers bellowing to penmates that were
departing in a truck. The cattle that were left behind watched as
their fat penmates walked up the ramp to get on the truck that
would take them to Burgerland. The two steers stared at the truck
as it turned out of the parking lot. One stretched out his neck and
bellowed at the truck, and his penmate on the truck bellowed
back."[145]

MR. BUDIANSKY: "Sadness, pity, sympathy, condolence, self-pity,
ennui, woe, heartbreak, distress, worry, apprehension, dejection, grief, wistfulness, pensiveness, mournfulness, brooding, rue,
regret, misery, despair—all express shades of the pain of sadness
whose full meaning comes only from our ability to reflect on their
meaning, not just their feelings."[146]

They cannot both be right. Dr. Grandin in *Thinking in Pictures* is telling
us that those two bellowing cows actually felt sadness and fear at their separation. Mr. Budiansky in *If a Lion Could Talk* is telling us that no such feelings are possible. She is telling us that animals do think in their way, a
conscious and meaningful way, in the memories of places, scents, and experiences. He is saying they can't think without language. She is describing a
world of real terror and real torment. He is saying that those emotions cannot
be, that this "wonderful gift and wonderful curse" of emotion has been
reserved only for us.

His own book, like similar studies, might better have been called *Thinking in Theory*. They amount to that and nothing more, so many vain conjectures piled one atop the other until we are all standing up there on "creation's

pedestal" proudly gazing down upon creation, a summit of sanctimony from which all the creeping things of the earth look so small, so worthless, so disposable, their suffering so mere and maudlin and meaningless.

Science conducted with this outlook has today become a project of violence and aggression toward nature instead of cooperative inquiry, of relentless assault instead of respect and revelation, and one fears the worst evils have yet to come. A project, as Saint Bonaventure described the spirit, of "speculation without devotion, investigation without wonder, observation without joy, work without piety, knowledge without love, understanding without humility, endeavor without grace."[147]

Missing above all is love, which the theorists mistake for utility. Love for animals, like our own love for one another, comes in seeing the worth and beauty of others apart from *us*, in understanding that the creatures need not be our equals to be our humble brothers in suffering and sadness and the story of life. We are asked, in theory, to believe that all these other beings in our midst dumbly traipse and dart and swim and fly about, preprogrammed to forage, hunt, and mate, denied even the smallest share in the world's gifts and griefs—a dreary, self-centered assumption that goes against everything we know about the Programmer himself, the Lord of Life who has made each one with care, counted them all, and delivered them into our hands.

I picture the lion, if he could talk, shaking his great mane in disbelief at the effrontery of it, and of all the canned hunts, baiting, high-tech safaris, factory farms, whale and dolphin slaughters, and endless array of other exploitative and cowardly things such theories are used to justify. Maybe he would advise them all to make better use of their own minds, and to just leave him be in his glorious lionhood.

—e—

DELIVER ME FROM
MY NECESSITIES

*How do the beasts groan! The herds of cattle are perplexed, because
they have no pasture; yea, the flocks of sheep are made desolate. O Lord,
to thee will I cry. . . . The beasts of the field cry also unto thee: for the
rivers of waters are dried up, and the fire hath devoured the pastures of
the wilderness.*

JOEL 1:18–20

Standing outside a factory farm, the first question that comes to mind is not a
moral but a practical one: Where is everybody? Where are the owners, the
farmers, the livestock managers, the extra hands, anybody? I have been driving
around the North Carolina countryside on a Thursday afternoon in January
2001, pulling in at random to six hog farms, and have yet to find a single farmer
or any other living soul. It is as if one of those vengeful hurricanes that pound
the Carolinas has been spotted, and I am the only one who didn't get word.
Who runs these places? Why aren't they here? Who's looking after the animals?

There are so many factory farms around here that they are easy to miss. I
doubt that the average visitor just passing through even knows what they are,
any more than the airline passenger descending into Raleigh knows that
inside each one of those barrack-like structures scattered below are four or
five hundred animals never let out. Exactly identical, differing only in the
number of long, drab, concrete and metal buildings that make up each of the
state's thirty-four hundred or so hog farms, these places seem by design to
repel any natural human interest or curiosity.

Murphy Farm 3547, on Route 41 southeast of Raleigh, has a four-row barracks a few hundred yards from the road—some kind of storage facility, as one might assume in a quick glance from the road, maybe garages for tractors, combines, and threshers. Mr. Holmes Finishing Complex on Route 242 has at least eight barracks, and despite the "Restricted Area—No Trespassing" sign there is not a trace of Mr. Holmes, his employees, or anyone else. Prestage Farms, just past Jamba's Exotic Ranch on Route 210 south, where evidently you can hunt some captive deer, buffalo and llama, has concealed its facilities with a wall of freshly planted pine trees, so that one notices nothing at all except the "P-16 Complex" sign pointing down a long dirt road. Venturing in, the entire complex appears unmanned except for one workman I see across a pond, fixing or adjusting something. Clear Run Farms off Route 41 would be better named Self-Run Farms: Not even a car or truck parked outside. The herd isn't "running" today either. Through a small airhole in the canvas siding of one barracks, all I see are five hundred startled faces staring at the eye that is suddenly staring at them.

It happened so quickly, this vanishing of hog and farmer alike. When I was last here, in 1992, there were a third as many hogs being raised as there are today—about three million then, ten million now. In the mid-1980s North Carolina had a hog population of around one and a half million. Go back another decade and we're talking fewer than a million of the creatures, most of them, in the Arcadian 1970s, actually visible, actually outdoors. Yet looking around today one has just the opposite impression, and if you did not know the reality you would wonder what plague had come to carry all of them off. Ten million pigs, more than the state's human population, and you can travel North Carolina end to end without seeing a single snout except through the grating of those triple-decker trucks constantly rumbling by.

Murphy is a big name in these parts, the hundreds of Murphy Family Farms a monument to the lifework of Wendell Murphy, a 62-year-old former state senator and the man generally credited with the concept of mass-confinement hog farming. Inspired by the poultry industry, which today can pack as many as a quarter million birds into a single building, he realized that with just a bit more ingenuity hog farmers could also eliminate the space, labor, and cost of raising pigs in open lots. He saw the possibility of barring their movements entirely—saving money on feed since confined pigs burn off less energy and require fewer calories than free-range pigs, deploying vaccines and antibiotics to control the diseases borne of mass confinement, and, five millennia after the first pig was domesticated, solving the problem that the animals are, well, animate. The crucial breakthrough came in the early 1960s when he conceived of how, by the simple device of slatted floors, their refuse could be collected underneath a climate-controlled confinement facility, flushed through a drainage channel, mixed with chemicals, and then sprayed onto the soil or carried off—somewhere—by the winds.

For Mr. Murphy and others who soon followed his example, in America and across the world, this innovation meant riches. For the pigs, it meant that not only must they be confined forever, now they could no longer have even straw to lie on. Straw would only clog the slats and pipes and mar the system. The creatures now live their whole lives on metal and concrete.

The state's forty-eight hundred active or abandoned waste lagoons have stirred bitter feelings here and elsewhere because of the pervasive odor, the ammonia discharge into soil and water and air, and the general suspicion that they just might have something to do with a high incidence of respiratory, gastrointestinal, and infant sicknesses among people who live nearby. Earthen pits filled with millions of gallons of urine and excrement, stretching at the larger farms two or three times the length of a football field, and collecting yearly at least five times the waste of the state's human population, the lagoons present one final challenge to the pork industry.

The pigs have all been locked away, never feeling soil or sunshine. The farms practically run themselves, making hogs, per unit, America's most profitable agricultural product. Scientific efficiency is transforming industry and creature alike, from the splicing of genes to the smoother sliceability of ham. There remains only the refuse to worry about, a final force of nature still uncontained and the last visible reminder of their existence as living beings. If only they didn't have to defecate so much, if only that need could be ignored as all of their other needs have been, the whole system would be just perfect.

Managerial Intensity

The offices administering these farms are the picture of modern corporate comfort. I stopped by Carroll's Foods, in a place called Warsaw two hours southeast of Raleigh. You can't miss it. Turn off Interstate 40, follow the procession of trucks past Wendy's, McDonald's, KFC (Kentucky Fried Chicken), and other town landmarks until the road narrows and you see a giant feed mill. Across from that is a sleek new office complex with landscaped grounds and a parking lot filled with Lexuses, SUVs, and BMWs. Entering Carroll's, you step out of rural America into the tiled lobby of what might be some prestigious law firm or rising dot-com, everything so stylish and spotless, so glassy and brassy and obviously expensive. The place sparkles.

A plaque in the lobby honors the man who started it all sixty years ago in the old headquarters nearby, a small red brick building now serving as a laboratory to inspect feed, and turned it into this cutting-edge, quarter-billion-dollar enterprise. No longer with us, his name was O. S. Carroll, and "His past creates our present and inspires our future."

As it turned out, the company's future after Mr. Carroll's passing was to be bought in 1999 by a rival company, Smithfield Foods, Inc., of Virginia. In 2000, Smithfield obtained Murphy Family Farms as well for $470 million in cash and assumed debt, making Wendell Murphy, already worth $750 million according to *Forbes,* among the richest men in the state and, as the *Raleigh News & Observer* calls him, "Boss Hog."[1] Both Carroll's Foods and Murphy Family Farms kept their names, but, like a dozen other pork producers Smithfield has acquired throughout America, are wholly owned subsidiaries of what is now the world's largest producer of the world's most popular meat.

The former Smithfield Ham and Products Company, a family enterprise tracing back to colonial times, this single entity brings to market 7 million pigs a year just in North Carolina. Ranked 341 on the Fortune 500 list, they report annual sales of five to six billion dollars.[2] They own 700,000 sows, of our national stock of four and a half million. They slay 82,300 pigs every twenty-four hours—not quite one every second—of the 355,000 killed across America to give us this day our daily meat.[3] They run eight packing plants, and a few years ago spent $76 million to raise up the world's largest slaughterhouse, the final destination of 32,000 creatures a day, down in Tar Heel on the Cape Fear River. If you buy Lean Generation Pork, or any pork product under the name of Gwaltney, Valleydale, Dinner Bell, Sunnyland, ReaLean, Patrick's Pride, Ember Farms, or Circle Four, that's them.

What happened here was a synergy of two amoral ideas. Mr. Murphy's vision had prepared the way. Once the "live" had been taken out of livestock, and all regard for the well-being of the animals had been abandoned, the next challenge was how to take the farmer out of farming. This Smithfield has accomplished through a strategy known as vertical integration. Smithfield president Joseph W. Luter III explains: "What we did in the pork industry is what Perdue and Tyson did in the poultry business. Vertical integration gives you high quality, consistent products with consistent genetics. And the only way to do that is to control the process from the farm to the packing plant."[4]

Similar to what we used to call "monopoly," vertical integration consists in absorbing rivals until only a few remain. Around here, Smithfield controls the farms. Smithfield controls transportation. Smithfield controls the packing plants. Through contracts with the grocers to which Smithfield sells some three billion pounds of fresh pork a year, including a deal in 2000 to sell Wal-Mart its "case-ready" pork, they control much of the market itself.

With other corporate farms such as its last sizable competitor, Premium Standard, Smithfield also controls advertising. Through the National Pork Producers Council they spend some sixty or seventy million a year—much of that money extracted in mandatory fees paid by small farmers—to promote "the other white meat" and sustain the current craze for the super-lean pork that only intensive farming can produce.[5] And, finally, through its sheer size as a feature of the North Carolina economy and unsparing political contributions, Smithfield usually gets its way in the state's legislature and regulatory agencies.

All of these trends, in the jargon of the university animal-science departments—themselves controlled by the livestock industry with grants and endowments—are driven by the need for ever greater "managerial intensity." Modern livestock production requires "highly coordinated flows of sophisticatedly produced raw materials arriving at a huge processing facility. . . . [the] movement to a more attribute specific raw material; the advancement of technology; the need to certify production methods; economies of scale in larger production and processing facilities; the need to reduce inefficiencies originating in hogs."[6]

Of course small farmers, doing things so much less "sophisticatedly" than their corporate competitors, cannot survive in this environment. Hog farms, once upon a time, were part of larger farms raising other livestock, feed, and a cash crop. A farmer might raise a few hundred hogs or just a few dozen to supplement his income—like young Harry S. Truman, who years later could remember the names of his pigs. As pork became more popular in the last generation many farmers turned exclusively to hog rearing, only to find themselves overwhelmed by the large-scale intensive operations. Personal care of livestock requires time, money, land, and character, and the Smithfields of the industry can always do it a lot faster for a lot less. Against these forces independent farmers have about as much say in their fate as the hogs have in theirs. In one recent year, reports our Department of Agriculture, 25,280 independent farms either phased out hog production or shut down altogether.[7] In North Carolina, most who survived did so by signing up as contract farmers working for Smithfield.

Contract farming works much like the fast-food franchises so successful at the other end of the meat business. The farmer applies to become a Smithfield "grower." On that basis he is able to secure a loan to build his new factory farm according to precise Smithfield specifications. He buys and is liable for everything, the barns, the machinery, the land, the lagoons. Smithfield provides only the pigs, the premixed feed, and a strict regimen of Smithfield-approved methods.

The larger farms have "farrow to finish" facilities with sows on-site, the smaller ones just do the finishing, operating very much like storage lockers: Smithfield trucks come by to drop off a thousand or so 15-pound piglets, who are driven down a chute into the finishing barns. Six months later, when their hour has come, other trucks pull up and the same thousand pigs, minus the usual casualties and each now at the market weight of 250 pounds, are driven up the chute and it's off to Tar Heel.

The system actually works out pretty well for farmers, as long as they do not mind being farmers in name only and, in effect, hired hands on their own property. Your average Smithfield contractor makes about sixty or seventy thousand dollars a year, guaranteed. A big farm might gross a quarter million. Better still, all the risks of livestock agriculture are suddenly gone, doubtless the most tempting aspect of the New Agriculture, as it is called, even for farmers otherwise wary of the deal. Smithfield, on the other end of the bargain, gets its 82,300 units per day, paying a fixed cost to farmers for their services while eliminating the costs of land, facilities, insurance, taxes, liability for waste disposal, and all the rest. Indeed the company makes even more money by its involvement in manufacturing and selling to farmers the factory barns and equipment required under the contract—another example of what an investment analyst calls Smithfield's "masterful job of diversifying their business."[8]

The difference between this and traditional corporate monopoly is that no conspiracy was needed. Just as Smithfield, and ConAgra with its own 72,600 kills per day across America, and Premium Standard with its 56,000, and all of our giant livestock companies protest in their defense, it was market driven, and might have come to pass even without malleable politicians and enormous public subsidies.[9] Corporate farming arose for the same reason all large corporations arise, as men like Donald Tyson, Frank Perdue, and Wendell Murphy realized that animals, too, could be produced on an economy of scale in which costs per unit diminished the more units they produced. Mass confinement met vertical integration to provide the cheapest goods for the greatest number in the most efficient way, and consumers rewarded it.

THE NEW AGRICULTURE

Running Carroll's Foods these days is a gentleman named F. J. "Sonny" Faison, with whom I had arranged a meeting. He lets me wait awhile, but I can see him and his impressive quarters from the reception room through the glass interior wall separating us. Starting here twenty-eight years ago in the old headquarters, he now presides over Carroll's from an office of mayoral dignity, dominated by an enormous wall unit, a credenza, and a desk of thickly varnished solid cherry. Mr. Faison is a distinguished-looking fellow of sixty or so, with silver hair and black pinstripe suit, reclining in a very ample executive leather chair as he talks on the phone and looks out the window, swiveling now and then to cast an expressionless glance at his waiting visitor. Though not from a farming family himself, his people have been in North Carolina since the 1600s, and just up the road is a town called Faison. A few years ago he had the honor of presenting a Smithfield turkey to President Clinton in the Rose Garden. He's a respected man around here, an employer to thousands running the enterprise on which the town and county depend, and carries himself as such.

Through the wide, full-length windows on the opposite side of his office, I can also see the lawn and trees and mill outdoors. This pleasant architectural touch is employed throughout the building. Even the smaller offices have full-sized windows to let the sun in. The corridors and waiting room have an atrium effect, roofed by steepled glass so that there is always blue sky above. The effect is to brighten things up. It takes the stuffiness out of the workplace. It lends a sense of freedom and openness to the employees. They like openness at Carroll's. They like the sunshine.

He comes out with a big, friendly "Hi, Sonny Faison!" ushers me into his suite, sits me down and then says nothing despite increasingly desperate promptings. No small talk. No "So how was your trip here?" What do I want?

A couple of minutes' fumbling about family farming, trends in agriculture and whatever else jumped to mind finally yields this observation. "Today, agriculture is simply producing and distributing proteins and food for the country," says Sonny. "Farming continues to get more sophisticated, based on science. It's evolved, like every other business. There's a passion in this country for the small family farmer, but it just happens that process has changed. And I think what most people do is cling to that same old vision of what farming is, rather than what the New Agriculture is. And of course when you look at agriculture, you look at it on a strictly business format. You don't look at it as a way of life. Farming today is a business arrangement. And that's the way we look at it, and we've got to make a profit. Today it's easy to see that in this country the food is the cheapest anywhere in the world. It seems like we overproduce everything. The biggest problem in agriculture today is just that, overproduction."

In the new *aggicultcha,* as it comes out in Sonny's rich Carolina accent, small farmers simply cannot offer superior quality at a competitive price. The only reason any small-scale livestock farms have survived at all, he tells me, is that the federal government keeps resuscitating them with billions of dollars in annual subsidies. Demand for pork is greater than ever, and worldwide expected to double within a generation. That's one reason Smithfield has located so many farms and plants in North Carolina and recently erected that 50,000-acre complex in Utah under its Circle Four brand name. They want to be near ports on our east and west coasts in anticipation of massive exports to come, especially to Asia where population will likely rise to four billion by 2030 as demand for meat quadruples.[10] Consumers, meanwhile, are getting more particular about the meats they buy and the prices they're willing to pay. This means that for any company to succeed it must produce in colossal quantities while guaranteeing, in the mantra of the New Agriculture, "consistency."

Perdue and Tyson, as always, have set the standard: "Poultry people have had a consistent product for years," Joseph Luter told *National Hog Farmer,* "Pork people have not." Consumers want a brand name they can always count on, and "you can't build a brand name unless you have a consistent product. McDonald's may or may not have the best hamburger in the world, but it is consistent, consistent, consistent."[11] Richard Poulson, Smithfield's vice president for media affairs, explained this *idée fixe* to me when I called to arrange this sit-down with Sonny. "What we find is that consumers will not put up with the undisciplined way hogs are raised on small farms. They want products that are uniform in appearance, size, and quality. They want specialized types of meat. They want their meat a certain color. They want it lean."

What they want, they must have. And consistent texture in the meat requires consistent torture at the farm. Small farmers, as seen from Smithfield, are hopelessly undisciplined, hopelessly behind the curve in consumer tastes. In Mr. Poulson's analogy, to persist in small-scale farming today is like trying to make cars in one's own backyard, refusing to automate and mass produce and get with the global program. Smithfield, he tells me, is like the Ford Motor of livestock agriculture. "Our farms are run by Ph.D.'s, guys in white coats. We're the biggest company, and big is not bad. Big is efficient. If you wanted to add a couple of dollars to the price of a pork chop at the counter, you can do it very quickly. You can put them at free range."

Nor is it just the cost of raising the animals that has rendered traditional farming obsolete. Small farmers today can hardly afford to kill them. The final cost in hog farming comes in the purchase of "shackle space." To each farmer shipping his pigs to be slaughtered and processed, the packing plant is selling the disposable commodity of time and space, like a hotel. Overproduction of hogs in a given region gives packers the edge. They can keep raising their prices because the line is long and if you don't buy that space then step aside because somebody else will. In the U.S., the last of our independent hog farmers were nearly ruined a few years ago when supply overtook demand, driven in part by a corporate rush to build more confinement operations before new state and local restrictions could take effect. Shackle space was at a premium and the small producers were going broke, reprieved in the end only by another few billion in "emergency" funds. Corporate farmers don't have that problem because they own the plants, production is so precisely calibrated to demand, and they have enough money to ride out the inevitable ups and downs in price and demand.

"Here's the thing that's so hard to understand about agriculture," Sonny explains. "It's ten months [before slaughter] when we start deciding how many hogs we're going to grow. Ten months, that's how long it takes to grow 'em. So we can't stop. When we produce 'em, we got to sell 'em, no matter what the price. And as farmers get bigger, they'll understand that you don't need to produce more than is needed. And when there's not so many farmers, there won't be as much overproduction, because they'll have more information and more ability to control the market. It's all a supply-and-demand price question, that's all it is. The meat business in this country is just about perfect, uncontrolled, supply-and-demand free enterprise. And it continues to get more and more sophisticated, based on science. Only the least-cost producer survives in agriculture."

So corporate farming, I remark, is inevitable, and it's always going to be like this, only more so, and the future of the livestock business is right here in Warsaw, North Carolina—"growing" heavier animals with leaner meat in smaller spaces on bigger farms. "It will continue on just this way, yes sir," says Sonny.

A mix of tolerance and pity describes the Smithfield attitude toward the traditional farmer. They'll let him linger on awhile, sponging off the government until his affairs are in order and he is ready to face his final extinction. At the same time they do not mind at all if consumers still think of their own corporate operations as small farms like the ones Smithfield has been systematically killing off. They understand the deep sentimental value of family farming, with its connotations of land stewardship and decent treatment of animals. That's why so many of our meat labels still bear the images of happy little farms with animals grazing afield. That's why the New Agriculture still trades on the reputation of the old with its countrified corporate brand names, all of this "Murphy Family Farms," "Clear Run Farms," "Sunnyland," and "Patrick's Pride" when the more apt designations would be Murphy Factory Farms, Never Run Farms, Sunlessland, and Patrick's Shame.

Only two forces stand in the way of the New Agriculture, Sonny warns: more meddling by government, and more harassment from environmental groups over the alleged affects of intensive farming on public health. Does he worry about this? A grave look comes over Sonny. "Oh yeah, we worry a lot about that."

Fears over the public health hazards have already brought a moratorium from the North Carolina General Assembly on the construction of new mass-confinement facilities. Iowa, Oklahoma, and a few other states have since taken up similar measures. Smithfield fears more laws to come, leading perhaps to a phasing out of mass-confinement operations altogether. Mr. Luter, a Smithfield heir who runs the business from Aspen, Colorado, and a Park Avenue office in New York City, has threatened to move more operations abroad, and has already begun building factory farms in Mexico, Brazil, and Poland ("the Iowa of Europe"[12]). With so much government regulation already, he recently griped to the *Des Moines Register,* "there's not a whole lot of opportunities left in this country. Farmers think we're robbing them blind, and the environmentalists would put us back in caves if they could. . . . There are so many people with an agenda."[13]

The pork industry's own agenda lately has involved seeking a federal subsidy of more than a billion dollars annually to pay for the costs of environmental damage left by its own untreated sewage. Proposed by Republican Representative Frank Lucas of Oklahoma for the 2002 federal budget, this additional aid from taxpayers is justified, says one North Carolina hog farmer, because thanks to his industry "We eat cheaper than anyone else in the world."[14] And it's true, meat in this country certainly seems cheaper than anywhere else. You just have to overlook the costs that don't appear on the label, each consumer's share of the tens of billions of dollars in annual subsidies Americans pay to keep their meat so cheap.

For Sonny, public concern over the sewage and spillover is a problem of misinformation "promoted mainly by extreme environmentalists." This propaganda campaign peaked after Hurricane Floyd in the fall of 1999, when floods in eastern North Carolina entombed hundreds of thousands of hogs in their pens and more than two million chickens and turkeys in their cages. Hundreds of lagoons burst with a toxic purple swill of waste and blood and bloated carcasses, requiring still more federal money for cleanup and repair. It looked bad, in pictures published across the world, including a particularly poignant one on the front page of the *New York Times* showing thirty-five pigs swimming and clinging to the roof of a factory barn. But in the end, Sonny asks, what harm did it really do? Today, he tells me, everything's right back to normal.

"You want to talk frankly about the floods? Have you ever heard of Ocean View, that one big spill?"

Ocean View is an aptly named farm whose giant lagoon burst in 1995, excreting 25 million gallons of nitrous sludge (compared to the 11 million gallons of oil spilled by the *Exxon Valdez*) into the state's New River and killing some eight to ten million fish.[15]

"All right, what damage did that do? Just as many fish in the New River today as there was before. I mean, I'm not a scientist, but I know that the most pristine waters in this country, probably, flow right through this area. Now how is that possible with the hogs we've got around? We just don't contaminate. We just don't believe it. It's just like that spill. That spill was a terrible thing, and I don't know the true situation there, but I think that probably a lot of it was mismanagement as much as any other thing. I don't say we should exonerate the hog business from that. But yet once it spilled out and was gone, there was no lasting results from that. It wasn't toxic waste that got out. It wasn't the greatest thing in the world. It kills fish, but the fish grew back. The river's as good as it ever was. Beach property is higher than it's ever been. I mean, when you really try to look at lasting damage, it's hard to prove."

In Sonny's vision of the world—Sonnyland, as we might as well call it—everything appears in the collective, and everything just keeps growing. Hogs grow, no matter what privations you inflict upon them. Fish and other aquatic creatures grow back, no matter what filth you pour into the river. People keep growing too, no matter what's in the meat they eat or in the soil and air and water around them. Property values grow, companies grow, profits grow, exports grow, life keeps going on if only we all stay focused on what matters, which is business.

We haven't quite connected, Sonny and I. An idle remark about Wendell Murphy being the first to think of all this only makes matters worse. I've raised a sore point. "For one thing, I wouldn't say it was Mr. Murphy that started that. I'd say Carroll's Foods. We've always said we were the first. We were using hog growers early on. In 1974 we started putting everything in-house. We phased out all outside production to total confinement. But even prior to that, Mr. Carroll, the founder of this business, had some of the first confinement buildings—they were called 'hog parlors' back then—in the country."

All right, then, so Carroll was first, not Murphy. Can't we all just *share* the credit? I decide to roll the dice by asking what these "parlors" are like for the animals. I understand the economics of mass confinement, I tell Sonny. And I'll grant that if one company is going to kill a million pigs every twelve days, there is no kind way to do it. But man to man, I ask, isn't there something, you know, just a little sad about locking millions of animals away like that?

"They love it," Sonny replies.

"They do?"

"Yeah. They don't mind at all. They're in state-of-the-art confinement facilities. The conditions that we keep these animals in are much more humane than when they were out in the field. Today they're in housing that is environmentally controlled in many respects. And the feed is right there for them all the time, and water, fresh water. They're looked after in some of the best conditions, because the healthier, and [more] content that animal, the better it grows. So we're very interested in their well-being—*up to an extent.*"

I had been hoping for a look at these state-of-the-art facilities, and finally the invitation is offered. Just then Sonny springs from his chair, declaring "Come on, I'm going to show you one of our farms right now!"

STATE OF THE ART

We left Carroll's in the biggest car in town from Sonny's private garage and are now pulling into Farm 2105 a few miles away. One of about thirteen hundred farms in the company's regional network, the place is owned, he tells me, by one Perry Smith. There is a lovely white house with a large front porch. On the lush green lawn is a child's swing set. Fifty yards away stand eight brand-new, state-of-the-art confinement facilities. On approach, before the sounds can reach you, one's first impression is a tidy picture of pastoral prosperity. It is such a pretty snapshot of the New Agriculture that suddenly I realize why I've been granted a tour. They've got a showpiece farm.

"See," says Sonny, "that farm doesn't look like it's bothering anyone, does it? Wouldn't mind living here myself. You talk to Perry. For him it's a good income. It's tuition for his kids, maybe some vacation money and that kind of thing. He's just tickled to death."

Perry is not here, however, if he exists at all. This morning, exactly one person is here looking after four thousand incarcerated animals. It takes us ten minutes of driving back and forth around the complex to find him. And he's just making the rounds, one of Smithfield's farm inspectors who comes by once a week to see that everything's in order.

"How's it going?" Sonny inquires.

"Oh, pretty good," he reports. "But lots of tail biting today."

"Well, they're about done anyway."

"Yeah, just about."

As they chat by the car I ask if I might step inside the hog parlor for a quick look, and opening the door I ignite a squealing panic that sweeps across the barn. They draw back, as if I am a wolf. At least they try to draw back. There isn't room to draw back. At twenty per pen, and twenty-five pens each at 7.5 square feet, they can only crouch and huddle and try to hide behind one another.

"They don't get many visitors," says Sonny from outside. "But they'll quiet down."

And he's right, they do. A moment later a stillness fills the barn. You can hear the breathing of five hundred animals as slowly they begin pressing forward. Those in the nearest pen edge up for a sniff. Eyes appear between the slats of the fences. Heads pop up in the back, then more, and more, until there is an audible press forward, two thousand hooves on concrete, everybody now rising and jostling and straining to see the god. Some are up on their hind legs, forelegs curled over the fences of their pens, ears half-erect, eyes filled with fear and life and what any man with eyes of his own to see will know as intelligence. Temple Grandin's words come to mind. They are just like puppies.

Why do they come forward like that when they're so afraid? I ask Sonny.

"They're interested. They're bored. But when you close the door, they'll go back to sleep."

I reach down to stroke a snout sniffing my feet. But the "stroke snout" impulse from my brain has barely reached my hand before the hysteria begins again, a split-second stampede back, away, almost upward against the walls like a splash of bodies. Then the stillness, then the breathing and stirring and again the scramble forward to see and sniff their visitor.

Closing the door on five hundred faces, I wonder how Perry gets any sleep himself over in that pretty new house of his. How does a man rest at night knowing that in this strawless dungeon of pens are all of these living creatures under his care, never leaving except to die, hardly able to turn or lie down, horror-stricken by every opening of the door, biting and fighting and going mad? This is how the hurricane found them too, all packed in like this, and what was that scene like?

We left the Smith place and headed for Farm 2149, a "multi-site, all-in/all-out stocking" facility, where once again, upon arrival, the search begins for traces of human life. Only the vultures are here to greet us, hovering above the interrupted meal of a dead possum lying in the dirt parking lot. And this time we can't even show ourselves around because enclosing the entire complex, except for the lagoon, is a 10-foot-high barbed-wire fence—designed not to prevent escapes, but to keep the curious away and all human sympathy at a distance.

What's the attrition rate in your average farm? I ask Sonny, noticing other vultures swirling over a barn some distance from the possum. "Oh, we lose some, the sows mostly." What becomes of them? "They get rendered. The ones with disease, a truck comes by every day and we take 'em to the dead hole."

He gestures to an area beyond the farm, indicating there's a dead hole nearby. There are lots of dead holes in North Carolina, mass graves holding the remains of hundreds of thousands who never even made it to Tar Heel, the corpses each enshrouded in an airtight bag. Part of the federally funded emergency cleanup after Hurricane Floyd consisted of incinerating and disposing of fields full of bodies into the dead holes.

Rendering—the grinding-up of animal remains into livestock feed and other products such as gelatin for Jell-O and Gummy Bears—is still permitted for the pork industry. The U.S. Food and Drug Administration prohibits the rendering of most ruminant animals in fear of "mad cow" disease. But swine and poultry remains may still be fed to their own kind and to cows, sheep, and goats. And the remains of those other animals, our share of the 40,000 metric tons of slaughterhouse leavings collected and rendered every week across the world,[16] may legally be fed to pigs and birds. It is confidently assumed within the industry that no porcine equivalent of bovine spongiform encephalopathy will ever appear. And they just can't see any other reason not to feed dead herbivores to live ones.

There's a little office up front. Sonny gets out and knocks on the door, which is locked. No answer. He walks over to the fence, hollering, "Hello? Hello?" Still no answer, except for a wave of squeals and snorts across the complex. Next we drive around back, where he gets out again, suppressing his irritation. When he's in his country gentleman mode Sonny can be real friendly-like, but I have the impression he can also get mean in a hurry. "Hello? Hello?"

There is movement. A door opens and out comes a slight man of thirty or so named Roberto, which we know only because of the employee badge on his shirt. Roberto doesn't speak English. He can only stand there holding a pail on the other side of the fence helplessly nodding and shrugging at Sonny's questions: "Is anyone here? Do you know who I am? Can you get someone else to come here? Is . . . there . . . anyone . . . else . . . *here?*"

Roberto retreats into the barn. Maybe he's gone to get someone. So we wait in the car, in a lovely nook between the barbed-wire fence and the waste

lagoon, and time passes. "We got a lot o' hawdworkin' people workin' fo' us,"
is Sonny's commentary on the situation.

Perhaps Roberto came across one of the ads that Carroll's runs on its
Web site and on flyers in the poorest neighborhoods of North and South
America: "The Pork Production Career You Are Looking for Is Looking for
You!!! If you're looking for a fulfilling swine production career that offers
opportunities for professional development, look no further. Carroll's Foods is
one of the largest pork producers in the world. We have swine farms in North
and South Carolina, Virginia, Utah, Iowa, Mexico and Brazil."[17] Some nine
thousand Mexicans who learned of this chance of a lifetime are today
employed on North Carolina hog farms under a special temporary visa program run by the North Carolina Growers Association in cooperation with the
Immigration and Naturalization Service.[18]

The 2000 federal census revealed a growth of 700 percent in the His-
panic population of North Carolina, the largest of any southern state. It's the
same in parts of other states, towns in Iowa and South Dakota and Utah that
today look like the rural outskirts of Sao Paulo and Mexico City, employing
altogether hundreds of thousands of resident or temporary aliens. To run our
modern factory farms and charnel houses, you need people actually willing to
do the soul-killing work it requires. In America we have turned to our brothers to the south. Just as in Saint Thomas More's *Utopia* the bloodletting is left
to the slaves, today, here and in Western Europe, we have our immigrants.

Packing plants have long relied on the unskilled labor of immigrants, but
only now are their services also needed in the rearing of livestock. They make
fine "associates." They don't ask a lot of questions. They don't make
demands. Deportable at any moment, they don't start unions or any of that
nonsense. They keep to themselves, especially the illegal ones, and don't
make trouble. Typically they don't know the first thing about pigs or other
farm animals, either. But what does that matter when there is no tending or
herding or caring to be done? All you need is hawdworkin' people, people
without choices, people so poor and desperate that seven or eight dollars an
hour for cutting throats and filling dead holes seems like a break in life. Best
of all, immigrants disappear. When they've saved enough and endured
enough, you can send them back and feel like you've done them a favor. We
don't have to see them, either.

Still no sign of Roberto. Finally Sonny reaches for the car speakerphone
and dials for help.

"Carroll's Foods, Mr. Faison's office."

"Yeah, Teresa, this is Sonny. I'm down at Farm, let's see, two-one-four-nine. Can you call and find out if anyone's here to let us in?"

We circle round to the front office again to wait with the vultures. Teresa calls back. Someone's on the way.

Does he inspect the farms much himself these days? I ask. "Not nearly as much as I'd like to," says Sonny, trying to sound engaged and happy to be here with me. "I should try to get out more often, I guess."

This outing is dragging on more than Sonny had expected. His eyes keep returning to the dashboard clock, and he seems to be doubting this allocation of today's working hours. We'll just go inside for a few minutes, he tells me, then head back. No need to go inside the barns. We'd need to shower first anyway so as not to introduce any "exotic germs" into the stock. These are not only finishing barns like Perry Smith's, he explains. They're breeding, farrowing, and nursing barns, and it's all a very delicate process.

Oh, I don't mind at all, I assure him. I'd love to see the whole process and a shower would do me good. Well, says Sonny, there's really not all that much to it, but if I insist, then, okay, suppose he just leaves me here and comes back in forty-five minutes? That'll work, I tell him.

A large round face materializes in the front window. The door unlocks and Sonny turns me over to a woman named Gay. As he departs she hands me a towel, boots, underclothes, and official "Carroll's Foods" coveralls. I scrub up and slip into the uniform of the gods.

Lean Generation

A hefty girl in her late twenties, Gay has the disheveled, effusively perky manner of someone just rousted from a furtive nap. She's an agricultural scientist, Gay tells me as we begin our tour. Just got her doctorate in animal science from N.C. State. Loves her career. Loves animals. Really excited to be part of this, working for Smithfield and all. Gay hasn't a clue why I'm here, only that her boss showed up out of nowhere and said show this guy around, and is full of nervous chatter.

The complex is divided into five parts: the Isolation Barn, the Gestation Barn, the Farrowing Barn, the Nursery Barn, and the Finishing Barn. And once you know your way around here you will never get lost at any industrial hog farm in the world, because they're all identical. In Germany, Holland,

Denmark, Belgium, France, Ireland, Spain, Portugal, and the UK some 70 to 95 percent of pigs are raised by the same methods, with Italy, Greece, and Hungary not far behind.[19] If you live in just about any country except Sweden, as of 1994 alone in forbidding mass-confinement hog farming, this is how your pork is made. These are your farms, too.

Gay leads me first to the Isolation Barn back near the lagoon for a look at the pride of Smithfield, the "seed stock" almost ready to produce the next Lean Generation of cuts. Just four or five months old, they are direct descendants of the original "nucleus herd" of two thousand swine imported from England to give Smithfield its American patent on the prized NPD— "National Pig Development"—line of meats. One day in 1991, these two thousand creatures were actually loaded into cargo planes bound for the New World, and from this purest of breeds have come new generations ever more pliant on the farm and pleasing to the palate. As patented by God, the pigs would be ready to bear young well after age one. New and improved by Smithfield, they'll start bearing next month. Under the company's state-of-the-art genetics program, these eighty young sows, not even adults themselves—and indeed exactly the age at which their ten thousand or so offspring will be slaughtered—will then go forth into the gestation and breeding barns to be fruitful and multiply. And multiply, and multiply, and multiply until they expire.

"These are our babies," says Gay. "They get special care."

The mothers-to-be are crowded inside with as little room for movement as in Perry Smith's finishing barn. But they're not as startled when we appear. They don't go crazy at the sight of a human being. They actually seem eager to receive guests, and soon are snuffling around my feet. They're cleaner and pinker, too, lavished here in the Isolation Barn with the closest thing they will ever know to human kindness—in cramped but clean pens, under veterinary monitoring and the daily supervision of Roberto, who is here now spraying them with a hose as if they were so many plants in a greenhouse.

No patting allowed. The strictest "biosecurity" procedures are observed to keep out exotic germs. The whole system depends on the survival and reproductive capacity of this seed stock, isolated here to protect them from flu, pneumonia, or other infections before risking introduction into the system. A pig displaying signs of illness is taken out, dispatched by one of the associates with a captive-bolt gun or other means, and trucked either to the dead hole or a rendering plant, yet those who stay healthy have it relatively good. Three to five years from now, if these creatures do any thinking in pictures on the truck to Tar Heel, they will recall in these pictures a time of wondrous peace before all the pain.

What awaits them is next on the tour, the Gestation Barn.

A bedlam of squealing and chain rattling and guttural, roaring sounds I didn't know pigs could make greets us as Gay throws open the door. They are locked, about six hundred of them, not only in the barn but each between bars fitted to size. "Confinement" doesn't describe their situation. They are encased, pinned down, unable to do anything but sit and suffer and scream at the sight of the gods.

"They're scared," Gay informs me.

These four-sided encasements are still called "crates," from earlier versions of sow confinement back when Murphy, Carroll, and others were only getting started. And what a merciful change real, old-fashioned wooden crates would be for the sorrowful beasts imprisoned here before us in six rows of iron crates stretching the length of the building.

"We keep it nice and warm in here," says Gay. "They're completely protected from all the elements."

It takes an extra moment for the eyes and ears to register a single clear perception. But you can tell just by their immediate reactions which sows have been here the longest. Some of them are still defiant, roaring and rattling violently as we approach. Some of them are defeated, motionless even at the touch. Some of them are dead.

"They don't get a lot of exercise," says Gay. "But at the same time, that's good because they can carry more fetuses. We get rid of them after eight litters."

Their exercise regimen consists in being driven or dragged from these crates every sixteen weeks to give birth over in the Farrowing Barn for a week to ten days of confinement, then returning here for sixteen weeks of confinement, then back to the Farrowing Barn, and so on. They don't even leave the crates for conception. To get them pregnant, Gay explains, a group of boars— briefly relieved of their own confinement—are run through the place from crate to crate, and when each sow in turn is sufficiently receptive a thrust of the "AI rod," for artificial insemination, does the rest. How is the fluid obtained that's inserted by the AI rod? It cannot be explained elegantly. Suffice it to say that there are actually people employed full time arousing boars and collecting the seed—though here, too, Richard Poulson's Ph.D.'s and men in white coats are busy improving upon nature. Soon most sows will be inseminated with genetically engineered replicas, not even the real stuff from real boars.

After that brief human involvement, the machines take over. Computers monitor temperature and ventilation. Automated misters and drip coolers water them. Automated heat lamps are their sun. An automated feeding system delivers scientifically formulated food, fresh from the mill, into long iron troughs. These piles of pellets are rich in growth hormones, laxatives, antibiotics, and the rendered remains of other pigs—as many of the sows here now, in the wonderful Smithfield cycle of life, will themselves get sick and be slain and rendered into feed for their progeny to eat. There are even machines to monitor all the other machines, automated sensors to correct the least rise or fall in temperature, moisture, or food and water consumption—all of this data collected into regular reports for study by the Carroll's team staring at computer monitors in their tidy, sunlit offices.

The automated flushing system still needs some refining, and the odor could not be more disagreeable if one were outside doing laps in the lagoon. What must it be like for them, lying here covered in their own dung? Pigs are sloppy but they are not suicidal. They like to root in dirt and roll in mud. That's how they find food and manage to stay wet and cool without sweat glands like ours. But they have olfactory powers many times our own, snouts that can detect truffles ten feet beneath the ground, have even been used to sniff for contraband and land mines, and in nature they do not leave their droppings near where they live and sleep. Among the earlier woes for some sows in confinement is constipation because they refuse, at first, to foul their own stalls.[20]

We walk up an aisle, my guide tossing off a bewildering assortment of comments alternately kindly and callous. "They're very smart," she tells me. "I was reading in a magazine the other day where it said they're as smart as your cat or dog."

Gay embodies in her ample frame all of humanity's contradictions about animals, capable of touching solicitude one moment and staggering disregard the next. "This'll be your first time farrowing, won't it, baby?" she says to a sow I pause to inspect, identified on a tag above the cage as NPD 88-308. "Baby" is lying there covered in feces and dried blood, yanking maniacally on chains that have torn her mouth raw, as foraging animals will do when caged and denied straw or other roughage to chew. She's hurting herself with the chains, I remark. "Oh, that's normal."

What happened to this one? I ask, pointing to NPD 50-375, whose legs are swollen and body covered with open sores. "Probably a crate injury," says Gay, without breaking stride. Following her further down I realize how silly the question must have seemed. They are all covered with sores. They all have crate injuries.

The sows each weigh 500 pounds. The crates are seven feet long, and in width less than twice the length of my 11¾-inch legal pad. Not much room, is there? I ask. How can they even lie down on their sides? Gay gives a baffled shrug, like it's some kind of trick question or she has honest to God just never thought of it before. "I don't know. They just do."

The answer can be seen in the swollen legs of the sows standing or trying to stand. To lie on their sides, a powerful inclination during months of confinement in twenty-two inches of space, they try to put their legs through the bars into a neighboring crate. Fragile from the pigs' abnormally large weight, and from rarely standing or walking, and then only on concrete, their legs get crushed and broken. About half of those pigs whose legs can be seen appear to have sprained or fractured limbs, never examined by a vet, never splinted, never even noticed anymore.

What's that on the thigh of NPD 45-051? I ask. "That's a tumor," says Gay. The tumor, I observe, is the size of half a soccer ball. "Yeah, and she's just one year old," says Gay. "Getting thin, too. So, she's not desirable anymore." What causes these tumors? A shrug. What happens when they get tumors? "She goes into the cull pen after her next litter." The sow herself may not even survive till birth, Gay explains, but they have a new method, called "superovulation," of harvesting the eggs and getting the live babies from the dead mothers.

NPD 40-602 appears to have a tumor as well, I tell Gay. "That's just a pus pocket. They all get those." The pus pockets are smaller, only the size of half a baseball. How are they treated? "Kopertox," says Gay, pulling from the pocket of her coveralls a bottle of this all-purpose remedy with which, she tells me, abrasions, hoof infections, and other maladies are also treated. A topical fluid that forms a hard coating over the wound, but made of copper naphthenate and dangerous if licked by another pig or absorbed into the flesh and ingested by a human, Kopertox carries the warning: "Do not use on animals which are used for food production."

We keep walking. Sores, tumors, ulcers, pus pockets, lesions, cysts, bruises, torn ears, swollen legs everywhere. Roaring, groaning, tail biting, fighting, and other "vices," as they're called in the industry. Frenzied chewing on bars and chains, stereotypical "vacuum" chewing on nothing at all, stereotypical rooting and nest building with imaginary straw. And "social defeat," lots of it, in every third or fourth stall some completely broken being you know is alive only because she blinks and stares up at you like poor NPD 50-421, creatures beyond the power of pity to help or indifference to make more miserable, dead to the world except as heaps of flesh into which the AI rod may be stuck once more and more flesh reproduced. When they have conquered the "stress gene," maybe the Ph.D.'s and guys in white coats can find us a cure for the despair gene, too.

A single piece of rubber tire hangs by a string over one crate in the entire barn, apparently someone's idea of "environmental enrichment," yet out of reach unless NPD 88-283 has been genetically engineered to leap five feet in the air. One of those "soft pliable objects" recommended by Temple Grandin, whom Smithfield has paid for consultation, I have an awful hunch it was put there just so they can tell her, yes, Dr. Grandin, we've applied your findings, our pigs now have toys and they're happier than ever! NPD 39-215 is bleeding profusely from a gash above her eye. Nothing a little Kopertox won't fix. NPD 45-066 has a bright pink "X" painted on her back, indicating an imminent birth and transport to the Farrowing Barn. New life on the way, as the expectant mother noses at straw that isn't there to make a nest she'll never have for another litter she'll never raise. NPD 38-453 pulls back, shaking and screaming wildly, as I lean down to look at a perfect little spiderweb between an iron bar and a wooden board at the base of her crate. No Charlotte to bring help.

Gay trundles ahead, directing my attention to this and that with the AI rod she has been using as a pointer, cheerfully unaware, apparently, of the profound betrayal of veterinary ethics everywhere around us—the sworn obligation of every veterinarian "to protect animal health [and] relieve animal suffering."[21] Who cares for these creatures, besides Gay and Roberto and whatever other poor soul reports here every morning? Some Smithfield shill of a vet comes by every few days to check on the stock. But for the vets, too, they are not even animals anymore. They're piglet machines. And tumors, fractured bones, festering sores, whatever, none of these receive serious medical attention anymore. If the ailment threatens a particular production unit's meat-yielding capacity, like the vaginal and urinary tract infections apparent from discharge stains on some of the sows, that'll get treated. *That* can be justified by the return on labor and costs—though only if the unit isn't too old to even bother, "old" meaning three or four years instead of one or two. Otherwise, it's a quick cull and sale to the renderer. There is no sick ward here. For most, it's either Kopertox or the cull pen. Nothing in between, no care anymore for animals as such, no regard for their suffering or for the most minimal duties of ordinary decency.

Conscientious medical care, indeed, would only add another layer of madness to the scene—armies of veterinarians running around our industrial farms ministering to the mass suffering necessarily inflicted by mass confinement and mass slaughter. A vet, like a doctor, must first ask what is the cause of the injury or sickness, and then recommend that those causes be removed. But how is that possible when the caregivers work for the company, and the company itself willfully and systematically inflicts the suffering, and if it didn't then costs would edge up and profits edge down? Once set in motion, there is no turning back in an enterprise like this. Moral disengagement on this scale requires moral disengagement at every stage, from farrow to finish to food market, or else basic assumptions are suddenly open to question, and human kindness and mercy enter like exotic germs to destroy the whole system. Here, too, consistency is everything.

NPD 41-132 is lame and losing weight and dying in the cull pen—here, at last, able to stretch out her limbs. She never made it to her eighth litter, Gay tells me. By the miracle of fertility drugs she had eighteen piglets in her first litter—twice what a sow will normally carry—thirteen in her second litter, but then started losing weight and aborting, and now, says Gay, "has served her purpose" and will be killed. Lying near her is another sow who left us this morning, dying of pneumonia, and strewn elsewhere in the cull pen the bodies of six others who for some reason just never learned to love it. The man in the truck will come by soon to take care of them all. "Most of the culls go to market," says Gay as we survey the day's casualties, "but the ones with disease don't go to Smithfield at all. These are, like, trash." The diseased ones don't go to market because at Smithfield they have standards. They make only quality products here. You, the consumer, deserve only the best.

FOR THEIR OWN GOOD

Lots of people "come by" our factory farms—to turn a valve or check a pump, to inseminate these sows or eliminate those, to collect the finished ones and cull the weak. But intensive farming, at least until the slaughter begins, is intensive only for the creatures. The corporate farmer is the absent farmer, the stranger on his own property, too important to worry about little details like whether a pig has room to turn or straw to sleep on. He is our modern hireling, too busy with bigger business than the care of his own animals, and we were warned about him long ago:

> The hired hand—who is no shepherd nor owner of the sheep—catches sight of the wolf coming and runs away, leaving the sheep to be snatched and scattered by the wolf. That is because he works for pay; he has no concern for the sheep.[22]

Far from being an aberration, moreover, some dark corner of the New Agriculture where standards have grown lax, Smithfield *is* the standard, modern animal science literally by the textbook. Professor Bernard Rollin of Colorado State University, in his perceptive writings on the subject, reminds us that until a few decades ago there wasn't even any such thing as "animal science," much less "meat science." If you studied livestock agriculture at N.C. State or any other rural university in America, you studied "animal husbandry."

The chief virtue of traditional husbandry was an acceptance and understanding of the nature of the animals in one's charge. "[T]he essence of good husbandry," Professor Rollin observes, "was keeping the animals under conditions to which their natures were biologically adapted, and augmenting these natural abilities by providing additional food, protection, care, or shelter from extremes of climate, predators, disease, drought, and so on, and by selectively breeding better survival traits into their natures."[23] The term *husbandry* itself means "bonded to the house," conveying commitment, mutuality, a sense in which the interests of farmer and animal were meaningfully, if not entirely, bound together in a symbiotic enterprise. On the traditional farm at its best, writes Professor Rollin, "ethics and prudence were closely intertwined: the biblical injunction to rest the animals on the Sabbath expressed both concern for animals and prudence; exhausted animals would not reproduce, produce, or work as well as rested ones. Ethics and self-interest were organically united. . . ."[24]

Traditional farmers had some fairly ruthless practices of their own before the corporate farmers came along, like ringing the snouts of pigs to prevent them from rooting up pasture grass. But we need not romanticize either the lives of these farmers or the lot of their animals to see the crucial point. By the terms of basic husbandry, the animals served our needs and in return we showed a regard for theirs. We assumed certain rights, and with those rights certain obligations. There was honor in it. We didn't "grow" animals. We raised them, took the trouble to understand them, respected their needs and natures.

Now, as industrial farming spreads, mankind has broken that trust. At every stage, with every new innovation, it is just assumed that whatever the cost-benefit analysis requires is acceptable. What can be done, however harsh, must be done, or else the competition will do it first. And then in that way the mind sometimes works self-interest and conscience became indistinguishable, and factory farming now seems not only necessary to the owners, but good and right and humane, and it's common knowledge in agricultural circles that the animals are happier than ever. "The key to sow welfare," explains Paul Sundberg, a veterinarian and vice president of the National Pork Producers Council, "isn't whether they are kept in individual crates or group housing, but whether the system used is well managed. Science tells us that she [a sow] doesn't even seem to know that she can't turn. . . . She wants to eat and feel safe, and she can do that very well in individual stalls."[25] How coincidental that the sows—who don't know they can't turn but for some darned-fool reason keep *trying* to turn—want exactly what factory farmers want. How comforting it must be for them to believe that, when they look around and see how their money is gained. How low we can sink when, in the human mind, duty and profit seem suddenly and miraculously to speak as one.

We can blame technology, or economics, or global demand among the many available excuses. Whatever the cause, we, humanity, have not kept up our end of the bargain. Now we think only of ourselves, *our* need to cut costs, *our* ambitions for higher profits, *our* taste for leanness, *our* desire for consistency. And them? In exchange for their service they get exactly nothing, no days of nurturing, no warm winds, no sights and sounds and smells of life, but only privation and dejection and dread.

The material incentive for care is simply gone. Not only can factory farmers afford to lose some of the stock—they're counting on it. The cullings have all been factored in. If a certain number weren't dying every week they would start to wonder why, to question whether somewhere along the line the units were not being exploited to maximum efficiency. The whole system now presupposes a high attrition rate outweighed by a massive production rate. At every stage, the system requires of farmers not only new techniques but an entirely new outlook. "Factory farmers are all Cartesians," as novelist Joy Williams observes. "Animals are no more than machines—milk machines, piglet machines, egg machines—production units converting themselves to profits."[26] "Everything that is done with and to the pigs," writes Professor Lowell Monke of Ohio's Wittenberg University, himself from a hog-farming family,

> is determined by narrowly conceived, quantitative measures of effi-
> ciency. Transformed into biological machines in the eyes of the
> farmer, hogs are abstracted onto the ledger sheet as numbers per-
> taining to inputs and outputs, rates of attrition, pounds gained per
> pound of feed, cost per head versus price per pound, and so on. The
> sterility of the hog's living environment is merely a reflection of the
> sterility of agribusiness: a manufacturing process guided by the need
> to reduce the growth of living creatures to as little uncertainty, as
> much human control, as possible.[27]

In the next chapter, addressing animal rights, I want to reflect a bit more on the natures of animals and how that might guide us again in caring for them. Enough to say here that such ideas have now been completely aban-doned. So far removed are modern factory farmers themselves from nature, and especially corporate hog farmers, that you wonder if they would even know how to care for the animals under any conditions other than radical deprivation. What would pigs *do* if they were not constantly confined? What would they need?

"Pig sense," as it used to be called, is known to the small farmers still with us, and dying now like an ancient oral tradition. Everything that the best minds at Smithfield know about pigs, they know from observing pigs squeezed into narrow stalls and pens, and from trying to devise still narrower stalls and pens, and from inspecting every facet of confinement and slaughter with a view to minimizing input and maximizing output. As in all forms of tyranny, management intensifies as knowledge, interest in, or even curiosity about the subjects passes away. The average consumer, rarely seeing live pigs anymore, is in much the same position as producers, knowing that pigs forage and wallow in mud, but otherwise possessing only the sketchiest knowledge of what a pig actually does or needs or is. And a child playing with a toy barn-yard set, putting all the little horsies and piggies outside the barn to graze, dis-plays a firmer grasp of nature and reality than do the agricultural experts who today can prove to a scientific certainty that farm animals prefer confinement to freedom, heat lamps to sunlight, and concrete to grass.

Two agricultural scientists, Professors Alex Stolba and D. G. M. Wood-Gush of Edinburgh University, back in the 1980s conducted a study I'd like to have witnessed for myself. They were trying—to their great credit, but to no avail—to design a cost-efficient group-housing system for pigs that could be used on a large scale by corporate farmers. So they took a control group of hogs raised in confinement and simply let them loose, into a park complete with a stream, a pine copse, and a swampy mud bog. The professors' report, drawn from three years' observation, reads like the fieldwork of zoologists describing some previously unknown species:

> It was found that pigs built a series of communal nests in a coopera-tive way. These nests displayed certain common features, including walls to protect the animals against prevailing winds and a wide view that allowed the pigs to see what was approaching. The nests were far from the feeding sites. Before retiring to the nests, the animals brought additional nesting materials for the walls and rearranged the nests. On arising in the morning, the animals walked at least 7 meters before urinating and defecating. . . .
>
> The pigs formed complex social bonds between certain animals, and new animals introduced to the area took a long time to be assim-ilated. Some formed special relationships—for example, a pair of sows would join together for several days after farrowing, and forage and sleep together. Members of the litter of the same sex tended to stay together and to pay attention to one another's exploratory behav-ior. Young males also attended to the behavior of older males. Juve-niles of both sexes exhibited manipulative play. In autumn, 51 percent of the day was devoted to rooting.[28]

To relieve the miseries of factory farming, in other words, and to design conditions more suited to the needs and habits of hogs, the researchers actu-ally had to go back and establish just what those needs and habits are. The study ends with this startling conclusion: "Generally the behavior of . . . pigs born and reared in an intensive system, once they had appropriate environment, resembled that of the European wild boar."[29]

The pigs, in short, still bear an amazing resemblance to pigs. They're just like the ones we started with millennia ago. They remain, miraculously, living creatures with a nature all their own.

At Farm 2149, the difference between husbandry and science is clearest in the Farrowing Barn. Here are the hardest privations of all, at least for the observer to witness. "For their own good," Gay explains to me, the sows must remain in confinement before, while, and after they give birth, barred even from caring for the piglets emerging from their bruised bodies.

They get the same twenty-two inches, with one difference: The bar is raised slightly at the rear, and beside each crate is a little area where the piglets are deposited from the womb, slipping out one by one onto concrete and with great labor crawling back to suckle from their immobilized mothers, who can hardly turn to see them. This is for their own good because, if the mothers could move about, they would only crush their young.

In the literature this crushing of piglets is described as a simple, unavoidable fact, as if it were some law of nature or tragic flaw in the sows themselves that they kill their young. It's another of those unfortunate "vices" pigs display, leaving our corporate farmers no choice but to keep the birthing mothers between bars. Just as confinement during gestation "protects sows from aggression" by other sows, as the *Swine Care Handbook* puts it,[30] and just as stuffing them all with antibiotics protects them from the effects of stress in crowded conditions, here the narrow stalls are necessary to protect piglets from their clumsy mothers.

It makes such perfect sense, provided you have accepted as normal and reasonable all of the preceding agonies to which the sows have been subjected. If one were to suddenly remove the bars here in this room, yes, the sows would roll over and crush many of their piglets. I imagine you and I would lose our physical coordination too if we were released from prolonged confinement, our bodies grossly enlarged from massive doses of growth hormones, our bones fragile or broken from injuries and lack of exercise. "Vice" is certainly the problem here, but it isn't porcine vice.

What the sows have not lost, somehow, is their maternal instinct, an apparently indestructible desire to care for and protect new life. They would be very comfortable here, the newborn piglets, if only they, like their mothers, could see and feel straw where there is only air. We entered to a shrieking panic as in the Gestation Barn, but now, in both aisles of this smaller facility, nests are again being prepared. In some stalls the work is done and the mothers lean crumpled against the bars, or on their sides with legs through the bars, or actually on their foreheads, as if bowing before the gods, to shift some of the weight forward and off their legs and ankles, warmed from above by fluorescent lamps that give the place a sickly orange glow.

NPD 88-956, distinguishable by a bleeding eye and an enormous tumor on her side, has just given birth, aided by a drug called Prostamate injected into sows who are not producing on schedule. Eight or nine piglets still wet from the womb scuttle blindly around her body in search of a nipple, one of them wandering far afield behind his mother's back while he wrestles to free himself from the umbilical cord. Asking "Wanna hold one?" Gay leans down, flips him up by the hind legs, and hands him to me. A frail, quivery being whose eyes will not open for another week to the world around him, even in nature this one probably wouldn't make it, and Gay, walking on, rates him a likely casualty too weak to survive even the Nursery. I'm not sure it is a kindness, but this time nature is overruled, the gods have decided in his favor, and he's going first in line at the nipple.

No such miracles for the dead piglets born to NPD 41-110, whose stillborns have marked her own fate, or for one forsaken creature born this morning to NPD 38-967, a "starve-out," as Gay calls this piglet, struggling from underneath three or four other piglets who have piled on top to prevent her from feeding. What happens to the starve-outs? I ask. Someone will come by to "knock her head." Finding no leniency even from her penmates, who if they could remember this deed would soon envy their victim, she lived less than a day, reminding us in her few hours here that the world has enough pain without our adding more.

The survivors will all stay here for a week or two, depending on how long it takes. Smithfield gives the piglets seven to ten days before weaning, compared with the thirteen to seventeen weeks that nature had planned and the three to four weeks still allowed by some intensive hog farms in Europe. When the barn is full of piglets, like a popper filled with popcorn, somebody will come by to collect them. The mothers will be tethered, as some already are. The rear gates of their stalls will be opened. And the little ones will all be swept away. Up one chute, down another, pouring into the Nursery Barn for an orientation of vaccinations, ear notching, teeth cutting, tail docking, and, for the males, castration. All of this, in a place so full of state-of-the-art scientific technologies, without the use of a local anesthetic. On a shelf in the Nursery there is only a bottle of good ol' Kopertox. Six or seven weeks after birth, the piglets will all be ready for "finishing."

As the sows' confinement is the necessary consequence of prior pains, all of these measures are for the youngsters a necessary preparation for afflictions to come. Docking, for example—an amputation of the lower part of the piglets' tails, performed with an instrument known technically as a "pliers"—is necessary because premature weaning has left them constantly searching for something to chew or suck, and because their five or six months on earth will be spent in a crowd staring into the behinds of fellow captives, snapping at the tails in front of them while the guys in back are doing the same to them. Termed in the field a "short-term stressor," docking doesn't remove the target: The idea is to leave each tail more sensitive, so that the pain of a bite is sharper and the pigs will therefore try harder to avoid attack. Otherwise the pigs display what is known in both animal and human psychology as learned helplessness. They just give up, their tails get chewed and infected, the infection spreads, and they die an unauthorized death.

Castration—usually by hot knife—is necessary even though death will come right about the time of puberty. Castration is done to check early signs of aggression, and to accommodate prickly consumers who used to complain of the "boar taint" caused by sexual pheromones in the males. The teeth clipping, removing the tips of incisors, is another "protection" measure for the mother, whose udders get lacerated by twice the number of mouths they're designed for, and to protect the piglets themselves from being injured in twice the competition for suckling space. The struggle for milk only intensifies when mothers die here and, as Gay explains, their piglets are dropped into other pens.

New punishments in this way are invented to solve problems caused by the punishments already in place. "Managerial intensity" here suddenly requires more managerial intensity over there. There's a reason for everything in factory farming, everything necessitates everything else, one privation or mutilation inevitably requires others before or later in the system, which operates like some moral biosphere with its own dynamic and ethic, insulated from the standards and judgment of the world beyond the barbed wire.

Throughout our industrial farms you find the particular madness of trying to make all of one's other madnesses fit together rationally. Agricultural scientists are even now trying to solve the lagoon problem by genetically engineering pigs to produce less phosphorus in their manure, thereby lessening the harm of spillage into rivers and ponds.[31] A still more ambitious scheme seeks to trap the smelly fumes, convert them to methane, and use that gas to fuel the facility itself.[32] This, in turn, would allow for the multilevel barns also under discussion today—the factory-farm high-rise with thousands of pigs stacked atop one another in a single facility. With these ultimate cost savers, the self-containment of the system and subjugation of its victims would be complete: billions of creatures across the earth not only confined in our factory farms, but powering them too. If our corporate farmers could figure out a way to eliminate feed costs entirely, and leave the pigs to subsist upon their own refuse, I have not the least doubt they would do that, too.

Complaints about the smell of our factory farms, and only the smell, are the final insult. We like to assume that pigs, being pigs, don't mind such conditions. We may even half believe Sonny Faison when he says they love it here, or the Pork Producers Council when it insists modern agribusiness is "very animal friendly,"[33] or agricultural scientist Dennis Avery when he assures us they're "becoming healthier and happier" in confinement, they crave this life, just can't get enough of it. We notice these places, many of us, only when the odors reach our homes and new subdivisions, affecting our own quality of life. We create these animals for our profit and pleasure, playing with their genes, violating their dignity as living creatures, forcing them to lie and live in their own urine and excrement, turning pens into penitentiaries and frustrating their every desire except what is needed to keep them breathing and breeding. And then *we* complain about the smell. But no one who has seen the inside of a modern hog farm will find comfort in these assurances of their happiness. And no one who has seen how they are treated will ever again dare to use "pig" as a synonym for filth and greed and ugliness.

PIECE BY PIECE

"So what'd you think?" Sonny asks. A real eye-opener, I tell him, and thanks for the hospitality. We part back at headquarters, Sonny pointing out all the trucks coming and going from the Carroll's mill perpetually grinding out the 2.9

pounds of hog feed it takes to produce one pound of hog flesh. "Twenty-four hours a day, seven days a week, something's always happening at Carroll's."

I had one more appointment to keep, at Murphy Family Farms down in Rose Hill, N.C.—"Home of the World's Largest Frying Pan." Sonny said that afterward somebody might show me around the plant at Tar Heel. This hope began to slip away, however, from the moment I sat down in a comfy little conference room with Murphy's president Jerry H. Godwin.

I had considered requesting an interview with Mr. Murphy himself, but doubted the great man would consent to it. Besides, his work is done and his day is passing. Even Sonny strikes one as a transition figure in the New Agri-culture, a man just going with the times but who deep down probably knows better, knows that the whole business is beneath him as a farmer, a gentle-man, a Faison.

Mr. Godwin, I'm not so sure about. Sitting here in his starched cotton shirt, no tie but all business, a self-described conservative and doubtless, too, a churchgoing pillar of the community, he is alarmingly earnest about it all. He was hired, as he tells me, precisely because he is not a farmer, and he will soon be placed in command of both Murphy Family Farms and Carroll's Foods in a consolidation planned by Smithfield. Hailing from the town of Kenly some sixty miles from here, Mr. Godwin's background is in the tool business as an executive at the Champion Spark Plug Company and as presi-dent of the Cooper Automotive Company. "I'm not a pig specialist," as he puts it. "I'm a businessman. And that is exactly what Mr. Murphy was looking for."

I tell him that I'm not a pig specialist either, but I was at a Smithfield facility yesterday and it struck me, walking around there, that the company could use a few pig specialists, because as it is they're all stored in narrow lit-tle spaces like, well, tools, and they don't seem to like it.

"We are the best in the world at doing what we do," Mr. Godwin says. "And it's not because we're big, it's because what we really have done is taken the information, the science-based information and a system, put a group of people, a cadre of people that are intelligent, are open-minded and want to make that best balance work for everyone and being able to use that system and have sustainability of that system. Now we've done that, and if anybody in the world wants to learn modern pig production and that proper balance, they'll come to this location. They will come to the office you're sitting in today. We are known as the best in the world if you want to learn a system that has a proper balance. If you want one that has free-range pigs, we don't have that system. But we have a lot of Ph.D.'s, we have a lot of specialists."

"Ph.D.," in North Carolina corporatese, is a synonym for "oracle"—an all-wise, all-knowing being at the mere mention of whom one is expected to fall silent, furrow one's brow, and just keep nodding.

"This company and Smithfield as a whole," Mr. Godwin continues, "are very open to change, very willing, have a very open mind, but I think we must always keep in mind, we raise animals and process those animals for profit. We have shareholders. It is a customer-driven business all the way through; customers are saying 'I want consistency, I want continuity, I want traceability.' Food safety is an issue. And we're coming to the point that people are saying—and the Japanese are doing this already, and have—but they are really, really putting tremendous emphasis on 'I want to know about that animal from the day it is born, and how it is bred and the sow is kept,' all the way through the chain until it's in the store, and I can tell the person that buys it, 'This is what it was fed, this is what happened to it, this is how it was cared for.'

"Everybody today—not everybody, but there is a movement that says, 'Oh, we don't like this so-called factory farming.' And I would tell you, it is not that at all. Most of our production is done by family farmers who actually are grower-partners with us. But we're asked for this traceability, to do all these things, and have consistency, make sure that animals are not medicated beyond a point. All these things . . . are being required, but yet everybody wants it done on an individual farm with no consistency or continuity. You can't have today a group of pigs from a family farm, twenty pigs every week being delivered to a slaughter plant from thousands of places, and have consistency. So it's a consumer, customer-driven business, with requirements being placed on the people that are growing and processing the product, but yet you want it done in a different way. Those two are not compatible in today's economy.

"It's science-driven. We're not raising pets. We're raising animals for profit. But everything we do is based on scientific fact. It is not emotionally driven. We have a business. . . . The best institutions in the world—not just in the United States but in the world—have said—I mean, we didn't invent these systems. It's not that a group of farmers that have never been to school go out and say, 'Oh, we want to cram all these animals into this small space.'

The fact is that those are the plans and what people have studied and said on balance, 'This is the best way for these animals to be treated, to be handled, to be managed.' I mean, there's no way, if you want to look at an animal in one of our systems, at the way it is housed, you look at that and say, 'Oh my gosh, that's terrible.' Well, the fact is that to that animal it may not be so bad. That animal seems to live longer, to prosper, to do well. Its comfort is there. If you put it outside, I would suggest to you that the most cruel thing you could do to these animals in the summer, in North Carolina, is to have them outside and, in the winter in Minnesota, is to have them outside. Because if you want to see them die, you try that. . . .

"I mean, you put 'em out, they kind of scrounge around in the mud, and in the summer, around here, animals that are outside risk getting mosquito bites and things. Our animals don't have that. I mean, we don't have that kind of thing. People tend to forget that just because they're outside and they can roam around, it may not be the best environment for them. You lose pigs, they're freezing in the winter. Even around here they're cold. You know, this idea of having these sows in pens. Everybody says, 'Oh, that looks terrible.' But there's a reason for that as well. And again, it's balance. It's balance.

"Now, to keep them inside, there are certain ways you need to do that. But I can tell you that the systems that are used today are systems that were not invented by Smithfield or its companies. They are systems that have evolved over time through the land-grant universities that are scientifically based that say, 'This is the proper way of doing this.' Now, if we progress, and if there is a different or a better way that really is scientifically based, then I can tell you, this company is very open to those considerations. I mean, it's not that we want—there's a misconception that people that have larger-scale operations somehow, automatically, want to mistreat animals, and I can assure you that is not the case. It's really quite the opposite."

To sum up, factory-farm animals aren't suffering, and Smithfield is not to blame for the suffering of factory-farm animals. It's all the consumers' fault. It's the shareholders' fault. It's the economy's fault. It's the competition's fault. It's the fault of the Japanese. The scientists. The weather. The mosquitoes. It is the fault, the misery of factory-farm animals, of everything and everybody except the people who actually own the animals and control the farms.

I ask about Temple Grandin, since she understands modern agriculture and Smithfield has hired her for consultation. She advises extra space so the animals can turn around, "soft, pliable" objects to chew on, and toys so they can play. She's a Ph.D. too. Yet to all appearances, Smithfield has put none of her recommendations into practice.

"Temple," he replies, "is a person that we pay to come in and say, 'How is the best way to deal with these animals?' We seek that advice. We pay those people."

Exactly. They pay animal-welfare consultants for the privilege of saying that they have paid for animal-welfare consultants, without actually heeding any of the recommendations.

"It depends on where your view is. If you are totally against consuming meat of any kind, then I could never convince you or anyone else that raising pigs the way we raise them is the proper way of doing it. But if you are on balance, what the economics of the system—with the proper food-safety aspects, and consistency and quality, leanness, the health aspect, all the way through to the traceability, the identification, and how we care for the animals, and make sure the animals are well fed and watered, we control the temperature, the climate, we control the heat for the baby pigs, we change the diets nine times through this feeding regimen. . . . So I would tell you on balance we have a great system. But if your sole purpose is animal welfare, then our system probably wouldn't satisfy you. . . .

"Pigs get bored. They get bored, and Temple Grandin and others can tell you, would say, well, you need to give 'em something to play with. So what do you do? You take a piece of chain, and you put in front of 'em so they can reach up, play with it, and that's about the extent of occupying their time. I mean, it sounds crude to you and me, but I think the people that seem to know more about it, and have studied the issue say that is a proper way of getting rid of the boredom and keeping them busy. It would be no different from having them go out and biting at a tree limb."

From there it was on to a description of exciting new scientific projects to make this "great system" even greater. The "stress gene" apparently under control, Smithfield has hired a biotechnology firm called ProLinia, based at the University of Georgia, to prepare its new cloning program for the ultimate in consistency. The upshot is that unless it is stopped by some act of God or law, the very codes to life will now and forever be in the hands of men who can tell you with a straight face that confinement for animals is comfort, and endurance is contentment, and the chains on their cages are toys.

It was an awkward parting, after Mr. Godwin left to make a few phone calls and returned with the news that no one would be available after all to conduct the tour of Tar Heel. I told him that if I ran a place like that, I wouldn't let people in either.

They come at night, when the pigs are sleeping. They move fast, shouting and prodding and hitting the creatures to get them into the trucks. Sometimes they play country music, Mr. Godwin tells me, to soothe them when they arrive at the plant, greeted by men in hard hats and steel-toed rubber boots waiting at the end of the lighted chute leading from the truck. The antibiotics are withdrawn a week before slaughter, so that many of the pigs, on their journey to Tar Heel, are suffering from pneumonia. Trembling and shaking, many lose control of their bowels and the floors must be constantly washed of excrement. *New York Times* reporter David Barboza, who came here in early 2000, describes their arrival:

> Squealing hogs funnel into an area where they are electrocuted, stabbed in the jugular, then tied, lifted and carried on a winding journey through the plant. They are dunked in scalding water, their hair is removed, they are run through a fiery furnace (to burn off residual hair), then disemboweled and sliced by an army of young, often immigrant laborers.[34]

The electrocutors, stabbers, and carvers who work on the floor wear earplugs to muffle the screaming. What it's like for them we may gather from the 100 percent turnover rate every year reported by another *Times* writer, Charlie LeDuff, who worked at the plant undercover in the summer of 2000. "Slaughtering swine," he writes, "is repetitive, brutish work. . . . Five thousand quit and five thousand are hired every year. You hear people say, 'They don't kill pigs in the plant, they kill people.'"[35]

Smithfield recruiters, the *Times* found, "comb the streets of New York's immigrant communities . . . and word has reached Mexico and beyond. The company even procures criminals. Several at the morning orientation were inmates on work release in green uniforms, bused in from the county prison."[36] He quotes an employee, a convict from a nearby prison who figured it all out after just two days on the job: "Man, this can't be for real. This job's for an ass. They treat you like an animal."[37] Inside, Mr. LeDuff reports, the plant "reeks of sweat and scared animal, steam and blood."

> Kill-floor work is hot, quick and bloody. The hog is herded in from the stockyard, then stunned with an electric gun. It is lifted into a conveyor belt, dazed but not dead, and passed to a waiting group of men wearing bloodstained smocks and blank faces. They slit the neck, shackle the hind legs and watch the machine lift the carcass into the air, letting its life flow out in a purple gush, into a steaming collection trough.[38]

At 16,000 kills per eight-hour shift in the Tar Heel plant, 2,000 per hour, and 33 every minute, all of this done by transient, unskilled laborers, there are mistakes. Gail Eisnitz of the Humane Farming Association came down here for her 1997 book *Slaughterhouse*. She didn't make it inside either, but did talk to some employees at this and other plants. "Does it ever happen," she asked a fellow named Nathan Price, a worker for Carolina Foods, "that hogs aren't properly stunned?"

> "All the time," Price laughed. "Because if you're killing 16,000 hogs a shift, those guys aren't going to stun all them hogs all the time. Some hogs come out kicking and raising hell."
>
> "Is kicking the only sign that they're not stunned properly?" I asked.
>
> "Running across the table or floor isn't a good sign neither. See, they use this four-pronged stunner. And if you don't hit that hog precisely, that hog runs across the table."[39]

At this point, you'd almost expect that some mighty instinct would make them charge the throat slasher, the sooner to escape a world that never gave them anything but hurt, but they don't, they still want to live, and so, as Mr. Price explained, they have to be chased and beaten. There are beatings? asked Ms. Eisnitz. "That's all the time. You get a stubborn hog that doesn't want to go, employees can get to beating that hog all they want to. They use a shackle, a pipe, anything they can get their hands on."[40]

The pigs are then downed and shackled alive, as he described it, hanging by the ankle bracelet as they move down the production line. Often, we learn, they still can't be killed because they're still moving and flailing. So they are dropped alive into the scalding tank. A hidden camera at one Iowa plant recently captured this scene, the hogs still squealing and kicking as they are being lowered into the water.[41]

These mistakes, we're assured, happen with but a slight fraction of the total hogs slaughtered every year. Yet every year, just in America, 103 million pigs are slaughtered, and what is a slight fraction of that? Supposing the very minimum of 1 percent, that's more than a million right there, 3,550 creatures condemned every day, *today,* to this most merciless of deaths. Not by "mistake," either. Each time, it is the predictable and necessary consequence of a system deliberately designed to operate at this pace.

Meanwhile, 38 million cows and calves are slaughtered annually in the United States. Ten years ago the typical American slaughter plant operated at 50 kills per hour. Now, at newer plants, it is 300 to 400 per hour.[42] The same immigrants man these places, with a comparable turnover rate and identical problems in production. As Martin Fuentes, an IBP worker, told *Washington Post* reporter Joby Warrick in 2001, "The line is never stopped simply because an animal is alive."[43]

Mr. Warrick, formerly of the *Raleigh News & Observer,* spoke to another worker at the IBP abattoir in Washington State, Ramon Moreno, whose job is to cut off the hooves of strung-up cattle passing by at 309 an hour. When they reach him, they are supposed to be stunned and killed already, but often they're not, as Mr. Moreno tells it. "They blink. They make noises. The head moves, the eyes are open and still looking around. They die piece by piece."[44]

Shown videotapes of cows in the company's plants being processed alive and conscious, an IBP spokesman called it an "aberration," suggesting to the *Post* that the scenes had been staged by "activists trying to raise money and promote their agenda." But if radical activists are staging these scenes, the conspiracy is great, and they are everywhere. Larry Gallagher, another journalist who worked undercover, was employed in 1996 at a typical midwestern beef factory. He describes cattle routinely fighting after the first "knock," hanging by their legs from the processing rail for minutes, kicking and bellowing:

> The "knocker," as he's known, stands on the platform holding a
> pneumatic gun, like a giant stapler. The cattle are funneled through

corrals until they are in single file, straddling a rubber conveyor. When a cow's head emerges into the light of the kill floor, it is greeted with a blast from the gun, which shoots a bolt of steel into its forehead, stunning it in a single mechanical blow. "Stunned" is the appropriate word to describe the expression on the animal's face: eyes and mouth frozen open, tongue sticking out, teeth biting into tongue—an expression which, were it human, would be asking, "How could it all come to this?" The pathos of that look catches me by surprise. I thought that a few weeks of gut cutting had numbed my feelings. I know I am anthropomorphizing, but I still have to bite down on my own tongue to keep the tears from welling.[45]

Elsewhere in America, 250 million turkeys are processed annually and no fewer than 8 billion chickens, or more than fifteen thousand beheadings with every tick of the clock. We can safely assume some slipups at that pace, too. Just how bereft of human feeling that entire industry has become was clear at a municipal court case heard in Warren County, New Jersey, in the fall of 2000. A poultry company, ISE America, was convicted of cruelly discarding live chickens in trash cans. The conviction was appealed and overturned, partly on the grounds that ISE America (short for "International Standard of Excellence") had only six employees overseeing 1.2 million laying hens, and with workers each left to tend two hundred thousand creatures it remained unproven they were aware of those particular birds dying in a trash can. The company's initial defense, offered to Judge Joseph Steinhardt by an attorney named Kevin M. Hahn, asserted outright that this is exactly what the birds were anyway—trash:

> MR. HAHN: We contend, Your Honor, that clearly my client meets the requirements [of the law]. Clearly it's a commercial farm. And clearly the handling of chickens, and how chickens are discarded, falls into agricultural management practices of my client. And we've had—we've litigated this issue before in this county with respect to my client and how it handles its manure. . . .
> THE COURT: Isn't there a big distinction between manure and live animals?
> MR. HAHN: No, Your Honor. Because the Right to Farm Act pro-

tects us in the operation of our farm and all of the agricultural management practices employed by our farm.[46]

Here, at last, an honest man, stating in plain language the ethic that we have now come to accept in practice.

I can't say that I really regret missing the tour at Tar Heel. Just seeing it from the outside is enough for me, watching truck after truck line up outside this single structure running almost a quarter mile in length, as other trucks leave packed with fresh meat. Even if you had no idea where you were, you would sense that something bad happens here. The feel of the place, the size of it and this busyness late at night make you want to flee.

Delivery for slaughter is supposed to be so precisely calibrated that the trucks hardly come to a stop until they are at the chutes, which are in the back of the plant, facing the Cape Fear River. It's just like the back of a supermarket, where the docks and bins are, the plant itself serving as a giant wall to shield us from what is going on. But tonight the line is long, so they have to wait their turn. Hundreds of eyes look out from between the grating at me, at the plant, at the other trucks and eyes. The line is backed up because Easter is approaching. And in the South, Easter means ham. And all that ham, after all the curing and treating, must be ready when folks gather at their tables to celebrate the hope of the world.

Leaving here, one feels a terrible loneliness. It is a scene of abandonment. Thomas Hardy in *Jude the Obscure* describes the last moments of a pig Jude and his wife Arabella have slaughtered, and how after the struggle "the dying animal's cry assumed its third and final tone, the shriek of agony; his glazing eyes riveting themselves on Arabella with the eloquently keen reproach of a creature recognizing at last the treachery of those who had seemed his only friends."[47] Now, one might say, there is no more element of surprise because there is no more kindness. The treacheries begin on the day they are born. From the start they must feel they are in the hands of an enemy. No creature of the factory farm goes to its death feeling betrayed by friends.

SEVEN

NATURE AND
NATURE'S GOD

The present-day mentality, more perhaps than that of people in the past, seems opposed to a God of mercy, and in fact tends to exclude from life and to remove from the human heart the very idea of mercy. The world and the concept of "mercy" seem to cause uneasiness in man, who, thanks to the enormous development of science and technology, never before known in history, has become master of the earth and has subdued and dominated it. This dominion over the earth, sometimes understood in a one-sided and superficial way, seems to leave no room for mercy.[1]

POPE JOHN PAUL II, *THE MERCY OF GOD*

Turning to the question of animal rights, I confess that I could hardly care less whether any formal doctrine or theory can be adduced for these creatures. There are moments when you do not need doctrines, when even rights become irrelevant, when life demands some basic response of fellow-feeling and mercy and love.

Walking around a place like Farm 2149, I do not need some utilitarian philosopher to do the moral math for me, adding up and subtracting the suffering of the world to determine which lives have value and which do not. I do not need a contractualist philosopher to define for me an "appropriate object of sympathy." I do not need behavioral scientists or cognitive theorists to distinguish which pains are "real" pains and which are not. I do not need experts in evolutionary ecology or some other faddish field of the day to explain the hard and remorseless demands of natural selection. I require no advice from theologians on where mercy may be granted and where withheld. Confronted with this wholesale disregard and destruction of life, all attempts to justify it strike me as vain talk, miserable excuses that cannot cover the iniquity, the ungodly presumption of it, the scale and sorrow of it.

Only effete "urbanites," we are admonished, care about such things because we are so estranged from nature's harsh realities. But these particular realities are not of nature's design, and in every corner of our factory farms one finds the most casual disregard for the nature of the animals themselves. Nature has its own hardships, but its own kindnesses, too, like straw and room to sleep and the care of a mother for her young. When we take even those away, we are smothering the inmost yearnings of these creatures and the charity in our own hearts.

Pigs and lambs and cows and chickens are not pieces of machinery, no matter how cost-efficient it may be to treat them as such. Machinery doesn't cry or feel frightened or lonely. And when a man treats them this way, he might as well be a machine himself. Something dies in him, too. Something is lost in a society that rewards and enriches him, driving him on at this pace and in this spirit.

Without animal rights groups, moreover, it would all go almost completely unremarked, except by economists who welcome industrial farming as a stage of progress, stock analysts who recommend it as a smart investment, trade representatives who want to export it, and environmental and consumer groups who worry only about our sullied waters. Who would be left to speak for the creatures themselves? Feared for the truths they might tell, animal rights champions do not deserve our scorn. They deserve our admiration and our gratitude, here above all. Sometimes the most courageous thing is to state the obvious, and that is what they are doing when they tell us that to treat animals in such a way is cruel, abhorrent, and inexcusable. "We do not need a zoological proletariat," writes one commentator in dismissing the rights of farm animals,[2] to which the obvious reply is that we do not need zoological gulags, either.

NECESSARY EVILS

What we need here are standards, bright, clear lines beyond which none may pass. Whether we call those prohibitions "rights" possessed by the animals themselves becomes at a certain point purely academic, and indeed can distract us from present duties more readily agreed upon. The first thing to notice, however, is how the factory farms and our acceptance of them today prevent any hard standards at all.

Factory farming isn't just killing: It is negation, a complete denial of the animal as a living being with his or her own needs and nature. It is not the worst evil we can do, but it is the worst evil we can do to them. It confronts us with the animal equivalent of Abraham Lincoln's condemnation of human slavery: "If slavery is not wrong, nothing is wrong."[3]

Take anything else I have described in this book—elephants ambushed at the water hole, baby monkeys ripped from their mothers and eaten alive, dolphins trapped and clubbed to death—and the reality is that none of it is any worse than anything we tolerate in our corporate farms. Perhaps you share my opinion of people who do those other things. You may call them cruel. You may call them reprehensible. But they all have a ready answer: "You eat *meat,* don't you?"

If we buy and eat factory-farmed meat, we are left without any rational reply. With every new proposal to curtail or abolish one or another form of cruelty, opponents may simply point to our modern farms and ask why we do not favor abolishing those, too. "Leave us to our whale," as the whalers say, "and we will leave you to your McDonald's and pork chops." They have a point. If you can have your favorite treats from the factory farm, why on earth can't others have their whale meat, or others their "racks" or ivory or fur coats or macaque brains or whatever? By what moral standard may we condemn any practice?

The sole difference—that in the one case we are dealing with wild animals, and in the other with animals bred and born just for our use—actually works to the favor of the killers. Their prey at least enjoyed some modicum of freedom. Their victims, at least, were not subjected to lives of unremitting pain and privation. And they, at least, were willing to do the job themselves.

We claim, in defense of our laboratory experiments, that it is all justified by vital moral goods. We claim, in defense of our slaughter of wildlife, that important human interests are at issue. Yet the worst sufferings we inflict, we inflict to extract pork rinds, veal, and assorted other pounds of flesh. How are we to be believed when our claims are serious, if we act just the same when our claims are trivial? We have what, in a court of justice, would be called a serious credibility problem, casting doubt on the integrity and good faith we bring to all questions of animal welfare.

Cruelty and mercy both have a logic of their own, the farms in both cases compelling an account of first principles. William F. Buckley, Jr., captures this logic in a quote he passed along in a 1998 column about England's fox hunting controversy. If fox hunting were banned, Mr. Buckley asked a British friend, what next? "Will they . . . then call for outlawing bird-shooting?"

> Well, he thought this inevitable. Why protect foxes and not birds?
>
> He then leaned over and spoke in tones that suggest: "Don't let out what I'm about to tell you." What he preceded to tell me was: Had I ever seen an abattoir in operation? No, I said, but in my youth I read Upton Sinclair's *The Jungle,* which was the first American twentieth-century muckraking book, about the horrible end of cows and bulls in the slaughterhouses of Chicago.
>
> "Well, when they notice what happens in abattoirs, there will be a serious movement against the eating of meat."[4]

This British man's perfectly sound point being that nothing done to foxes could possibly be worse than how we get our meat, that many of those protesters doubtless eat meat, and that, therefore, it seems awfully silly to get so upset over a little thing like a fox hunt—or over fur farming, or trapping, or vivisection, or bullfighting, or rodeo, and on and on. Yet at the same time he acknowledges that if we looked at modern farming many of us would be so appalled as to give up meat entirely.

People have always said this about the abattoir, the actual scenes of slaughter, though only in our age could it be said about the farm itself, of every pitiless stage of it from birth to death. And either we can quit whispering about these facts and start acting upon them, or, as in the case of this man, we can take the view that such is the way of the world, there's not much we can do about it, best to drop the subject and hope that more people don't notice.

Yet where does this worldly-wise outlook leave us? It leaves us silent, compromised, exchanging knowing glances at the barbarities that lay out of view, unable to judge the conduct of others because we are unwilling to judge our own. Saddest of all, it leaves us useless. It leaves decent and humane people silent as the creatures and their world fall ever more under the heel of the careless or wicked.

The worst becomes the standard. Tolerance of the factory farms dictates a tolerance of just about everything else, in effect moving the ethical bar lower and lower until, after a while, the critical faculties break down and one cruelty is used to justify another—new "necessary evils" defended and permitted merely because the old ones still go on. We can't seriously question fox hunting because then we must seriously question bird shooting. We can't seriously question bird shooting because that would oblige us to seriously question other blood sports. And we can't seriously question blood sports, though just a fraction of humanity engages in them, because then we would have to seriously question the factory farm. We cannot seriously question anything because we are not thinking seriously at all.

In South Africa a few years ago, some enterprising farmers and businessmen actually dreamed up a "primate abattoir," which is under construction at this very moment. Primates will be caught, caged, transported to the abattoir, placed on a conveyor belt, stunned, killed, and butchered. (Imagine the sight and sound of that!) It all makes perfect sense, as a spokesman for the Warmbaths Development Initiative explained. And, of course, there are important "conservation" advantages:

> The businessmen argue that the animals should be trapped, slaughtered and their meat canned for sale in west and central Africa—where its use could prevent the killing and eating of endangered gorillas, chimpanzees and other primates—or cured for sale as a delicacy in western Europe. The group also believes that the animals' genitalia could be sold in Asia as aphrodisiacs in traditional medicine.[5]

Why not? Why not start butchering and eating primates, too? Once accepted, the logic of the factory farm knows no limits. Indeed, every argument we have heard in defense of other cruelties is just as easily applied here. This will help us to "conserve" primates, to keep up the stock. We need an "incentive" to keep primates alive, a little bonus for all our good works. Primates, too, must "pay their own way." Throughout Africa, chimpanzees, orangutans, and even gorillas are picked off anyway by poachers and hunters—who illegally ship at least a thousand tons of primate meat every year to Britain alone.[6] Why not make the whole thing more orderly, systematic, and profitable with primate farms?

For many in the West, this idea of primate abattoirs may take some getting used to. Yet we are hardly in a position to object. We might recoil at the
thought, believing that conscious, feeling creatures should not be treated that
way, but we are well advised to keep our own counsel. We might say of those
European consumers with a taste for primate flesh that they are thoughtless
and decadent, indulging frivolous appetites at the cost of unspeakable cruelty. Since when did that become the standard? They have traditions and
preferences of their own. They like their primate meat. And who are the customers of Smithfield to lecture them on the virtues of self-restraint?

Take another example, a bill debated not long ago in the Congress of the
United States. Nothing in mankind's use of animals has been left untried, no
degradation unexplored, and this piece of legislation, sponsored by Representative Elton Gallegly, a Republican from California, involved something so
vile I will spare you the details beyond this description by co-sponsor Representative Bill McCollum, Republican of Florida, here addressing the House
in October 1999:

> At a hearing on this bill in the Subcommittee on Crime of the Com-
> mittee on the Judiciary, a California State prosecutor and police offi-
> cer each described how they came to learn about the growing industry
> that deals in the depiction of animals being tortured. In most
> instances, videotapes are offered for sale that show women wearing
> high-heeled shoes slowly and sadistically crushing small animals, such
> as hamsters, and in some cases even cats, dogs, and monkeys.
>
> The witnesses explained that these types of videos, together
> with other visual and audio depictions of similar behavior, appeal to
> persons with very specific sexual fetishes who find these depictions
> sexually arousing. . . .
>
> During the . . . hearing, one of the witnesses played a short clip
> from one of these videos. In it a small animal was slowly tortured to
> death. And let me say to my colleagues that most of those in atten-
> dance had a hard time looking at it, and I do not believe in my entire
> time in Congress I have ever seen anything quite like this that is as
> repulsive as the videotape that I had to watch a portion of. . . . [7]

Forty-two members actually voted against a bill to ban these videos, including California Representative John Doolittle, a Safari Club member in good standing—though in fairness it must be said that another legislative friend of SCI, Collin Peterson of Minnesota, voted for it. The dissenters cited "free expression" objections, Representative Bobby Scott of Virginia arguing that "fundamental constitutional rights" were at risk, and that "films of animals being crushed are communications about the acts depicted, not doing the acts."[8] But with 372 yeas the bill passed, moving swiftly through the Senate to be signed into law on December 9, 1999, by President Clinton, who in characteristic form deplored "wanton cruelty to animals" while directing his Department of Justice to "broadly construe" the bill's free-speech exception, thereby narrowing the scope of the law lest anyone's artistic freedom be hindered.[9] The result went down on the books as follows:

> *Be it enacted by the Senate and House of Representatives in Congress assembled,*
>
> SEC. 1. PUNISHMENT FOR DEPICTION OF ANIMAL CRUELTY
>
> (a) IN GENERAL—Chapter 3 of title 18, United States Code, is amended by adding at the end the following:
>
> *Sec. 48. Depiction of animal cruelty*
>
> *(a) CREATION, SALE, OR POSSESSION—Whoever knowingly creates, sells, or possesses a depiction of animal cruelty with the intention of placing that depiction in interstate or foreign commerce for commercial gain, shall be fined under this title or imprisoned not more than 5 years, or both. . . .* [10]

When we speak of the rights of animals, we are talking as a practical matter about legal protections within our power to grant or deny, and that is what such a law actually looks like. Was the moral world upended? Was radicalism loosed upon society? Did Reason totter on its throne? No, a law was passed saying that you can't crush hamsters and mice and monkeys and puppies for fun or profit, and if you do then you are going to jail.

And why would anyone oppose such a thing? Because they see the logic of it. Because those forty-two members, mostly from western and rural states, know where that logic must lead. Although one hesitates to put even the most

maniacal trophy hunter into quite the same category as a crush-video enthu-
siast, rationally there is not all that much difference between crushing and
filming a small animal for the thrill of it and hunting and filming a large one
for the thrill of it. In the pain inflicted and the pleasures gained, there is no
great moral distinction to be made between a crush video, now illegal, and
With Deadly Intent, Double-Barreled Zambezi Adventure, and all the rest of
that sadistic filth we saw in Reno being made and sold by perfectly legal
means.

Fears over any such legal gains for animal welfare are well founded, for,
once it is granted that our pleasures, preferences, and profits alone cannot
justify the suffering of animals at our hands, that line of reasoning cannot
stop there. If we seriously question a "crush video," then we must seriously
question a sport-hunting video. If we can seriously question a sport-hunting
video, then we must seriously question sport hunting itself. And so on until
we are seriously questioning what goes on at our farms.

Here, too, consider any argument we have heard to justify animal cruelty,
and it applies just as well to crush videos. "Animals have no rights," British
philosopher Roger Scruton argues, because "we are rational beings, who exist
by negotiation and by reciprocal recognition of duties. A creature that cannot
recognize the rights of others cannot claim rights for itself."[11] Obviously these
small creatures being crushed for fun can't claim any rights for themselves, so
that doesn't help them.

To grant an animal legal protection, as Stephen Budiansky argues, we
must have some economic motive for doing so. We must "make it pay." The
folks making and buying crush videos are certainly motivated, economically
and otherwise. And the creatures featured in the films are certainly paying. So
that all adds up, too: The whole thing can easily be defended as a hamster,
chimp, and puppy conservation program.

Besides, these folks like their videos. The experience gives them pleasure,
a feeling of freedom, maybe even a chance to be "like boys again." And once
the government starts meddling in their recreations, then what's next?

THOU SHALT NOT

To take things in their turn, we must pick up where we left off earlier, asking
what moral obligations follow from an acknowledgment of animal suffering.
The idea that animals do not experience physical pain comparable to our

pain, as Stephen R. L. Clark observes, "has never satisfied anyone without something to gain."[12] That assumption may now once and for all be discarded as rubbish. Animal life will always retain much of its mystery, but on the matter of suffering their feelings are not "unknowable territory." Modern science has confirmed what mankind suspected all along with a prima facie case that of course animals suffer, of course they have emotions, and of course they are conscious beings.

That is not an expression of sentiment. It is not a statement of ideology. It is neither an avowal nor a denial of any tenet of religion or philosophy. It is a statement of fact, objective reality as best we can discern it. And it is a big fact. Three centuries after Descartes likened the crying of animals to "broken machinery," no serious person can say that anymore. Wherever people argue or act on the assumption of "mere pain," they are arguing and acting on a falsehood.

But how to get from this biological fact, "Animals suffer," to the moral statement, "It is wrong to inflict suffering on animals"? Upon what, ultimately, can we base any moral claims for the life or feelings of any animal? Might we call those claims "rights"? In examining the scientific evidence, at least we were dealing with tangible, measurable things like stress and squeals and neurological reflexes. Here we're dealing with moral values, and we humans have trouble enough finding agreement on the moral values governing our conduct toward one another. What hope is there of ever finding agreement on moral standards in our conduct toward the creatures, much less for imposing those standards in the laws of different societies?

It only gets more complicated when we consider that by far most people, in the abstract, would surely agree with the proposition that "It is wrong to inflict suffering on animals." It's the specific cases that cause problems, for in each instance the people involved are asserting another value they assume takes precedence over the value of the animal, whatever that value might be. "It is wrong to inflict suffering on an animal," they would say, except where some overriding value lay in the balance. For the factory farmer it is the value of foods for human nourishment, for the vivisectionist it is knowledge to be used for the relief of human suffering, for the whalers it's their livelihood and what they regard as a good and time-honored way of life, and so on.

Usually, then, what we're debating is not so much value as comparative value, the moral claims of animals weighed against our own claims upon them. We do the same in moral questions concerning human welfare, with the difference that at the end of the day we are prepared, in countries with advanced systems of law, to assert the value of innocent human life as non-negotiable. For all of our differences in faith, history, and culture, this, in theory at least, is held universally as a first principle of society, and we use a common vocabulary in defending it. When we call something unfair or indecent or unconscionable or evil, when we speak of mercy and pity and compassion, those words have meaning, regardless of our particular faith or moral philosophy. They appeal to common standards we all are expected to understand and accept, standards without which we could not live any common life at all. One is permitted to invoke them without having to explain all of life's ultimate mysteries. They compel our assent, if only because the alternative, moral chaos, is intolerable.

With animals we accept no such claims of absolute value, and so are left without any common and consistent standards. Ultimately, in the weighing of goods and interests, there's nothing on their side of the scale to counterbalance our demands upon them. Anyone with the right license can come along and deposit on our human side of the scale the slightest velleity: a "rack," a money-saver at the farm, a bowl of whale soup, tasty nibbles in the Churchill Room, a new shampoo to be poured into the eyes of laboratory rabbits, even the "free expression" of a crush video. And, just like that, all of the creatures' humble little claims are scattered as the scale plops down, without fail, resoundingly in our favor. Whatever high-minded motives we profess, in practice we recognize no intrinsic evils, acts that are wrong no matter who commits them or what the motive. Our laws concerning animals are a system of inconsistencies, special privileges, and arbitrary dispensations best described as codified caprice. Faced with the worst enormities a man might contemplate, where the creatures are concerned there are no inviolable prohibitions, no Thou Shalt Nots to make him draw back.

We do, in most places and in all Western societies, have cruelty statutes like the one quoted above, and it's easy to forget just how revolutionary these laws are all by themselves. In most times and places animals have been viewed as property, and only as property, even wildlife as the property of the state or sovereign. With these laws, first appearing in colonial Massachusetts and in nineteenth-century England, came the decisive moral concession from which all of our debates today quite naturally follow.

Having granted some protections to some animals, we are constantly confronted with the logic of our own laws, troubled by perfectly rational connections between the random or "wanton" acts of cruelty the law forbids and the systematic, institutional cruelties it still permits: If this animal is to be protected, why not that identical one, too? If it is cruelty to confine or mistreat a dog, a cat, or even a pet lamb or pig, why is it not cruelty to confine and mistreat millions of equally sensitive animals at Smithfield, IBP, ConAgra, and other such places? When we speak of the unavoidable severity of livestock production or laboratory experiments or trapping, and so on, just how rigorously are we defining "unavoidable"? By what standard of reason do we judge our own demands upon the creatures, the goods we place on our side of the moral scale?

Even as we debate whether animals have rights of their own against the cruelty of man, in effect, then, we have already admitted as much through laws forbidding cruelty. If a man beats, neglects, starves, or abandons a dog, and the dog belongs to him, there are no grounds to punish that man except by recognizing some independent moral claim of the dog. The dog, in fact, occupies two conflicting legal categories—that of property, as if he or she were just a thing, and that of a legal subject who may be the victim of a crime or even, in thirty-six of the fifty states, a felony. The same is true of our farm animals. They are protected, but only as property, like a tractor or a thresher. Under separate statutes, however, we impose certain very minimal standards asserting even their moral claims in rearing, transport, and slaughter. Now and then, in the rare cases where there are witnesses or video evidence, these statutes are actually enforced and the offenders prosecuted, as when one employee at a Florida dairy farm was charged in 1999 with dragging thirteen newborn calves into a muddy pit filled with rainwater and shooting them as they thrashed and kicked and gasped for air.[13] How often do things like that happen when no one is filming?

What we are really debating today is just how far the assumption of moral claims or rights may reasonably extend, when they are of lesser moral value than the claims we assert and when of greater value. Philosophers, as we will see, still labor at great length to produce other, "indirect" reasons for prohibiting cruelty, but the sheer exertion required of these arguments makes them suspect. If cruelty is a wrong, one immediately assumes that it is a wrong done to the animals. Certainly in cases where specific cruelty statutes apply the creatures must have some standing that the law asserts on their behalf, as we would naturally say were we to witness the animals being abused. We would say the abuser was being mean and unfair. We would say the creatures deserved better. We would say they had been victimized and mistreated. Why not also say they had a right to be treated better?

Where our own fundamental interests are at stake, in short, and our suffering in the balance, we are moral absolutists, and with animals and their suffering we are moral relativists, a position made explicit by the Japanese delegates back in Adelaide. All standards governing our treatment of animals are relative, they insist, the moral regard some of us feel for whales merely a narrow and irrational cultural prejudice. Everything depends on the value we care to place on their suffering or well-being, a matter, essentially, of preference. As Professor Peter Carruthers argues, "[I]t is wrong (in our culture) to cause suffering to an animal for trivial reasons, or to obtain sadistic pleasure."[14] It is wrong only in our culture, he believes, and then only owing to the delicate sensibilities of humans who falsely assume that animals actually do suffer conscious pain. Other people and cultures have different ideas, so that what one society calls sadism is for another normal and not to be judged.

To run through this once more for the benefit of Professor Carruthers, the problem here is very simple. While we are dealing with different people, different cultures, and different standards, we are still dealing with the same whale. Whales, when they swim into Japanese waters, do not assume a different nature, transformed at that instant from beings with moral claims into moral nonentities whose individual suffering or collective extinction suddenly becomes meaningless. Morally, a whale is one thing or the other. It's not whatever we decide it is at any given moment in any given culture.

There are wrongs against human beings we now regard as morally intolerable under any circumstances and regardless of local customs. Slavery comes to mind, or *suttee,* or foot-binding, or female circumcision, or, at the extreme, what in the last century we learned to call "crimes against humanity," atrocities for which the guilty can be prosecuted in international courts no matter what the laws of their own culture and country. Even if we do not attach the same moral importance to human welfare as to animal welfare, it is still human conduct we are talking about, and one wonders on what sacred tablet is it inscribed that there cannot be at least a few universally accepted standards to govern human conduct toward animals as well. There is not a culture in the world, including Japanese culture and certainly all Buddhist cultures, that does not have at least some concept of unacceptable cruelty to an animal. Indeed Japan's own "collective-guilt" argument against Western critics assumes such elementary standards by way of demonstrating that

Japan is not alone in disregarding them. Just what are we all guilty *of*? In the same way, when we condemn cruelty to animals, we don't call it un-American, or un-European, or un-Japanese. We call it inhumane.

SELF-EVIDENT TRUTHS

I'm going to leave the theories to the theorists, but in passing we might well wonder from what authority we get even these most basic of moral standards and prohibitions we think of as common decency and the minimal requirements of law. On what rational grounds do we make the simplest moral statements about ourselves—that our own lives have value, that there are certain things one must never do to a human being, that we have fundamental moral rights and claims and responsibilities, and that we all have them equally? Whatever the moral claims or rights of animals, after all, and however these might differ from our own, it would stand to reason that they come from the same source and by the same logic as our own moral claims and rights. So where do we get ours?

Well, there's the Bible, but we're not all Christians or Jews, and we don't live in theocracies. The sacred texts of other faiths and moral traditions have their own standards and admonitions—all, for example, offering some version of the Golden Rule. But these, too, are religious tenets, and we are not all bound to them. Then we have the wide array of current theories explaining the source of morality and rights, all the various modern "isms" from Professor Singer's preference utilitarianism to Professor Carruthers's contractualism. Trouble is, they're very different theories, and none of them were even around when our fundamental traditions of law and morality began to take shape.

Historically, the short answer is that we get our belief in human rights and human equality from the tradition of natural law. And there's a reason this tradition survived so long and influenced so much before our modern theorists got to work. It marks the key insight of mankind in our understanding of the world and our moral progress within it, the insight that makes other insights possible. Natural law doesn't explain every question about our existence or solve every last moral quandary, but it does have the great virtue of giving us a few solid assumptions to start with. It lays down a set of non-arbitrary standards and laws on which to base the standards and laws we make for ourselves.

This key insight is that all moral truth arises from the nature of things, true in themselves and in crucial respects accessible to reason. Every being has a nature, and that nature defines the ends and ultimate good for which it exists. In discerning these purposes we perceive what that being is, what it can do, what it must do to find its completion and fulfillment, and therefore what its moral interests are and how they may be advanced or hindered. Suddenly all is not arbitrary and we have a fixed point of reference, an intelligent basis for calling one thing good and another bad. That which advances a being onward toward its natural fulfillment is good. That which frustrates or perverts its natural development is bad.

In our case, as all the sages have reminded us over the centuries, what sets us apart is reason and in particular reason's ability to perceive the very moral order to which it belongs. You and I have many different needs, desires, and capacities in common with other animals. But what defines our nature is this power of reason to discern the design of our own and other lives, and then deliberately and cooperatively to seek their fulfillment. That is why when we observe ourselves or others giving in to impulse or desire at the expense of reason, we can call it wrong and unworthy. That is why we can call all wrongs by their name, greed greedy, sloth slothful, and vice vicious, and all the virtues by their names. All such words would be meaningless unless we had some objective standard of what a human being is and is supposed to do.

Natural rights in this way all presume natural standards, a good for which each right is the necessary means. Without the rights to property, free speech, free movement, free assembly, free worship, or freedom from the threat of violence we are hindered from achieving the good intended for each human life. We cannot live fully as human beings, obtaining the things we need and doing the things we ought.

Without recourse to any religious doctrine we can still speak of a fundamental moral difference between us and other animals. The adage "Better Socrates unhappy than a pig happy" is true, and no insult to the pig. We humans find our ultimate fulfillment in moral goodness, developing our capacities to the full and sharing those gifts with others. Pigs find their happiness in rooting, playing, and rolling around in the mud. Nature has given them less and demanded less. Nature has given more to us and demanded more, and human excellence is achieved exactly when the things that make us animals are governed by the things that make us human.

From natural law, too, we derive our understanding of human equality. When we say we are equal, really we are saying nothing more complicated than that we are each the same kind of being—that "nature," as John Adams observed, "throws us into the world all equal and alike."[15] Differences in gender or race or in our specific traits and capacities are accidental differences having nothing to do with the essential rational and moral nature that makes us all one kind of creature and not another. Since we all have the same moral nature, we must have the same moral purposes and ultimate good, and therefore also the same natural right to the means of living out those purposes and, in our many different ways, seeking that good.

Antiquated though "natural law" may sound, it holds up. It provides the only rational grounds I know of for claiming any one thing better than another, without reliance on religious belief or intuition or the constructs of theory. Whether or not we have ever even heard of the term, natural law provides formal support for the commonsense morality we all invoke whenever we speak of anything as just plain true or wrong or good or bad or just or unjust. Here in America it is what our Declaration of Independence means by "inalienable rights" and "self-evident truths" and "the Laws of Nature and Nature's God."

Modern philosophers tend to view the assumption of natural law as an archaic obstacle to enlightenment and progress because it obliges us to acknowledge some things as simply true whether we like it or not. But they have carried mankind a long way, the assumptions of natural law, and for that reason alone command our careful attention. Whether natural law accords with one's own bold new theories or not, it still happens to be the central moral principle underlying Western civil society, democracy, and the rights and protections we all claim for ourselves. Natural law is more revolutionary than any scheme of rights ever conceived precisely because it does affirm an authority higher than ourselves and those who rule over us.

Natural law is just that, a law and not a theory. If anything it serves as a kind of anti-theory, an understanding of natural proprieties, an acceptance of things as they are prior to man's attempts to intellectualize them and make them his own. It compels us by reason to perceive purposes and goods beyond our own desires and decrees, to heed natural boundaries, to respect and live within an order of which we are a part but not the center. It asserts what the philosophers call a teleological view of a moral universe with a detectable structure, direction, and broad design beyond our power to alter or escape. Our lives do have a purpose, written into our very nature. We are defined by our reason, not by our urges, passions, or preferences. Some moral statements are true, others false, and we can know the difference.

✑

Those same thinkers who reject the assumption of natural law have demonstrated again and again what happens without it, Professor Singer being only the latest. If there is no law above our own laws, then nothing inherently has value and nothing inherently is right or wrong. We have no standards above the ideals, aspirations, and preferences of the day, no fixed principles allowing us to speak of "unjust laws" when wrongs are apparent or even of "human rights" beyond whatever rights are accorded us in whatever society we happen to live. Everything in the end comes down to power, and one by one the prohibitions fall away.

Of course, as Professor Singer would be the first to point out, many of the philosophers and theologians who shaped our natural-law traditions viewed the creatures as fit only for natural enslavement, as Saint Thomas Aquinas believed. One answer is simple enough. Wise as they were, Aristotle, Aquinas, and others just didn't know as much about animals as we do. They helped to give us our understanding of rights as a reflection of the nature of things, but did not fully understand the nature of animals as conscious beings capable of thought and feeling. It was an error of fact, but not an error of principle. And once that is corrected it seems to me that natural law still makes as sound a guide in understanding the animals as it is in understanding ourselves.

After all, they have natures too. Exactly as we can discern our own high place and purpose in the world, we can discern that they have each a place to fill and a purpose to live out as well. For them, too, there is such a thing as the good, such a thing as dignity, in simply being what they are and doing what they do. We sense this, I think, when we step out of our abstractions and actually witness cruelty to animals. Just as Blake's "Robin red breast in a cage / Sets all heaven in a rage," in seeing a creature mistreated we sense that some wrong has been done, some good has been ignored, some law violated even if it's not in the local statutes.

The fact that animals cannot themselves understand all this is irrelevant. How often in our own lives do we stop to reflect on "the good"? Most of the time, like them, we just experience the goodness of life and the natural purposes for which we were made, or the hurts and frustrations that come when we are prevented from doing so. And for us, who can see the good in things and call it such, you would think that in some very uncomplicated way we could acknowledge in our laws the right of all creatures under our power to have their natures respected and their dignity as living creatures recognized.

Far from being some new idea of mine, Catholic teaching asserts this very rule—"We are bound to act towards them in a manner comfortable to their nature"[16]—and even in our secular age one is hard put to think of any principle of Christian moral conduct so thoroughly or casually disregarded.

It is as simple as saying that nature has made birds to fly—therefore we should not raise them in cages for release at the pleasure of "gentleman hunters" positioned for the shot. Nature has made elephants and giraffe and rhinoceros to inhabit the plains—therefore we should not shoot them, stuff them, and stick them in our ballrooms for display. Nature has made whales and dolphins to swim the seas away from man—therefore we should not track them down by helicopters and attack or electrocute them from factory ships until they are almost gone from the waters. Nature has made pigs and cows and lambs and fowl to nurse from their mothers and walk and graze and mix with their kind—therefore we have no business confining and torturing and treating them like machines of our own invention.

The "nature of things" is an awfully broad standard, but at least it's something, and rigorously applied might help us to avoid the worst of evils we inflict on the creatures, like trying to make them what they are not with our monstrous genetic programs, or hiding them from the world in the prisons we call farms. The standard narrows, moreover, when we turn it back on ourselves and the goods we assert on our side of the moral scale, for cruelty is not only a denial of the animal's nature but a betrayal of our own. If we are defined by reason and morality, then reason and morality must define our choices, even where animals are concerned. When people say, for example, that they like their veal or hot dogs just too much to ever give them up, and yeah it's sad about the farms but that's just the way it is, reason hears in that the voice of gluttony. We can say that here what makes a human being human is precisely the ability to understand that the suffering of an animal is more important than the taste of a treat.

Likewise, when a thinking man's hunter like Roger Scruton launches into one of his breathless descriptions of the "centaur hour" of the kill, then we must ask him to please explain the moral value of a centaur hour, and just where exactly do such ecstasies fit into his own assumption of human beings accountable to reason and what he calls the "moral law"? And if they don't fit, then they don't fit, and he must concede his pleasures as the base and disordered appetites they are.

If natural law is what informs our own laws and moral codes among one another, in short, then it should also inform our laws and moral codes regarding animals. And its most basic and revolutionary insight is the same for them as for us. Any moral claims we have, we have simply because of what we are. Any moral claims that animals have in relation to us, they, too, have simply because of what they are. We don't each get to decide their moral claims for ourselves. The moral value of any creature belongs to that creature, acknowledged or not, a different value from our own but just as much a hard and living reality. Just as our own individual moral worth does not hinge on the opinion of others, their moral worth does not hinge upon our estimation of them. Whatever it is, it is.

Add a little old-time religion and natural law has the further advantage of being an affirmation of life as good and purposeful, instead of treating life, in the way of so many contemporary philosophers, as some gnawing problem to be solved or escaped. It sees every life, ours and the lives around us, even in trial and sorrow as the gifts they are—no creature slighted in being what it is, all exactly as they are meant to be. It reminds us that creation is not just a colorful backdrop for human action. It turns our minds to first things, helping us to ally ourselves with something good, permanent, and infinitely greater than any plan we could ever conceive or any profit we could ever gain. One needn't be a Buddhist to share in the sense that "All beings seek for happiness; so let your compassion extend itself to all." Nor must we be Catholics, or even to profess any particular faith at all, to feel with Pope John Paul II "the joy of creation":

> God, who in creating saw that His creation was good, is the source of joy for all creatures, and above all for humankind. God the Creator seems to say of all creation: "It is good that you exist." And His joy spreads especially through the "good news," according to which *good is greater than all that is evil in the world.* . . . Creation was given and entrusted to humankind as a duty, representing not a source of suffering but *the foundation of a creative existence in the world.*[17]

When this sense of the goodness of life passes away, what's left is the "horrifying nothingness" we have felt in scenes of farm animals being led outdoors by the hundreds of thousands to be shot, heaped into flames, and shoveled into pits. For whatever purpose Nature designed them, for whatever good Nature's God created them, it could not have been for that.

THE MIRROR TEST

It should tell us something important all by itself that animals have this way of constantly confronting us with ultimate questions—about truth and falsehood, guilt and innocence, God and sanctity and the soul—forcing us to define ourselves and our relationship to the world.

Earlier I asked this question: Does any creature have any place and purpose in the world beyond its usefulness to us, any inherent value or claim to existence that we are bound to honor and respect? That is what the rights matter comes down to. And though science and reason can lay down some boundaries and definitions for us, ultimately I cannot answer the question, fully and finally, any more than you or Peter Singer or anyone else can. It is beyond both my capacities and the aim of this book.

The reason it is so difficult is that we cannot answer without giving some final and authoritative account of ourselves, of the meaning of our own existence, our own place and purpose in the world, and that only the Author can give. Here as elsewhere, we should be wary of anyone who knows all the answers. "He who is unaware of his ignorance," it is wisely said, "will only be misled by his knowledge." When philosophers, theologians, or scientists inform us that animals are of absolutely equal moral value to humans or of absolutely no moral value, that we may never use animals, even cooperatively and humanely, or that we may use them without end, they have all overstepped themselves. They are asserting ultimate values beyond anyone's knowing, venturing into regions where even natural law and the most profound insights of man are to sovereign truth as a baby's building blocks are to language. All the more reason, in our dealings with the other creatures, to draw back and be sparing. "Heav'n is too high to know what passes there," as the angel Raphael says to Eve in *Paradise Lost*; "be lowly wise."[18]

This is sound advice in matters of human morality, and it can serve us just as well in our treatment of animals. Whatever they are, however they stand in their Maker's judgment, we know that up close there is something about them that seeks our moral attention, something that can make even the cruel mourn their cruelties. We feel a connection, a fellowship of common origin, and try as one might to dismiss them as nothing, in fact we can never quite figure out their moral status until we have truly contemplated our own.

How often, when we describe animals and pronounce judgment on them, we are really talking about ourselves, judging what it means to be human.

When, as I think has happened with many people today, we come to see ourselves primarily as consumers and conquerors, then the creatures will mirror that vision, appearing only as commodities, resources, and production units to be governed only by the laws of supply and demand. This is the attitude that demands to know, for example, "what is so special about whales"— as if a whale, to achieve significance, has to *do* something for us, to serve little man, and just being a glorious and innocent creature is not sufficient. It doesn't end there, either, this grasping vision of life that sees only things to buy and sell and exploit. We live in an age when you can prowl the streets of major cities and find human beings offering themselves in store windows, or just reach for the yellow pages and have them delivered. It is the same mindset at work, spreading in our world, and after a while this attitude can find nothing very special about anything or anybody, let alone whales.

Likewise, when we see ourselves as the product of blindly amoral evolution, as a kind of global superpredator, the creatures will mirror that vision, too, appearing as enemies of progress, mere prey to be caught and used and made to pay. Darwin himself, a member of the RSPCA, was more modest in his views and actually quite empathetic toward animals, often describing in his letters and journals their capacity for misery and happiness alike. But today's evolutionary scientists seem to remember only the survival-of-the-fittest part, just as many Christians and Jews remember only the go-forth-and-subdue part of their Bible. In a strange way, on questions of animal welfare, the fundamentalist and the evolutionist speak a common language of power, appropriation, and consumption. Mankind's preeminence in the world, as Mr. Budiansky writes, depends ever and always on "the strength of mind to slaughter."[19]

When, like Professor Singer, we see ourselves as sovereign beings, defined ultimately by sentience and not by soul, by the search for pleasure and the fear of pain, animals will mirror that vision, too—calling to us as fellow victims with equal claims to be heard in a universe without purpose or design or a designer. When, like Mr. Scruton, we think of ourselves as "self-created beings," inevitably our every whim will seem a divine decree, the creatures around us all so many interchangeable "generic beings," and the delight we find in killing them a high and noble form of recreation.

And, whatever our faith or basic moral outlook, when we see ourselves as beings created by God, who knows us and loves us and has a plan for us, so we will tend to see them—entirely dependent beings just like us, made to some purpose beyond our full knowing, formed of the same dust and fated for the same death. We have a way of forgetting this in talking about the animals and their rights, forgetting our own ultimate dependence and entirely contingent existence. The reality is beautifully expressed by Felix Salten at the end of *Bambi: A Life in the Woods,* when the fawn's father leads him up to the body of a dead hunter:

"Come near," said the old stag, "don't be afraid."

He was lying with His pale, naked face turned upward, His hat a little to one side on the snow. Bambi, who did not know anything about hats, thought His horrible head was split in two. The poacher's shirt, opened at the neck, was pierced where a wound gaped like a small red mouth. Blood was oozing out slowly. Blood was drying on His hair and around His nose. A big pool of it lay on the snow, which was melting from the warmth.

"We can stand right beside Him," the old stag began softly, "and it isn't dangerous."

Bambi looked down at the prostrate form whose limbs and skin seemed so mysterious and terrible to him. He gazed at the dead eyes that stared up sightlessly at him. Bambi couldn't understand at all. . . .

"Do you see, Bambi," the old stag went on, "do you see how He's lying there dead, like one of us? Listen, Bambi. He isn't all-powerful as they say. Everything that lives and grows doesn't come from Him. He isn't above us. He's just the same as we are. He has the same fears, the same needs, and suffers in the same way. He can be killed like us, and then He lies helpless on the ground like all the rest of us, as you see him now."

There was a silence.

"Do you understand me, Bambi?" asked the old stag.

"I think so," Bambi said in a whisper.

"Then speak," the old stag commanded.

Bambi was inspired, and said trembling, "There is Another who is over us all, over us and over Him."[20]

There's probably some truth in the idea that killing for sport is an act of rebellion against one's own mortality, as if in possessing the power of death one somehow defeats or deflects it. As bow hunters are urged in a catalog of the trade: "Life is short. Hunt hard."[21] But, of course, there in the end lies every last sovereign one of us, as powerless before death's dominion as the lowliest creature that creeps upon the earth. Only before one another do we ourselves even have a right to life. Before our Maker we are rightless, our very existence an act of divine generosity. Many environmentalists today share, I think, this basic outlook of reverence even if they would reject such explicitly religious language as unsophisticated.

It is to no avail, in any case, to argue over the details of animal welfare where the basic premises are violently opposed. One could go on and on with long weepy appeals for kindness toward animals to Mr. Budiansky, but it's probably pointless because, in theory at least, he sees a universe ruled by raw force, and indeed with his "covenant of the wild" has managed to redefine human compassion into human conquest. He, in turn, could fault me for living in some childish fantasyland of chirping birdies and capering lambs, blessing their Maker and giving Him glory, but again we're operating from entirely different premises.

Short of answering life's eternal questions to everyone's satisfaction, all we can really do is examine each basic outlook on its own terms, seeing where it leads and whether that particular view is in fact the view we hold, an attitude and set of principles that we are prepared to defend and to live by. Having tabled ultimate matters, moreover, it actually becomes easier to think clearly about our duties to animals. For there is a logic to these basic assumptions about animals and, taking each in turn, we are then in a position to test it against our vision of ourselves.

If animals are the products of blindly amoral evolution, then of course Mr. Budiansky is correct and we, too, are shaped and driven by the same amoral forces. If they are victims in a universe without purpose or meaning or a Creator who made them, then so are we, and rights and entitlements become everything. If animals are just commodities, then we are just consumers, with no greater good than material pleasure and no higher law than appetite. And if there is a God and they are His creatures, not ours, then there is indeed a higher law regarding their care and we must answer to it—not just when it suits us, not just when we feel the spirit upon us, and not just when it's cost-efficient, but always.

We have, in short, the standard of internal consistency. We need not agree on everything to identify specific contradictions and falsehoods. You can operate by one or another of these basic assumptions, but you cannot operate by a mix of them—here acting in blindly amoral fashion and there in the spirit of religious piety, here extending kindness and there spreading terror, here treating animals with respect and there treating them like refuse. We may not know or agree upon ultimate moral truths. But we do know that opposite things cannot at the same time be true: identical creatures at the same time capable of suffering and incapable of suffering, worthy of moral consideration and unworthy of such concern, within the reach of God's love and beneath it.

Many people when they examine their beliefs about animals will find, I think, that they hold radically contradictory views, allowing for benevolence one moment and disregard the next. And the reality is that we have a choice of one or the other. As a practical matter we are free, of course, to do more or less as we please absent further changes in law. As a matter of conscience, however, we must each ask ourselves which outlook is truer, which is closer to our heart, which attitude leaves us feeling better and worthier when we act upon it, and then follow that conviction where it leads. And when we fail to act consistently with our own moral principles, when we profess one thing and do another, we must be willing to call that error by its name. It is hypocrisy.

Kindness to animals, as columnist Jeffrey Hart writes, arises from "the imperative duty as rooted in the concept of the fully human. Does it not diminish the human to abuse an animal? Who wants to see in the mirror the man who tortured an animal?"[22] Most of us know just what he means. And for us that is usually enough—the mirror test, simple decency, a functioning conscience.

But, of course, most public forms of cruelty have now been banned. Most of the practices we're talking about here take place out of view. And those who do the foulest things have different ideas about what it means to be fully human. So the mirror test is not enough unless applied everywhere, just as in the case of wrongs done to human beings. We must apply the basic demands of common decency not only to ourselves but to others, not only to the cruelties we see but to the ones we don't see. We cannot bestow our kindness on the animals we name and know while viewing as nothing the nameless, faceless beasts we condemn in our farms and labs to lives of ceaseless misery.

Like so many philosophical questions today, animal welfare presents a choice between sovereign man and sovereign truth, moral truth as our unyielding standard or as a convention of our own making, to be observed at our convenience. Just as in logic a thing cannot be and not be at the same time, in moral reasoning identical creatures cannot be worthy of moral consideration and unworthy of moral consideration; this dog or dolphin or elephant morally significant and those others not. Whatever moral status we grant one, we must grant to all that come within the scope of our power.

For good reason have sport hunters, whalers, furriers, and others who commit and promote acts of cruelty lately adapted the rhetoric of the "pro-choice" movement, and for good reason must we reject it. There are truths greater than our own wishes. Things are what they are. And standards that are left for us to observe or not observe are not standards at all. The biological and moral realities—to say nothing of God's own plan, whatever it may be—do not change with our own wishes, though prayers must certainly help. A person is a person just as a dog is a dog, a deer a deer, a pig a pig, and so on through the animal kingdom. And either they suffer or they do not suffer. Either that suffering has moral value or it does not have moral value. Either there is a God or there isn't. Either He cares about animals or He doesn't. Either we have duties of kindness or we do not.

That does not mean there are no other moral considerations in the balance where animals are concerned, such as our own human needs. Nor does it give us some sort of unerring formula to solve each and every moral question regarding the welfare of animals. It just means that we are obliged in every instance to call things what they are and to observe the standards they require. When we assert reason as our authority for dominion, we must use that authority reasonably. When we assert free will as our distinctive human quality, we must *use* our free will not only in acts of self-interest but in acts of self-restraint. When we call something a "necessary evil," something requiring the suffering or death of a fellow creature, the evil is real and it had better be necessary.

This principle of treating natural equals equally is not some abstraction pulled from nowhere to make a case for animals. It is, in the tradition of our own laws, the rational basis for the legal protections we place upon human life, too—for our belief in the moral equality of human beings. It states simply that reality is reality, that the moral claims of other creatures are facts about those creatures, regardless of when or where or whether it pleases us to recognize them. It is the law behind all laws, commanding consistency, coherence, order, humility. Indeed, absent the tenets of revealed religion it is the last safeguard of reason against the worst abuses of power—the spirit declaring that things have only the value we choose to give them, and that even the most innocent life on earth, a baby waiting to be born, may be destroyed if we wish it so.

You will find no theory in this book, then. It would be enough if the lines of division were clearer, if people on both sides of the debate would examine their own moral attitudes while taking a careful look at the company they are keeping and the things they are defending, excusing, or ignoring altogether. It would be enough if more of us would simply compare our own principles, our own vision of life and nature, whether secular or religious or somewhere in between, with the reality of how animals are actually treated, often in our name. If such things cannot be justified, if the great majority of us find them reprehensible and wrong and unworthy of humanity, then why on earth are they all permitted? Why do we tolerate them, in our lives and in our laws?

In the same way, animal liberationists who turn to Peter Singer for guidance must ask themselves how we can protect vulnerable animals from the caprice of man if we do not protect vulnerable people, the sick, the aged, the newborn, and the unborn—how it is possible to love cats and dogs and baby seals if we do not love the most innocent and defenseless of human beings. I saw a car recently with two bumper stickers, "Save the Whales" and "Every Child a Wanted Child." But something is amiss there. Why not also Every Whale a Wanted Whale? And why not also Save the Children?

Nor are duties, the things we *must* do, even the final standard in our treatment of animals. There is the morality of duty and there is the morality of aspiration. Often the latter is the best guide of all, opening our eyes to new possibilities. We do not, in thinking about our own lives, simply ask what minimum effort is required of us and then content ourselves with that. In our better moments we try to go beyond that, to exceed the standard, to stretch ourselves and thereby become better people.

We do this as fathers and husbands and mothers and wives. We do this as Christians and Jews and Moslems and Buddhists and Hindus, in our duties to one another and to conscience. We do it in our work and careers, whatever that calling may be. We do it as friends and neighbors. We do it simply as human beings trying to leave our mark in the world, to spread a little love and goodwill where we can. Why should we not also do it as stewards of the earth, the caretakers of creation? Why should we not also carry that same spirit, that same moral vision of ourselves and our possibilities, into our dealings with the creatures of the world?

A Crime Against Nature

In the case of Smithfield, then, and the entire way of life it stands for, the question is simple and blunt: Looking into that mirror, what do you see? Where is the charity in it, where is the humanity? How does it square with the kind of society you wish to live in and the kind of person you hope to be? If you are a religious person, where in that scene is the God who loves these creatures and asks us to do the same?

For my part, even if it were demonstrated to me that these poor beasts have no rights at all while I have every right to subject them to such privation and torment, and to delegate that authority to the gentlemen of Smithfield, it is a right I do not want, a power I gladly surrender. That is the whole idea of mercy, after all, that it is entirely discretionary, entirely undeserved. "It drop-peth as the gentle rain from heaven."[23] There is no such thing as a right to mercy, not for the animals and not even for us.

We tell ourselves that all this carnage is inevitable, traditional, the way of the world. And until our own day, when we have removed all compassion from the process even as a wide array of meat substitutes appear, this was a plausible position. Hunting and raising animals for meat, as the historian Will Durant observes,

> were not stages in economic development, they were modes of activ-ity destined to survive into the highest forms of civilized society. Once the center of life, they are still its hidden foundations; behind our literature and philosophy, our ritual and art, stand the stout killers of Packingtown. We do our hunting by proxy, not having the stomach for honest killing in the fields. . . . In the last analysis civi-lization is based upon the food supply. The cathedral and the capitol, the museum and the concert chamber, the library and the university are the facade; in the rear are the shambles.[24]

As a hard fact of human experience, this is true enough. Yet it is also part of civilization to question and to challenge and to change. History is full of other "hidden foundations" too long unexamined, old ways that people could not part with, practices about which they were proud and sure and defiant when they should have been ashamed.

Before you dismiss vegetarianism as radical animal rights nonsense, contradicted by ages of custom and habit the world over, reflect for a moment on our own human experience, on all the violence and brutality and ceaseless subjugation from which our own concepts of human rights arise. Sometimes we speak of human rights and human dignity in terms of such elegant certitude that we forget the facts of the matter—as if these truths and natural laws have always been understood and appreciated by man, advanced and refined through some Aristotelian inquiry calmly conducted across the centuries: Man the seeker of truth, Nature's Nobleman in his constant quest for wisdom. Human beings, as Desmond Morris writes in *The Naked Ape*, "find the contemplation of our humble origins somehow offensive. . . . Our climb to the top has been a get-rich-quick story, and, like all nouveaux riches, we are very sensitive about our background. We are also in constant danger of betraying it."[25]

Of course these truths we declare to be self-evident are relatively new to human history, and they are not everywhere held as self-evident, as in corners of the world where even today we find human slavery. They seem self-evident now, but it sure took us a while to figure it out. The reason we proclaim human rights with such fervor is that always there have been, and always will be, human beings constantly seeking to crush them, to vanquish, to destroy, and to exploit other human beings, often enough in the name of civilization and economic advancement. Our own human rights, in other words, are not an abstract proposition but rather a practical response to the most fundamental of all moral problems: Human evil.

Christians and Jews call this the problem of the Fall, rarely reflecting on its implications for man as steward of the earth, never, as it seems, acknowledging that here, too, man is capable of mischief and evildoing. Dominion, in religious orthodoxy, has become a quest for subjugation without limits, cruelty to animals a sin without judgment. The Tempter is strangely silent on this front.

Along the way, in our understanding of human rights, some traditions that once seemed perfectly normal and natural have, in fact, been cruel and mean and oppressive. "It is a totalitarian morality," says Roger Scruton of today's animal protection causes, "which inverts the old scheme of values and makes them into crimes."[26] But, historically, that is a better description of

Christian morality, and every great moral advance we now take as a given was once derided as the radical and meddlesome project of a few cranks. Everyone, even Aristotle himself, once assumed that human slavery was part of the natural moral hierarchy. Roman law sanctioned slavery by the *jus gentium,* loosely translated as "Everyone does it," and it is probably no coincidence that animal welfare as a serious moral cause had to wait until the 1800s when human slavery was abolished. Everyone, in some places and ages, once thought human infanticide was a reasonable option, as some maintain even today—Peter Singer being only the most explicit among them. Everyone except a few Christian moralists once assumed that deliberately killing civilians was a legitimate tactic of war. Everyone except a few cranks once thought it acceptable to use children for factory labor and to treat women and dark-skinned people as second-class citizens, or indeed as mere things, as chattel—and so on through the ages.

History affords ample evidence as well that even when the greatest enormities are committed against innocent human beings, majority opinion can be indifferent, and even the best of people stone-blind to the cruelties in their midst. Every age, as Allan Bloom observed, is blind to its own worst madness.

It may be adamantly objected that I am equating injustice to animals with injustice to human beings, a sign of my own misplaced priorities and moral confusion. This rejoinder only cuts the other way. It is only further evidence of our own boundless capacity for self-delusion, especially where there is money involved. For if so many wrongs once thought right can fill our human story, such unbounded violence and disregard of human life, how much easier for the human heart to overlook the wrongs done to lowly animals, to tolerate intolerable things. Tradition with all its happy assumptions and necessary evils, all of its content majorities and stout killers, is not always a reliable guide. "We had stopped short at Comfort, and mistaken it for Civilization," as Disraeli remarked in another context.[27] Sometimes tradition and habit are just that, comfortable excuses to leave things be, even when they are unjust and unworthy. Sometimes—not often, but sometimes—the cranks and radicals turn out to be right. Sometimes Everyone is wrong.

In passing we may note the rare exceptions, including what Durant in his *Story of Civilization* describes as perhaps the closest thing in human history to an herbivorous society—for we vegetarians of today, our own little golden age way back in the third century B.C. in the time of an Indian ruler named Ashoka. Overcome, as lore has it, by remorse at the violence of his own conquests and ruthlessness at home, his reign known abroad as "Ashoka's Hell," he set free his slaves and captives, reformed the criminal code, ordered that animals be treated with leniency, renounced the royal pastime of tiger and elephant hunting, commanded an end to all blood sports, opened the world's first animal clinics, declared himself a vegetarian, and had his new creed— the "Eightfold Noble Way"—inscribed on rocks and pillars throughout the realm. "Now," read one of these imperial edicts,

> by reason of the practice of piety by His Sacred and Gracious Majesty the King, the reverberation of the war-drums has become the Reverberation of the Law. . . . As for many years before has not happened, now, by reason of the inculcation of the Law of Piety by His Sacred and Gracious Majesty the King, there is increased abstention from the sacrificial slaughter of living creatures . . . seemly behavior to relatives, seemly behavior to Brahmans, hearken-ing to father and mother, hearkening to elders. Thus, as in many other ways, the practice of the Law of Piety has increased, and His Sacred and Gracious majesty the King will make such practice of the Law increase further.[28]

"Half the empire," we are told, "waited hopefully for Ashoka's death."[29] But I like to think of the other half, who perhaps discovered, as many have today, that life really is possible without extracting the suffering and flesh of animals, now so punitive and unrelenting, and that this abstinence belongs to a broader vision of gracious and seemly behavior.

Philosophically, one can look at it this way. Broadly speaking, for as long as people have engaged in moral thought, mankind has acted upon two funda-mental beliefs: (a) It is morally permissible to raise and slaughter animals for our own consumption—a material good—because doing so is necessary for our survival and well-being—a moral good. But this very claim of moral sanc-tion attested to the belief that there was a sacrifice involved and that (b) even in livestock production we do have at least certain minimal obligations of kindness to animals—a moral good.

Whether these are direct or indirect obligations is for the moment irrele-vant to the fact that they exist, that they require certain restraints on our part, and that before the age of industrial farming one could act upon both (a) and (b) at the same time. And the problem is just this simple. The moral component of (a) is gone. We have no valid claims of need anymore, only our claim to the material good of fare to which we are accustomed. Meanwhile, in a global, high-tech economy of six billion consumers—perhaps nine or ten billion by the year 2100—livestock animals simply cannot be raised under humane conditions. We are left, then, with exactly one material good and one moral good, our pleasure weighed against our duty of compassion. And these can no longer coexist. One or the other must be abandoned.

Among those who have noticed this shift in the scales is environmentalist Robert F. Kennedy, Jr., who writes of how, "like other Americans, I've reconciled myself to the idea that an animal's life has been sacrificed to bring me a meal of pork or chicken. However, industrial meat production—which subjects animals to a life of torture—has escalated the karmic costs beyond reconciliation." Mr. Kennedy, who is leading a campaign against Smithfield for environmental negligence, buys only meat raised from small farms that "treat their animals with dignity and respect."[30]

I think that is a decent compromise, and it is good to hear such a prominent voice taking the side of animals. How rare to hear anyone today speak of the "dignity" of these creatures. But this middle ground is vanishing with our small farms. More and more, consumers are left with a choice between two radical alternatives. The way I figure it, we can be radically kind or we can be radically cruel.

I know, of course, that we vegetarians are still considered an eccentric minority. It is always hard to raise the subject without feeling a little awkward, the skunk at every party and barbecue. Frankly I have felt a little uneasy just writing about the matter, forcing unpleasant details upon the reader, a task that can be mean and spiteful if done in the wrong spirit. As harsh as the process of industrial farming may be, the motive, after all, is not cruelty. It's not as if anyone *wants* the creatures to suffer. We would all wish it otherwise. And in a way the standard vegetarian argument that the average person eats meat, and yet could not bear to see how it was produced, actually speaks well of the average person. Imagine a world in which most people *enjoyed* hearing and seeing the details.

I think this is why even the most impassioned vegetarian arguments often miss the mark: Because we tend to judge ourselves by motive and intention rather than by means and result. We vegetarians, in our defense, are at least prepared to look at actual consequences and inconvenient realities, understanding that he who wills the end wills also the means. At least we have confronted the seriousness of the matter, thought about it, made a conscious and deliberate choice, and how many people can actually pinpoint some moment in their lives when they *decided* to eat meat? From the first bits of flesh placed on the tray of our high chairs, most people go through life never once questioning that this is natural and necessary, the way things are and must ever be. Everyone does it, so it must be right.

Here's a good question to ask yourself: Would you give up eating meat *if* you were persuaded that factory farming was cruel and unethical? Hypothetically, in other words, how difficult and inconvenient would it be to act upon your own moral concerns? Or indeed how socially embarrassing would it be, how troublesome to have to make a choice and explain and stay with it? The next question would be whether it is, in fact, the absence of moral concerns that prevents the change, or the prospect of the difficulties and inconveniences.

Likewise, if you must have meat, regarding it as a right and necessary thing while viewing factory farming as a bad and unnecessary thing, do you, like Mr. Kennedy, act on that distinction by buying only meats raised by humane standards? And if not, why not? Why is industrial farming wrong by your own standards, yet not a serious enough wrong to warrant a change in your own daily choices? Think of the effect that this decision alone would have on modern agriculture, more millions of consumers making that one little effort every day to spare the creatures from needless misery.

Marjorie Kinnan Rawlings in *The Yearling* captures a feeling many people will recognize, here describing the boy, before he has befriended his fawn, gazing upon a deer his father has just slain:

> Jody examined the deer hide. It was large and handsome and red with spring. The game seemed to be two different animals. On the chase, it was the quarry. He wanted only to see it fall. When it lay dead and bleeding, he was sickened and sorry. His heart ached over the mangled death. Then when it was cut into portions, and dried and salted and smoked; or boiled or baked or fried in the savory kitchen or roasted over the camp-fire, it was only meat, like bacon,

and his mouth watered at its goodness. He wondered by what alchemy it was changed, so that what sickened him one hour, maddened him with hunger, the next. It seemed as though there were either two different animals or two different boys.[31]

Later in the story the boy expresses the wish that "we could git our meat without killin' it." His Pa replies, "Hit's a pity, a'right. But we got to eat."[32] In the end the child must kill his own deer, Flag, whom he had found orphaned by a sinkhole in the woods. That night Jody was filled with sorrow, "but a man took it for his share and went on." He called out for him in his sleep, but "it was not his own voice that called. It was a boy's voice. Somewhere beyond the sinkhole, past the magnolia, under the live oaks, a boy and a yearling ran side by side, and were gone forever."[33]

I find this very beautiful, for it is true that part of being an adult is to understand that there really are necessary evils in the world, that life does present things that are sad and hard to bear but nevertheless unavoidable, like the punishments of law or many of our own griefs or the crying of lambs in distress. It is part of being an adult to accept these along with life's joys, to take them all for our share and go on. Predation itself, the intrinsic evil in nature's design of creatures devouring and absorbing one another to survive, is among the hardest of all things to fathom. One falls back in the end on the idea that it was not God's design at all, that there lies a hope and expectation beyond creation's "groan of travail," as we are promised, not only mankind but all creatures delivered from our "bondage to decay."[34]

It is an interesting thing all by itself how much animals are bound up in our ideas of manhood, as with the *man's* dinner of steak and potatoes and his general impression of us scrawny little vegetarians, nibbling away at our rabbit food, as somehow weak and effeminate. "I am like a cougar," as James Swan puts it in his *In Defense of Hunting*. "I must have meat."[35] You find this even in the writings of sophisticated thinkers like Freud, who diagnosed the vegetarianism of Leonardo da Vinci as the sign of a feminine personality, or the philosopher Spinoza, who scoffed at "womanish pity" toward animals.

This kind of manly realism is like the "civilization" argument, just a little too easy, and how fragile that kind of manhood which requires such huffing and puffing, such constant affirmation and wearisome self-display. The hunter must hunt, Mr. Swan continues, to feel himself "fully alive"[36] (only more so with a bow, "for it is the twang of the bowstring that calls me"[37]).

"Hunting as self-actualization seems like psychopathology to some people. Yet, for many passionate hunters, one of the few areas in life in which they can feel fully alive is the hunt. We need to understand the passionate hunter, for it is in the passions that people achieve their potentials of being human."[38] Roger Scruton, you'll recall, offers the similar justification of hunting and meat eating as "deeper than choice,"[39] in its possessive violence a kind of "homecoming to our natural state."[40]

Of course it is *not* in the passions and appetites that we achieve our highest potential, at least as moral beings, but more often just the opposite, in the passions that we sink to the lowest depravities, and in the denial of moral choices that we commit our worst offenses. It is part of being an adult to understand this. It is part of being an adult to give up a few things now and then, to make moral judgments and to exercise self-control. And it is part of being a man to take responsibility, to face the consequences of one's own actions, to measure and to weigh things and sometimes to do without. I wonder if this doesn't explain why, even as they are incessantly strutting their masculinity, our modern hunters talk so much about being "like boys again," because in young boys cruelty may be forgiven. "Self-actualization," for a man, is self-mastery, the strength to govern his appetites and passions and not be governed by them.

I once did a column on the subject for *National Review* and was amazed by the volume and indignation of the letters that came back, almost all of them from men. Invariably they conceded that factory farming raises serious moral problems. Almost invariably, the same readers informed they had no intention whatever of changing their habits, they *liked* their meat and would I please drop the matter and mind my own business. "In the future," concluded one fellow, "I'll take greater care to thank God for what he's provided whenever I enjoy my favorite dish—pork loin stuffed with prunes and dried apricots. Mmmmm, it's so good." "I would submit to Mr. Scully," wrote another, "that if one does not have the stomach to chop the head off a Cornish hen, then perhaps one should forgo the pleasure of eating it. As for the rest of us, *bon appétit!*" "Like it or not," said a third, "we humans are predators. . . . You keep your mitts off my bacon-cheese-venison burger and I'll promise not to touch your tofu."

What are all these hardy menfolk really defending here? A pleasure. A flavor. A feeling in their bellies. And what does this say of them? Here life has presented them with a moral problem, maybe by their lights a little one but a moral problem all the same, and this is all they can think about, hens and burgers and pork loin stuffed with the prunes and dried apricots. It's just too inconvenient, too much trouble to change. I hear this a lot, even from people I admire, the voice of appetite unwilling to brook the least hint of criticism, not only indifferent to the animals but scornful of those who are. And frankly, faced with the trials and terrors inflicted on our farm animals, faced with lagoons of filth and that godawful squealing, *Mmmmm, it's so good* is not my idea of a man's reply.

I enjoy a good feed as much as anybody, and am rarely the first to pull back from the table. Yet nothing so convinces me of the soundness of my own choice to do without meat as to be told again and again, in a thousand ads and cultural cues, that I have no choice at all, that I *must* have meat to be strong and stout and hardy. I *must* have animal flesh, and yet somehow, with little sense of privation or struggle or self-mortification, I have managed to go twenty-eight years without it, never suffered a single nutrition-related medical problem, and, if I may strut a bit myself, have been known to bench press a respectable 355 pounds.

All you are getting from meat, after all, is the protein converted by the animal from its own herbivorous diet, at a massively inefficient ratio. The idea that we need it is a superstition, only less sustainable with today's abundance of tasty meat substitutes. Plutarch called meat eating a kind of "unnatural second nature," not a necessity but an option for the chief of creatures, and I think there's something to it.[41] We may be predators, but we are the only predator with a choice in the matter.

Our bodies, too, do not appear to have been designed for eating flesh, a point easily established by examining the statistics on heart and vascular disease, or by asking why the meat industry must constantly *remind* us how necessary their product is, or by going to the mirror, opening your mouth, and asking yourself why it is that you do not see fangs. Indeed, what is all this genetic tampering with animals today, to make their flesh paler and leaner and softer, but an admission that normal meats are not, after all, particularly healthy?

In any case I just cannot imagine attaching so much importance to any food or treat that I would grow irate or bitter at the mention of the suffering of animals. A pig to me will always seem more important than a pork rind. There is the risk here of confusing realism with cynicism, moral stoicism with moral sloth, of letting oneself become jaded and lazy and self-satisfied—what used to be called an "appetitive" person.

That is when we can sink to new depths, for cruelty is rarely a vice in itself but rather the end result of other vices. I notice even among people I know a certain flippancy on the topic of farm animals. You hear it too in popular culture. I was very sorry one night to see, for example, a skit on the Comedy Central channel involving jokes at the expense of veal calves. The gag involved one of the cast members, Adam Carolla, locked in a crate while pretending to suckle from a shapely farm maiden, showing us that, hey, maybe life isn't so hard after all for those calves, and Adam doesn't mind it at all, and ha ha ha. The lighter side of factory farming.

We have all made jokes we later regretted, and I think Mr. Carolla would regret doing that skit if he ever saw the real thing, what their four months on earth are really like for those creatures. It is bad enough that they are treated that way. Must we laugh at them too?

Somehow it has become mawkish and weak to dwell upon the details of animal suffering, and strong and sensible to ignore them—to disregard "the sentimental maunderings of animal rights extremists," as Larry Katz, Safari Club's president for the year 2000, puts it.[42] This is a twisting of plain words, an excuse and an evasion. A realist is someone who wants to know the realities, the facts of the case, what is actually taking place and how it feels to the victim. A sentimental person is one who follows desire, emotion and impulse, often in disregard of the facts.

For my part, it has always seemed a good rule never to support or advocate any moral act that I would not be prepared to witness in person. I apply that to questions of human welfare and I see no good reason not to apply it to animal welfare as well. When we shrink from the sight of something, when we shroud it in euphemism, that is usually a sign of inner conflict, of unsettled hearts, a sign that something has gone wrong in our moral reasoning. Curiously, it was one of those *National Review* readers quoted above, right before his *bon appétit* sign-off, who made this point for me:

> As for the consumption of factory-processed meat and fowl, the real problem is that consumers are separated completely from the reality of what they are eating and how it found their plates. I would assert that today, fewer meat-eating Americans would be able to kill their

meals than ever before. They have the stomachs to eat meat, but not to kill it. In much the same way in which society is repulsed by images of aborted fetuses, yet continues to demand the right to "choose," so too we are horrified by the plight of veal calves but unable to curb our appetites.

Americans consume, on average, 51 pounds of chicken every year, 15 pounds of turkey, 63 pounds of beef, 45 pounds of pork, 1 pound of veal, and 1 pound of lamb.[43] "More than ever," reports our U.S. Department of Agriculture, "we are a nation of meat eaters."[44] And now, with help from Dr. Atkins and his wonder diet, we have millions of consumers gorging themselves on nothing but flesh, one excess to correct their other excesses—no thought whatever of taking their *portion* of meat even if we grant that meat production and the sufferings involved are necessary.

So, in my own moral reasoning, I try to personalize this broad statistic, just as I would in the case of human suffering. I try to locate my own particular part in the big picture. I simply imagine what it would be like to see those creatures every day—the ones, in effect, being prepared just for me. Suppose that the morally irrelevant facts of distance and ignorance were removed and I had literally to live with my own choice to eat meat, seeing my very own pig and cow and lamb and chickens every day.

Once, in the little town of Bastrop, Texas, I pulled into a gas station to find, parked nearby, a small trailer packed with cattle, almost piled one upon the other, twisting and stepping over one another to see me as I approached. There was a calf, separated from the others, trying to nuzzle his mother. One cow had lost an eye, apparently from ocular cancer—an unimaginably painful disease spreading today because of overbreeding. She just lay there staring up at me, her entire chest and right shoulder covered with fresh blood. All of this on a sweltering afternoon while the driver of the truck yakked on the payphone with a nice, frosty Big Gulp in hand, utterly indifferent to the scene.

Suppose that trucks like that were parked every day outside of every restaurant, grocery store, and meat market the world over? What would it be like, I ask myself, to face such sights every day, every day to see creatures like that being raised in these same conditions—in a miniature factory farm, let us say, right near my house?

Each morning, as I stepped out to greet the day, I would observe them being readied for me, peering into their crates and cages and pens, seeing their eyes begging me to let them out, out of the darkness and into the sun. It would be hard and I would probably try to convince myself that they're just animals, for heaven's sake, they can't "think thoughts about thoughts," they can't really think or feel or want anything. After a while I might actually start believing that. I might become inured to their whimpers and cries like the men of Smithfield. It's just a job, just a product.

We are constantly told that concern over "the supposed cruelties of farming," as Stephen Budiansky puts it in *The Covenant of the Wild,* is a product of the soft "urban" mind-set, unaccustomed to the harsh realities of rural life.[45] Another way of looking at this is that the "urban" types are not steeped in the ways of blood spilling and have no financial and emotional attachments to the practices in question. In other contexts, that's usually called objectivity.

Confronted each day with the objective facts of industrial farming, I might search for comfort in Mr. Budiansky's "covenant" theory—that by the great and mysterious workings of evolution these creatures have somehow "chosen" this fate for themselves. *They* chose it, not me. Invoking Roger Scruton, I might confidently declare that the "animals that we eat have the best chance of competing for space on our planet. We therefore have a duty to eat meat—as much meat and in as many varieties as possible. Every vegetarian meal is a crime against nature."[46] So, by accepting the facts of industrial farming, I am simply doing my bit, being a good conservationist. With Digby Anderson, the British culinary critic and intrepid bunny hunter we encountered in Chapter 3, I might brush off objections to animal pain and death as "barmy" sentimentality, the prattle of a few weak-minded "cranks."[47] Or with Mr. Swan in his hunting *pensées* I might angrily declare that to hell with my doubts, I am a cougar too, a real man, and I *want* my meat.

Up close, however, I doubt these would set my mind at rest. I know a "crime against nature" when I see one. It is usually a sign of crimes against nature that we cannot bear to see them at all, that we recoil and hide our eyes, and no one has ever cringed at the sight of soybean factory. I also know phony arguments when I hear them—unbridled appetite passing itself off as altruism, and human arrogance in the guise of solemn "duty." We must, as C. S. Lewis advises, "reject with detestation that covert propaganda for cruelty which tries to drive mercy out of the world by calling it names such as 'Humanitarianism' and 'Sentimentality.'"[48]

If I had pets, I would see them lolling and roaming freely about the yard, basking in my care and affection while, inside the factory farm, animals of comparable feeling and intelligence received no comforts, no names, no affection, no nothing, only my silent and resolute indifference. Day by day I would observe a little stream of waste pooling outside of the factory farm, this refuse the only external evidence that inside are living creatures never themselves allowed to touch soil and grass. Night after night, as I drifted off to sleep in my warm, comfy bed, I would hear them, hear the shuffling and stirring and yanking of the tethers, the groans and bleats and bellows.

All of this not to obey some inexorable force of evolution or biology, not by divine decree, not to meet some unstoppable market demand, not for Everyone—no, all of it done just for me. Each creature bred and born just for me. Confined and isolated just for me. And then in lonely terror packed off to die, just for me. And every time I saw and heard them I would have to remind myself just why I was doing this, to ask if my taste for pork loins or ham or steak or veal was really worth this price, to ask if this was really my choice and there was no other way.

I know that I could not abide the sight of animals being treated so harshly, much less inflict such punishment myself. If I were "a cougar" perhaps it would not trouble me. But I am a man and so it does. I know that I would feel mean and selfish and mediocre. I would want my animals to roam and feed and play outdoors, to be what they are and do what they should.

Therefore, I want no part in any of it. I do not want this product. And I damn sure don't want someone else doing the confining and beating and killing for me so that I am spared the unpleasantness of it all. The only thing worse than cruelty is delegated cruelty. It is colder than if I were doing it myself. When you eat flesh extracted in this way, as novelist Alice Walker puts it, "You're just eating misery. You're eating a bitter life."[49]

That is the reality, exactly the same moral situation in which you and I both stand, involving exactly the same degree of complicity and exactly the same degree of choice. And it is the cheapest kind of sentimentality to ignore it. Far from being an emotional response, this is reason, a direct confrontation with the facts about the animals, about ourselves, and about our own actual needs and legitimate moral claims upon those creatures. The whole sad business, even while defended in terms of reason and realism, is designed precisely to prevent that engagement with the facts, to keep information and conscience as far apart as possible, to soothe and satisfy all at once, now even to the point of eradicating "cosmetic defects" like bloodsplash lest Everyone be troubled by the thought that pain was felt and blood was shed.

I know many people far more upright and conscientious than I am who disagree, who think nothing of it. I know that vegetarianism runs against mankind's most casual assumptions about the world and our place within it. And I know that factory farming is an economic inevitability, not likely to end anytime soon.

But I don't answer to inevitabilities, and neither do you. I don't answer to the economy. I don't answer to tradition and I don't answer to Everyone. For me, it comes down to a question of whether I am a man or just a consumer. Whether to reason or just to rationalize. Whether to heed my conscience or my every craving, to assert my free will or just my will. Whether to side with the powerful and comfortable or with the weak, afflicted, and forgotten. Whether, as an economic actor in a free market, I answer to the god of money or to the God of mercy.

Taking pity on livestock may not be among the most profound moral choices I will make in my life. It may, as the world regards animal welfare in general, be a small, trivial matter I can slough off or not worry about at all. It may be nothing for all I know, as, for all that any of us will ever quite know, our own suffering goes unheard in an indifferent universe. But I don't think so. And it is a terrible thing that religious people today can be so indifferent to the cruelty of the farms, shrugging it off as so much secular, animal rights foolishness. They above all should hear the call to mercy. They above all should have some kindness to spare. They above all should be mindful of the little things, seeing, in the suffering of these creatures, the same hand that has chosen all the foolish things of the world to confound the wise, and the weak things to confound the things which are strong. "Who so poor," asked Anna Kingsford more than a century ago, "so oppressed, so helpless, so mute and uncared for, as the dumb creatures who serve us—they who, but for us, must starve, and who have no friend on earth if man be their enemy?"[50]

A FRESH START

Mercy is a concept we all understand, however we might weigh its relevance to animals. The anticruelty statutes already on the books have come, I believe, from just that spirit. So will future laws protecting animals. Reforms will come as all great reforms have always come in ridding us of evils against both man and animal—not as we change our moral principles, but as we discern and accept the implications of principles we already hold.

Yet there is something in our current debate over the status of animals that needs examination, a certain spirit that has failed to change hearts where it has not, in fact, hardened them. And Professor Singer with his recent defense of human infanticide, assisted suicide, and euthanasia—his "New Commandments," as he calls them—has not helped matters.

All of us who care about animals owe Professor Singer a debt of gratitude. *Animal Liberation,* with its details of how laboratory and farm animals are treated, its tone of confrontation and intellectual confidence, was a first in mainstream publishing, forcing a lot of people to think as never before about animal pain, and inspiring many to take action. There were pictures, too, of the kind that even today people rarely see. Rereading the book twenty-five years later, and leaving aside his deeper theoretical scheme, it still strikes me as a work of great compassion, intellectual integrity, and moral courage. Often, for whatever philosophical reasons, Professor Singer was and is simply advocating little decencies like the right of chimps not to be bludgeoned or repeatedly electrocuted, or the right of a pig to be left "with other pigs in a place where there is adequate food and room to run freely."[51] What's so radical about that?

We are confronted, however, with the fact that for all of his good work the most prominent writer on the subject, lately described by the *Atlantic Monthly* as the "world's most influential living philosopher," has somehow reasoned his way from a principled defense of kindness to animals to a principled defense of killing babies. "Simply killing an infant," as he told a Princeton audience, "is never equivalent to killing a person."[52] This new turn can only spell grief all around. The suspicion is that Professor Singer's attack on the sanctity of human life follows a natural trajectory from his case for animals, that they are one and the same moral project. Though this criticism overlooks the many thoughtful arguments of contemporary animal rights philosophers, the defense of animals has come to be identified with one man's theories, and with the degradation of human life instead of with our uplift and enlightenment. By what madness, people wonder, can we seek to protect calves in their cages from human cruelty but not children in their cribs?

Professor Singer is a serious man and formidable intellect, with his own purposes and principles. But he offers a vision of humanity that is in crucial respects degrading and dangerous, and not very flattering even to animals. He has, if nothing else, needlessly complicated the subject, while alienating religious people and furnishing a handy strawman for groups eager to portray animal protection causes as radical nonsense. Anyone wishing to avoid cruelty to animals as a serious moral problem will find in his writings the excuses they are looking for.

For many critics, too, Professor Singer confirms the impression that to make a case for animals one must draw a new circle, that no rationally compelling challenge to such things as factory farming, recreational hunting, or modern whaling can be made within the parameters of common moral standards. Often his theories are not an appeal to morality or justice in any recognizable form, but a redefinition of justice. He requires of his readers, not that they apply common standards of morality, but that they accept an entirely new set of standards, and indeed a new and improved set of Commandments produced *ex nihilo* from the mind of a modern intellectual.

His critics are correct, then, to say that his rejection of the sanctity of human life follows from his view of animals. But this misses the larger point that Professor Singer rejects sanctity, period, any assumption of God or the soul or any kind of natural or divine law to guide our choices and our lives—a vision of life he would now extend into our intensive-care units and nurseries. "The traditional ethics," he writes in his 1994 *Rethinking Life and Death: The Collapse of Our Traditional Ethics,* his case for euthanasia and infanticide, "is still defended by bishops and conservative bioethicists who speak in reverent tones about the intrinsic value of all human life, irrespective of its nature and quality of life. But like the new clothes worn by the emperor, these solemn phrases seem true and substantial only while we are intimidated into accepting that all human life has some special worth or dignity."[53]

From *Animal Liberation* on, his basic enterprise has been to liberate not only animals, but all of us, from the influence of religion and, more directly, of Judeo-Christian morality: We are just one face in the evolutionary crowd, our belief in God and the sacredness of human life an illusion. Nothing at all, in Professor Singer's theories, has any intrinsic moral claim or value. The universe is planless, meaningless, with no other purpose than that we choose to give it. Even human equality, our own claim to have inherent rights among one another, is a fantasy. The principle of human equality is a prescriptive convention, an assertion of what ought to be rather than a statement of fact: "[I]f the demand for equality were based on the actual equality of human beings, we would have to stop demanding equality."[54]

You still find critics like Mr. Scruton brushing off Professor Singer's theories on the grounds that obviously animals and humans cannot be equal in capacity, and that, therefore, to grant them equal treatment would be absurd—as a chimp, for example, could not exercise the right of free speech or of voting even if we attempted to extend such rights. But that was not the argument. His argument was that the interests of each creature are defined ultimately by a capacity for self-awareness, for enjoying its life and expressing conscious preferences, and that these preferences form the basis of its particular rights. Where natural law bases value on the distinctive faculties of each creature, and surmises as "the good" the fulfillment of every creature in the use of its gifts, for Professor Singer there is no good, no purpose, no *telos* or ultimate moral destination for any of us, on four legs or two. There are only particular relative goods like pleasure and choice, with no final standards to govern their use. His golden rule is that any ethical decision one makes must agree with the preferences of anyone, man or beast, whose interests that action will affect. Cruelty to animals becomes "speciesism," an ideological sin, an unjust distribution of power. "Our isolation is over," he writes,

> Science has helped us to understand our evolutionary history, as well as our own nature and the nature of other animals. Freed from the constraints of religious conformity, we now have a new vision of who we are, to whom we are related, the limited nature of the differences between us and other species, and the more or less accidental manner in which the boundary between "us" and "them" has been formed. . . .
>
> The new vision leaves no room for the traditional answer to these questions, that we human beings are a special creation, infinitely more precious, in virtue of our humanity alone, than all other living things. In light of our new understanding of our place in the universe, we shall have to abandon that traditional answer, and revise the boundaries of our ethics.[55]

He never does, in any of his writings that I know of, get around to arguing the matter of religious belief directly. He simply takes it as a given that intelligent people do not believe in God or, if they do, know better than to bring it up in serious philosophical discussion. Nor need we traverse that ground here, except to note two very grave problems.

First, and understandably enough, Professor Singer has difficulty comprehending the terms of faith outside of his own utilitarian assumption of man as a fundamentally selfish being. He can understand human dominion only in terms of power and subjugation. This is apparent, for example, when he interprets the Sermon on the Mount for us. Religion, he writes in his 1995 *How Are We to Live? Ethics in an Age of Self-Interest,* is concerned above all with reward and punishment, and thus arises ultimately from self-interest. "It began with Jesus, whom the Gospels portray as preaching a morality of self-interest."[56] He cites the passage in Matthew's account about doing acts of charity without "a flourish of trumpets," merely to win the admiration of men. This sounds like a call to goodness for its own sake, writes the professor, but the reason that Jesus gives for such behavior "is less elevating."

> Throughout the sermon, Jesus hammers home the same message: about loving your enemies, about praying in private, about forgiving others the wrongs they have done, about fasting, about judging others, and more generally, about doing "the will of my heavenly father." In each case, the reward of heaven is held out as an incentive—a reward, moreover, that, unlike treasure on earth, cannot grow rusty, or be stolen by thieves.[57]

This interpretation somehow reminds me of the behavioral and cognitive theorists we saw trying to make sense of animals—able to note the sounds and motions and yet so deaf to the meanings, seeing everything in terms of stimulus and response, and for exactly the same reason: Because they cannot conceive of any reality independent of their own theories. The whole passage is steeped in the very kind of materialistic egotism from which the words of the gospel seek to liberate the hearer. Doing God's will, pleasing our Creator and gaining salvation thus become so many more self-interested calculations, more pleasures to be sought, and the Lord himself a kind of motivational speaker up there "hammering home" his package of incentives and rewards.

Because the whole thing seems so preposterous to him, Professor Singer cannot put himself in the place of the believer to perceive the different meanings of words like reward and treasure and goodness when the speaker himself is Truth. The same difficulty is evident in a similar passage in which he attempts to explain the life of Mother Teresa not by her "implausible beliefs" but from a more sophisticated "evolutionary perspective."[58] Why her implausible beliefs always seemed to bring such plausible results, turning orphans into family members and scabrous human discards into patients loved and cared for, goes unexamined.

A still bigger problem is finding rational grounds for his own ethical theories. Unlike Stephen Budiansky with his "rocket" theory of human conscience—we blasted clear of evolution and somehow invented ethics—Professor Singer at least understands his dilemma and is trying valiantly to pull from his root assumption of human selfishness an ethic of altruism and concern for the suffering of other beings. But they're both in the same fix, for all the usual reasons that moral relativism ends in intellectual incoherence: How can we assert *anything* as true or false, just or unjust? How can we assert even that it is wrong to inflict suffering on others? If individual preference and subjective desire are the sole basis for ethics—a term Professor Singer prefers to "morality" precisely because the latter implies actual truth—how do we distinguish good from bad desires? Somehow he must create a system of moral values without being able to assert any moral values, even his own, as true. "If the universe has not been constructed in accordance with any plan," the professor writes,

> it has no meaning to be discovered. There is no inherent value in it, independently of the existence of sentient beings who prefer some states of affairs to others. Ethics is not part of the structure of the universe, in the way that atoms are. But in the absence of belief in God, what other options are there for finding a basis in ethics? Is it possible to study the nature of ethics in a secular fashion and find some philosophical grounding for how we should live?[59]

In the short version, he winds up with something called "the point of view of the universe," a sort of empty throne from which we can imagine how things *would* appear from the divine standpoint. There is still no actual moral order or reality. We can still assert nothing as absolutely true or false. Life is still meaningless. But if there were truth or meaning to life, this is how it might appear. "From this perspective," he explains, "we can see that our own sufferings and pleasures are very like the sufferings and pleasures of others; and that there is no reason to give less consideration to the sufferings of others."[60]

It is a nice thought, only it doesn't solve the problem, as witness that last equivocation that "there is no reason to give less consideration" to others.

Reconstructing this double negative into the positive claim that *there is a reason* to care for other beings, we're exactly where we were before. We are unable, by Professor Singer's own terms, to make the simplest assertion of moral value upon which everything else depends.

The historian Gertrude Himmelfarb describes such arguments as "the self-conscious, analytic, purely rational mode of thought and behavior."[61] Accepting no first principles of nature or reality, they keep crumbling because there's nothing in the end to support them, like trying to construct a building from the top down. Indeed, by the end of *How Are We to Live?* we find Professor Singer bidding us to follow the example of Sisyphus, doing good for no good reason, finding some semblance of dignity in a posture of stoic defiance against the very meaninglessness of our existence.

How, in the end, do we know right from wrong in preference utilitarianism? We don't. We just need a little faith. For all of his scoffing at traditional ideas of natural or divine law, in other words, it turns out Professor Singer's ideas are pretty shaky themselves, and before we start scrapping the guiding ideas of human civilization he is going to have to do better than that.

The trouble started when Professor Singer turned his attention from animal to human suffering, applying his theories to the ethical dilemmas arising in intensive-care units and maternity wards the world over. If the lives of fully healthy and alert people are ultimately meaningless, obviously, by Singer's terms, the lives of the sick, defective, or unwanted are going to be very precarious indeed. Faced with these dilemmas, he views himself as the unapologetic truth-teller, "ripping the veils aside" to expose our belief in the sanctity of human life as "a farce," and indeed one of the criticisms from conservatives has been that Professor Singer is merely advocating outright ideas applied in practice in the matter of abortion.[62] "In the modern era of liberal abortion laws," he writes in *Rethinking Life and Death,*

> most of those not opposed to abortion have drawn a sharp line at birth. If, as I have argued, that line does not mark a sudden change in the status of the fetus, then there appear to be only two possibilities: oppose abortion, or allow infanticide. I have already given reasons why the fetus is not the kind of being whose life must be protected in a way that the life of a person should be. Although the

fetus may, after a certain point, be capable of feeling pain, there is no basis for thinking it rational or self aware, let alone capable of seeing itself as existing in different times and places. But the same can be said of a newborn infant. Human babies are not born self-aware, or capable of grasping that they exist over time. They are not persons. Hence their lives would seem to be no more worthy of protection than the life of a fetus.[63]

If parents desire even their healthy infant's death, then it is so ordered. The child has no natural, prior moral claims of his or her own. There is no higher law to which anyone is accountable, only the prevailing wishes and interests of the people involved. In Professor Singer's theories, everything is a zero-sum proposition, and everybody always seems to be in conflict with everybody else, one interest group always pitted against the other—A's good always coming at B's expense, with C hovering closely by to make sure he doesn't lose out on any pleasure or get more than his share of pain. Having abandoned the only rational basis there is for human equality, he ends up with a scheme of perpetual division and distrust, the sick and hungry and aged all just "interest groups" out to get their share—an ethical alphabet of fractious interests even when A is a doctor, B is Mom, and C her blameless newborn child.

In *Rethinking Life and Death* Professor Singer lays it down "that a period of 28 days after birth might be allowed before an infant is accepted as having the same right to life as others."[64] In a bizarre aside he then informs us that any such line-drawing will tend to be arbitrary. This arbitrariness alone, he writes, may be "enough to tilt the balance against a change in the law in this area. On that I remain unsure."[65]

Thanks for the warning. And never mind that the whole thing is arbitrary, or that this single admission calls into question the entire speculative enterprise. Maybe he was just thinking aloud here, ripping away more veils while drawing his own tentative lines to guide us in life and death. He just wants us all to "rethink" things. But there is a recklessness even in that. With the lives and death of innocent children lying in the balance, let him keep his thought experiments to himself.

Skipping a bit, we arrive at what Professor Singer calls the "New Commandments." For example: "First New Commandment: Recognize that the worth of human life varies." This will replace what he calls the "First Old Commandment: Treat all human life as of equal worth."[66] The Third Old

Commandment of Western morality declared that you should "never take your own life, and always prevent others from taking theirs." Our Third New Commandment enjoins us to "respect a person's right to live or die."[67] And so on, each commandment arising from what turns out, in preference utilitarianism, to be the nearest thing to universal truth: We are each a sovereign being, our own pleasure the highest good, our own choices the final authority.

Of course, it's the same old problem: If we are each our own final authority, then we have no authority at all, and we're left in practice with something very like blindly amoral evolution. How, moreover, can we assert the moral claims of animals if we have not first affirmed the moral claims of human life? How can we believe that their lives and their suffering have meaning and moral relevance if we're not even sure about our own?

There are certain assumptions without which reasoned debate must sooner or later break down, and one of them is the validity of reason itself. Here I am, for instance, writing this book, here you are reading it, and there might be a world of difference between what we regard as just and unjust conduct toward animals. Whatever those differences, the whole exercise depends on a common belief that there is such a thing as justice. We must both assume, going in, that we are individually and socially obliged to pursue justice; that, if we can agree upon a reasonable standard of justice governing animal welfare, then we would have to conform ourselves to that standard; and that failing to do so we would be guilty of injustice. Even to define the differences in application, there must be some final standard of value to apply. We must believe that there is such a thing as truth, and that reason can give us at least a partial glimpse of it, otherwise what is the point of debating at all?

With Professor Singer we step into the abyss, denying that moral truth exists and we must answer to it. Having once so skillfully exposed human capriciousness toward animals, he now finds himself defending the ultimate act of human caprice ("simply killing an infant") in a case of what Leo Strauss, the great expositor of natural law, called "retail sanity and wholesale madness."[68] It is a view of morality as purely instrumental and arising from blind preference, an intricate system of ethical rules drawn up in the belief that there is no good and no evil.

There is not space enough to examine every turn in Professor Singer's theories. Let us simply recall the final turn—his justification for killing an unwanted child already born. Here again choice becomes a good in itself and whim takes the guise of freedom. Nothing is left to help us distinguish moral from material goods, and when all the earnest speculating is done the practical result can be lawless egotism. Intellectuals are a pretty unique species all by themselves, given to advocating things out of sheer brazenness that they could not themselves stomach if they were ushered in to witness the scene. Doubtless this is true of some of the theorists we have seen who contend that animals feel nothing and so we may do with them as we please. I like to think the same is true in Professor Singer's case, as for example when he weighs the fate of a child with Down's syndrome. No one who has not had a child with disabilities should speak too freely on the subject. We can say with confidence, however, that Professor Singer's approach in *Rethinking Life and Death* is the wrong one:

> Shakespeare once described life as an uncertain voyage. As parents, or intending parents, we want our children to be as well equipped as possible for whatever it may bring. . . .
>
> To have a child with Down syndrome is to have a very different experience from having a normal child. It can be a warm and loving experience, but we must have lowered expectations of our child's abilities. We cannot expect a child with Down syndrome to play the guitar, to develop an appreciation of science fiction, to learn a foreign language, to chat with us about the latest Woody Allen movie, or to be a respectable athlete, basketballer or tennis player. Even when an adult, a person with Down syndrome may not be able to live independently; and for someone with Down syndrome to have children of their own is unusual and can give rise to problems. For some parents, none of this matters. They find bringing up a child with Down syndrome a rewarding experience in a thousand different ways. But for other parents, it is devastating.
>
> Both for the sake of "our children," then, and for our own sake, we may not want a child to start on life's uncertain voyage if the prospects are clouded. When this can be known at a very early stage of the voyage we may still have a chance to make a fresh start. This means detaching ourselves from the infant who has been born, cutting ourselves free before the ties that have already begun to bind us to our child have become irresistible. Instead of going forward and

putting all our efforts into making the best of the situation, we can still say no, and start again from the beginning.[69]

This would be the "Fourth New Commandment: Bring children into the world only if they are wanted."[70] The passage is notable for being one of few occasions when we find Professor Singer succumbing to euphemism. Everyone gets "a fresh start," except the baby who gets no start at all. To spare this infant all the travails of his or her uncertain voyage (in that entirely needless allusion to Shakespeare, expressing the commonplace that life is uncertain), parents may hand their little bundle of grief back to the doctor, who in disregard of a few millennia worth of medical ethics may— well, let's just say that no one has to watch. With any luck it all happens before those "ties" begin to bind us, ties known as "love" outside the world of theory. We can "start again from the beginning," put the matter behind us and be "free." It was all in the baby's own interest. What was the point of his going on anyway, the little stranger, off on a voyage through this world where he would only be a burden to others, never attain full personhood, never read science fiction or play guitar, never even sit around one day chatting about Woody's latest work of genius—all of those things that give life its meaning?

Professor Singer is touching on hard questions, but with a hardness of his own, and I'll take the "solemn pieties" of bishops any day over this gauzy, quality-of-life sanctimony, with its blurring of lines between caregiving and killing, doctor and executioner. He has ripped away the veil only to replace it with another, concealing something that not even he can bring himself to describe in plain language. It was Dickens, in the words of his Ghost of Christmas Past, who warned us against this view of anyone on earth as unviable surplus to be disposed of:

> "Man," said the Ghost, "if man you be in heart, not adamant, forbear that wicked cant until you have discovered What the surplus is, and Where it is. Will you decide what men shall live, and what men shall die? It may be, that in the sight of heaven, you are more worthless and less fit to live than millions like this poor man's child. Oh God! To hear the Insect on the leaf pronouncing on the too much life among his hungry brothers in the dust."[71]

Though in person a mild and considerate man, Professor Singer needs to be more careful here. One detects in his writings of late the same kind of arrogance by which people today justify the wrongs inflicted upon the creatures. It is the same permissiveness passing itself off as high principle—a sophisticated rationale for putting one's own pleasure and convenience over the suffering of others. It is the same fundamentally negative, hostile, imperious stance toward the universe. The same mercilessness, with the same maudlin air of altruism. The same blindness to the face of innocence.

Most revealing of all, there is the same hiding of things we cannot bear to see. The sportive slaughter of wildlife as "conservation," one might say, is the perfect ecological counterpart, and our factory farms the perfect agricultural counterpart, to the "quality of life" ethic we find at work in our own world, putting self-interest first and disposing of inconvenient realities. In all of them there is despair, ingratitude, a loss of love for life and of humility before the Giver of life. The Reverend Andrew Linzey has put the matter plainly:

> Are not animals now sacrificed for a species that increasingly takes to itself God-like powers and who regards its own interests as unquestioningly the goal and purpose of creation itself? Demythologized, we might say that our idolatrous tendency consists in thinking that our own estimation of our own worth and value can be the main or exclusive criterion by which we judge the worth and value of all other species. If we find this language disconcerting, it may be because we have come to accept, bit by bit, the utilitarian position even in its enlightened Singerian form, which accepts axiomatically that the interests of the weak can be traded against those of the strong.[72]

Philosophical theories can in this way become a destructive venture, confusing matters with false choices and sterile power schemes the cruel are only too happy to accept. In hostile hands, they become a pretext for doing nothing, for brushing off real and urgent moral duties in the care of animals. "The campaign against 'speciesism,'" as Father Richard John Neuhaus writes, "is a campaign against the singularity of human dignity and, therefore, of human responsibility. . . . The hope for a more humane world, including the more humane treatment of animals, is premised upon what [animal liberation theorists] deny."[73]

Lost, too, in such theories are the only terms of debate in which animal welfare can be truly understood, and, as I think, the truest terms in which morality in general is to be understood. Professor Singer's is the language of autonomy, personal sovereignty, self-assertion, and preference. Man and animal alike will always fare better when our thoughts center on compassion, charity, benevolence, generosity, hospitality, and even pity with its noble Roman root in *pietas*, the virtue and vision from which mercy comes.

Professor Singer's is a well-intentioned yet ultimately barren and unsparing vision of life. He would extend that spirit into matters of human welfare. Religious people whose traditional ideas he dismisses hold a kindly and merciful vision of life, the faith of the broken, the hounded, the hopeless. Yet too often they will not extend that spirit to our fellow creatures. More than anything else, I hope with this book to speak to those people. A sign of moral truth is that it has a familiar ring, telling us what deep down we knew already. I hope they might find at least a bit of that here, even where reasonable differences remain.

Animals are different, too, and if there are disagreements over the moral claims of some then let us start where agreements are clearest. The elephants we have seen taunted and tormented and slaughtered by the likes of Safari Club do not have time to wait while the world's ethicists work out some centuries-long paradigm shift in moral thought. The creatures just need specific protections from the specific human evils against which they are so helpless. And if we are ever going to rescue them, we must rescue them now.

AN OBLIGATION OF JUSTICE

Peter Singer could have become the best known defender of animals only in a moral vacuum, only for the lack of clear moral alternatives among those philosophers and theologians who have even troubled themselves to address the problem of cruelty to animals. Many of these writers and thinkers now express their shock and indignation at his ideas and influence. There is something a little hollow about their objections, and they would do well to reflect on their own silence on the subject.

One strain of thought understands the problems of cruelty, and is forever expressing sympathy for animals, yet resists any and all attempts to act against it, fearful of confusing the moral and legal status of animals with the moral and legal status of humans. This was apparent, for example, in a June

2001 debate between Professor Singer and Richard A. Posner, a judge on the U.S. Court of Appeals, in which the latter expressed his disapproval of factory farming while stopping short of legal prohibitions: "[I]f it is true that alternative methods of producing meat would substantially reduce animal suffering at trivial cost, I am for adopting them, because I like animals and therefore don't want to see them suffer gratuitously. But I would not be inclined to force my view on others who disagree. I don't see either the necessity or the justification for coercion."[74] Factory farming should be left, Judge Posner adds, to "consumer preference."[75]

It fell to Professor Singer to point out that "liking" animals has little to do with whatever human obligations their gratuitous suffering entails. If we have duties concerning animals, one would assume, moreover, those duties are shared and may without injury to our special status be translated into hard law of just the kind that Judge Posner imposes every day—including cruelty statutes already on the books and still regarded by some as needless coercion from the state. Regardless of the philosophical differences over the status of animals, in practice it comes down to this. All we need to affirm is the right of the law to intervene on their behalf. Call it a right inhering in animals, call it a duty exercised by us, call it anything you want, but that is the test. Are we prepared to *act* against cruelty to animals?

Invariably trotted out here is the British historian Thomas Macaulay, who famously observed that "the Puritan objected to bear-baiting, not because it gave pain to the bear, but because it gave pleasure to the spectator."[76] Animal cruelty, on this view, is wrong because it is bad for us, bad for our character and our soul. John Henry Newman, even while discerning "something so very dreadful, so Satanic" in tormenting animals, settled on the similar view of animal welfare as incidental in the virtuous life, important more as a reflection of human goodness than of the creatures' own interests:

> We have no duties toward the brute creation; there is no relation of justice between them and us. Of course we are bound not to treat them ill, for cruelty is an offense against the holy Law which our nature has written on our hearts, and is displeasing to Him. But they can claim nothing at our hands; into our hands they are absolutely delivered. We may use them, we may destroy them at our pleasure, not our wanton pleasure, but still for our own ends, for our own ben-

efit or satisfaction, provided we can give a rational account of what we do.[77]

Still further back, we have our old friend Aquinas expressing the Scholastic moral tradition, and more or less the assumption of Christian thinkers today, holding that animals can figure into human affairs only incidentally. In and of themselves, they have no standing:

> If any passages in Holy Scripture seem to forbid us to be cruel to brute animals, for instance to kill a bird with its young, that is either to remove men's thoughts from being cruel to other men, or lest through being cruel to animals one becomes cruel to other human beings, or because injury of an animal leads to the temporal hurt of man, either the doer of the deed, or of another, or because of some symbolic signification. . . . [78]

This is the tradition Professor Peter Carruthers follows when he informs us that while animals cannot have direct moral rights, they have "indirect moral significance nevertheless, in virtue of the qualities of moral character they may evoke in us. Actions involving animals that are expressive of a bad moral character are thereby wrong."[79]

I used to hold similar views myself, until I started noticing how many people who take this position then proceed, just like Professor Carruthers, to explain that in practice it requires "minimal" constraints on human conduct.[80] I also began to wonder how something so very bad for one's moral character could not itself be bad. What exactly is the difference, to take Cardinal Newman's words, between having a "duty" to refrain from cruelty to animals and being "bound not to treat them ill"? As a practical matter, just what is the difference between having a "relation of justice" and violating "the holy Law which nature has written on our hearts"? A person refraining from cruelty to animals, for either reason, would do and not do exactly the same things. Indeed if, as Cardinal Newman believed, animal cruelty can plummet a man into the realm of the "Satanic," I'd say that alone is reason enough to steer clear of it.

Likewise, examining Macaulay's saying, why is it wrong for the spectators to derive pleasure from bear-baiting unless, at some level, the bear-baiting is wrong in itself, regardless of whether one enjoys the spectacle or not? Exactly *what* in the act of mistreating an animal leads to cruelty toward human beings? You'd think there must be an evil, or at least some event that evokes evil in the spectator's heart, and that this thing would make the act inherently bad. "Evil events," as Aristophanes observed, "from evil causes spring."

In and of itself, we are to believe, it is not an unjust *act* to torment an animal. Yet we're also told that the doer of the act is at that very moment an *unjust person*. It is a moral separation easier to state than to actually imagine: We have our unjust person standing there, say, with his whip or gun over some poor bear he has just tortured or killed. But we don't have an injustice, in this view, and we don't have a victim. When happened, then? And what's the bear doing there?

In any case, as I observed earlier, one need only split the difference, acknowledging our own duties regarding animals, and it comes to the same thing as rights. Whatever the semantic, philosophical, and theological nuances, duties *in respect of* animals and duties *to* animals are, in application, identical. The fact that the creatures cannot act morally toward us in no way diminishes our ability to act morally toward them. The creatures are *owed* dutiful human care. As a moral restraint to be observed by us, it matters little, least of all to the objects of cruelty, whether we say they have a "right" not to be mercilessly confined, beaten, dissected, or neglected. The point is that we should not mercilessly confine, beat, dissect, or neglect them. Whatever one chooses to call it, precisely the same conduct is or is not permissible.

These pious men were trying, of course, to lead the faithful away from a confusion between animals and us, between the unreasoning beasts and man made in the image of God. But whatever reasons might be given or theological distinctions made, back in the world of everyday life we are still left, on the traditional Christian account, with pleasures the enjoyment of which is depraved, and practices the doing of which either is evil or leads to evil.

From all three of these thinkers we get the same set of relevant facts: There is such a thing as pain or injury to an animal. There is such a thing as cruelty to animals. And directly or indirectly, cruelty to animals is bad. It is the act of an unjust person. That is enough, we are informed by *The Catholic Encyclopedia*, to establish not only a personal duty but a clear and binding obligation of justice: "While the scholastics rest their condemnation of cruelty to animals on its demoralizing influence, their general teaching concerning the nature of man's rights and duties furnishes principles which have but to be applied in order to establish the direct and essential sinfulness of cruelty to the animal world, irrespective of the results of such conduct on the character of those who practice it."[81]

A more recent version of the argument for duties, not rights, comes to us from Professor David Oderberg in *Applied Ethics,* who along the way offers this sweeping indictment of our time:

> Millions of animals are caused horrific suffering in experiments that, while some may and indeed do benefit humans, are for the most part pointless if not positively harmful to us. . . . In this technological age where utilitarian reasoning all but predominates, animals are treated far more viciously and with far more cruelty than at any time in the history of civilization. We have found ways never before imagined to torture and maim animals and make their lives a misery, almost a living hell for many thousands locked in cages in the multinational food industry, in government establishments devoted to finding the newest and best weapons for humans to kill each other, and in laboratories where often the most important thing being researched is the latest in lipstick or face cream.[82]

The problem, Professor Oderberg writes elsewhere, is not one of rights we fail to recognize but of our own capacity for "moral degeneracy," "the lack of virtue and flowering of excess."[83] For all of that, he will not allow that these sins amount either to a direct duty to animals or a direct, intrinsic right against human cruelty. "We may not, as a matter of strict moral theory, be committing an injustice against these victims of human vanity and greed. We may not, as I have argued, be violating their rights."[84] We have no duties *to* the creatures, but only "duties *in respect of* animals."

In *Applied Ethics* he offers the natural-law definition of a right as "a kind of moral protection provided to an individual in his pursuit of the good."[85] Rights are conditioned upon a recognition of moral goods in the person himself or herself and in the things we need to fulfill our nature. Animals can neither perceive nor pursue moral goods like justice and liberty and virtue, observes Professor Oderberg. Thus, they neither possess nor have need of rights. They do, he believes, have moral claims upon us, falling under the category of duty—our obligations as moral beings. From this he draws the useful distinction between a moral good and a right. Moral goods are things like benevolence and charity that we have a duty to perform, with no corresponding right on the part of others to expect it of us. We owe these to animals, too, says Professor Oderberg, but they have no more a moral right to kindness and charity, much less a legal right, than we have toward one another.

It's a good argument, and conscientiously applied would give us the hard standards of conduct we are looking for. Alas, it can also make for a very good evasion. When, for example, the New Zealand parliament debated an animal-welfare proposal in 1999, we heard once again from Roger Scruton, now warning that if the law were passed

> chimpanzees will not only have a right to life, but also a "right not to suffer cruel or degrading treatment," and "a right to take part in only benign experiments." Well, why not? Few of us are happy with the idea that chimpanzees should be exposed to cruel or degrading treatment, or subject to malign experiments, and most of us would welcome a law that protected them from such abuses. The problem lies in the language of "rights."[86]

Chimps cannot have rights because rights and duties can be exercised only by moral beings, and chimps aren't moral beings. "If chimpanzees had rights, they would be moral beings just like us. In which case, they would have liabilities and duties, which could be enforced by law."[87]

Mr. Scruton would "welcome" a law protecting chimps, and yet for some reason has never once lifted a hand to promote one, in New Zealand, Britain, or anywhere else. In all his many writings on the subject, he has never, so far as I can tell, championed a single specific animal-welfare reform meeting even his own criteria. This generous concession toward laboratory chimps comes only by way of dismissing the particular bill in question. It is nice to hear—the chimps would welcome some reforms too—but a fat lot of good his words will do them without specific statutes protecting them from needless experimentation.

Over and over again Mr. Scruton argues that primates and other creatures cannot be said to have moral rights because they cannot be said to have and exercise moral duties. Yes, he allows in *Animal Rights and Wrongs*, we have individual duties regarding the creatures arising from piety and from "the ethic of virtue [which] condemns those ways of dealing with animals which stem from a vicious motive."[88] Society, too, has an interest in preventing cruelty on the grounds of "moral corruption, since law is the guardian of society and would be ineffective in a world where the sources of social feeling had all been polluted."[89]

This is helpful, and the reader assumes it will lead Mr. Scruton to some clear and inviolable standards prohibiting cruelty. But no, he adds, it does not follow from this that the creatures themselves have any sort of rights, any natural claims of their own against human cruelty, for unlike us they are not "self-created beings" capable of understanding rights; they are not "sovereign" beings, creatures possessing "sovereignty over the life that is theirs."[90] All rights, he tells us again and again, are reciprocal, existing by negotiation, granted only to the extent that we get something in return, his variation on Immanuel Kant's categorical imperative. "If animals possessed the self-consciousness and autonomy of the moral being, then they would also have rights and duties."[91] Animals, in other words, can't go into court or file briefs or hire lawyers to assert rights, therefore they cannot conceivably possess rights. Just as we were elsewhere told that outside our world of language there can be no conscious feeling, now we're told that outside our world of contracts there can be no moral standing.

There is a range of possible replies to this contention, one of which is to note its resemblance to Peter Singer's theories. Both of them define the rights and value of human life in terms of personal choice, self-interest, and sovereignty. This leaves Mr. Scruton with the same ambivalence toward marginal cases, retarded and severely handicapped people who are unable to reciprocate. If rights belong only to beings capable of discharging duties under mutual contracts and agreements, what are we to say of people who are retarded and disabled?

This section of *Animal Rights and Wrongs* just sort of trails off without a clear answer. The best Mr. Scruton can do is to warn against a "cold and calculating attitude to the human species and the human form," which is comforting, although his own use of designations like "imbeciles" and "congenital idiots" in referring to people with mental disabilities doesn't set much of an example.[92] And it falls far short of declaring what needs to be said, and cannot be said by the terms of his own "sovereignty" argument, namely that physical and mental capacities, and man-made contracts, have nothing whatever to do with moral value or equality or the right to protection from cruelty and exploitation. Just as in Professor Singer's outlook, there is a whole realm of moral action missing from this construct of sovereignty and reciprocity—the realm of generosity and empathy and special consideration for the weak. But once that door is opened, where does it lead in our approach to animals?

Another response to Mr. Scruton's reasoning is to recall again the sense in which we ourselves, whatever theories of sovereignty we might dream up, cannot be said to have rights either. We live partly in the animals' world of nonrights too, the world of decay and plagues and diseases and natural disasters against which we have no claims of fairness, free will, kindness, or justice. If I am traipsing along in the woods and a grizzly charges me, I do not have any rights in the matter, nor will it help at all to invoke my sovereignty as a "self-created being." Though there have been cases in which predatory animals have for no apparent reason spared defenseless humans from attack and death (a mystery movingly depicted in the French film *The Bear*), Stalkers of the North are not moral actors answerable to our notions of rights.

Rights, and even the right to life, apply only to human action because we alone are moral actors capable of deliberate good and evil, as Mr. Scruton and other debunkers of animal rights never tire of reminding us. They have not paused to consider what follows from this, namely that rights exist, by definition, as a check against human wrongdoing. They attach to all human conduct, wherever human beings are capable of doing wrong. Once it is granted, therefore, that humans can act wrongfully in our power over animals, what grounds are left for denying that animals have a right not to be treated wrongfully at our hands? If a right is a prohibition on human wrongdoing, and if animals can be the object of wrongful human action, then to precisely that extent animals have rights—not, of course, among one another, but only in their encounters with us.

The alternative is to suppose that man the creature of reason and morality, when he enters the forests or factory farm or comes upon any animal, is somehow liberated from his own moral nature—which indeed seems to be the idea of that "therapy for guilt in guiltless killing" that Mr. Scruton relishes in the chase. His reciprocity argument, on close examination, turns out to be the moral counterpart to the language fallacy examined in Chapter 5. Mr. Scruton's conclusion ("animals cannot have rights") is merely a restatement of the premise ("rights are exclusive to beings capable of understanding the concept of rights"). He hasn't proved a thing except what we all knew going in, that animals are not philosophical or moral beings capable of understanding any moral claims they possess against human wrongdoing.

The next objection to Mr. Scruton's argument would seek a clearer definition of "vicious motive." Whether the issue is industrial farming or trapping or vivisection or hunting, everything depends, in his view, on the motives of the people involved, much like the wounded-dog theory of Peter Carruthers we also encountered in Chapter 5. Even fox hunting, says Mr. Scruton, if its chief enjoyment were derived from the suffering of the fox, would be a moral wrong.

Yet nowhere does he offer any sort of fixed criteria for judging what he himself calls the "wicked pleasures" of cruelty.[93] The law, he says, should forbid only "deliberate cruelty" in which the suffering of the animal "becomes an object of interest for its own sake."[94] Otherwise, the law should be silent on animal welfare, for, as it is, "modern societies suffer from too much legislation concerning matters in which lawyers and politicians are not necessarily the highest authorities."[95] Professor Oderberg in *Applied Ethics* makes the similar point that "it is wrong to cause pain to an animal for the sake of causing pain."[96] It depends on the motive, he argues, to be weighed and discerned according to a rather bureaucratic rule he calls the Principle of Double Effect:

> [O]n the Principle of Double Effect, it is permissible to allow foreseen but unintended pain or suffering for the sake of a beneficial purpose if the achievement of that purpose does not have as its means the doing of an act intrinsically wrong in itself, and if there is a proportion between the benefits conferred for that purpose and the evil of the suffering. So, if fox hunters can prove that what they aim at is the eradication of a pest that destroys farmers' livestock, and/or the benefits conferred by horse-riding in the fresh air, the "thrill of the chase" . . . and the like, then their pastime is legitimate. But cruelty for the sake of it is not, and a practice such as bullfighting seems to aim precisely at the pain and suffering of the bull. The point is that each case of the use of animals must be assessed on its merits, with due attention to whether what is aimed at is cruel, degrading, or otherwise set against the virtuous life that human beings are duty-bound to live.[97]

To take just the two most obvious problems here: First, how exactly are we to establish "deliberate cruelty" or "cruelty for its own sake"? I have yet to meet anyone who will confess to being deliberately cruel, toward man or animal. And it's pretty clear that Professor Oderberg has never read *Death in the Afternoon* or heard matadors or their fans explain the deeper meanings of bullfighting. Everyone who derives pleasure from tormenting animals, or watching the torment, insists they do so, like Mr. Scruton, for only the loftiest motives. How, moreover, would this Principle of Double Effect apply to factory farming, when the motive is nothing higher than extracting the perfect pork loin, or saving a dollar here in production, or a dollar there in consumption, and the line fades between deliberate and unintentional cruelty?

Motive, in normal moral and legal reasoning, is viewed as a criterion in measuring punishment for wrongdoing, but not for wrongdoing itself. Whatever the different motives, say, in the case of two assaults, the same event has occurred, causing the same degree of violence to the victim, and the law makes no distinction between the two. Both are crimes to be prevented, their moral gravity depending not on the motives of the offender but on the harm to the victim. Only in judging culpability for that objective wrong do the subjective motives of the offender count for anything, to be weighed by evidence of premeditation, mental competence, and so on. We apply this principle even to acts of self-defense or killings committed in war, which are not viewed as positive moral goods but, of course, as necessary evils. Circumstances, we say, left no choice.

In Mr. Scruton's reckoning, and to a lesser extent in Professor Oderberg's argument, where violence to animals is at issue, the event itself is colored entirely by motive. We are prohibited from assuming the intention directly from the act itself; an act, on their account, is transformed into an evil if the motive is evil, and a good if the motive is good. To this argument, in the case of sport hunting, Mr. Scruton piles on other "complex moral goods" such as the camaraderie and "tribal" bonding among hunters, the "hospitality" of the property owner, and on and on. In his own mind, at least, he thus manages to separate the motive of the hunt (recreation) as far as possible from the objective of the hunt (death), and farther still from the necessary consequence of the hunt (suffering). Called to account, hunters who make such arguments may then indignantly protest that the direct consequences of their own actions were all along an incidental detail, like the Christian Hunters in Reno explaining how their sport offers a chance to bond with their sons or "share the gospel" with one another between shots. Lately in England, Mr. Scruton and his fellow huntsmen have taken to raising money from fees to donate to rural charities—an attempt, like Safari Club with its "Hunters for the Hungry" program, to engraft their wicked pleasures onto the nearest moral good and thereby obscure actual motive and intention, perhaps even from themselves.

Both very learned men, Mr. Scruton and Professor Oderberg in any other context would recognize and decry in such twists of logic a useless mush of situational ethics and, in Mr. Scruton's case, a dreary utilitarianism very like Professor Singer's. Throughout *Animal Rights and Wrongs* he holds forth on the "moral law," the understanding of which sets man apart from the creatures. Yet somehow, in our moral regard for animals, this translates into practical lawlessness, every man left to discern his own motives, answer only to his own judgments, and face punishment only if he confesses first. Whereas in Professor Singer's scheme we get all kinds of specific rules without any moral law, here we get the moral law without any specific rules.

The second problem is that motive depends on knowledge, and knowledge varies. Suppose that one acts on the assumption that no animal can feel conscious pain, torturing some creature in ways that Mr. Scruton himself would find reprehensible. The motive in that case would be perfectly pure, but only because the offender is perfectly ignorant. How, if motive is the deciding factor here, are we to condemn that act? Cruelty is like any other vice, a quality reflected in specific acts, and a man can be cruel without knowing it.

Like other sport hunters, too, Mr. Scruton carries his moral relativism a step further in his constant appeals to *experience*. To "understand" hunting and the delights of the "substantial minority" of people who enjoy it (5 to 7 percent), we must hunt, submerge ourselves in the raw, choiceless passion of it all. We, too, might then know that sense of "homecoming to our natural state."

Of course, this is an argument equally available to enthusiasts of bull-fighting, cockfighting, bear-baiting, hare coursing, crush videos, or, for that matter, pornography in general. Since when do we have to indulge in vice before we may adjudge it as such? And if human beings are rational creatures defined by our accountability to the moral law, then you would think our "home" lay in exactly the opposite direction, not in these spasms of passion Mr. Scruton celebrates but in acts of self-restraint.

We can reject the "deliberate cruelty" argument, therefore, and all of its many variations, if for no other reason than because they are hopelessly ambiguous and accomplish nothing. Such arguments amount to an honor code. We have plenty of those already in our dealings with animals, and would not be discussing the matter at all if they were being observed. They rest upon a "rarified, intellectual brand of free will" and of other qualities by which moral claims are recognized, as Mary Midgley observes, obscuring the basic things we have in common with animals such as an aversion to being bullied, beaten, or confined.[98] Such arguments treat human cruelty as an interior state of mind or heart, like pride or envy, instead of as a quality of character expressed in specific acts, events, or institutions to be judged by their actual need and on the objective merits of each case. They are based on a concept of human dignity, yet leave the law silent on acts of human degradation at the expense of innocent creatures. They assert human freedom and our unique status as moral actors, while giving the worst among us license to act on pure appetite, or will, or even malevolence if they wish. They grant inherent rights only to man because he is the rational creature, and then let any man do just about anything to any animal provided his professed motive is pure. They condemn "wanton cruelty," letting every man decide for himself what "wanton" means.

Professor Oderberg, concluding his case for "strict moral theory," eloquently urges us to think beyond rights to moral duties. "[W]e must stop thinking that only by violating a right can we be cruel, malicious, avaricious, conceited, vainglorious, envious and plain degrading. Every act of cruelty for cruelty's sake disgraces and degrades us."[99] That is a humane and defensible position, though only if it can be translated into real remedies and protections under law. Otherwise the most abhorrent practices remain just as they are—disgraceful, degrading, cruel, and legal.

One can endlessly argue the ultimate moral or spiritual implications of animal cruelty, "direct" and "indirect" rights, and all the rest. It is not on point. These distinctions become after a while meaningless and tiresome, and there is something rather prideful and pedantic in this insistence that even in committing wrongs against other creatures, the *real* wrong is to ourselves or the moral law or whatever. Morality usually consists in precisely the opposite, in recognizing goods and values beyond ourselves and giving them their due—in respecting and obeying the order established by the Creator. And sin, by its very definition, *always* hurts the sinner more than the victim, estranging the offender from God and risking an eternal fate far worse than any hurt he or she has caused. But it is the temporal realm we are concerned with here, addressing specific evils and holding the offenders to account under the law. When "strict moral theory" fails to do that, when strict moral theory can merely comment on unjust acts without forbidding them, then maybe it is time to reexamine the theory. Maybe the theory is not strict enough.

The whole case against the direct moral claims of animals has the ring of a Zeno's Paradox, one of which proved the theoretical impossibility that any object could ever reach its goal. Before it arrives at the target, it must first travel half the distance, and then again half the remaining distance, and so on in an infinite number of smaller and smaller distances, never getting more than halfway to the end. It's an intellectual problem that still keeps mathematicians busy, while the rest of us safely assume that motion actually is possible, and objects actually can meet their targets. In the same way, while the philosophers argue over the finer points of the animals' moral claims upon us, we can safely assume that the creatures really can be wronged, and that the victim of bear-baiting really is the bear.

All that animals need, and what we owe them under our laws, are specific, clear, and above all consistent criminal sanctions declaring Thou Shalt Not subject them to human cruelty, as a matter of simple decency and an obligation of justice. The ultimate philosophical and spiritual questions we can each ponder for ourselves. The spectators and participants who delight in cruelty to animals, so far as I am concerned, can worry about their own souls.

EIGHT

JUSTICE
AND MERCY

And also for these, O Lord, the humble beasts, who bear with us the heat and burden of the day, we beg thee to extend thy great kindness of heart, for thou hast promised to save both man and beasts, and great is thy loving kindness.

SAINT BASIL

When an ape points to a swan, and using the signs we have taught her says "Waterbird," that is a revelation, and she is telling us more than that a swan is present. We have in such evidence what journalist Jeremy Paxman calls "the moral equivalent of the Missing Link."[1] When we know that elephants among other animals communicate danger to one another, and sorrow for their dead, and have nightmares, then we know too much to leave these creatures any longer at the mercy of sport hunters. When standard agricultural practice treats billions of animals as unfeeling flesh, at the very moment when humankind has established beyond reasonable doubt their conscious mental and emotional lives, it is no good to go on as if nothing had changed.

C. S. Lewis, reflecting on the moral problems raised by animal suffering, asks "What shall be done for these innocents?"[2] Trying to answer that question myself in this book, I have felt at times that I was venturing into forbidden territory, and at other times that I was saying things almost too obvious to bear mentioning. Often I have had both feelings at once. An author describing the methods of intensive farming, or the excesses of sport hunting, or even the harsher uses of animals in science writes with confidence that most readers will share his sense of concern and indignation. Sounding the call to action—convincing people that change is not only necessary, but actually possible—is more problematic. In protecting animals from cruelty, it is always just one step from the mainstream to the fringe. To condemn the wrong is obvious, to suggest its abolition radical.

But let us, in this parting chapter, try to think through some practical reforms addressing the problems described in the preceding pages. We have seen a wanton disregard of wildlife and, in some nations, of marine mammals. We have witnessed a collapse of standards in livestock farming. We have examined the abuses of genetic experimentation, and seen in the extremes of biotechnology an inherent cruelty that disregards the integrity of animal life. We have considered the primary arguments by which such things are defended—animals feel only "mere pain," exploiting them is "for their own good," only "deliberate cruelty" is really cruelty—and these claims do not survive rational inquiry. No religion gives sanction to the abuses we permit, least of all the faith of prophets. No self-respecting code of morality defends them—they're merely overlooked, or tolerated, or dismissed as unworthy of serious attention. In short, we have run out of excuses. Yet still hanging in the air is the apprehension that even if we were disposed to enacting serious reforms in law, the project would simply be too impractical, too costly, too disruptive of our way of life, and for that reason alone must be refused. "We shall be living the life of beasts once we give up the use of beasts," as this fear was long ago expressed. "No civilized pursuit, no refinement of living, could survive."[3]

I myself doubt that most of us would even notice serious reforms in animal-protection laws, much less object to them. And those we did notice would meet, I am sure, with the sincere and resounding support of a great majority. Sometimes reform is just a matter of enforcing already existing laws protecting animals, or else of slightly revising existing legal boundaries to reflect beliefs already shared by most people in most societies. A reader skimming the preceding pages might never know it, but most people *like* animals and often love them, and indeed we live in a time of great change in attitudes about the care and treatment of animals. Animal protection in this way is like many other great moral and social causes now adopted into custom and law, ideas once viewed as a threat to civilized values but now accepted as the extension of civilized values.

I think of Jim Carmichel, the big-game hunter who confides in *Outdoor*

Life about his reluctance to tell others, even fellow sportsmen, that his "consuming passion" is stalking elephants.[4] Why the reticence? "The reason I'm evasive is because even a hint of my true hunting passion invariably provokes shocked outrage or a cascade of questions."[5] People just don't understand him, says Mr. Carmichel. The very fact that "no wild creature on earth is as fascinating or as intelligent,"[6] for most of us a reason to avoid harming elephants, evidently for him only heightens the enjoyment of the hunt. One doubts it really takes all that much to get Mr. Carmichel talking on the subject. But here, at least, we do have an admission of overwhelming public disapproval, raising the obvious question: Why does the law reflect his values and not those of the vast majority who find the whole thing repugnant? Why do we let him do it?

In the same way, most readers had probably never even heard of many other practices mentioned in this book, or didn't know that others were legal. You will excuse, I hope, a liberal use of "we" here and there in describing cruelties that almost always turn out to be the doing of a perverse few who inflict the worst abuses and oppose the simplest reforms. "Our" worst offense is permissiveness, inattention, or, in the case of industrial agriculture, complicity. Among those few, however, while the nonviolent majority looks politely away, there is no self-restraint and very little in the way of legal restraint. What is true of violence in general, in any given society, is true of cruelty to animals: Ninety or so percent of the problems come from five or so percent of the population.

We all know the person who is never wrong, never at fault, and can never have enough of anything. Examine most every animal-welfare problem and you will find this type standing athwart reform, people so completely absorbed in their own pursuits and passions that the meekest defense of any animal will be met with anger and indignation. In a way, those sows we have seen in crates, unable to turn around because corporate farmers want to squeeze the last dime out of them—granting not even a few lousy inches on each side—are the perfect metaphor for much of the needless animal suffering we tolerate today. So many are the victims not only of rank cruelty but of pride and selfishness, of a petty, unyielding spirit that takes all and gives nothing.

You and I may not always agree on the precise moral standards that must obtain. But most will agree that where there is no standard at all the law must supply one. As I argued in the last chapter, we can assert such standards without recourse to any new doctrines or theories regarding animals. The moral and religious principles of the great majority would do quite well if we actually enforced them, if all were held to the standards that most profess. In free societies this will usually come down to a counting of votes. If enough of us can agree that certain practices are no longer justified or acceptable, then that's that, and the law must speak.

Animal issues can be complicated, and though I do not myself claim to know where all the answers lie—say, in the case of elephants today being driven from the earth by development and hunting—I do know what the answers are not. I know that it is mean and unjust to treat such creatures in such a way. As in judging egregious wrongs committed against human beings, I start with the thing itself, the act and its results, the spirit and its fruits, and work my way back from there. Some things cannot under any circumstances be justified, even in our dealings with animals. When we find them we must call them what they are, evils, and then set about ridding those evils from our midst.

GAME BUTCHERY

Baiting wild animals, for instance, is still legal in many places, and where illegal seldom punished. As we have seen, entire companies exist just to make and sell the "feed" for deer hunters, along with an array of ever more sophisticated lures and decoys. Though such devices are condemned even by most hunters, in their informal codes of "fair chase," advertisements for every imaginable kind of bait or lure today fill the pages of every hunting magazine including the two most widely read, *Outdoor Life* and *Field & Stream*. Somebody is buying all those products, and our more affluent hunters are going afield with things like heat sensors and satellite positioning systems.

If we're looking for common ground, then, and if hunters themselves claim to disdain such practices, then how about starting right there? We can enact state and federal cruelty statutes banning all forms of baiting, or the manufacture, distribution, or sale of any product serving that purpose. Civilization will also survive a prohibition on the "fawn distress" signal and similar high-tech gadgetry used in locating and pursuing wildlife, all of which can be forbidden on the general grounds that if a man insists on hunting, let him at least hunt like a man.

Bear-baiting, even as moral philosophers are still mulling over its precise implications, is becoming more common, not only because of trophy hunting in the "Bears of the World" competition, but because of a growing demand for bear gallbladders among the affluent of Asia, where the stuff is considered of medicinal value and—what else?—an aphrodisiac. The Asiatic black bear has already been wiped out to meet this demand, and in China there are actually 247 bear farms where, at this very moment, some seven thousand of the creatures live in narrow cages just like our pig farms, their bile constantly drained through surgically implanted catheters.[7]

Supplying the same market today are thousands of American and Canadian men who go forth every spring and fall to bait bears, using their Wayne-Carleton cub callers and the like, or by the time-honored method of leaving jelly doughnuts or other scraps of food, and then hiding somewhere to lie in wait. Neither gender nor age is a factor in the gallbladder market. They kill the females and cubs, too. In America, bear-baiting is legal in nine states, and hunters even do their baiting in many of our national forests. Hunters in North America legally kill in excess of forty thousand bears annually, and perhaps just as many illegally. Senator Mitch McConnell, a Republican from Kentucky, has several times introduced a bill to ban any interstate commerce in bear viscera, with penalties of up to $25,000 per offense and a maximum one year in prison, only to see this measure fought back by the hunting lobby with little public attention.

Federal law should go farther than that, outlawing all bear-baiting on federal lands for any purpose whatsoever. For baiting and all other abuses of wildlife, moreover, let the penalties be serious criminal sanctions under cruelty statutes, and not just game laws casually enforced by our various fish and wildlife departments, as is usually the case. These sanctions should include a disqualification for both gun and hunting licenses—for a first offense, say, five years, for the second offense ten years, and a lifetime disqualification after that.

Bow hunting, another form of the "game butchery" Teddy Roosevelt condemned, is also legal, and in our own age of Ted Nugent has become an all-out mania among sportsmen who live for that sweet "twang" of the bowstring, the "wet gurgling" of stricken deer, and those thrilling extra hours following the blood trail. A broadhead arrow kills like a knife, torturing the creature with a slow death by hemorrhaging. Bows wound as often as they kill, even in the hands of the rare expert, and are a favorite of poachers. Employed precisely to maximize the pleasure of the hunter, at the cost of maximal animal suffering, they are of no conceivable "conservation" value. Yet except for a rule here and there barring crossbows (which lock the waiting arrow in place, allowing for a noiseless aim), the law has looked the other way, and in the U.S. actually permits bow hunters a season of four or five months—longer than for any other weapon.

Mr. Nugent, the "master whacker," holds himself out as a champion of basic American rights and liberties, often invoking America's founders. But there is no constitutional right to torture wildlife, and the distinction our Founding Fathers made between the free man and the libertine must find a place here and in all laws governing the modern sportsman. Bow hunting is a good example of how our traditional notion of "wanton" cruelty, in contrast to unavoidable pain inflicted on an animal, might correct a current problem if only we acted upon it. Arguably, many statutes already on the books could be applied to prohibit bows, but an explicit ban is in order here and we should restrict their use to nonliving targets, just like in the Olympics. Archers can still enjoy the twang all they want, just not the gurgling.

Into the same category of gratuitous torture of wildlife we can put the steel-jawed leg-hold trap still legal in parts of America, Canada, and elsewhere. Our Trappers Association celebrates the "valiant and heroic exploits"[8] of its trade, which today consist in subjecting an estimated four million animals every year, including uncounted "non-target" victims like cats and dogs, to slow death by shock, bleeding, or strangling even in our supposedly protected national wildlife refuges. To date, eighty-eight countries have banned these traps, including all members of the European Union. The practice could easily be abolished throughout the U.S., as five states have already done by ballot initiative. Local ordinances like the one proposed a few years ago in Beverly Hills, requiring labels on furs or other animal products explaining how the material was obtained—with no emotive language, but in hard nouns and verbs like "trap," "cage," "poison," "electrocution"—are also to be welcomed. Such proposals will sometimes fail, but they will always succeed in exposing deceit, complaisance, and willful ignorance.

Another recent mania in America is the shooting of swans, cranes, and especially mourning doves. Incredibly, the latter suffer the highest casualties of any game bird, accounting for a third of all animals hunted for sport in this country, some 45 million doves a year falling from the sky in a bloody spray of feathers. No one claims they're overpopulated. Doves are migratory birds, just passing through. Few claim to kill them for food. Doves yield little meat anyway, and for just that reason are often not even retrieved after being killed or wounded. They pose no problems to crops or vegetation, either. They're ground feeders, needing only seeds and spilled grain. Where legal, too, dove hunting starts in early September before the young have left the nests, leaving the little ones to die of starvation.

The hunting lobby calls the dove an "underutilized resource," meaning, basically, there are a lot of doves around so why not use them for target practice? Human decency regards doves as gentle songbirds of no harm to anyone, our very harbingers of peace on earth, and not just feathered skeets to be annihilated for recreation. Eleven states still prohibit dove hunting, including Iowa where, in 2001, it took a courageous veto from Democratic governor Tom Vilsack to stop a bill to open season on that state's doves. Here's another easy call, even by the terms of the hunters' "conservation" ethic. Let the laws of all fifty states protect these creatures—sparing, while we're at it, the equally beautiful and harmless swans and cranes.

Game farming and canned hunting are among the lowest practices described in this book, and also the most easily outlawed. Despite the good efforts of former senator Frank Lautenberg, a Democrat of New Jersey, both are not only legal today in thirty states but are standard procedure from Texas to upstate New York. Captive hunting is commonplace in Africa as well, especially in South Africa with its many private game farms where wildlife is bred for sport hunting. Often, as we saw, the private ranches lie adjacent to the protected areas, so that supposedly protected animals are routinely baited into the line of fire, even elephants lured away from safety by man-made water holes and reduced to frantically running back to the protected areas. Hunting ranches large and small are common as well in Namibia, Botswana, and Zimbabwe, and the practice is now spreading into South America, Australia, and the Canadian provinces of Quebec and Saskatchewan.

Few, if any, of these exotic ranches existed a generation ago. Wildlife farming is an entirely modern innovation. Millions of wild animals across the earth have today been reduced to "exotic livestock"—born, fed, and raised to be sold, shot, and stuffed. J. B. Hunt, the trucking magnate and owner of a large canned hunting ranch in Missouri, lays it out very simply: "There's no difference between this and raising cattle except the life of the animal is much longer."[9] The proprietor of a hunting ranch in Zimbabwe is even more blunt: "We want the elephant to be a commodity, because if it isn't, it might as well be dead."[10]

If we make no other reform in the treatment of wildlife, let us at least abolish canned hunting wherever it is found, and with it this insidious merging of farming and hunting, of protection and destruction, of species survival with systematic killing. "Sustainable use," "free-market conservation," and other notions offered in defense of canned hunting are based on a perverted view of both wildlife conservation and of human freedom. They seek to preserve not the animals, but old forms of violence that can no longer, on their own, stand the tests of reason and morality. They are not rational codes of human action, but expressions of an ideology that reduces all human action to economics and every animal to a production unit, as if all creatures of the earth must come before man to render fitting praise and justify their existence by commercial value. Driven not by "conservation" but by blind consumerism, today's canned-hunting industry also illustrates the logical endpoint of Professor Peter Carruthers's rule that "animals are worth preserving for their importance to *us*," which, in practice, will usually mean "for their importance to *me* and any damn thing I want."

The free market can and does in many ways join the interests of wildlife with our human interest in appreciating animals, as in photo safaris, whale-watching businesses, and other forms of largely benign use. Free-market societies over the past century were certainly more conscientious and successful than were statist regimes in safeguarding the natural world. But pure, rationalist economics can take us only so far. In the hands of a man like Mr. Hunt, who apparently can see no difference between wildlife and the commodities shipped and delivered by his trucks, the profit incentive will fail us. At a certain point, as Clive Hamilton writes in Australia's *Canberra Times*, the free market becomes "fundamentally at odds with a true conservation ethic, one that appreciates the intrinsic worth of the natural world and celebrates the ability of humans to participate in it."[11] Government, and only government, can lay down the basic boundaries and prohibitions—saying, just as it must in protecting human beings from cruelty and degradation, "This far and no farther."

We must think hard on the idea of breeding and farming wild animals for any commercial purpose, let alone for tawdry and silly purposes like culling ivory or harvesting "racks." In the case of game ranching in America and Africa, we are to believe that as human population and development expand, conservation of wildlife is possible only by creating economic incentives to breed and farm animals for the hunting of trophies in fenced parks, an abhorrent idea and cowardly beyond belief. Even if this notion were true—if mankind's only alternative in the century to come were to turn even the remaining elephants and lions of the world into "exotic livestock" for ivory and sport hunters—this would be numerical survival only for these species, and their disappearance a morally preferable alternative. We would then have lost all appreciation for the elephant and lion, and there are fates worse than extinction. The exotic livestock would only be tormented and degraded like our current livestock, or like the poor beasts in China's bear farms and America's own "deer factories," and it would be better to just let them all go.

In the United States, the Captive Exotic Animal Protection Act proposed by Mr. Lautenberg and now picked up by Senator Joseph Biden, a Democrat of Delaware, would very nearly shut down our domestic canned-hunting industry. The federal government should declare unequivocally—as states including California, Oregon, Georgia, Wyoming, and Montana have recently done—that the hunting of captive mammals, no matter what the size of the enclosure, will not be tolerated, and that all offenders will be held to account.

If you spent a typical day at the cargo terminal of Miami International Airport, or some other major point of entry into America, you would see a procession of chimps, lions, bears, and other imported animals passing under the inspection of the U.S. Fish and Wildlife Service, some of them en route to hunting ranches. (And they are the lucky ones—many others, including captured wild primates, are bound for laboratories.) The law should forbid all of that, barring the private ownership or commercial transport of wildlife altogether, exempting only sanctuaries and zoos of high repute. In the decades to come we may well find ourselves abandoning the idea of any animal as pure property, settling instead on the concept of guardianship implied by our current cruelty statutes, but for now we can at least draw the line at wildlife: No one has the right to own a lion or bear or any other wild creature. Addressing the problem of excessive breeding by zoos, moreover, some of which have been selling sick or elderly animals to hunting ranches, the law must better define their accreditation standards and corresponding ethical obligations—specifying, for example, the duty to care for all zoo animals regardless of age.

Laws against canned hunting should also apply to the caged fowl favored by "gentlemen hunters" in America, the United Kingdom, and elsewhere. About four thousand such businesses operate today in the U.S., raising tens of millions of pheasant, quail, partridge, mallard ducks, and other birds for release at the shooters' convenience. Often, as the gun waits, the cages are shaken up to dizzy the birds and assure they can't fly too fast or too far. Like other canned-hunting concessionaires, the people who run these businesses will protest that their livelihoods depend upon such practices. The answer is that they should find honorable work, that no man has a right to make his living from wanton cruelty, and henceforth a felony charge will await any gentleman found raising birds or any other creature for blood sport, or patronizing any establishment that does so.

How to deal with Safari Club International? For starters, Congress and the IRS can undertake a brisk review of the group's tax status, along with kindred "conservation" groups today enjoying the privileges of charitable and educational enterprises. Wherever Safari Club belongs in our law, it does not belong in the same category as the Sisters of Charity, the Salvation Army, and the Humane Society of the United States.

A change in import policy would also go a long way in checking the spread of game butchery by American citizens traveling abroad. Here we have as our model the largely successful bans on other wildlife products. If a ban on the importation of ivory products can help take the money out of ivory poaching, if a ban on products from endangered species can help take the money out of the illegal wildlife trade, and if a ban on marine-mammal products can help take the money out of whaling and dolphin killing, guess what can help take the money out of exotic trophy hunting?

With the merest fraction of one percent of the American people going abroad every year to haul back elephant, lion, giraffe, and other "mounts" by the thousands, this is one market easily dealt with. Just as America was once the primary market for ivory, we are today the chief market for the trophy-hunting trade. A ban could be accomplished by a revision of the 1988 African Elephant Conservation Act, which prohibits the importation of ivory and other elephant parts while specifically exempting, thanks to Safari Club lobbyists, "the importation into the United States of sport-hunted trophies from elephants."[12] This change would not find much support among elephant slayers like Johan Calitz and Jim Carmichel, or by fans of "The Big-Tusker Trilogy." And it would come as a serious blow to taxidermists. But such a reform will be welcomed by many other American hunters, the ones who still hunt for meat alone, and have long despised big-game trophy hunters as a disgrace to their ranks. Similar laws in the United Kingdom and Germany—the other primary destinations of big-game trophies—would kill the industry. Also, where in our Second Amendment does it say anyone has the right to carry guns *abroad*?

An Abomination

Recalling the exploits of Mr. Calitz, who cannot feel a special concern for the elephants? We are told they have to be sacrificed, to help people in need. We are led to believe that the material uplift of developing societies depends upon their further destruction by hunters from abroad. This professed solicitude for the struggling poor—one elephant-trophy fee, as Mr. Carmichel puts it, paying for "a desperately needed schoolroom" in Africa[13]—is as phony and as insufferably sanctimonious as their professed concern for animals. There is a difference between alleviating the desperation of poor people and exploiting it. You cannot take an evil thing and make it good by association. You cannot put human cruelty at the service of human compassion.

Representative Richard W. Pombo, a Republican and member of Safari Club, wrote to Secretary of State Colin Powell in May 2001 seeking assurances that American policy toward elephant conservation would treat them as a "renewable resource." He urged "that any future policy regarding various species—whether the subject species are elephants, whales, turtles, or trees—be based on sound science," meaning "limited harvests that would have no adverse impact on stocks."[14] Secretary Powell was too busy or too polite to reply explaining to Mr. Pombo the difference between an elephant and a tree, but there is a danger that such ideas will prevail by default. Our president and secretary of state have many other responsibilities in the world, and the fate of the elephant might seem one of the smaller ones. But I hope that in any decisions they might make on the matter, they will disregard Mr. Pombo and the creed he represents. I hope they will choose a different way— the true conservation of protection and respect for these beautiful creatures who already have withstood so much.

There is much truth to the idea of elephants, like whales, as the martyr animal whose fate will decide the future of other wildlife and our treatment of them. They are not only a prime moral symbol in the eyes of humanity, one of the charismatic animals that draw our particular attention and empathy, but a giant ecological force. If they are protected in Asia and Africa, other wildlife will survive in their wake. If they go, many others go with them.

There is truth, too, in one argument that safari hunters and their defenders have made. They are correct when they say that wildlife conservation in developing nations must give the people who live in those regions a stake in its success. It is not enough to merely eulogize the elephants, bemoan their suffering, and idly deplore the cruelties of man. We have to offer clear alternatives. And we have to be prepared to see those policies through with whatever financial aid and investment they require.

One cannot draw a tidy little picture of the African elephants and their troubles that leaves out all of the terrible human travails around them. Indeed, with official corruption and persistent poverty in many parts of Africa, with violence, malaria, and now by some estimates twenty million young men and women on the continent carrying the AIDS virus, it is more difficult than ever to make a case for the elephants and other animals. But the fate of elephants and other wildlife need not be as urgent as all of this human suffering for us to respond to both with compassion, moral seriousness, and whatever material aid can be offered. In the end, the well-being of both the people of the continent and the wildlife around them often depends on the same things—on honest and stable governments, long-term economic enterprises, secure and orderly civil and financial institutions to encourage such enterprises, law enforcement and the control of violence.

We have the basic problem in sub-Saharan Africa that human populations and agricultural settlements are competing for land with wildlife and with elephants in particular. The willingness of villagers in Zimbabwe, Botswana, Namibia, and elsewhere to accept large trophy fees from American hunters is entirely understandable, no matter what we or they might think of the hunters themselves. Elephants for them are not a poignant symbol of vanishing wildlife, as they seem to us from afar. They're the neighbors. And they're in the way, lumbering around eating a couple of hundred pounds of food a day. Then along come all these rich westerners offering to pay thousands of dollars just to kill those elephants, sums it would take months or years to earn farming or ranching. In the place of those villagers, what would we do? More to the point, what have we already done? As an African game manager asked American author Douglas Chadwick, "And what of your Great Plains? Didn't it once have even more wildlife than Kenya? Where are your animals?"[15]

America and other industrialized nations must help these countries to repeat our successes without tempting them to repeat our sins. It's not as if America's extermination of the buffalo and other wildlife, for example, is some sort of economic model to be followed. Nor do Americans today point with pride to that chapter in our history, or believe that killing off those creatures in order to starve and scatter the Native Americans who relied upon them was justified. The question is not whether to help developing nations but how to help, and whether economic aid can come only in the form of men with guns. We're told that hunting either for trophies or ivory is the only alternative in Africa. But it is not the only alternative. It is not even the most profitable alternative. It is just the easiest alternative. It's easy money, with all of the long-term economic value that term usually conveys.

Our best example is Kenya, which banned sport hunting in 1977. As Kenya's main newspaper, the *Daily Nation,* reminded us in a 2000 editorial, the safari hunt itself is a colonialist invention alien to the values of most Africans. Even more abhorrent to them are canned and competitive hunting. "The massacre of animals for sport," declared the *Daily Nation,* "is un-African and an abomination. . . . Countries such as South Africa and Zimbabwe refuse to see what is essentially a simple truth: The only way to guarantee the future of the world's wildlife is to ruthlessly destroy the market for animal products."[16]

Kenya each year receives more than a million tourists. They come not to shoot animals, much less captive animals, but to see free-roaming wild animals in the country's fifty-nine protected parks and reserves. They leave behind more than a billion dollars in revenue. That revenue, nearly 10 percent of the continent's total $9.5 billion income from tourism, depends precisely on the absence of hunting, which elsewhere has the perverse effect of keeping nonviolent tourists away. If hunting and in particular legal ivory hunting were ever introduced in Kenya, cautions the archeologist Dr. Richard Leakey, who oversaw that nation's wildlife service at the height of the ivory slaughter, it would destroy tourism. "Men will roam the countryside with rifles. Elephant viewing will become more difficult, because they will be skittish and frightened and tourists will not be safe. It will put us back 10 or 15 years."[17]

Hunters and game managers, with their hard "realism" and purely numerical and commercial calculations, never even pause to consider this particular reality. They don't think of the trauma that systematic killing inflicts upon intelligent mammals with no natural predator. They take no note of the vacancies left in families and herds, the juveniles left with no mothers to raise them, the long-term effects of all this slaughter on the ecological well-being of elephant populations.

Somehow, too, Kenya has managed to hold to its ban on hunting and the quick profits it offers even while experiencing the same hardships found elsewhere on the continent. The difference, where wildlife is concerned, is that Kenya has not surrendered its wildlife department to international hunting or ivory interests. Over the years, often showing great vision and courage, Kenya has proved that human interests can be protected and advanced in Africa without turning preserves into game ranches for the hunting elite.

Sometimes the nonlethal approach is as simple as building, when the money is available, really, really strong fences around either the elephant preserves or the human settlements and farms—or digging protective trenches, as India has done around its Bandipur park elephant preserve. With a grant of $7 million from the U.S. Agency for International Development (USAID), the Kenya Wildlife Service recently erected such a fence around human developments abutting the Kimana Wildlife Sanctuary, containing one of the country's largest elephant populations, near Mount Kilimanjaro. The project even opened up to the elephants land and migration routes they had abandoned during the ivory pogrom of the 1980s. In this way the local Masai government continues its farming and cattle ranching, with little or no loss of crops to elephants, while receiving additional revenues from a growing tourism concession. Other such projects are either in the works or planned for six other areas where most of Kenya's elephants roam, with as much as 400 kilometers of special fencing to be constructed if enough money can be raised. "The landmark approaches to the human-elephant conflict in Kenya," reports an observer,

> show that the protection and promotion of human livelihoods can be addressed in the absence of elephant hunting, culling, or the ivory trade. Human lives are the top priority, and the government shoots dangerous elephants. Conflict with agriculture is addressed with a dramatic, growing fencing strategy that sacrifices ecology for human needs where necessary. Co-existence in pastoral areas is pursued through negotiations with local communities, while keeping land available for elephants outside protected areas. Tourism provides many communities with a stake in local conservation.[18]

Even as USAID is helping Kenya with this lenient and cooperative approach, the same agency oversees America's financial support of the CAMPFIRE program promoting trophy hunting in Zimbabwe and elsewhere.

Though accounting here is sketchy, and a U.S. government audit found that only one in ten dollars actually reaches local villagers,[19] some income surely is going to people who badly need it. But we should choose one policy or the other. Though conditions in these two nations vary, our own guiding principles in both cases are the same, and the U.S. government should assert them without apology—making it clear that certain practices are simply outside the bounds of decency and we will no longer support them, much less subsidize them. If money will solve at least the immediate problem with fences, and if America is spending money anyway, then let us direct our efforts there instead of to hunting concessions. Grants through the UN, the World Bank, and other international agencies could likewise promote private tourism ventures that capitalize on live elephants, while also promoting investment in the schools, roads, hospitals, and sanitation infrastructure that will allow African villages to expand their economies beyond both tourism and sport hunting.

Elsewhere, elephants can be spared from hunting and culling by taking down fences no longer needed, as South Africa has done in the northeast edges of Kruger Park, allowing the herds to move back into Mozambique now that the civil war is over and the ivory poachers have largely receded. With money donated from private charities like the Elephant Trust, the William Holden Wildlife Foundation, and the International Fund for Animal Welfare (IFAW), other elephants pressed in by human development have been moved to other areas where they can "pay their own way" by just being elephants for tourists to appreciate. Foreign aid, both public and private, could help here, too. In September 2000, private researchers in South Africa announced the first successful test in the wild on a dart-delivered contraceptive vaccine for African elephants, reducing pregnancies by half.[20] So now, facing problems of population and overgrazing, we have yet another alternative. This, of course, will be mocked as a foolish extravagance and a waste of time—by men whose idea of time and money well spent is to fly across the world, kill an elephant, hack off the head, haul it home, hang it on a wall, and then go back for more. Thanks, but we don't need their advice on practicality.

One wonders, too, as long as America and other industrialized nations are devoting millions of dollars in foreign aid to Africa, why we could not also use some of that money, acting through private, nonprofit organizations, for the leasing or outright purchase of land where today elephants and other endangered animals are routinely shot by ranchers and farmers. The millions of dollars in payments and tax revenue this would bring might allow villagers to invest not only in job-creating tourism centers, but also in other enterprises of greater long-term value to their economies while at the same time protecting both their land and its wildlife.

A company named Conscorp, short for Conservation Corporation Africa, has set a good example here. Conscorp has so far converted some twenty-seven hunting lodges in six southern and east African nations, including Kenya and Zimbabwe, into tourism facilities supporting more than 20,000 people in rural areas. "It builds schools," as the *New York Times* describes the company,

> and clinics near its lodges, and it employs as many local people as possible, not just as cooks and chambermaids, but as builders, iron-workers and trackers. It buys seeds from local farmers and teaches them to plant vegetables which it then buys for its tables. It buys materials for local artists and sells their work to its local curio shops. It hires people to clear trees, then buys the charcoal they produce from the wood they carry home. . . .
>
> The rationale is partly neighborliness and partly a gamble that the bigger the stake local people have in the lodge, the less likely they will be to poach, take the company to court or even object when the occasional elephant herd runs amok in their cornfields.[21]

Tourism of this kind accounts for less than 1 percent of the gross domestic product of most sub-Saharan African nations, compared to nearly 6 percent of America's GDP and as much as 25 to 50 percent for other developing nations that have learned to capitalize on their natural beauty. Only four of every hundred tourism dollars spent across the world go to Africa, even though the continent accounts for nearly 20 percent of the world's landmass and holds some of the earth's most beautiful sights.[22] Given the current $9.5 billion in total annual tourism revenue for Africa, we can safely assume a potential of at least twice that within a decade were the conditions right for more companies like Conscorp. Africa's chronic civil strife is the gravest problem here. But skittish elephants and snipers lying in wait by the water hole are not the right conditions either.

Some environmentalists actually prefer hunting tourism because it keeps other tourists away and can involve less disturbance to wild places. Better one trophy hunter in a jeep, they reason, than a bus full of people with cameras. This is not a very practical outlook. It bears an unfortunate resemblance to the elitism of trophy hunters themselves, who would divvy up all of Africa's natural lands into private trophy farms for the rich. And it overlooks the fact that people across the world are more likely to take an interest in Africa, in the welfare of its people and the fate of its wildlife, once they have actually been there.

The issue here is not whether the people of rural Africa are entitled to use the natural wonders of their own countries for economic advancement. Of course they are. The question is which economic incentive is of greater long-term value to Africa—the desire of one person, on one visit, to kill an elephant, or the desire of thousands of people over the years to come and appreciate that same elephant? And safari hunting is nothing if not a short-term enterprise. As one reporter puts it, describing the economic impact of a single elephant hunter: "While he spends more money than the tourist who shoots with a camera, he also becomes the last tourist to enjoy that elephant."[23]

Conservation of African land, made available only for benign tourism, could also be made a condition of the billions of dollars of debt relief America and the G-7 nations agreed to provide in July 2001. The U.S. has already made such an arrangement, the first of its kind, with the government of Belize, and plans similar pacts in South America to help preserve rain-forest lands. Working with the Nature Conservancy, our U.S. Treasury agreed recently to halve Belize's debt obligation in exchange for the protection of 23,000 acres of forestland inhabited by endangered wildlife. With another $5.5 million authorized by the Tropical Forest Conservation Act, America will assist a local private conservation group in the purchase of an additional 11,000 acres of forestland. If a few million dollars in debt relief will secure 23,000 acres of publicly owned habitat in one Central American nation, thereby helping that nation to thrive through eco-tourism, what will many billion dollars in debt relief secure on the African continent?

The Nature Conservancy itself, a private foundation based in Arlington, Virginia, is probably the most successful of all conservation programs, public or private, and all by itself disproves the notion that conservation requires an incentive to exploit and kill wildlife. Since the 1950s this foundation and its many local chapters have purchased some 80 million acres of land across the world, including 12 million acres in America. In Montana, for example, the

Nature Conservancy has acquired rangeland where grizzly bears are known to wander. They pay ranchers, in effect, for the development rights, and then leave the land as it is, while also paying the property taxes so as to contribute to the area's economy. America's state and local governments have lately taken a similar approach to preserving open spaces and guarding against suburban sprawl.

Government in this way can help to turn private, free-market incentives in favor of conservation. In Africa, such a strategy would have the further advantage of directing many millions of dollars straight to those who need it most, without it passing first, as in CAMPFIRE, through the hands of private outfitters, tribal chieftains, and government officials. America could fund such efforts through the African Elephant Conservation Act, reauthorized in 2002 by Congress and President George W. Bush for another five years, under which we still furnish up to $5 million annually to projects like Kenya's new fences.

That law, signed by President Ronald Reagan, was one of the great triumphs of the modern wildlife-protection movement. It came about after years of campaigning to "Save the Elephant" by both American, European, and African environmentalists and animal-welfare groups. But public attention understandably turned elsewhere and, well, as with many good laws we just haven't followed through. Make it forty or fifty million a year in public and private dollars for fencing, law enforcement, and the purchase of land rights through local nonprofit agencies—with strict accounting, and diminishing by not one dollar our humanitarian efforts elsewhere in Africa—and perhaps humankind really can save the elephants.

In a generation or two the nations of Africa may well become more politically stable, economically advanced, and involved in the affairs of the world. If forced by circumstances to build and farm over their savannas and forests, Africans may look back on this time with the same regret we in North America now feel in recalling the destruction of the sequoias in California and the killing of the buffaloes, grizzlies, wolves, and other creatures we are now trying to spare from extinction. Selling off elephants to ivory and trophy hunters is the kind of scheme that seems to make sense only in times of desperation. At the very least, public and private financial help from the industrialized nations could give the African people the luxury of real choices, buying both them and the elephants the time they need.

NOAH'S CHOICE

Attempts to resume legal ivory trading must likewise be firmly repelled, at future meetings of the Convention on International Trade in Endangered Species (CITES) and elsewhere. Illicit trade in ivory and other wildlife products is today a vast global enterprise, more lucrative even than trade in illegal firearms and second in scope only to trade in illegal narcotics. Only if nations known to cater to it—and not just rivals of America like China, but even allies like Taiwan—are held to account can this trade ever be controlled and endangered wildlife saved from extinction.

Given the injustices committed against human beings by the Chinese regime in particular, one can't be too hopeful that wildlife will ever count for much either. If hundreds of forced labor camps, the torture of political prisoners, the persecution of Christians and other religious people, the subjugation of Tibet, the theft of nuclear secrets, and thirteen ICBMs aimed at the continental United States cannot hinder trade deals that profit China's regime, chances are that the woes of bears and elephants won't do it either. But that is what it would take, the full economic weight of the industrialized nations. All evidence of trade in ivory or other illicit wildlife products by any nation, or by private dealers unpoliced by that nation, must meet with serious trade sanctions, and all offenders must be properly punished. Trade sanctions should not be used lightly in foreign policy, and we would not be doing so here. In dealing with the governments of Japan and China in particular, we simply have to make it clear that protecting wildlife is not some elaborate joke or a game, but actually an important public priority shared by many of their own people. These governments must know that we are prepared to see those policies through even at the risk of profits from trade and other commercial relations they depend upon far more than we do.

The alliance now pushing for renewed ivory hunting and trading first appeared at the 1997 meeting of CITES. Support for lifting the ivory ban, reported the *Sunday Times* of London, came "from strange affliations" including "the All-Japan Seamen's Union, Fur Information Council of America, National Institute of Fisheries, National Rifle Association, Safari Club International, Zimbabwe Association of Tour and Safari Operators and, most bizarrely, the Ringling Bros. and Barnum & Bailey Combined Shows."[24] Of course there is nothing at all strange about these affiliations. These groups represent the elephant's longtime persecutors—led by men like Eugene Lapointe, the sustainable-use advocate we met in Adelaide—who think it is their divine right to sit around international conferences and hotel suites parceling out elephants and whales and whatever other creature will turn a profit.

Their new pretext for legalized ivory hunting is the "overpopulation" of elephants, meaning the relatively stable elephant populations resulting from the very success of an ivory ban that these same people once told us would never succeed. Their new arguments cast the debate in terms of entrepreneurial freedom and property rights versus statism and regulation, perfectly tailored to win the support of conservatives in America and Europe. "There is a schism at the heart of the environment movement," declares the libertarian *New Scientist*. "On one side sit the preservationist and animal rights advocates with their parks, fences, bans and armed game wardens. On the other, sit the advocates of sustainable development who are determined on local control of wildlife."[25]

They don't like fences, our sustainable users, except when those fences surround hunting ranches. They don't like parks and bans and armed game wardens and other things like that. Of course they don't like those things. Those are the signs of *law*. Those are the signs of standards, and effective government, and criminal penalties, and other things we normally associate with civilization. A lawless, corrupt, and chaotic Africa has always suited the ivory and trophy trades much better.

Lending help from abroad, our strategy must be wildlife protection, money for law enforcement, and assistance by all available means in tracking, prosecuting, and punishing offenders in the manner of Kenya. Tens of thousands of ivory carvers and retailers still operate in Japan, Hong Kong, Taiwan, China, Thailand, Indonesia, Malaysia, and elsewhere, demanding more and more of the stuff, more and more slaughter for their all-important trinkets and curios, exactly as Christian churches for centuries helped to sustain the trade with their demand for ivory statuettes, crucifixes, and other adornments. Asia's population is rising fast, in number and affluence. So long as ivory is available, and the carvers can keep their skills and trade alive, demand for these luxury goods will only keep growing too—as witness the 1.8 tons of smuggled ivory found by Kenyan customs at Dubai airport in 1999, all of it bound for the Far East. The elephants can sustain only so much human vanity, avarice, and corruption. Without complete legal protection, swift and severe enforcement, and, as Kenya's newspaper advises, "ruthless" trade sanctions against offending nations, the slaughter will never end until the last elephant has taken the last brain shot for the last trophy or pair of tusks.

America, meanwhile, can set a better example in the treatment of elephants with a law like that proposed in 1999 by Representative Sam Farr, a Democrat of California, barring their use in traveling road shows and circuses. Circus elephants, sometimes the captured orphans of elephants hunted in Africa, spend about twenty-two hours a day in chains. They pass much of their lives on trains, shuttled from city to city in cramped travel cars. They're trained to do their tricks by the use of electric prods, denial of nourishment, and, as in a case documented in 1998, severe beatings even of calves.[26] Go to Black Beauty Ranch in Texas, a sanctuary for mistreated animals, and you will see a fifty-year-old elephant named Tara who for hours on end just stands there, rocking back and forth, as if still in the chain she wore while locked alone indoors for thirty-five years. Of course some trainers are very kind people who give their best care to the three hundred or so elephants employed in entertainment in America. But thriving companies like the Cirque du Soleil have demonstrated that circuses do not need animal acts at all. In India the high court of Delhi recently did away with the entire institution of training or using any wild animal for entertainment, and other nations may soon follow. America ought to do the same, especially in the case of the elephants as we try to protect them from cruelty abroad.

The remaining whales of the world are likewise a test of mankind's capacity for clemency, our ability to admit a wrong and work cooperatively to right it. Governments have a clear standard here in the form of a commitment that we, most of humanity, have already made through the International Whaling Commission to spare them from further grief. Whales, we must remind the government of Japan, are no country's private stock, or perpetual resource, or "brave fish" or *isana* or national symbol in some anti-imperialistic struggle, or any other such nonsense. They are just whales. They belong to no one. And they have suffered enough. We, a majority of mankind, care about them and have decided therefore to grant them a reprieve.

The U.S. Congress has long been resolutely opposed to commercial whaling anywhere in the world. This cause has lately been led by Senator John Kerry from Massachusetts, whose harbors were once the launching point for our own whaling industry and are today given over entirely to whale-watching. In Japan, one hopes that the reformist prime minister elected in

2001, Junichiro Koizumi, will find similar possibilities for his nation. Calling the fleets home once and for all would require defying some powerful financial interests in his country, but the rewards in public support, across the world and among the Japanese people themselves, would be great and lasting. Otherwise, to make good on our commitment, we shall have to be as serious about protecting whales as Japan and Norway are about destroying them, saying to their IWC representatives, without further diplomatic parrying or time-wasting, "Gentlemen, agenda item 1: From now on, 'sanctuary' means sanctuary, and 'science' means science. These are not arbitrary standards and they are not just Western standards. They are the standards of law, reason, and humanity, and all nations seeking our goodwill are expected to observe them. Should your fleets kill one more whale—any whale, anywhere, under any pretext—then your goods, and those of your confederates, are no longer welcome in any market of any IWC nation, effective immediately."

Let Masayuki Komatsu, Odd Gunnar Skagestad, and their governments issue indignant statements, make threats, boycott the IWC, summon home a few diplomats from London and Washington, stage protests against this act of "cultural imperialism," etc. When it's all over both Japan and Norway will do just as they did in 1986 when their tedious little game of power politics was briefly turned against them. They will cease the slaughter at once, and start acting again like the fine and civilized countries they are.

All of this must be seen against the background of a great vanishing of wildlife that the people of Africa, India, Asia, or anywhere else will welcome no more than Americans or Europeans. Environmentalists today are justified in their sense of alarm, and also in their conviction that it involves all of us, in all nations, no matter what other hardships and challenges we face. They are right in affirming common interests here, common obligations shared by all of humanity.

Nature, as the libertarian writer Virginia Postrel assures us, has no fixed boundary for human action, "no stopping point, no final shape."[27] Whatever that might mean for us, it certainly doesn't apply to the animals. For them, nature definitely does have a stopping point, and some are very near it. We have come to a sad pass where mankind's advance may spell, for many species, their final and permanent undoing.

Africa, its own human population expected to double within two generations, in this way is no different from most other parts of the world where the sheer pace of human development may already have numbered the days of many wild animals. Throughout thirteen nations of Asia just forty thousand or so elephants remain, scattered in loosely guarded preserves and patches of forest. In Thailand, the hundreds of elephants once used in logging have been abandoned and can today be found begging and scrounging for food on the outskirts of Bangkok—despite the valiant efforts of a Thai man named Roger Lohanan to secure them a refuge. A snapshot of their global situation can be seen today in Sri Lanka, where 60 percent of the island's jungle has been razed for farmland over the last few generations. The elephant population during that time fell from about 12,000 to fewer than 2,000. These survivors today inhabit shrinking forestland between the ranchers who shoot and poison them on one side and the rebel guerrillas who kill and terrorize them with guns and grenades on the other. Where can they go? What hope is left for them?

In central Africa's Republic of Congo at this moment, what's left of the gorilla population is beset by other armies in that nation's horrific civil war, and by villagers suddenly in possession of automatic weapons. Young men now hunt the apes for meat to sell, or for reasons described by a Congolese researcher named Inogwabini Bila-Issia, who has given us this perfect summary of the creed of sport hunters the world over: "They think that if you kill a gorilla you become very strong and your power as a man grows."[28] Bonobos are caught up in the same human strife, as well as being the chief victims of illegal exotic pet traders who shoot the mothers and steal the infants. A similar fate carries off thousands of monkeys and lemurs every year in other parts of the world. Across Africa, East Asia, and South America, meanwhile, other primate habitat is being razed or fatally fragmented by logging, mining, and other development.

Tigers? Even the estimated five thousand still in the wild aren't safe. They, too, live in small and broken remnants of forest in India, East Asia, and the Russian Far East. As their numbers decline, their market value as "aphrodisiacs" only rises, so that a single dead tiger is today worth a fortune,[29] and it would take a Secret Service detail to protect each one of them. African poachers today are killing off lions, too, and storing up the powdered bones and other parts in expectation of the day when all the tigers are gone and these become the next-best alternative for the Asian market.

To know where it is all leading would take a gift of prophecy not given to me, but it doesn't look good. We hear estimates that by the close of this new century some two-thirds of the species now with us will be gone. That figure may not be as apocalyptic as it sounds, counting as it does particular sub-species of creatures the ornithologists and mammalogists will mourn, but whose extinction was perhaps predestined and irreversible anyway. The cerulean warbler and the northern flying squirrel, for example, will pass from the scene. But, of course, birds and squirrels will live on. And I am not among those who view it as mankind's sacred duty to keep every existing species of life-form on the ecological respirator at all costs, a project well beyond our reach even if we tried.

Among the departed, however, will also be many more familiar faces, fellow creatures we shall truly miss. One hundred years from now, Paul Theroux matter-of-factly predicts, the waters will be emptied of marine mammals, no more whales or even dolphins. "There will be fewer of them and fewer other wild animals—no gorillas, no rhinos, no elephants, no tigers. But given the birth rate, the world's population is projected to be 9.5 billion."[30] It may come to pass that such creatures as the tiger, rhino, wolf, grizzly, panda, giraffe, and even many primate species will exist only in refuges and game parks here and there. Our genetic scientists are already preparing for this, storing up the DNA of each species against the day when they are gone at least as wild, free-roaming animals, a project one author in his book title has aptly described as *Noah's Choice*.

There is the temptation, as Douglas Chadwick writes in his beautiful book *The Fate of the Elephant*, to become "a professional mourner," composing useless and self-serving elegies to dying species. Worse, however, is the temptation to become a professional apologist, ignoring these mass extinctions or pretending they are somehow normal and natural developments—as if automatic rifles, drift nets, factory ships, or industrial pollutants could in any sense be natural forces in the life of the world.

The elephants above all—in their sheer size, their harmlessness when left alone, and the moral claims that come with our new understanding of them—stand as a test of our willingness to share the earth and leave room for the animals. Without inviolable barriers protecting them, without the humility and human generosity such barriers reflect, we may ourselves be nearing what Mr. Chadwick calls "the end of natural history." "From there on," he cautions, "we would be pinwheeling into an unfathomable era with no reference point other than the shifting impulses and convictions of humankind."[31]

This sounds like one of those panicky overstatements environmentalists are often faulted for. Actually it is a sober analysis. I had a glimpse of this strange new world myself in April 2001 on a visit to the widely heralded Project Noah's Ark at Texas A&M University. It's one of those genome banks storing away the DNA of endangered species, though at the moment the genome bank consists of sixteen steel canisters stored like old milk bottles in a back room of the university's Department of Veterinary Physiology and Pharmacology.

Within these tanks, explained my host, a distinguished veterinarian named Duane Kraemer, are the sperm, embryos, and skin cells of animals headed for the brink. Humankind does not yet have the technology to clone all of them, Dr. Kraemer tells me, though in theory it can be accomplished one day through the use of surrogate mothers. They'll use equine mothers for zebras, domestic sheep for bighorn sheep, bears for pandas as Chinese scientists are trying now, and so on. The important thing, he and his colleagues believe, is that posterity will have the DNA, like negatives from which they can one day print out pictures of their own. Now, while gene pools are still sufficiently diverse, we must go forth and collect samples of the type. For all of these creatures, Dr. Kraemer tells me, "There's not going to be any more diversity than there is now, so we might as well get them in storage."

Each tank, a kind of ultimate wildlife refuge, is filled with fifteen gallons of liquid nitrogen, cooled to $-360°$ Celsius. A cloud of vapor rose as Dr. Kraemer removed the lid to show me the green plastic straws stored inside. The straws have a label bearing the name of a species expected to die off: Chimp. Lowland Gorilla. Baboon. Giraffe. Bison. Bighorn Sheep. Oryx. Kudu. Tortoise. Other straws contain the makings of Lion, Leopard, Rhinoceros, Cape Buffalo. The sperm, embryo, and skin cells of an African elephant will be arriving soon, and with that the scientists here will have themselves the genetic "Big Five."

It concentrates the mind, a scene like that, and perhaps a little sentimentality is in order. Quite literally, they are going away, many of the animals, never to return as we once knew them. A century from now, all that may be left are zoo specimens and genetic blueprints to tell of their world and its vanished glories. How will Asia's lovely little ivory carvings look then? What will people in that lionless, elephantless world make of *The Official Record Book of Trophy Animals*? Let us be sure as well to preserve for posterity a few copies of *With Deadly Intent* and other such evidence, so that they can know the full story, and see for themselves how these intelligent, beautiful, and peaceable creatures were treated even in the very last decades of their existence on earth. Posterity, no doubt, will be impressed by our foresight and our works of science, and glad to have at least the genetic codes of the elephant. But how much better to have the elephant.

SINNING BRAVELY

On that very same campus, as Dr. Kraemer and his team at Project Noah's Ark labor to save the world's wildlife, another scientist is at work trying to minimize muscle growth in pigs, and thereby reduce their need for nourishment. "Bringing home the bacon," reports the university's promotional magazine, *Advance,* in an item entitled "This Little Pig Went to Market,"

> may soon be a little cheaper as Texas A&M University researchers attempt to genetically engineer pigs that produce more meat than the average pig, while requiring the same amount of feed. "The end result is that you get more meat for less grain," said Dr. Jorge Piedrahita of Texas A&M's college of Veterinary Medicine. "Obviously, this benefits the consumer because you are going to be able to produce more meat for less cost." The key to producing a meatier pig is to suppress the animal's production of the protein that regulates muscle growth—Growth and Differentiation Factor Eight (GDF8). Piedrahita said he is still developing the technology to create a GDF8-deficient pig. He estimates it will be two years before the public sees one.[32]

Who is going to save those poor beasts from Dr. Piedrahita and his conscience-deficient profession? Perhaps Project Noah's Ark should preserve their genes, too. Posterity might be curious to know what a pig was like—a simple, genuine, real-life *pig*—before modern scientists took upon themselves the godlike power to remake these and other creatures.

They do a lot of cloning at Texas A&M as well, a must these days for every animal science department. The university has been trying, for example, to create the perfect cow, with the girth of a beef cow and the udder of a Holstein. So far, no perfect cow, but only hundreds of spontaneous abortions, miscarriages, disfigured fetuses, and horribly malformed live births to show for their efforts—pictures of these creatures, scarcely recognizable as calves, lining the walls inside the department. I saw one of the rare successes in a little pasture outside the lab, a cloned calf of eight or nine months old grazing beside his surrogate mother. They made him, Dr. Kraemer explained, by scraping some skin cells off a carcass at a nearby abattoir and inserting those cells into the egg of a surrogate—the new cells, as he puts it, in effect "asking the egg to start all over again." The creature's biological father, in other words, was dead before he was conceived. His life literally began in a slaughterhouse.

"The public," Dr. Kraemer tells me, "has a tendency to overemphasize what evil things can be done by cloning, and give less consideration to the good." Dr. Kraemer, who earned his degree forty-six years ago not in animal science but in "animal husbandry," is himself a fine and well-intentioned scientist, but I think he is mistaken. In the case of cloning and genetically altering farm animals, there is no good to find, and the evils have hardly begun to reveal themselves. Inspired by hubris alone, and by the profit motive divorced from scientific scruple, such projects are in fact destroying the perfect cow, pig, sheep, chicken, turkey, and other animals as formed over the ages by evolution and the hand of their Creator.

In the laboratories of our animal science departments, the right of researchers to do anything to any agricultural animal goes unquestioned. Since April 15, 1987, the day when America's highest court gave permission for the patenting of animal life, just about every conceivable experiment has been carried out on every kind of farm animal. And now comes "pharming," raising animals to be human blood and organ donors. A biotechnology company in 1999 was granted a patent for what are called "chimeras" (pronounced ki-*mera*), sheep, pigs, primates, and other animals in which human cells will be implanted to grow human tissues and organs for transplantation.[33] The spirit of the enterprise was best expressed by Dr. Frederick Coulston, a toxicologist in New Mexico who presides over the world's largest captive population of chimpanzees, some four hundred in all: "I wouldn't even rule out in the far future having a colony of chimps providing blood for human transfusion. How many chimps do you want? You can raise them like you do cattle. In ten years you could have half a million."[34] (Dr. Coulston, apparently, was unmoved by viewing *Planet of the Apes*.)

A bold step in this direction occurred in late 2000 when the first genetically engineered primate came into the world, a rhesus monkey fashioned at the Oregon Health Sciences University by inserting the fluorescent gene of a jellyfish into the egg of a surrogate mother, and playfully named "ANDi" for DNA spelled backward. Elsewhere, frogs and other creatures are engineered without heads, mice with human ears growing from their backs, fish and plants with both human and animal genes, and who knows what other such projects yet to be reported. The ethicists earnestly wonder in what sinister experiments this awful power might one day be turned back on man himself—as if inserting human genes and organs into animals has not already crossed the fatal line. Whether anyone should have legal sanction to use such power at all, re-creating creatures to suit the designs and pleasures of man, hardly comes up for discussion.

In much of medical science and biotechnology, the pattern is the same as in modern livestock agriculture: our New Economy is making our own lives easier, cheaper, more pleasant and risk-free, while adding to the burdens borne by the animals who serve us, and little by little removing the need for human care and self-restraint. In the same way, too, most any criticism or call for reform is heard as an accusation and assault on science itself. Such efforts, says Frederick King, formerly the director of the Yerkes Regional Primate Research Center at Atlanta's Emory University, "represent a bizarre elevation of a touchy-feely, do-gooder's view of the world that ignores all understanding of ethical complexity. Such agitation is anti-intellectual, anti-science, and anti-human."[35] Actually, it is the other way around: Many of our scientific researchers have lost all appreciation for ethical complexity, while animal rights advocates, almost alone today, are left to remind us that there are other values beyond scientific progress of which we must at least be mindful. Nor must one be a scientist to know that something has gone seriously wrong, any more than one must be a farmer to know that veal crates are cruel or a skilled marksman to know that canned hunting is cowardly.

We pay incredibly little attention to our laboratories, perhaps because they raise the most complex and painful questions of all. "Animal rights groups," warns conservative columnist Cal Thomas, "want us to believe that all research involving any animal is cruel and unnecessary."[36] Content to scold the "radicals," as he describes them, and leave it at that, Mr. Thomas himself makes no attempt to delve further into the moral problems of animal research, or to note the alternatives to animal subjects of which he seems entirely unaware. He might have told us, too, which animal experiments are unnecessary so that we might know what the standard is for necessity. With blind faith, he just takes it as a given that if Science says research and testing are necessary, then it is not for us to question, and those who presume to do so must be radicals, misfits, and, sure enough, as he notes in the same column, "vegetarians," too.

Let me give Mr. Thomas an example of the use of laboratory animals that just might fall into the category of cruel and unnecessary, one among thousands that could be pulled from our journals of science and listings of government grant applications. And it's one he will understand, because it involves our federal government doing something costly, irrational, and reckless, a project being conducted at this very moment by America's Environmental Protection Agency (EPA). For decades our government has required the testing of industrial chemicals and other commercial products by injecting or force-feeding them into animals. We now know that there are other ways of establishing toxicity—testing on cell cultures, for instance, or basic molecular analysis, or computer and mathematical modeling. The Congress itself, in a 2000 law encouraging such alternatives, has determined that these methods should be developed and employed, and established an interagency committee to meet that objective.

Yet right now, under the direction of the EPA, a project is under way called the Chemical Right-to-Know Program, calling for new testing of 2,863 industrial chemicals produced or imported in the U.S. in annual amounts of more than one million pounds—known as High Production Volume chemicals, or HPV. Leaving aside the question of whether, given the current universe of 87,000 man-made chemicals in air, soil, and water, any more are needed at all, the agency assures us that for these particular chemicals "data needs remain unmet."[37] Yet perusing the government's own list we find one chemical after another that has not only been tested already, but tested many times over in America and elsewhere. These include known carcinogens like butadiene and benzene, and known toxins like turpentine, lead, and cyclonite rat poison. They have to test rat poison again, to see if it's poisonous; and gasoline, to make sure we shouldn't drink it; and propane and butane, to have a look just once more at what happens when they're inhaled in large quantities.

Worse, the European Commission has meanwhile mandated its own new tests for many of the very same chemicals. Worse still, all of this was the doing of environmentalists, demanding these new tests as a means of setting back the chemical companies. And so, in labs that neither they nor we will ever see, more millions of animals must endure internal bleeding, convulsions, seizures, paralysis, and slow death. A stroll through the laboratories of Pfizer or any other pharmaceutical company, of Emory or many other universities, of the EPA, Consumer Safety Commission, Food and Drug Administration, Department of Defense, and a dozen other federal agencies would reveal similar scenes. It is easy to say, *a priori,* "It has to be done—it's the price we pay for human safety and progress." But we ourselves neither pay that price nor even look at the cost. And until you see the cost, you cannot rationally weigh what is essential and what is not.

Poisoned, scalded, electrocuted, dismembered, emotionally deprived, or genetically reconfigured by the tens of millions every year in laboratories across the world, these are truly our least of creatures. They are accorded not even the certain intimacy we share with animals we eat, no blessing or saying of grace, but simply yanked from their cages, worked over, and discarded. Even your dog or cat, should the creature wander off without a tag and fall into the hands of a dealer supplying laboratories, enters a different moral world where cruelty statutes no longer apply.

The March of Dimes, for instance—unlike the Easter Seals and other charities that have moved beyond animal research—each year devotes millions of dollars to experiments of the kind carried out by a team of scientists at the Massachusetts Institute of Technology. The team published its findings in a report bearing the impressive title, "The Morphology of Retinogeniculate X- and Y-Cell Axonal Arbors in Dark-Reared Cats."[38] What does this mean? For the researchers, it meant taking a group of kittens, sewing shut the eyelids of half of them while rearing the others for one year in total darkness, and then killing them all to examine the effects of this experience on their brains. The March of Dimes has also funded experiments administering massive doses of cocaine, nicotine, and alcohol to animals, as if mankind has not himself provided sufficient data on the harmful effects of these substances.[39] Still another experiment involved implanting wires into the uteri of pregnant monkeys who spend fifty to sixty days at a time in a cage, in a straitjacket, tethered to a wall.[40]

The philosopher Paul Ramsey spoke of "sinning bravely" in the name of science—that is, knowingly disregarding moral restraints in order to achieve great advances in medicine. Yet so much of what passes today under the name of scientific research is commercially driven, having nothing whatever to do with human health and welfare, or is motivated by our thousands of research journals and the professional imperative to be published regardless of the worth or redundancy of one's experiments. And appeals to medical progress cannot be used as diffuse accusations when the use of animals is called into question for unworthy ends or where—through these very advances in medical knowledge and technology—animal research simply cannot be medically or morally justified. Who gave anyone the right to create a fish-primate hybrid? Since when does science, much less charity, require the torment of blinded kittens? When, we must ask, is "sinning bravely" just sinning?

We have a presumptive respect for the scientific professions, so often deserved but here and there in need of serious examination. The researchers today busily cloning animals and suddenly so restless, some of them, to begin cloning human beings, are little more than businessmen with medical or veterinary degrees—science's counterpart to the grasping personal-injury lawyer. "Meat scientists" vie to create the featherless chicken or the fear-free pig, the genetic engineers of ProLinia to clone a new "lean generation" for Smithfield, Dr. Deer to design the must-have "rack" for sportsmen, and we're all supposed to stand back in awe as if it were Dr. Jenner or Dr. Salk at work. The most trivial of experiments are today carried out with a holy air, the mere mention of "science" has become an incantation to hush the least doubt or moral reservation, in a spirit G. K. Chesterton saw among the scientists of his own time:

> Now, it seems to me that this is the weak point in the ordinary vivi-sectionist argument, "Suppose your wife were dying." Vivisection is not done by a man whose wife is dying. If it were it might be lifted to the level of the moment, as would be lying or stealing bread, or any other ugly action. But this ugly action is done in cold blood, at leisure, by men who are not sure that it will be of any use to any-body—men of whom the most that can be said is that they may con-ceivably save the life of somebody else's wife in some remote future. That is too cold and distant to rob the act of its immediate horror. That is like training a child to tell lies for the sake of some great dilemma that may never come to him. You are doing a cruel thing, but not with enough passion to make it a kindly one.[41]

In our own day, we might with justice call most animal testing and experimentation "meat science," for the researchers seem to have lost all regard for their subjects as anything more than that. The same attitude that can view wildlife only as commodities, and livestock only as production units, can see in primates, dogs, cats, rabbits, mice, and rats that dream only research tools there to serve their every inquiry, however idle, repetitive, or purely commercial. It is as if every animal, in our day, is falling a level in the order of creation—wildlife to the level of farm animals to be raised for slaughter, farm animals to the level of plants to be "grown," and laboratory animals to the level of microbes or cell cultures one need not even treat as living, feeling beings at all. Today, observes our finest writer on the problems of cruelty, Joy Williams in *Harper's* magazine,

> in labs with names such as Genpharm International, Inc., Genzyme Corporation, and Pharmaceutical Proteins . . . we distance ourselves more and more from animals as we use them in increasingly bizarre ways. Animals are being subsumed in a weird unnaturalness. Indeed, technology, which is forever pressing to remove animals from nature, to muddy and morph the remaining integrity of the animal kingdom, has rendered the word "natural" obsolete. A side benefit of the new and developing technologies is that soon we won't have to feel guilty about the suffering and denigration of the animals because we will have made them up. . . . Any sentience they possess will have been invented by man or eliminated altogether. An animal will have no more real "life" than a lightbulb.[42]

Conservatives in particular should be wary of such enterprises. My wise friend Paul Greenberg, in a column against the harvesting of human embryos for stem-cell applications, observes that "there is something unthinking, something almost frivolous, in the unexamined assumption that Science should do something because it can be done." How, he wonders, have so many scientists come to view life as "more a product than a creation"?[43] The answer is they had a lot of practice, and unlimited material to work with.

"Be alert to the beginnings of evil," writes Catholic theologian Michael Novak in his case against the use of embryonic human stem cells in research. "It never comes under the appearance of evil, but always under the appearance of the beautiful, the promising, the idealistic, the pleasant. . . . The fatal mistake often comes as a result of unexamined moral sentiments: affects and feelings that serve as moral guideposts without submitting to interrogation by reason."[44] In twenty-five years of reading conservative commentary, and many of Dr. Novak's own profound writings, I cannot recall any serious questioning of the use of animals in any type of experiment for any purpose. Even now as we debate the legalized cloning of human beings, and dread the likelihood that some scientists are at this moment trying it anyway, the "moral guidepost" of cloning and patenting animal life is passed over as a perfectly licit and noncontroversial enterprise, with no thought whatever that just maybe *that* was the fatal mistake.

One would think that in scientific research, if anywhere, there is wisdom in the traditionalist's own argument that cruelty to animals is wrong, not because of moral equivalence, but because of a moral continuity that leads inexorably to cruelty to humanity. When scientists abandon moral scruple in the treatment of animals, growing numb to the disfigurement and suffering before their eyes, regarding life itself as a mere instrument to be used and discarded, used and discarded, the habit is hard to shake. "You can dispose of these animals," says one biomedical researcher in arguing for a prohibition against human cloning, "but tell me, what can you do with abnormal humans? You can probably keep them alive with medical intervention, and they'll probably be miserable, and even the ones who look normal probably won't be. It's an outrageous criminal enterprise to even attempt."[45] I certainly agree with him that human cloning is a bad business. But this spirit he warns against, this callousness among his fellow scientists, their utilitarian view of life and the arrogance to even contemplate human cloning—where did that attitude come from? What encouraged it? Where did the ethical barriers first begin to fall?

Reform, in America, would be most effective in a revision of our current Animal Welfare Act (AWA). That law actually began as the Laboratory Animal Welfare Act, signed by President Lyndon Johnson in 1966 to answer public concern about the abuse of animals in scientific research and commercial product testing, in particular cats and dogs being sold by shelters and private dealers to laboratories. Through various amendments over the years it has became our governing body of law regulating the use of warm-blooded animals for most scientific and commercial purposes. In its current form, however, the AWA is a collection of hollow injunctions, broad loopholes, and light penalties when there are any at all. The Department of Agriculture, for example, is statutorily empowered to define the very word "animal":

> The term "animal" means any live or dead dog, cat, monkey (nonhuman primate mammal), guinea pig, hamster, rabbit, or such other warm-blooded animal, as the Secretary may determine is being used, or is intended for use, for research, testing, experimentation, or exhibition purposes or as a pet; but such term excludes horses not used for research purposes or other farm animals, such as, but not limited to livestock or poultry, used or intended as food or fiber, or livestock or poultry used or intended for improving animal nutrition, breeding, management or production efficiency. . . . [46]

"Sinning bravely" has here required lying bravely in this completely arbitrary removal of all legal protection for the small animals used by the millions in laboratories across America. Certain animals are animals, under the AWA, only when such determination is made by the secretary of agriculture. Otherwise they are, well, something else. And the entire AWA is left for our Department of Agriculture to interpret and enforce. The same officials and financial interests who view our factory farms as acceptable forms of animal husbandry are entrusted with deciding what constitutes acceptable treatment of laboratory animals.

Let us at least call things what they are, no matter what else the law permits or prohibits. It may be inconvenient and at times even costly to treat our littlest laboratory animals like animals, living creatures to be spared from needless stress and suffering and death. But the law does not deal in convenient fictions. The law must speak in the language of truth, and science always the language of reality, even when they are humble realities like Mouse and Rat and Bird. They are animals too, with or without the blessing of the secretary of agriculture.

No warm-blooded animal, according to the AWA, may be experimented upon repeatedly, or without anesthesia, or kept conscious while enduring paralytic tests, except in cases of "scientific necessity."[47] This is left in practice for the experimenters themselves to decide, never mind that they would not be proposing the test in the first place if they thought it unnecessary. An amended AWA must lay down some basic definitions to be observed by all, according to the objective standards of science and the clear requirements of public health.

Research facilities, under the AWA, are to establish a committee of three or more members to assess the treatment of animals, only one member of which must have no affiliation with a given facility.[48] In practice this means that any lab can do basically anything it wants. With just seventy or so animal-welfare inspectors employed by the Agriculture Department to keep an eye on the thousands of laboratories public and private, there's little to fear from public oversight. While Congress funds the National Institutes of Health (NIH) at about $20 billion a year, it appropriates all of $15 million a year for enforcement of the AWA. This is not the sign of a good-faith effort. In both the law and in public expenditures, there must be a correspondence between the commitment to research and the commitment to assuring that experimentation is conducted humanely, or that it is even necessary.

Scientifically sound alternatives to animal experimentation are becoming available, the Congress declared in a 1990 revision of the AWA: "Methods of testing that do not use animals are being and continue to be developed which are faster, less expensive, and more accurate than traditional animal experiments for some purposes and further opportunities exist for the development of these methods of testing."[49] These alternative methods—only better now, more than a decade later—include computer modeling to predict toxic hazards, noninvasive scanning technologies like magnetic resonance imaging (MRI) to observe internal disorders, molecular analysis and gene studies like the Human Genome Project to understand the effects of chemicals, and *in vitro* techniques that are often more sensitive and accurate than the traditional tests on rats and mice.

Many scientists and researchers themselves now advocate these methods, most prominently the Physicians Committee for Responsible Medicine. There is no longer any rational basis, they tell us, for the Draize test, dripping chemicals and personal-care products into the eyes of immobilized rabbits. We can now test for eye irritancy by use of human tissue systems mimicking characteristics of the eye. We can stop pouring commercial and industrial chemicals into animals. Acute toxicity is determined more accurately by *in vitro* methods using human cell cultures obtained from cadavers. Damage to DNA can be studied in bacteria, as in the Ames assay developed thirty years ago, adopted slowly by the EPA and yet now internationally accepted. Further experiments on animals for diseases of the heart, nicotine addiction, obesity, and many other disorders are unwarranted because we have already identified their primary causes by studying human populations.

We hear in "alternative" research or testing a synonym for second-rate, as if forgoing animal experiments must always compromise scientific standards. But often, according to physicians and researchers who advocate reform, it is just the opposite. Science has its cautionary stories of animal research as well as successes. The tobacco industry for decades traded on research showing, correctly, that their product did not have cancerous effects on the dogs and primates they had used in forced-inhalation experiments. Defenders of unrestricted animal research commonly cite such cures as penicillin and the polio vaccine as evidence for their case. Yet it turns out the discoverer of penicillin, Alexander Fleming, observed as early as 1929 that penicillin killed bacteria in a petri dish but not in bacteria-infected rabbits, falsely concluding the drug would not cure humans until a decade later when he used it, in desperation, to save a dying patient.[50]

Experiments infecting monkeys with the polio virus in the early 1920s and 1930s, by the account of Albert Sabin himself, also proved futile because primates and humans contracted the disease differently. It was only in human autopsy research that Dr. Sabin established the correct pathology. "Paralytic polio," he said, "could be dealt with only by preventing the irreversible destruction of the large number of motor nerve cells, and the work of prevention was long delayed by the erroneous conception of the nature of the human disease based on misleading experimental models of the disease in monkeys."[51] The polio vaccine itself, likewise, is now grown in human cell culture because the original vaccine, drawn from primate tissue, had harmful and sometimes lethal side effects. Insulin for diabetics once came from pigs and cows, but has now been replaced by human insulin—not to spare the pigs and cows, but simply because it works better.

Here one does need scientific training to judge all of these alternatives, and I myself can only parrot what many experts say. I proceed, too, on the assumption that few doctors, scientists, and researchers are capable of intentional cruelty, and certainly not the ones I have met. But this much is certain. Every profession and institution knows the pull of simple inertia, refusing to shake off old assumptions and part with settled ways. Often, too, the old ways no matter how needless or unreasonable take on a dynamic of their own, with financial interests dependent upon their preservation. There is no reason to believe medical science is any different. And there is every reason to believe that government can act that way. Where alternatives to animal testing and experimentation can indeed serve the purpose, then in each and every case changes must no longer be delayed. Every scientist today experimenting upon animals, or using animals for any marketed product, has an obligation to use these alternatives. That is a professional obligation, an ethical obligation, and it must be made a legal obligation.

As it is, under the AWA and related laws and regulations, scientists are bound only to "consider" alternatives to painful or lethal experiments, with no objective criteria laid out to establish the necessity of such experiments.[52] We would all like laws telling us what we must "consider" doing, but it doesn't work that way. The law makes a clear finding of fact and on that basis determines the standard of acceptable practice. Here, the fact is real and conscious pain by animal subjects. And here the standard—not the option—must be utter necessity and nothing less. The same question confronting us in the factory farms must be asked in our labs as well: When you start with a necessary evil, and then over time the necessity passes away, what's left?

One good reason to believe that testing and research alternatives are equal or better is that some governments, private industries, and laboratories around the world are already adopting them. The United Kingdom no longer requires, while still permitting, the lethal-dosage testing of commercial and industrial chemicals. The U.S. Congress passed a law in 2000 making it the stated goal of our government to find and adopt alternatives. America's NIH banned the use of mice in monoclonal antibody production, sparing, just like that, a million of these creatures every year from induced tumors and painful procedures extracting the fluid. Our Food and Drug Administration recently approved a plant-based estrogen, Cenestin, as an alternative to Premarin, a drug derived at the cost of great suffering from the urine of pregnant mares. Some two-thirds of America's medical universities, including Harvard and Johns Hopkins, no longer use live-animal experiments for instruction. The government of Israel banned animal experimentation and dissection in high schools, as some local school districts have done in the United States. The government of Slovakia outlawed the use of animals in cosmetic testing. And in New Zealand, despite philosopher Roger Scruton's warnings that granting explicit rights to primates would blur the species barrier, parliament went ahead and outlawed the use of great apes in research, teaching, or testing, except for benevolent purposes, and many nations may soon do the same. So far, none of Mr. Scruton's fears have been realized. The chimps show no signs of abusing their new rights or aspiring to be anything other than chimps. In sparing these intelligent creatures from needless torture, however, perhaps New Zealand's leaders felt a little more human.

The British pharmaceutical company Pharmagene elected in 1996 to end all animal testing, using instead leftover tissue from human operations to test their products.[53] Colgate-Palmolive in 2000 announced a voluntary moratorium on the use of animals in testing personal-care products, following Gillette and many other companies that once insisted animal tests were essential. Mary Kay Cosmetics recently pledged to end animal testing entirely, the largest of more than six hundred corporations to do so. Many other companies now proudly inform us on their labels, "Not Tested on Animals," while other corporations persist in the practice only under pressure from insurance companies as a safeguard against possible lawsuits—under liability laws also in need of revising to acknowledge the existence of alternative tests.

With changes such as these a standard is taking shape. We now know that for each of these enterprises animal testing was either unnecessary in the first place or has now been rendered unnecessary by alternative methods. In each case it took years of prodding from animal rights and welfare groups. In each case, too, there were undoubtedly scientists, laboratory suppliers, and other interested parties warning that any changes in research policy were outrageous, intolerable, unscientific, antihuman, and we must never cave in to PETA and all those animal rights extremists! But now, by the admission of these very companies and laboratories, animal research and testing actually *isn't* necessary. They really can do without it. So who was right all along? Who were the real extremists? And where else are we told animal experimentation, testing, or research is essential when, in fact, it isn't?

The AWA was last amended in 1990, just before we began to grasp the possibilities of biotechnology and its implications for animal welfare. Here, above all, a change in policy is in order. In every law and every regulation governing the use of animals in any laboratory, we must recognize that while the profit incentive is often essential to scientific pursuit, it is not sufficient all by itself. Economics must serve the rightful aims of science, and not the other way around, or else cruelty abounds and science itself is corrupted.

When we observe no limits in the trivial things, we lack credibility in defending the serious. It is one thing to argue that animals might still be needed in research for cures and treatments for AIDS or Alzheimer's or cancer—though in these cases, too, there are many abuses and the need must be proven, not taken on faith. It is another proposition entirely to claim they are needed in research to take the fear out of pigs, and the fumes out of their refuse, and other such madnesses. In all things the law must make this distinction, giving sanction and financial support only to projects aimed at important social, moral, and medical goods, while prohibiting frivolous, unnatural, and inhumane ventures.

That will not always be easy to define, but we can start with the livestock industry and its many new projects of the "stress-gene" variety. We can prohibit xenotransplantation, the placing of organs or DNA from one species into another. And, advancing a cause admirably led by Peter Singer and put into action by the Seattle-based Great Ape Legal Project, we can place an absolute prohibition on any further experimentation or genetic tampering with primates, if for no other reason than that they are genetically almost identical to ourselves and entitled as such to have their integrity respected.

The U.S. House of Representatives voted in 2001 to restrict all types of human cloning and many uses of human embryos, imposing, if the bill becomes law, fines of a million dollars and prison terms of ten years for offenders. That was an assertion of government's authority and responsibility to guard against the excesses of medical pursuit, not just in the eight hundred or so federally funded labs but in all laboratories public and private. The dignity of animal life need not be as profound or fundamental for Congress to assert exactly the same authority and responsibility in preventing cruel and monstrous abuses of animals for commercial gain.

Biotechnology carries complicated moral questions we are all still trying to understand, with enormous possibilities for good and boundless possibilities for mischief and evildoing. "Complicated," however, must not bar us from rational inquiry, from asking what are the limits in our use of animals, and are there any at all? Addressing European farmers in the fall of 2000, Pope John Paul II had some advice about biotechnology in agriculture that all societies would do well to heed: "Resist the temptations of productivity and profit that work to the detriment of respect for nature. When you forget this principle, becoming tyrants and not custodians of the Earth, sooner or later the Earth rebels."[54]

They Know Pain

Through the same legal fiction obtaining in our laboratories, farm animals in the U.S. are also denied the status of simply "animals" as covered by the Animal Welfare Act and many state anticruelty statutes. Denying the *ought,* as natural-rights philosophers have observed, always ends in denying the *is.* We know by the commonest standards of human kindness that the methods of intensive farming are no way to treat animals. So, in the statutes, they had to be reclassified into something less than animals.

Meat is today a luxury item, large-scale livestock farming an irrational and inefficient enterprise, and the suffering it inflicts morally untenable. It will not do to say, with writer David Plotz in the online magazine *Slate,* that "Calves are adorable, but veal is delicious. . . . God gave man dominion over the beasts of the earth [and] if an animal has economic utility, we should farm it."[55] That is not a serious argument. It is an excuse for evading serious argument, for doing what he pleases and getting what he wants, the whims of man in their familiar guise of the will of God. Nor is it any answer to say, with Judge Richard Posner, that the law should be neutral and let corporate farmers answer to "consumer preference" alone. When the law sets billions of creatures apart from the basic standards elsewhere governing the treatment of animals, when the law denies in effect that they are animals at all, that is not neutrality. That is falsehood, and a license for cruelty.

In a familiar political problem, institutional cruelty has an active and influential constituency while kindness has only broad, ineffectual sentiment on its side. Reporters in both the print and broadcast media can help here, not by advocacy but by hard investigative journalism. With outstanding exceptions like the *Washington Post,* the *New York Times,* and several of our television and news magazines, in America our media often shy away from cruelty stories, if only because the subject can be so painful and depressing for reporter and reader or viewer alike. A little more reportorial courage is needed, of the kind displayed by *Times* writer Charlie LeDuff and the *Post's* Joby Warrick in their exposés of the pork and cattle industries and their brutality to man and animal alike. There are many other problems to be explored, many injustices and abuses of power to be uncovered, and it is trite but true that the greatest enemy of the cruel is an informed electorate.

Even today, however, candidates and political leaders might be surprised at the support they would find for reform in livestock agriculture—as we are seeing already in state ballot initiatives like that in Florida where, in November 2002, citizens may have a chance to vote on whether to ban mass-confinement hog farms. State and federal officeholders are like the rest of us, troubled by factory farming when they pause to reflect on it, but pressed on every side by many other concerns and responsibilities. I have no doubt that President George W. Bush—a man, in my experience, of extremely kind and generous instincts, and back in Austin even a rescuer of stray animals— would be appalled by the conditions of a typical American factory farm or packing plant. I know of a Republican senator, of evangelical Christian faith, who toured a hog factory in his home state and was aghast at the scene. The venerable Senator Robert Byrd of West Virginia, addressing the United States Senate in 2001, spoke these powerful words:

> Our inhumane treatment of livestock is becoming widespread and more and more barbaric. Six-hundred-pound hogs—they were "pigs" once—raised in two-foot-wide metal cages called gestation crates, in which the poor beasts are unable to turn around or lie down in natural positions, and this is the way they live for months at a time.
>
> On profit-driven factory farms, veal calves are confined to dark wooden crates so small that they are prevented from lying down or scratching themselves. These creatures feel; they know pain. They suffer pain just as we humans suffer pain. Egg-laying hens are confined to battery cages. Unable to spread their wings, they are reduced to nothing more than an egg-laying machine. . . .
>
> God gave man dominion over the Earth. We are only the stewards of this planet. We are only the stewards of His planet. Let us not fail in our Divine mission. Let us strive to be good stewards and not defile God's creatures or ourselves by tolerating unnecessary, abhorrent, and repulsive cruelty.[56]

This from a man who himself has raised and slaughtered pigs, who understands the hard demands of farm life, but also its hard obligations. And when a rural, eight-term senator speaks this way, we know that change is in the air.

In the decades to come perhaps the free market, more than any changes in law, will prove the undoing of the factory farms. In America some seventeen million people are already vegetarians, most of them teenagers and college students whose influence in the world has yet to be felt. In Europe the foot-and-mouth nightmare of 2001 converted millions, and you can today find soy-based meat substitutes even in French supermarkets where just a few years ago they were unheard of or disdained. McDonald's, Wendy's, and Burger King have lately shown a sensitivity to public concerns over cruelty in farming, and the latter now even offers veggie-burgers. While some higher-end establishments like La Colline in Washington, D.C., and the White House mess continue serving veal, many others, like New York's Tavern on the Green and Russian Tea Room, no longer do so. This is all to the good and shows the power of conscience to influence market forces—as millions now, and one day soon tens of millions of consumers choose of their own accord not to buy meats or dairy products from corporate farms.

In the meantime, that does not relieve government of its own duties to protect animals from the scandalous abuses Senator Byrd describes. In 1958 Congress asserted the obligation of every farmer and rancher to minimize the suffering of livestock with the Humane Method of Slaughter Act, an unprecedented reform championed by the great Senator Hubert Humphrey. The rise of industrial farming in the years since, and the routine disregard of that very humane-slaughter law, today call for a Humane Farming Act. The law has recognized our duty to give farm animals a merciful death. The law must now recognize our duty to give them a merciful life.

A Humane Farming Act—and perhaps Senator Byrd is just the man to author it—would explicitly recognize animals as sentient beings and not as mere commodities or merchandise. It would uphold elementary standards of husbandry by codifying the obligation of every farmer, rancher, and slaughterer to raise and kill every animal according to clear and unbending standards of human decency. Under explicit cruelty statutes, and not just industrial regulations, it would carry specific provisions as to the space afforded to each animal, following no more complicated a principle than that pigs and cows should be able to walk and turn around, fowl to move about and spread their wings, and all creatures on our farms to know the feel of soil and grass and the warmth of the sun. No more mass confinement. No more veal crates. No more gestation crates. No more battery cages. If we cannot do something humanely, without degrading both the animals and ourselves, then we should not do it at all.

A Humane Farming Act should also:

- Define acceptable feed ingredients according to the nutritional needs of animals, barring practices such as the deprivation of iron and fiber for veal calves, starvation-induced molting of egg-laying hens, or the force-feeding of ducks and geese to produce foie gras.
- Prohibit waste products from being used in animal feed, including manure and the ground-up remains of dead livestock.
- Define other proper living conditions appropriate to each species, such as mud and straw for pigs, bedding and pasture for cattle, perches and nest boxes for chickens and other fowl.
- Prohibit tail docking, ear notching, de-horning, de-beaking, hot-iron branding, unanesthetized castration, and other such mutilations designed to conform animals to the unnatural conditions of factory farming.
- Bar the use of hormones, drugs, cloning, and genetic technologies today necessitated by intensive methods and applied to maximize production at the expense of animal welfare.
- Restrict the pace and method of slaughter to spare the hundreds of pigs or other creatures who each day, under current conditions, leave this world being butchered and boiled alive.
- Hold veterinarians to the sworn oath of their profession, reminding them that they are caregivers for animals and not technicians for production units.
- Allocate all necessary funds for government oversight at production faciltes and for more inspectors at packing plants.
- Instruct all federal agencies that purchase farm products, like the USDA in the billions of dollars it spends on our school lunch program or the Department of Defense in the billions it spends feeding our 800,000 troops, to contract exclusively with farms practicing humane methods.
- Define the minimal qualifications of agricultural employees, and establish the right of all farm and slaughterhouse workers to form unions as a protection against their own exploitation.
- Require of all agricultural trade partners comparable standards of animal husbandry, with the right of inspection to assure compliance.

- Impose upon violators of agricultural cruelty laws heavy fines and criminal penalties.

A lot of barring, defining, and imposing there, but that is what laws do. As in other legal prohibitions against human wrongdoing, we would be protecting important moral and social goods, framing standards we can live by and defend—while extending, in the phrase of the day, a little "compassionate conservatism" even to the lowly animals. In practice, a Humane Farming Act would make family farming the model, as is slowly happening already in the laws of the European Union—barring over the next decade, for example, battery cages for poultry and veal crates for calves. In America it will take a law of this sweep to save the small farms now just barely surviving, and to end the moral race to the bottom—cutting costs by any and all means—that corporate farmers will always win.

Yes, it will also mean paying higher prices for meat and dairy products, and therefore, for many consumers, consuming less of both. But the meat you buy, when you eat it, will not have the taste of a bitter life. Even the most voracious meat eaters might discover that moderation has its own enjoyments. And that is an option available to every consumer, in every country, right now.

THE GOOD SHEPHERDS

These past couple of years I have had the privilege of meeting many people involved in today's animal-protection movement. As so often happens when one finally gets off the mark and tries to be useful, I discovered all around me men and women who for years had been working against cruelty while I was busy worrying about it. Take any harsh practice I have described in this book and there is somewhere a group or solitary person devoted to its abolition, often against great odds and in the face of derision. Cruelties unique to our age, in scope and intensity, have inspired their opposite in a movement of compassion just as far-reaching and just as unique.

There are always, in every area of life, human beings who can be counted on to act recklessly and selfishly, leaving behind them a trail of trouble and hurt. And then there are always those others who come along to repair the damage. Where there is human suffering, they're the ones who found and run orphanages, homes for beaten wives or unwed mothers in need of help. They found ministries for prisoners and their children, like Charles Colson and his thousands of volunteers. They open training centers for the jobless, refuges for the addicted or destitute, hospitals for the sick, and hospices for the dying in every corner of the world. We honor these people, even when we ourselves may lack their heroic idealism, because we know that theirs is a calling and bears witness to the best in humanity.

You will find all across the world the same kind of people helping neglected or mistreated animals. Theirs, too, is a special calling, not a distraction from the work of human love and charity but very much a part of it. They take in the orphans and give shelter to the stray, neglected, beaten, or malnourished. They follow in the path of sport hunters, trappers, whalers to help the "wounded or lost." They collect the discards from our farms, zoos, and laboratories. They follow debates in Congress and all the legislatures of the world, on the scene to make a case for forgotten animals. And though their efforts are often belittled, if all of a sudden they stopped their work, we would notice. Without such people we would see everywhere the hurt, harshness, and abandonment they rise to answer every day. Surely the most tired of all criticisms is that they must care more about animals than about people, as if for every dolphin spared from the net a homeless person must go unfed, or as if the people who *make* such accusations are themselves to be found devoting every spare moment to the uplift of their fellow man.

Such criticism is usually intended to divert attention from the critics' own doings or their own complaisance in the face of suffering. Least of all should these idealistic people have to endure the caviling of hunters, whalers, factory farmers, and other such groups with whom they contend for public support—people who only take, who bring only more violence into the world, and measure out their own lives in things appropriated, crushed, and killed. And that really is the heart of the matter—the measure of a life, how we choose to fill our own short time here on earth. In a strange way the more insistent human beings are of our singularity among creatures, the more aggressive and vocal in denigrating animals, the more indistinct and small we ourselves come to seem. And somehow the more humble we are in outlook, the more attentive and appreciative of the life around us, the more acutely we will feel our uniqueness and the special calling it brings.

Every act of kindness or empathy is always a sort of defiance against the way of the world. In any leniency we extend to animals in particular there is always a hint of wild impracticality and rebellion against irresistible forces.

Reuters a few years ago ran a charming story about a fellow named Chandrasir Abbrew, whose whole mission in life consists in protecting the eggs of sea turtles on the western coast of Sri Lanka. The locals for as long as anyone could remember were in the habit of killing the hatchlings to make food or combs from the shells. But knowing sea turtles are going extinct, this man had a different idea. With a grant from the Swedish camera maker Victor Hasselblad, he formed the Kosgoda Turtle Hatchery, and now pays people to bring him the eggs for safekeeping. When they're hatched, he carries them down to the water. He has a very simple philosophy. "I like animals. I am a happy man. People come to see my turtles every day."[57] At last report Mr. Abbrew was still out there every day collecting a new batch of baby turtles, and each evening depositing them in the ocean, sending these creatures forth on "the incredible first journey on a life that can last as long as 200 years."[58]

It was said of Saint Francis that "he walked the earth like the Pardon of God," rescuing lambs from their fate in the marketplace, rabbits from the hunters' snare, pleading the case of mistreated creatures before popes and kings. Mr. Abbrew seems to be a man of similar spirit, walking the beaches of Sri Lanka like the Pardon of God. Yet in a world where these very creatures are routinely drowned by the hundreds in drift nets, hooked for the meat, or left for dead by watercraft, what is the point? Why be different? Why not just take the eggs and shells for combs like it's always been done—or, elsewhere, the blubber from whales and meat from dolphins and fur from seals? Perhaps he does it because the rewards are better and more lasting than eggs and combs. This man can know that in a brutal and vengeful world, he, at least, has taken the side of life. And long after he is gone the seas will be filled with silent witnesses to his kindness.

Across America, many thousands of rescued animals can likewise bear witness, just by being alive, to the goodness of a man named David Duffield and his wife Cheryl. Having lost a dog they loved very much, the Duffields were concerned about the many millions of other dogs and cats euthanized for lack of space in our animal shelters. Most shelters are run by caring people who every day must deal with hard realities and small budgets. Typical is the Austin Town Lake Animal Shelter I used to pass every morning on the way to work, an afterthought in the city government even while some forty creatures are disposed of each and every evening.

So the Duffields, having made their fortune with a successful software company, did something about this national problem with a start-up grant of

$200 million. And for decades to come, just because of two people and all the volunteers who help them, fewer strays will wander the streets, and millions of others will be spared, bringing companionship to people who adopt them instead of dying unwanted in the back room of a shelter. Mr. Duffield might have invested that money into more enterprises, perhaps turning a fortune into an empire. He might have raised up some giant museum or university annex to forever bear his name—"forever" meaning the forty or fifty years until it would be torn down and forgotten. Instead he shared his good fortune with millions of mangy animals scrounging around our streets. That is by my lights a very wise use of wealth, and a gracious mark to leave in the world. Animal charities are, if nothing else, a high-yield investment in the happiness within our power to grant and the suffering within our power to relieve.

I think with special admiration of my friends Gene and Lorri Bauston, who have taken up the most forlorn cause of all at a place called the Farm Sanctuary, rescuing animals the world has declared worthless alive. They have two sanctuaries, actually. One is in upstate New York and the other in northern California, with a third to open near Los Angeles. Gene, Lorri, and their staff and volunteers go to factory farms, stockyards, and slaughterhouses and take away "downed" animals, the injured or sick who would just be tossed aside anyway, and who can be seen at the sanctuary doing nothing, sweet and glorious nothing, to serve the ends of man.[59] Pigs root and roll around. Chickens and turkeys scratch in the dirt and mill about the grounds. Lambs and calves forage, play, or lie together on straw in scenes recalling the lines from Oliver Goldsmith: "No flocks that range the valley free / To slaughter we condemn / Taught by the power that pities us / We learn to pity them."[60]

Scoffers will be further amused to know how the Baustons earned their start-up money back in the early 1980s—by selling veggie hotdogs at Grateful Dead concerts. Even now they rely on contributions of money and land, and they've had some fund-raising help from actresses Kim Basinger, Lindsay Wagner, and Mary Tyler Moore among others. The animals at the sanctuary do pay at least a little of their own way by income from the guest houses, filled most every weekend by visitors in flight from city and suburb, but that's about it, and a modern agricultural scientist would be appalled by what he saw—all of these production units going to waste, all of this money being squandered on land and straw and nourishment and veterinary care. While Gene himself does have a master's degree in agricultural economics, he and Lorri do not think that way, and neither, once, did farmers think that way.

I admire both their practicality in detail and impracticality in aspiration—the exact opposite of factory farming, which pursues grimly realistic goals with insane disregard for detail. The Baustons accept the daily toil of caring for hundreds of animals, and also the nearness of death that comes with that charge. They are impractical only in their belief that by hard work and merciful love they might each day plant one seed that yields a hundred-fold, and show the world a different way. Hopeless or even foolish as this cause may seem, I think that if I were an executive at Smithfield, these are the kind of people I would fear the most, the meek ones. You may have doubts about their cause, but you can thank heaven for their kind of impracticality, for no great wrong has ever been overcome without it.

My favorite animal-rescue story comes courtesy of the Elephant Sanctuary near the town of Hohenwald, Tennessee—800 acres of green pastures, forests, and spring-fed ponds. They have four elephants living there and recently took in a thirty-eight-year-old female named Sissy, who in November 1998 had been videotaped undergoing a beating at the hands of keepers in the El Paso Zoo—this on top of many prior miseries that began with separation from her mother at age two. When the tape was aired, the El Paso City Council voted to turn her over to the Elephant Sanctuary, responding to the public outrage that always follows when such things are revealed. The sanctuary then posted daily reports on Sissy's journey to her new home and the elaborate production required to get her there. The founders of the sanctuary, Carol Buckley and Scott Blais, supervised the expedition. Two truck drivers named Alton Henson and Michael Knowles volunteered their services. A giant trailer was donated by a family named Pankow in Nashville. The Comfort Inn donated rooms for the drivers and caretakers. The caravan had to stop every few hours just to make sure Sissy was doing okay back there, and on the sanctuary's special "Road Trip!" page we got little updates like

Jan. 24, 11:30 A.M.—Stopped to offer Sissy a drink of water. She ate a few carrots and appeared calm. . . . Jan. 25, 2:30 P.M.—Just outside Little Rock, Scott spied some river cane growing alongside the road. He stopped and cut some for Sissy. She made a quick treat out of the entire pile. . . . Jan. 25, 5:30 P.M.—Sissy drank gallons of water, finished off the last of her river cane and is bedded down for the night. All is well. . . .

And so on until the joyous arrival, whereupon the enormous daily costs of feeding, housing, and veterinary care will begin. All told, an awful lot of work and money and trouble just to make one elephant happy.

Yet one has the impression that everyone involved is pretty happy about it themselves. That cheerful voice we hear from her helpers—so far away from the whispering of men lying in wait for the kill—is the voice of humanity, of men and women pouring their passion and labor and ingenuity into the relief of innocent affliction. Seeing her at peace, they can truly know that "all is well," at least there, and share with one another the gladness of bringing comfort and care where once there was only hurt and fear. None of us knows just where Sissy or any creature may stand in the grand scheme, what her ultimate value may be or what her ultimate destiny. We know only that the world today is a slightly gentler place because she was given a home, and river cane for the journey, and that's something.

Such people are a reminder that animal welfare is not just a moral problem to be solved in statutes, but a moral opportunity to fill our own lives with acts of compassion. Kindness to animals is not our most important duty as human beings, nor is it our least important. How we treat our fellow creatures is only one more way in which each one of us, every day, writes our own epitaph—bearing into the world a message of light and life or just more darkness and death, adding to the world's joy or to its despair.

"In a drop of rain can be seen the colors of the sun," observed the historian Lewis Namier. So in every act of kindness we hold in our own hands the mercy of our Maker, whose purposes are in life and not death, whose love does not stop at us but surrounds us, bestowing dignity and beauty and hope on every creature that lives and suffers and perishes. Perhaps that is part of the animals' role among us, to awaken humility, to turn our minds back to the mystery of things, and open our hearts to that most impractical of hopes in which all creation speaks as one. For them as for us, if there is any hope at all then it is the same hope, and the same love, and the same God who "shall wipe away all tears from their eyes; and there shall be no more death, neither sorrow, nor crying, neither shall there be any more pain: for the former things are passed away."[61]

NOTES

Introduction

1. Andrew Sullivan, "The Killing Fields," *New Republic*, April 9–16, 2001.
2. Verlyn Klinkenborg, "Pox Populi," *New York Times*, May 6, 2001.
3. *Congressional Record*, July 9, 2001.
4. Matthew Parris, "Eating Our Fellow Mammals May Not Be Wrong, but It Is Not Very Nice," *Spectator*, April 21, 2001.

Chapter One: The Things That Are

1. Desmond Morris, *The Naked Ape* (New York: Dell, 1973), p. 194.
2. Ibid., pp. 194–195.
3. Ibid., p. 195.
4. Stephen Budiansky, *If a Lion Could Talk: Animal Intelligence and the Evolution of Consciousness* (New York: Free Press, 1998), pp. 193–194.
5. C. S. Lewis, *The Problem of Pain: How Human Suffering Raises Almost Intolerable Intellectual Problems* (New York: Macmillan, paperback, 1962), p. 133.
6. Independent Newspapers, "Elephants Keep Watch over Two Caught in Trap," July 1997.
7. Jack London, *The Call of the Wild, White Fang, and Other Stories* (New York and London: Penguin, 1993), p. 257.
8. Peter Waldman, "Taste of Death: Desperate Indonesians Devour Country's Treasure Trove of Endangered Species," *Sacramento Bee* (reprinted from the *Wall Street Journal*), November 29, 1998.
9. Viktor E. Frankl, "Man Alive," *International Journal of Logotherapy and Existential Analysis*, Vol. 6, No. 1 (1998), p. 81.
10. Peter Singer, *Animal Liberation*, rev. ed. (New York: Avon, 1990), p. 187.
11. Saint Basil, included in *A Select Library of the Nicene and Post-Nicene Fathers of the Christian Church* (NPNF), edited by P. Schaff and Henry Wace (Edinburg: T. Clark, 1897), 2nd Series, Vol. 8.
12. Cited in Andrew Linzey, *Animal Theology* (Urbana and Chicago: University of Illinois Press, 1995), p. 56.
13. Quoted by Paul Waldau in *Encyclopedia of Animal Rights and Animal Welfare*, ed. Marc Bekoff (Westport: Greenwood Press, 1998), p. 291.
14. Will Durant, *Our Oriental Heritage* (New York: Simon & Schuster, 1954), p. 451.
15. Plutarch, "On the Eating of Meat," *Moralia*, 994E.

16. Saint Thomas More, *Utopia,* ed. Edward Surtz, S.J. (New Haven: Yale University Press, 1964), p. 78.

17. Ibid., p. 98.

18. Ibid., p. 144.

19. Quoted by Andrew Linzey and Bernard Unti in *Encyclopedia of Animal Rights and Animal Welfare,* p. 334.

20. John Wesley, Sermon Sixty, "The General Deliverance," ed. Sarah Anderson (Nampa, Indiana: Wesley Center for Applied Theology at Northwestern Nazarene University, 1999).

21. John Henry Newman, *Parochial and Plain Sermons* (London, 1868).

22. Lord Shaftesbury in letter of April 30, 1881, quoted by Andrew Linzey in *Encyclopedia of Animal Rights and Animal Welfare,* p. 314.

23. *Catechism of the Catholic Church,* Sec. 2415–2418 (Mahwah, New Jersey: Paulist Press, 1994), pp. 580–581.

24. Ibid.

25. "Cruelty to Animals," *The Catholic Encyclopedia,* Vol. IV (New York: Robert Appleton Company, 1908).

26. Malcolm Muggeridge, *Jesus Rediscovered* (Glasgow: Collins, 1969), p. 63.

27. Peter Singer, *Practical Ethics,* rev. ed. (New York: Cambridge University Press, 1993), pp. 169–171.

28. Ibid.

29. Naomi Schaefer, "Professor Pleasure—or Professor Death?" *Wall Street Journal,* September 25, 1998.

30. Don Feder, "Professor Death Takes Ideas to Princeton," *Boston Herald,* October 28, 1998.

31. *Centesimus Annus: Encyclical Letter of Pope John Paul II on the 100th Anniversary of Rerum Novarum,* reprinted in *Catholic International,* Vol. 2, No. 3.

32. "Message of Reconciliation," delivered by Pope John Paul II at Assisi on March 12, 1982, and reported in *L'Osservatore Romano,* March 29, 1982.

33. United Press International, "Pope Urges Respect for Animals," October 3, 1982. Associated Press the same day translated the words a little differently: "It is necessary and urgent that, following the example of the poor man, one decide to abandon inconsiderate forms of domination, capture, and custody with respect to all creatures."

34. C. S. Lewis, *Problem of Pain,* p. 130 (italics in original).

35. Theodore Roosevelt, *African Game Trails: An Account of the African Wanderings of an American Hunter-Naturalist* (New York: St. Martin's, 1988), p. 240.

36. Genesis 9:11–16 (AV).

37. Hosea 2:18–19.

38. Isaiah 11:6–9.

39. Leland Swenson, president, the National Farmers Union, in testimony before the House Judiciary Committee, September 12, 2000.

40. Fern Shen, "Md. Hog Farm Causing Quite a Stink," *Washington Post,* May 23, 1999, and Ronald L. Plain, "Trends in U.S. Swine Industry," U.S. Meat Export Federation Conference, September 24, 1997.

41. For all of these figures I have relied on Bernard E. Rollin's excellent study, *Farm Animal Welfare: Social, Bioethical, and Research Issues* (Ames: Iowa State University Press, 1995), pp. 8–9.

42. Dennis Avery, "Big Hog Farms Help the Environment," *Des Moines Register,* December 7, 1997.

43. Ibid.

44. Dennis Avery, Commencement Address, University of California, Berkeley, College of Natural Resources, May 21, 2000.

45. David Plotz, "Gimme Some Skin: Why Shouldn't Dalmatians Be Made into Coats?"

46. Avery, Commencement Address.

47. Ibid.

48. Paul Hacket, Reuters News Service, "Porkers on the Lam Brought to Heel but Spared Dinner Table," *Washington Times,* January 17, 1998.

49. Michael A. Fuoco, "Pig, Soooie! Weeping Porker Rescues Mistress," *Washington Times,* October 15, 1998.

50. E. B. White, *Charlotte's Web* (New York: HarperTrophy, 1980 edition), pp. 163–164.

51. Stephen Crane, "In the Depths of a Coal Mine," reprinted in *The Pennsylvania Sampler: A Biography of the Keystone State and Its People* (Harrisburg: Stackpole, 1970), p. 103.

52. Ministry of Agriculture, "Banning Fur Farming: Government Introduces Bill," November 23, 1999.

53. *Hansard Debates, House of Commons,* March 5, 1999.

54. *Hansard,* May 14, 1999.

55. *Hansard,* March 5, 1999.

56. Mark Daniels, "Distaste Should Not Dictate Law," *Western Morning News,* November 24, 1999.

57. *Hansard,* March 5, 1999.

58. "At Parliament Opening, Queen Unveils Bill to Ban Fur Farming," *Los Angeles Times,* November 18, 1999.

59. Farming of Animals for Fur (Prohibition) Bill, House of Commons, presented March 16, 1998.

60. Genesis 1:28.

61. Genesis 1:29

62. Linzey, *Animal Theology,* p. 114.

63. Ecclesiastes 3:19–20.

Chapter Two: The Shooting Field

1. All brochures and catalogs quoted are from the 1999 season and are available upon request.

2. Rudy Rosen, "SCI's Economic Impact Huge," *Safari Times,* July 1999.

3. James A. Swan, *In Defense of Hunting* (San Francisco: Harper, 1995), p. 35.

4. Ibid., p. 15.

5. Ibid., p. 144.

6. Tom DeWeese, "The Pagan Roots of Environmentalism," *Ready . . . Aim . . . Fire,* Christian Sportsmen's Fellowship International, Spring/Summer Edition, 1998.

7. George N. Wallace, "If Elk Could Scream," *A Hunter's Heart: Honest Essays on Blood Sport,* edited by David Peterson (New York: Henry Holt, 1996), p. 96.

8. Ibid., p. 99.

9. James C. Kroll, "Building Your Own 'Deer Factory': How a Deer Manager Did the 'Impossible,'" *North American Whitetail,* January 1999 (Vol. 18, No. 1).

10. Linda Goldston, "Animals Once Admired at Country's Major Zoos Are Sold or Given Away to Dealers," *San Jose Mercury News,* February 11, 1999.

11. David Beresford, "Bogus Hunters under Fire," *Guardian* (London), August 15, 1997.

12. Quoted in Chris Osher, "Open Market for Exotic Animals: Hunting Ranch Boom Sparks Push for Laws," *Arkansas Democrat-Gazette,* November 1, 1999.

13. Chris Osher, "Open Market for Exotic Animals."

14. Skip Donau, "Enemy's Response a Measure of Success," *Safari Times,* April 1999.

15. Safari Club International 1999 Budget with Forecasts through 2001.

16. Associated Press, "Bison Hunt an Experience of a Lifetime," February 24, 1989.

17. Ron Marlenee, "Legislative Wins & Missions Accomplished in 1998."

18. Douglas H. Chadwick, *The Fate of the Elephant* (San Francisco: Sierra Club Books, 1992), p. 454.

19. Dan Causey, "Tragedy in Zimbabwe, Big Mozambique Jumbo," *Hunting Report,* September 1998 (Vol. 18, No. 1).

20. "Hunters Red-Faced over Elephant Shoot," *Johannesburg Mail and Guardian,* April 23, 1999.

21. Skip Donau, "Enemy's Response a Measure of Success."

22. Declaration by the Mozambique Ministry of Agriculture and Fisheries National Directorate for Forestry and Wildlife, issued January 11, 1999, by National Director Arlito Cuco.

23. "Hunting Activities in Blocks A and B of the Buffer Zones: Preliminary Report on Available Information," issued by Niassa Game Reserve, October 19, 1998.

24. Maureen Dowd, "Under Fire as Hunter, Bush Finds Defender," *New York Times,* December 29, 1988.

25. "An Ideal Shooting Day," *The Shooting Field* (Holland & Holland), Vol. 8, pp. 18–19.

26. "Diary of a Management Safari," *The Shooting Field,* Vol. 8, pp. 20–21.

27. Ibid.

28. Jim Carmichel, "Hunting African Elephants," *Outdoor Life,* February 1999.

29. Ibid.

30. Ibid.

31. Ibid.

32. Ibid.

33. Ibid. (italics added).

34. Ibid.

35. Ibid.

36. Cited in Matt Cartmill, *A View to a Death in the Morning: Hunting and Nature Through History* (Cambridge, Massachusetts: Harvard University Press, 1993), p. 228.

37. Letter from Internal Revenue Service, Exempt Organizations Ruling Branch, to Safari Club International, August 29, 1985.

38. "SCI Trophy Mount Donation Program Guidelines," Safari Club International.

39. R. Bruce Duncan, "Secrets of Tax Deductible Hunting," Chicago Appraisers Association.

40. Ibid.

41. Ibid.

42. I leave it to the authorities to determine whether a corporate restructuring by Safari Club meets the demands of the law. Under a plan recommended by SCI's accountant, Arthur Andersen, a new "Safari Club Foundation" enjoys the 501(c)(3) status of a charitable and educational enterprise, while Safari Club itself becomes a 501(c)(4) nonprofit corporation. In the latter category, a group may engage in political lobbying but is still presumed to be performing some sort of social-welfare purpose. The basic question here is whether anything Safari Club does may in any sense be considered a charitable activity.

43. Theodore Roosevelt, *African Game Trails: An Account of the African Wanderings of an American Hunter-Naturalist* (New York: St. Martin's, 1988), p. 317.

44. Ibid., p. 486.

45. Ibid., p. 486.

46. Ibid., p. 299.

47. Theodore Roosevelt, *Hunting Trips of a Ranchman & The Wilderness Hunter* (Modern Library, 1998), pp. 759–760.

48. Roosevelt, *African Game Trails*, p. 489.

Chapter Three: Matters of Consequence

1. Julius Ames was an American abolitionist and among the first Americans to write about cruelty to animals. For this quotation in Ames's *The Spirit of Humanity* (1835) I am indebted to the excellent scholarship of Bernard Unti, "The Quality of Mercy: Organized Animal Protection in the United States 1866–1930," Bernard Unti (Ph.D. diss., American University 2002), chapter 1.

2. Ray Sasser, "Bonus-Tag Proposal Means More Bucks for the Rich," *Dallas Morning News,* March 11, 1999.

3. Genesis 1:20–26.

4. Genesis 2:19.

5. Genesis 7:15.

6. Psalms 145:9.

7. Exodus Rabbah 2:2.

8. Numbers 22:28.

9. Proverbs 12:10.

10. Psalms 145:16.

11. Psalms 104:10–18.

12. Luke 6:36.

13. Luke 12:6–7.

14. Matthew 12:11–12.

15. Mark 1:13.

16. Isaiah 53:7.

17. Hosea 6:6.

18. Matthew 12:7.

19. Mark 11:11.

20. John 10:13–16.

21. Mark 16:15.

22. Revelation 6:2.

23. Daryl G. Treat, "Bible Allows Eating of Meat," *Omaha World-Herald*, May 11, 1999.

24. José Ortega y Gasset, trans. Howard B. Wescott, *Meditations on Hunting* (Bozemen: Wilderness Adventures Press, 1995), p. 106.

25. Ibid., p. 130.

26. Ibid., p. 132 (italics in original).

27. Ibid., p. 128.

28. Ibid., p. 129 (italics in original).

29. Cited in Cartmill, *A View to a Death in the Morning*, p. 234.

30. Ibid., p. 238.

31. Swan, *In Defense of Hunting*, p. 127: "Each of us has an identity, as well as instinctual cravings that move us to action. If we do not heed the inner energies of our soul, frustration, anger, rage, and illness may result. . . . If we try to deny our instinctual drives, eventually we will cause harm to ourselves or others, for our foundation of identity is not there."

32. Quoted in Gary Cartwright, "Shooting Blanks," *Texas Monthly*, December 1996.

33. Eric Lipton, "Move against Flock of Geese for the Birds, Neighbors Say: Resident Has Great Falls Fowl Snatched, Slaughtered," *Washington Post*, July 16, 1997.

34. David Petersen, "Bears on Your Own," *Outdoor Life*, October 1996.

35. "The Most Effective Deer Call Ever Created," *Journal of the Texas Trophy Hunters*, November–December 2000, p. 203.

36. Study conducted by the Erie Insurance Company and reported by David J. Cantor, "White-Tailed Deer: The Phantom Menace," *Animals' Agenda*, September/October 1999.

37. Associated Press, "Three Deer Wander in Traffic Near White House," *Washington Times*, April 12, 1997.

38. Dave Samuel, "Start Your Own Suburban Deerhunt," *Bowhunter*, April/May 1997.

39. Peter Finn, "Hunters Bag Ten Deer at Hunt in Fairfax: First Event Is Underwhelming during a 'Nice Day in the Woods,'" *Washington Post*, January 27, 1998.

40. Peter Pae, "Sharpshooters Kill 107 Deer in 6 Nights," *The Washington Post*, February 17, 1998.

41. George N. Wallace, "If Elk Could Scream," *A Hunter's Heart: Honest Essays on Blood Sport* (New York: Henry Holt, 1996), p. 101.

42. Jeffrey Hart, "Exposing the Dark Side of the Zoo Business," *Washington Times*, October 10, 1999.

43. Quoted by William F. Buckley, Jr., "The Brits (Some Brits) Protest," *National Review*, April 6, 1998.

44. William Booth, "The Sound and Furry on Rodeo Drive: Beverly Hills to Vote on Listing Killing Methods on Fur Labels," *Washington Post,* February 4, 1999.

45. Walter Williams, "Fur Tyranny That Begins with a Label," *Washington Times,* February 11, 1999.

46. Ibid.

47. Digby Anderson, "Eat, Drink, Be Merry—and Revolt: Consumers Are Defying the Government's Warnings about Beef," *Daily Telegraph,* December 12, 1997.

48. Digby Anderson, "Why Get By without Our Rabbit Pie? How Pet Sentimentality is Interfering with the Ways of Man and Nature," *Daily Mail,* November 11, 1994.

49. Digby Anderson, "Cook the Rabbit's Goose," *Daily Telegraph,* July 2, 1994.

50. Ibid.

51. Ibid.

52. Anderson, "Cooking Children: Some Recipes: Start by Teaching Them How to Kill Things," *Ottawa Citizen,* August 8, 1997.

53. Anderson, "Why Get By without Our Rabbit Pie?"

54. Ibid.

55. Anderson, "Passionate Tastes: The History of Vegetarianism," *Guardian,* April 20, 1993.

56. Roger Scruton, *On Hunting* (London: Yellow Jersey Press, 1998), p. 79.

57. Ibid., pp. 130–131.

58. Ibid., p. 80.

59. Richard Wagner, from letters reprinted in "Human Beasts of Prey and Fellow Suffering," *Ethical Vegetarianism: From Pythagoras to Peter Singer,* eds. Kerry S. Walters and Lisa Portmess (State University of New York Press, 1999), pp. 89, 93.

60. Roger Scruton, *Animal Rights and Wrongs* (Metro Books, 2000), p. 136.

61. Scruton, *On Hunting,* p. 76.

62. Ibid., p. 122.

63. Ibid., p. 76.

64. Ibid.

65. Ibid.

66. Ibid., pp. 74–75.

67. Scruton, *Animal Rights and Wrongs,* p. xi.

68. Ibid., p. 127.

69. Roger Scruton, "Bibles and Broomsticks: The Rise of Neo-Paganism," *National Review,* September 27, 1999.

70. Roger Scruton, "Eat Animals! It's for Their Own Good: There Is No Better Way of Protecting the Habitat of Species Than by Systematically Hunting It," *Los Angeles Times,* July 25, 1991.

71. Ibid.

72. Phil McCombs, "The Deer Hunter: Tim Forster Loves Animals. So When His Arrow Flies, He Hopes His Aim Is True," *Washington Post,* December 4, 1997.

73. Ted Nugent, "Hunters Should Show Daily Pride," *Detroit News,* November 20, 1998.

74. Ted Nugent, "Hunting Is a Rock-and-Roll Adventure of Fun," *Detroit News,* April 25, 1999.

75. "Ban on Spring Bear Hunt Draws Fire from Rocker," *Ottawa Citizen*, January 21, 1999.

76. Cited in Wallace, *A Hunter's Heart*, p. 87.

77. Scruton, *On Hunting*, p. 7.

78. Roger Scruton, "Be Here Now with Reference to Oasis and Heidegger," *Daily Telegraph*, October 10, 1998.

79. Ibid.

80. Ibid.

81. Roger Scruton, "Dressed to Kill," *Sunday Telegraph*, October 15, 1989.

82. Scruton, *Animal Rights and Wrongs*, p. 161.

83. Scruton, "Be Here Now."

84. Scruton, *On Hunting*, p. 82.

85. Susan Bell, "New Foie Gras Rule Sticks in French Throat," *Times* (London), June 23, 1999.

86. William Aron, "Save the Whalers," *Wall Street Journal*, August 8, 1997.

87. Keith McDermott, "How to Save Africa's Wildlife," Letters to the Editor, *Wall Street Journal*, July 19, 1997.

88. Ike C. Sugg, "Elephantine Propaganda," *Weekly Standard*, June 9, 1997.

89. "Road to Survival: Forget Trade Bans, Just Make Wild Animals Pay Their Own Way," *New Scientist*, April 29, 2000.

90. Ibid.

91. Douglas H. Chadwick, *The Fate of the Elephant* (San Francisco: Sierra Club Books, 1992), p. 343.

92. Jeremy Watson, "Giants Born without Their Tusks," *Scotland on Sunday*, June 17, 2001.

93. Tom Bethell, *The Noblest Triumph: Property and Prosperity Through the Ages* (New York: St. Martin's, 1998), p. 286.

94. Antoine de Saint-Exupéry, *The Little Prince* (Harcourt Brace Jovanovich, 1982), pp. 45–46.

95. Friedrich Nietzsche, *Beyond Good and Evil: Prelude to A Philosophy of the Future*, trans. Walter Kaufman (New York: Vintage, 1966), sec. 259, p. 203.

96. "Practicing Conservation through Commerce," Web site of the Exotic Wildlife Association.

97. Tom Seery, Associated Press, "Small Hog Farmer Sticks to Old Ways," April 21, 1997.

98. Paul Johnson, *The Quest for God: A Personal Pilgrimage* (New York: Harper-Collins, 1996), pp. 90–91.

99. Charles Colson and Nancy Pearcey, *How Now Shall We Live?* (Wheaton, Illinois: Tyndale House, 1999), p. 132.

100. Ibid.

101. Dennis Prager, *Think a Second Time* (New York: ReganBooks, 1995), pp. 77–78.

102. Temple Grandin and Joe M. Regenstein, "Religious Slaughter and Animal Welfare: A Discussion for Meat Scientists," *Meat Focus International*, March 1994, pp. 115–123.

103. Prager, *Think a Second Time*, p. 21.

104. Ibid., p. 100.

105. Ibid., p. 294.

106. Ibid., p. 78.

107. Ibid., p. 80.

108. Alison Green, "McDonald's Unhappy Meals," Knight-Ridder/Tribune News Service, September 7, 1999.

109. Eric Felten, "Nature, Red in Tooth and Claw Dept.," *Regardie's Power,* September–October 1999.

110. Joseph Sobran, "Unmasking 'Animal Rights,'" Universal Press Syndicate, March 1, 1990.

111. Ibid.

112. Ibid.

113. Cited in Jeffrey Masson and Susan McCarthy, *When Elephants Weep: The Emotional Lives of Animals* (New York: Delta, 1995), p. 111.

Chapter Four: Riches of the Sea

1. "An Appeal to Those with Power," *Advertiser,* July 4, 2000.

2. Associated Press, "Suggestion That Keiko be Made into Hamburgers Raises Hackles," November 4, 1998.

3. Andrew Rowell, "Wise Use: An International Environmental Movement?" *Conscious Choice: Journal of Ecology & Natural Living,* Vol. 10, No. 1, pp. 14–15.

4. "A Timeless Rhythm Endures," p. 8, *Marine Hunters: Whaling and Sealing in the North Atlantic* (High North Alliance, 1997).

5. "A Timeless Rhythm," pp. 8–9.

6. Ibid., p. 8.

7. Shawn Donnan, "As Whales Recover, So Does the Push for More Whaling," *Christian Science Monitor,* July 5, 2000.

8. Alex Kirby, "Whaling Ban Set to End," *BBC News,* June 11, 2000.

9. Paul Rogers, "Long-Lived Whales Test Age-Old Theory: Bowheads May Be Earth's Oldest Mammals," *Houston Chronicle,* December 20, 2000.

10. Quoted by Richard Ellis, *Men & Whales* (New York: The Lyons Press edition, 1999), p. 86.

11. Bill Morrill, "Conservation and Elephant Hunting," IWMC World Conservation Trust, November 27, 1998.

12. Quoted by Ellis, *Men & Whales,* p. 128.

13. Cited in Ellis, *Men & Whales,* p. 257.

14. Quoted by Ellis, *Men & Whales,* p. 267.

15. Craig Van Note, "Death of a Blue Whale," *Outlaw Whalers* (Whale Protection Fund, 1979), p. 3.

16. Ellis, *Men & Whales,* p. 349.

17. Except for estimate of blue whale population, all figures come from "Whale Population Estimates," in "The Lives of Whales," International Whaling Commission, June 2000, p. 6.

18. "Interview with Takahiro Nakamae, First Secretary of the Embassy of Japan in Argentina," IWMC World Conservation Trust, January 24, 2000.

19. Cited in Ellis, *Men & Whales*, p. 500.

20. International Agreement for the Regulation of Whaling, article 6.

21. "Determined to Continue Whale Hunting, Saint Vincent Roundup," *Caribbean Week*, May 28, 1999.

22. Ibid.

23. "The Minke Whale, Medium Rare," *Living off the Sea: Minke Whaling in the North East Atlantic* (Norwegian Fishermen's Association; February 1994), p. 6.

24. Masako Fukui, "Australia, Japan at Odds over Whaling," *Nikkei Weekly*, March 6, 2000.

25. Belinda Huppatz and Michael Owen-Brown, "Whale Win So Japan Moves in for the Kill," *Advertiser*, July 5, 2000.

26. Government of Japan, "Response to 'A Comment on the Usefulness of Biopsy Techniques,'" IWC/52/31.

27. *Report of the Scientific Committee*, p. 77.

28. "Whaling: The Facts," Japanese Whaling Association, p. 7.

29. Joby Warrick, "At Sea, the Catchword Is Conservation: New Rules Force Fisheries to Reduce Destructive 'Bycatch,'" *Washington Post*, January 7, 1999.

30. Opening Statement of the Japan Whaling Association at the 52nd Meeting of the IWC (IWC/52/OS JWA).

31. "Cultural Significance and Needs of Japan's Small-type Coastal Whaling," Japan Small-Type Whaling Association Opening Statement at the 52nd IWC.

32. Ibid.

33. Associated Press, "Japan Whaling Ships Return Home with 439 Minke Whales," April 6, 2000.

34. "Sanctuary Too Far Away," *Age*, July 6, 2000.

35. Calvin Sims, "Japan, Feasting on Whale, Sniffs at 'Culinary Imperialism' of U.S.," *New York Times*, August 10, 2000.

36. "Cultural Significance and Needs of Japan's Small-Type Coastal Whaling," p. 4.

37. Ibid., p. 7.

38. Seth Robson, "Public 'Misled over Whaling,'" *Christchurch Press*, February 1, 2000.

39. Mark B. Orams, *The Economic Benefits of Whale Watching in Vava'u, the Kingdom of Tonga* (Centre for Tourism Research, Massey University at Albany, North Shore, New Zealand: 1999), p. 2.

40. Belinda Huppatz, "Our Whale Vote Was Bought, Says Minister," *Advertiser*, July 7, 2000.

41. Ibid.

42. Joseph Kahn, "15 Countries Named as Potential Money-Laundering Havens," *New York Times*, June 23, 2000.

43. "Whale of a Hunt," *Wall Street Journal*, May 20, 1999.

44. Quoted in Ellis, *Men & Whales*, p. 34.

45. Ibid., p. 81.

46. Sho Shibata, "Symbol of Global Environmental Protection," *Isana*, March 2000, No. 22 (Japan Fisheries Association, Japan Whaling Association), p. 9.

47. Terry Plane, "Whale Haven Harpooned," *Australian*, July 5, 2000.

48. Reuters, "Vote Snub to Japan's Whale Bid," *Australian*, April 17, 2000.

49. Suvendrini Kakuchi, "Greens React Angrily As Japan Ups the Ante in Whale-Hunt Row," *Asiaweek,* October 13, 2000.

50. "A Reprehensible Whale Hunt," *New York Times,* August 15, 2000.

51. "Japanese Whalers Refuse to End Hunting," *USA Today,* June 30, 2000.

52. "Norwegian Commercial Whaling: Issues for Congress," Congressional Research Service, December 31, 1996.

53. Grant Robertson, "Canada Backs Exclusion of Animal Welfare from WTO Talks," *Calgary Herald,* October 13, 2000.

54. Resolution on Whaling under Special Permit in the Southern Ocean Sanctuary, IWC/52/37, agenda item 13.

55. *Report of the Scientific Committee,* p. 43.

56. "Resolution on Whaling of Highly Endangered Bowhead Whales in the Eastern Canadian Arctic," IWC/52/38.

57. Ted Gup, "Trail of Shame: Elephants Face Grim Struggle against Greed and Deceit," *Time,* October 16, 1989.

58. Paul Brown, "Japan Admits Aid Link to Votes," *Manchester Guardian Weekly,* November 24, 1999.

Chapter Five: The Laws

1. Carl Ludwig Schleich, quoted in Viktor E. Frankl, *The Doctor and the Soul: From Psychotherapy to Logotheraphy* (New York: Vintage, 1986 edition), p. 33.

2. James Sterngold, "Urban Sprawl Benefits Dairies in California, *New York Times,* October 22, 1999.

3. As with babies, too, we usually adopt the personal pronoun once we know the gender. In this book I have stuck with the common usage, adopting the personal pronoun where it seemed natural to do so.

4. "Fur: It's Your Fashion Choice," Fur Information Council.

5. Virginia Postrel, *The Future and Its Enemies: The Growing Conflict Over Creativity, Enterprise, and Progress* (New York: Free Press, 1998), pp. 158–159.

6. Swan, *In Defense of Hunting,* pp. 171–172.

7. Jack London, *White Fang,* pp. 227–228.

8. Ibid., pp. 244–245.

9. Theodore Roosevelt, *African Game Trails,* p. 239.

10. David Hume, *An Enquiry Concerning Human Understanding* (Oxford: Oxford University Press, 1999), p. 167.

11. Cited in John Passmore, "The Treatment of Animals," *Journal of the History of Ideas,* Vol. 36, Issue 2, p. 201.

12. David S. Oderberg, *Applied Ethics: A Non-Consequentialist Approach* (Oxford and Malden: Blackwell, 2000), p. 116 (italics in original).

13. Ibid., p. 119.

14. Ibid., p. 101.

15. Stephen Budiansky, *If a Lion Could Talk,* p. xiii.

16. Ibid., p. xxvii.

17. Ibid., p. 19.

18. John S. Kennedy, *New Anthropomorphism,* p. 24.

19. Budiansky, *If a Lion Could Talk,* p. 189.

20. Ibid., p. 192.

21. Ibid., p 194.

22. Romans 8:26.

23. Daniel C. Dennett, *Brainchildren: Essays on Designing Minds* (Cambridge: MIT Press, 1998), p. 331.

24. Tim Ingold, "The Animal in the Study of Humanity," *What Is an Animal?* (London and New York: Routledge, 1994), p. 95.

25. Cited in Kennedy, *New Anthropomorphism,* p. 91.

26. Kennedy, *New Anthropomorphism,* p. 5.

27. Ibid., pp. 5, 9.

28. Ibid., p 4.

29. Ibid., p. 118.

30. Ibid., p. 5.

31. Budiansky, *If a Lion Could Talk,* p. xxii.

32. Kennedy, *New Anthropomorphism,* pp. 31–32.

33. Budiansky, *If a Lion Could Talk,* p. xxv.

34. E. J. Gong, Jr., "He Talks to the Animals," *ABCNEWS.com,* June 4, 1998.

35. Cited in Oderberg, *Applied Ethics,* p. 110.

36. Peter Carruthers, *The Animals Issue: Moral Theory and Practice* (New York: Cambridge University Press, 1992), p. 141.

37. Budiansky, *If a Lion Could Talk,* p. xxiv.

38. Herbert S. Terrace, *Nim: A Chimpanzee Who Learned Sign Language* (New York: Columbia University Press, 1987), p. 209.

39. Budiansky, *If a Lion Could Talk,* p. xxxv.

40. Ibid., p. 159.

41. Eugene Linden, "Can Animals Think?" *Time,* March 22, 1993.

42. Donald R. Griffin, *Animal Minds* (Chicago: The University of Chicago Press: 1992), p. 212.

43. Ibid., p. 212.

44. Representative Lincoln Diaz-Balart, interviewed on *Hardball with Chris Matthews,* January 10, 2000.

45. William J. Broad, "Evidence Puts Dolphins in New Light, as Killers," *New York Times,* July 6, 1999.

46. Joseph Sobran, "The Dark Side of Dolphins," *Chattanooga Times,* July 9, 1999.

47. Kennedy, *New Anthropomorphism,* pp. 85–86.

48. Budiansky, *If a Lion Could Talk,* p. 182.

49. Ibid., p. 159.

50. Ibid., p. 171.

51. Ibid., p. 192.

52. Cited in J. M. C. Toynbee, *Animals in Roman Life and Art* (Baltimore: Johns Hopkins University Press, 1996), p. 23.

53. Roosevelt, *African Game Trails,* p. 283.

54. Ibid., p. 392.

55. Kennedy, *New Anthropomorphism,* p. 106.

56. Cited in Kennedy, *New Anthropomorphism,* pp. 109–110.

57. Kennedy, *New Anthropomorphism,* p. 109.

58. Budiansky, *If a Lion Could Talk,* p. 169.

59. Rob Stein, "A Simian Social Surprise: Chimps are Multicultural," *Washington Post,* June 21, 1999.

60. Budiansky, *If a Lion Could Talk,* pp. 169–170.

61. David Derbyshire, "Dolphins, on Reflection, Are Smarter Than We Thought," *Daily Telegraph,* May 2, 2001.

62. Quoted in Griffin, *Animal Minds,* p. 89.

63. Budiansky, *If a Lion Could Talk,* pp. 137–138.

64. "All Things Considered," National Public Radio, September 17, 1996 (Transcript 2339-5).

65. Ibid.

66. René Descartes, Letter to Henry Moore, cited in *Ethical Vegetarianism: From Pythagoras to Peter Singer* (State University of New York Press, 1999), p. 264.

67. Professor R. Latto, quoted in Griffin, *Animal Minds,* p. viii.

68. Kennedy, *New Anthropomorphism,* p. 118.

69. E. A. Wasserman, cited in George Page, *Inside the Animal Mind: A Groundbreaking Exploration of Animal Intelligence* (Doubleday, 1999), p. 42.

70. F. M. Toates, cited in Kennedy, *New Anthropomorphism,* p. 120.

71. Budiansky, *If a Lion Could Talk,* pp. xxiii–xix.

72. Ibid., p. xxii.

73. Temple Grandin and Gary C. Smith, "Animal Welfare and Humane Slaughter" (Colorado State University, 1998).

74. Budiansky, *If a Lion Could Talk,* p. 74.

75. Alex Tizon, "Animal Rights Activists Want Great Apes Recognized As People Too," *Seattle Times,* March 29, 2000.

76. Budiansky, *If a Lion Could Talk,* p. 18.

77. Roger Scruton, *Animal Rights and Wrongs* (London: Demos, 2000), p. 21.

78. Clive Wynne, "Do Animals Think?" *Psychology Today,* November 1, 1999.

79. Budiansky, *If a Lion Could Talk,* p. xxii.

80. Ibid., p. xx.

81. Cited in Marian Stamp Dawkins, "The Scientific Basis for Assessing Suffering in Animals," *In Defense of Animals,* ed. Peter Singer (New York: Basil Blackwell, 1985), p. 27.

82. Kennedy, *New Anthropomorphism,* pp. 2–3.

83. William James, "Does 'Consciousness' Exist?" (Classics in the History of Psychology, York University, Toronto, Ontario).

84. Budiansky, *If a Lion Could Talk,* p. 190.

85. Ibid.

86. Ibid., p. 191.

87. Carruthers, *Animals Issue,* p. 171.

88. Ibid., p. 180.

89. Ibid., p. 184.

90. Rob Stein, "Sleeping Rats May Dream of Maze: Resting Brain's Pattern Mimics That of Lessons Learned While Awake," *Washington Post,* January 25, 2001.

91. Carruthers, *Animals Issue,* p. 171.

92. Kennedy, *New Anthropomorphism,* p. 106; Budiansky, *If a Lion Could Talk,* p. 169.

93. Oderberg, *Applied Ethics,* p. 132.

94. Ibid., pp. 131–132.

95. Kennedy, *New Anthropomorphism,* p. 94.

96. Cited in Budiansky, *If a Lion Could Talk,* p. 34; Dennett, *Brainchildren,* p. 292.

97. Cited in Passmore, "The Treatment of Animals," p. 204. For a complete account of antiquity's version of "mock anthropomorphism," see also Richard Sorabji, "Perpetual Content in the Stoics," *Phronesis,* Vol. XXXV/3 (March 1990), pp. 307–314.

98. Budiansky, *If a Lion Could Talk,* p. 34.

99. Kennedy, *New Anthropomorphism,* p. 93.

100. Budiansky, *If a Lion Could Talk,* p. 34.

101. Ibid., p. 194.

102. Ibid.

103. Stephen Budiansky, *The Covenant of the Wild: Why Animals Choose Domestication* (New Haven: Yale University Press, 1999), p. xx.

104. Stephen Budiansky, "Killing with Kindness," *U.S. News & World Report,* November 25, 1996.

105. Carruthers, *Animals Issue,* p. xi

106. Ibid., p. xii.

107. Ibid., p. xii.

108. Ibid., p. xii.

109. Ibid., p. xii (italics in original).

110. Ibid., pp. 190–191.

111. Ibid., p. 192.

112. Ibid.

113. On the very last page of his book, Professor Carruthers does urge "caution" of the kind he failed to exercise in the preceding 192 pages. "The views presented in this chapter," he writes, "are controversial and speculative, and may well turn out to be mistaken. Until something like a consensus emerges, among philosophers and psychologists concerning the nature of consciousness, and among ethologists over the cognitive powers of animals, it may well be wiser to continue to respond to animals as if their mental states were conscious ones. This is not a concession to philosophical scepticism, just a realistic assessment of the likelihood of swift success in intellectual domains as complex and intractable as these."

114. London, *White Fang,* p. 265.

115. Temple Grandin, "Handling Pigs for Optimum Performance" (Colorado State University, 1998).

116. D. E. Gerrard, "Pork Quality: Beyond the Stress Gene" (Perdue University, 1997).

117. Cited in Richard Milne, "Animal Liberation: Do the Beasts Really Benefit" (Probe Ministries, 1994).

118. John C. Forrest, "Line Speed Implementation of Various Pork Quality Measures" (Purdue University, 1998).

119. Temple Grandin, "Methods to Reduce PSE and Bloodsplash," Allen D. Leman Swine Conference, Vol. 21, 1994, p. 206.

120. Jane Hughes, "Stressed-Out Porkers Get Anorexia," *Independent* (London), July 4, 1999.

121. Temple Grandin, "Methods to Reduce PSE."

122. Ann Marsh, "A Kinder, Gentler Abattoir," *Forbes,* July 1998.

123. Ibid.

124. Temple Grandin, *Thinking in Pictures: and Other Reports from My Life with Autism* (New York: Vintage, 1995), p. 25.

125. Ibid., p. 37.

126. Ibid., p. 33.

127. Ibid., p. 33.

128. Ibid., p. 89.

129. Ibid., p. 164.

130. Marsh, "Kinder, Gentler Abattoir."

131. Temple Grandin, "Environmental Enrichment for Confinement Pigs," Livestock Conservation Institute 1988 Annual Meeting Proceedings, pp. 119–123.

132. Grandin, "Methods to Reduce PSE."

133. Temple Grandin and Gary C. Smith, "Animal Welfare and Humane Slaughter."

134. Grandin, *Thinking in Pictures*, p. 169.

135. "Integration of Welfare into a Competitive Animal Production Sector" (Institute for Animal Science and Health, 1998).

136. Johanna de Groot and Marco Ruis, "Stress and Immunity" (Institute for Animal Science and Health, 1998).

137. Grandin, "Environmental Enrichment for Confinement Pigs."

138. "Superior Pork," Babcock Swine, Inc. (April 1999).

139. Grandin, *Thinking in Pictures*, p. 154.

140. Ibid., p. 202.

141. Ibid., p. 159.

142. Budiansky, *If a Lion Could Talk*, p. 193.

143. Grandin, *Thinking in Pictures*, p. 160.

144. Budiansky, *If a Lion Could Talk*, p. 157.

145. Grandin, *Thinking in Pictures*, p. 168.

146. Budiansky, *If a Lion Could Talk*, p. 194.

147. Saint Bonaventure, trans. Ewert Cousins, *The Soul's Journey into God, the Tree of Life, and the Life of St. Francis* (Mahwah, New Jersey: Paulist Press, 1978), p. 55.

Chapter Six: Deliver Me From My Necessities

1. Tim Gray, "Pig Stymied," *Business NorthCarolina,* March 1999.

2. "Smithfield Earnings Up Sixfold: Murphy Farms Acquisition, Higher Hog Prices Helped Fatten Bottom Line," *Virginian-Pilot,* August 23, 2000.

3. Greg Edwards, "Going Whole Hog: Smithfield Food's Strategy Creates Pork Industry Giant, Bigger Target of Criticism," *Richmond Times-Dispatch,* August 14, 2000.

4. David Barboza, "Goliath of the Hog World: Fast Rise of Smithfield Makes Regulators Wary," *New York Times,* April 7, 2000.

5. William Claiborne, "Hog Farmers Target Pork Promotion Fees," *Washington Post,* April 16, 1999.

6. Chris Hurt, "Staying Competitive in Today's Pork Business!" (Purdue University).

7. Ibid.

8. Quoted in Dipka Bhambhani, "Meaty Smithfield Stock Has Little Left to Grow," *Washington Times,* August 28, 2000.

9. Figures for both sow "stock" and daily slaughter from Greg Edwards, *Richmond Times-Dispatch,* August 14, 2000.

10. David M. Juday, "Intensification of Agriculture and Free Trade," *Livestock Ethics and Quality of Life,* edited by John K. Hodges and K. Han (CABI Publishing, 2000), p. 159.

11. Dale Miller, "Straight Talk from Smithfield's Joe Luter," *National Hog Farmer,* May 2000.

12. Ibid.

13. Jerry Perkins, "Smithfield Fattens Business, Profits," *Des Moines Register,* June 18, 2000.

14. Quotation and account of additional federal aid sought by pork industry reported by John Lancaster, "For Big Hog Farms, Big Subsidies: Taxpayers May Foot the Bill for Environmental Cleanup," *Washington Post,* August 17, 2001.

15. Laura Orlando, "McFarms Go Wild," *Dollars and Sense,* July/August 1998.

16. Information found on Web site of National Renderers Association, Inc.

17. "The Pork Production Career You Are Looking for Is Looking for You," advertisement appearing on official Web site of Carroll's Group Companies, January 2001.

18. Ned Glascock, "Rights Group Targets Firms," *Raleigh News and Observer,* August 31, 2000.

19. *The Welfare of Europe's Sows in Close Confinement Stalls: A Report Prepared for the European Coalition for Farm Animals* (Compassion in World Farming Trust, 2000), Section 3.0.

20. *The Welfare of Europe's Sows in Close Confinement,* Section 6.2.

21. Veterinarian's Oath (American Veterinary Medical Association, approved 1969), *Veterinary Ethics,* 2d ed., Jerrold Tannenbaum (St. Louis: Mosby, 1995), p. 88.

22. John 10:12–13 (New American Bible).

23. Bernard E. Rollin, *Farm Animal Welfare: Social, Bioethical, and Research Issues* (Ames: Iowa State University Press, 1995), p. 6.

24. Ibid.

25. Quoted in Marc Kaufman, "In Pig Farming, Growing Concern: Raising Sows in Crates Is Questioned," *Washington Post,* June 18, 2001.

26. Joy Williams, "The Inhumanity of the Animal People: Do Creatures Have the Same Rights That We Do?" *Harper's,* August 1997.

27. Lowell Monke, "The Pigs of Iowa: Industrialization of the Hog," *Netfire* (publication of The Nature Institute), No. 114, November 30, 2000.

28. Rollin, *Farm Animal Welfare,* pp. 74–75.

29. Ibid., p. 75.

30. *Swine Care Handbook* (National Pork Producers Council, 1996).

31. Rob Stein, "Pigs with Less Polluting Waste," *Washington Post,* August 6, 2001.

32. Detailed in Brian Feagans, "A New Era in Hog Waste Treatment: Contest Underway to Replace Lagoons," *Wilmington Star-News* (North Carolina), August 6, 2000.

33. Quoted in Esther M. Bauer, "Cattle May Still Be King, but Here Come the Hogs," *Wall Street Journal,* December 1, 1999.

34. Barboza, "Goliath of the Hog World."

35. Charlie LeDuff, "In the Hog Factory, the Lines Are Clear," *International Herald Tribune,* June 29, 2000.

36. Ibid.

37. Ibid.

38. Ibid.

39. Gail A. Eisnitz, *Slaughterhouse: The Shocking Story of Greed, Neglect, and Inhumane Treatment Inside the U.S. Meat Industry* (Amherst: Prometheus, 1997), p. 265.

40. Ibid., p. 267.

41. Joby Warrick, "'They Die Piece by Piece': In Overtaxed Plants, Humane Treatment of Cattle is Often a Lost Battle," *Washington Post,* April 10, 2001.

42. Ibid.

43. Ibid.

44. Ibid.

45. Larry Gallagher, "Meat Is Murder," *Details,* March 1996.

46. *State of New Jersey vs. ISE America,* Central Warren Municipal Court, Warren County, New Jersey, October 17, 2000.

47. Thomas Hardy, *Jude the Obscure* (New York: Bantam, 1969), pp. 68–69.

Chapter Seven: Nature And Nature's God

1. *Encyclical Letter of Pope John Paul II: The Mercy of God,* I:2.

2. Daniel Johnson, "The Wrongs of Animal Rights," *Daily Telegraph,* October 30, 1999.

3. Letter to Albert G. Hodges, April 4, 1864, *The Portable Abraham Lincoln* (New York: Viking, 1992), p. 302.

4. William F. Buckley, Jr., "Will Meat Go the Way of Fox Hunting?" *Houston Chronicle,* March 5, 1998.

5. Greg Neale, "Apes Can 'Talk,' but Africa's Farmers Want Us to Eat Them," *Sunday Telegraph,* August 1, 1999.

6. Reuters, "Britain Urged to Crack Down on Ape Meat Trade," February 27, 2002.

7. *Proceedings of the House of Representatives,* October 19, 1999.

8. Ibid.

9. Statement by the President, Office of the Press Secretary, December 9, 1999.

10. One Hundred Sixth Congress, H.R. 1887, January 6, 1999.

11. Roger Scruton, "Eat Animals: It's for Their Own Good," *Los Angeles Times,* July 25, 1991.

12. Stephen R. L. Clark, *Animals and Their Moral Standing,* p. 161.

13. The Humane Society of the United States, U.S. Newswire, "Florida Dairy Farm Sanctioned by State in Killing of Calves," October 15, 1999.

14. Carruthers, *Animals Issue,* p. 165.

15. Quoted in David McCullough, *John Adams* (New York: Simon & Schuster, 2001), p. 71.

16. "Cruelty to Animals," *Catholic Encyclopedia,* Vol. IV (Robert Appleton, 1908).

17. His Holiness Pope John Paul II, *Crossing the Threshold of Hope* (New York: Knopf, 1994), p. 20 (italics in original).

18. John Milton, *Paradise Lost,* Book VIII, 172–173.

19. Budiansky, *Covenant of the Wild,* p. 161.

20. Felix Salten, *Bambi: A Life in the Woods,* trans. Whittaker Chambers (New York: Pocket Books, 1988), pp. 186–188.

21. *Bear Catalog 1993* (Shooting Industry).

22. Jeffrey Hart, "Exposing the Dark Side of the Zoo Business," *Washington Times,* October 10, 1999.

23. William Shakespeare, *The Merchant of Venice,* Act IV, Scene I.

24. Durant, *Oriental Heritage,* p. 7.

25. Morris, *Naked Ape,* p. 197.

26. Roger Scruton, "Mr. Blair Shows He Is a Master of Intolerance," *Sunday Telegraph,* June 11, 1999.

27. Cited in Anna Kingsford, "The Essence of True Justice," *Ethical Vegetarianism,* p. 108.

28. Durant, *Oriental Heritage,* p. 448.

29. Ibid., p. 449.

30. Robert F. Kennedy, Jr., "I Don't Like Green Eggs and Ham!" *Newsweek,* April 26, 1999.

31. Marjorie Kinnan Rawlings, *The Yearling* (New York: Aladdin, 1988), p. 72.

32. Ibid., p. 108.

33. Ibid., pp. 427–428.

34. Romans 8:21–22. My Bible, in a footnote, offers this hopeful formulation of the doctrine: "Adam drew down into his ruin the old creation, of which he was lord and head. Christ will bring into moral unity with God, and into eternal life, all of the new creation of which He is Lord and head (Eph. 1:22–23). Even the animal and material creation, cursed for man's sake (Gen. 3:17), will be delivered by Christ (vv. 19–22; cp. Isa. 11:6–9)." *New Scofield Reference Bible* (Oxford University Press, 1967).

35. Swan, *In Defense of Hunting,* p. 15.

36. Ibid., p. 128.

37. Ibid., p. 206.

38. Ibid., p. 128.

39. Roger Scruton, "Be Here Now with Reference to Oasis and Heidegger," *Daily Telegraph,* October 10, 1998.

40. Quoted in Ajay Close, "Dispatches from the Rural Front," *The Scotsman,* February 10, 2001.

41. Cited in Passmore, "Treatment of Animals," p. 207.

42. Larry Katz, "President's Message," *Safari: The Journal of Big-Game Hunting,* March/April 2000, p. 10.

43. U.S. Department of Agriculture, *Agriculture Fact Book 1998*, p. 8.

44. Ibid., p. 3.

45. Budiansky, *Covenant of the Wild*, p. xix.

46. Roger Scruton, "Eat Animals! It's for Their Own Good: There Is No Better Way of Protecting the Habitat of Species than by Systematically Hunting It," *Los Angeles Times*, July 25, 1991.

47. Digby Anderson, "Passionate Tastes: The History of Vegetarianism," *Guardian*, April 20, 1993.

48. C.S. Lewis, *Problem of Pain*, p. 56.

49. Alice Walker, "Am I Blue," *Ms.*, July 1986.

50. Anna Kingsford, "The Essence of True Justice," *Ethical Vegetarianism: From Pythagoras to Peter Singer*, p. 122.

51. Singer, *Animal Liberation*, p. 5.

52. Quoted in Paul Zielbauer, "Princeton Bioethics Professor Debates Views on Disability and Euthanasia," *New York Times*, October 13, 1999.

53. Peter Singer, *Rethinking Life and Death: The Collapse of Our Traditional Ethics* (New York: St. Martin's, 1996), p. 4.

54. Singer, *Animal Liberation*, p. 3.

55. Singer, *Rethinking Life and Death*, pp. 182–183.

56. Peter Singer, *How Are We to Live? Ethics in an Age of Self-Interest* (Amherst: Prometheus, 1995), p. 181.

57. Ibid., p. 181.

58. Ibid., p. 103.

59. Ibid., p. 108.

60. Ibid., p. 222.

61. Gertrude Himmelfarb, *On Liberty and Liberalism: The Case of John Stuart Mill* (ICS Press, 1990), p. 7.

62. Singer, *Rethinking Life and Death*, p. 5.

63. Ibid., p. 210.

64. Ibid., p. 217.

65. Ibid.

66. Ibid., p. 190.

67. Ibid., pp. 196–197.

68. Leo Strauss, *Natural Right and History* (Chicago: University of Chicago Press, 1965), p. 4.

69. Singer, *Rethinking Life and Death*, pp. 213–214.

70. Ibid., p. 200.

71. Charles Dickens, *The Christmas Books: A Christmas Carol/The Chimes* (New York: Penguin, 1985), p. 97.

72. Linzey, *Animal Theology*, pp. 40–41.

73. Richard John Neuhaus, "Animal Lib," *Christianity Today*, June 18, 1990. In his 1992 book *Doing Well & Doing Good: The Challenge to the Christian Capitalist* (New York: Doubleday, pp. 219–220), Father Neuhaus expands on the point: "In recent years there has been a growing interest in animal rights, often motivated by moral and aesthetic revulsion against egregious cruelties toward the creatures with whom we

share the earth. . . . What the animal rights ideologists and the devotees of the goddess Nature usually seem to miss is that only by affirming the biblical view of human beings as the stewards of the creation can the other creatures be protected. It is certainly right that we are called to greater respect and care for nature and other creatures. The fact that the call is, of necessity, directed to human beings, however, only underscores the utterly singular status and responsibility of the human in the order of creation. Were we to allow, for the sake of argument, that animals have rights, it is obvious that animals do not respect the rights of other animals; only human beings can do that. In other words, the well being of all the creatures of the earth depends upon the 'speciesism' and 'anthropocentrism' that are today so frequently derided."

74. Richard A. Posner and Peter Singer, "Dialogues: Animal Rights," *Slate*, June 13, 2001.

75. Ibid.

76. Cited in Passmore, "Treatment of Animals," p. 195.

77. Ibid., p. 203.

78. Saint Thomas Aquinas, *Summa Contra Gentiles*, Book II:112.

79. Carruthers, *Animals Issue*, p. 165.

80. Ibid.

81. "Cruelty to Animals," *Catholic Encyclopedia*.

82. Oderberg, *Applied Ethics*, pp. 141–142.

83. David S. Oderberg, "The Illusion of Animal Rights," *Human Life Review*, Spring–Summer 2000, p. 45.

84. Oderberg, *Applied Ethics*, p. 142.

85. Ibid., p. 121.

86. Roger Scruton, "Please Don't Give Me Legal Rights," *Evening Standard*, February 12, 1999.

87. Ibid.

88. Scruton, *Animal Rights and Wrongs*, p. 124.

89. Ibid., p. 137.

90. Ibid., pp. 28–32.

91. Ibid., p. 44.

92. Ibid., pp. 53–55.

93. Ibid., p. 95.

94. Ibid., p. 138.

95. Ibid., p. 138.

96. Oderberg, *Applied Ethics*, p. 142.

97. Ibid.

98. Mary Midgley, *Animals and Why They Matter* (Athens: University of Georgia Press, 1983), p. 70.

99. Oderberg, *Applied Ethics*, p. 142.

Chapter Eight: Justice and Mercy

1. Jeremy Paxman, "The Moral Catch," *The Guardian* (London), February 23, 1995.

2. Lewis, *Problem of Pain*, p. 136.

3. Passmore, "Treatment of Animals," p. 206.

4. Carmichel, "Hunting African Elephants."

5. Ibid.

6. Ibid.

7. The existence of these bear farms and the methods employed are well known. The estimate of more than 7,000 bears I owe to Francoise Giovannangeli, "An Unbearable Prospect," *Japan Times,* September 2, 1998. The estimate of 247 such farms currently operating comes from Susan McClelland, "Illicit Sales of Animal Parts Are Putting Species at Risk," *Maclean's,* January 2001.

8. Quoted from preamble to *NTA Trapper's Handbook* (American Trappers Association, Bloomington, Illinois).

9. Quoted in Chris Osher, "Open Market for Exotic Animals: Hunting Ranch Boom Sparks Push for Laws," *Arkansas Democrat-Gazette,* November 1, 1999.

10. Quoted in Wendy Marston, "The Misguided Ivory Ban and the Reality of Living with Elephants," *Washington Post,* June 8, 1997.

11. Clive Hamilton, "Nurture Nature at What Price?" *Canberra Times,* July 2, 2001.

12. 16 United States Criminal Statutes 4222 (b) (3).

13. Carmichel, "Hunting African Elephants."

14. Letter from Richard W. Pombo to Secretary of State Colin Powell, May 3, 2001.

15. Chadwick, *Fate of the Elephant,* p. 98.

16. Cited in Joseph R. Berger, "The African Elephant, Human Economies, and International Law: Bridging the Great Rift for East and Southern Africa," *Georgetown International Environmental Law Review,* Winter 2001.

17. Quoted in Rob Ryan, "Back to the Hunt?"

18. Quoted in Joseph R. Berger, "The African Elephant, Human Economies, and International Law: Bridging the Great Rift for East and Southern Africa."

19. "Elephant Killers," *San Francisco Examiner,* April 14, 1997.

20. Associated Press, " 'Pill' Curbs Pachyderm Pregnancy," *Toronto Star,* September 14, 2000.

21. Donald G. McNeil Jr., "Packaging Luxury with Wildlife: Company Draws Rich Eco-Tourists to Africa," *New York Times,* June 25, 1997.

22. Figure cited in Donald G. McNeil, Jr., "Packaging Luxury with Wildlife."

23. David Olinger, "Big Game, Big Money," *St. Petersburg Times,* June 9, 1997.

24. Rob Ryan, "Back to the Hunt?" *Sunday Times* (London), June 8, 1997.

25. "Road to Survival: Forget Trade Bans, Just Make Wild Animals Pay Their Own Way," *New Scientist,* April 29, 2000.

26. Ross Herbert, "Training of Elephants Triggers Outrage: Animal Groups Say Methods Are Barbaric," *Washington Times,* November 12, 1998.

27. Virginia Postrel, *The Future and Its Enemies,* p. 152.

28. Alex Kirby, "Dire Outlook for Many Primates," *BBC News,* May 12, 2000.

29. John Tuxill and Chris Bright, "Protecting Nature's Diversity," *Futurist,* June 1, 1998.

30. Paul Theroux, "Traveling, Shoulder to Shoulder," *New York Times,* December 9, 1999.

31. Chadwick, *Fate of the Elephant,* p. 7.

32. "This Little Pig Went to Market," *Advance: Research, Scholarship, and Creative Achievement at Texas A&M,* 1998, p. 31.

33. Antony Barnett, "Patent Allows Creation of Man-Animal Hybrid," *Observer International* (London), November 26, 2000.

34. Quoted in David Berreby, "Unneeded Lab Chimps Face Hazy Future," *New York Times*, February 4, 1997.

35. Quoted in Mark Muro, "When Animal Rights Go Wrong: A Well-Intentioned Movement for Humane Treatment Has Lost Perspective," *Boston Globe*, October 30, 1988.

36. Cal Thomas, "Will Radicals Rule and Humans Suffer?" *Los Angeles Times*, June 24, 1997.

37. "Data Collection and Development on High-Production Volume (HPV) Chemicals," *Federal Register*, Vol. 65, No. 248, December 26, 2000.

38. P. E. Garraghty, D. O. Frost, and M. Sur, "The Morphology of Retinogeniculate X- and Y-Cell Axonal Arbors in Dark-Reared Cats," *Experimental Brain Research* (1987) 66:115–127.

39. E. D. Levin and F. J. Seidler, "Sex-Related Spacial Learning Differences after Prenatal Cocaine Exposure in Young Adult Rat," *Neurotox* 1993; 14(1):23–8. E. D. Levin, F. J. Seidler, S. E. Lappi, and T. A. Slotkin, "Fetal Nicotine Exposure Ablates the Ability of Postnatal Nicotine Challenge to Release Norepinephrine from Rat Brain Regions," *Dev. Brain Research* 1992; 69:288–91. E. D. Levin, S. J. Briggs, N. C. Christopher, J. E. Rose, "Prenatal Nicotine Exposure and Cognitive Performance in Rats," *Neurotox and Teratol* 1993; 15:251–60.

40. Miles J. Novy, "Notice of Intent to Use Live Animals in Research or Instruction for Experimental Model for Mycoplasma Chorioamnionitis and Preterm Labor," submitted to the Oregon Regional Primate Research Center Institutional Animal Care and Use Committee, August 28, 1998.

41. *The Quotable Chesterton*, eds. George J. Marlin, Richard P. Rabatin, and John L. Swan (San Francisco: Ignatius Press, 1986), p. 360.

42. Joy Williams, "The Inhumanity of the Animal People," *Harper's*, August 1997.

43. Paul Greenberg, "Forever Drawing the Line," *Washington Times*, August 7, 2001.

44. Michael Novak, "The Stem-Cell Slide: Be Alert to the Beginnings of Evil," *National Review*, September 3, 2001.

45. Quoted in Rick Weiss, "Human Cloning Bid Stirs Experts' Anger: Problems in Animal Cases Noted," *Washington Post*, March 7, 2001.

46. Animal Welfare Act, Section 2 (g).

47. Animal Welfare Act, Section 13 (3) (D) (i).

48. Animal Welfare Act, Section 13 (8) (B) (I).

49. Animal Welfare Act as Amended (7 United States Code, 2131–2156), Section 1 (b) (2).

50. "How fortunate," Fleming later reflected, "we didn't have these animal tests in the 1940s, for penicillin would probably never have been granted a license, and possibly the whole field of antibiotics might never have been realized." Quoted by Dennis V. Parke, a student of Fleming and professor of biochemistry at the University of Surrey, in "Clinical Pharmacokinetics in Drug Safety," *Alternatives to Laboratory Animals*, Vol. 22 (1994), pp. 207–209.

51. Albert Sabin, statement before the subcommittee on hospitals and healthcare, Committee on Veteran's Affairs, House of Representatives, April 26, 1984.

52. Animal Welfare Act, Section 13 (7) (b).

53. *Journal of the American Medical Association,* 276 (1996) 87–88.

54. Frances D'Emilio, "Pope Cautions about Risks from New Agricultural Technology," Associated Press, November 12, 2000.

55. David Plotz, "Gimme Some Skin: Why Shouldn't Dalmatians Be Made into Coats?" *Slate,* December 6, 1996.

56. *Congressional Record,* July 9, 2001.

57. Reuters News Agency, "One Man's Quest to Save Sea Turtles: Beach in Sri Lanka Is Nesting Ground for Five Species," *Washington Times,* September 6, 1997.

58. Ibid.

59. I am here indebted to reporter Aline McKenzie for her lovely turn of phrase in describing the atmosphere at a different animal sanctuary, the Black Beauty Ranch in Texas ("There is nothing going on today. Sweet, glorious nothing"). "Beasts Unburdened: Menagerie of Mistreated Animals Finds Sanctuary at Writer's East Texas Ranch," *Dallas Morning News,* October 14, 1997.

60. Oliver Goldsmith, "The Hermit."

61. Revelation 21:4.

ACKNOWLEDGMENTS

One day in August 1997, after I had published a column on elephant hunting in the *New York Times*, I received a call from Wayne Pacelle of the Humane Society of the United States. I had never met Wayne, but have since come to know him as a gifted and fearless advocate for mistreated animals, and I draw a straight line from his appearance in my life to the completion of this book. I relied on him at every turn, and I am grateful for the help and encouragement of a true friend.

Many others involved in animal protection lent their knowledge to me. I thank in particular Gene and Lorri Bauston, Bernard Unti, Andrea Lane, Nicolette Hahn, Nicole Cardello, Naomi Rose, Patricia Forkan, Regina Hyland, Craig Van Note, Amy Trakinski, Eric Sakach, Franz Danzler, Becky Robinson, Bruce Friedrich, and the authors Douglas Chadwick and Richard Ellis. To all of these new friends I am indebted not only for their practical assistance, but for their examples of compassion and their years of perseverance in the cause of animal protection.

I also leaned heavily on friends of long standing. Mark Simpson, Vivian Dudro, Bob Heiler, Robert J. Loewenberg, John Evans, John Stevens, Maria Baier, Ben Sanders, Nancy Uhrbrock, Laura DeWitt, John Castellano, George Hamm, Bob Hamm, and my parents-in-law, Wil and Anne-Marie Boers, all came through with crucial edits, sound advice, or just some badly needed moral support. Other longtime friends like John O'Sullivan, William F. Buckley, Jr., Bill Kristol, Rich Lowry, and Mike Gerson had no hand in the book—and may be enormously relieved that I have made that clear—but I am much in their debt all the same for the confidence, opportunities, and guidance they have given me in years past. My friend Richard Brookhiser of *National Review* gave me some simple and well-timed advice once—to write appreciatively, not just critically—that I have tried to follow here, and I am grateful to him as well.

Many friends and relatives were subjected to my extended monologues and unsolicited readings from the manuscript, enduring these with patience and fortitude. In this respect my speechwriting colleague John McConnell, trapped in the same office with me for three years, took the worst of it. Amazingly I cannot recall a single complaint, but only a daily example in the virtues of cheerfulness and equanimity. I will always be in John's debt for the kind and judicious counsel of one of the finest men I know.

My agents, Lynn Chu and Glen Hartley, have also been tested by my frequent calls and needless worries. From the start Lynn and Glen placed their confidence in me, and have earned my complete confidence many times over. Their greatest service was to point me in the direction of St. Martin's Press. My editor, George Witte, improved the book with his careful pruning, and helped to shape it from the start with the sense of trust, professionalism, and high standards he gives to an author by his own example. He and his assistant, Brad Wood, have also given me more time and consideration than a first-time author was due. I thank Marie Estrada, Michelle McMillian, Philip Pascuzzo, Donna Sinisgalli, Geraldine Van Dusen, Ethan Dunn, Jeff Capshew, Joan Higgins, Lisa Herman, Anna Navarra, and all the talented people at St. Martin's, especially George and Brad, for the skill and enthusiasm they brought to the project. The book is also better for the fine touch of my cousin Bill Moran, who helped with the jacket, and for the sharp eye of Ellis B. Levine.

I could not have finished the book without the gracious help of four of my oldest and best friends, Jay and Carol Heiler and Greg and Mireille Hamm. I could not have begun the book without a timely gift from my oldest brother, Chris Scully, the most generous man I know. I am grateful as well to my brother Steve for his example and wonderful way with animals, especially his years of care for Lucky; to my oldest sister, Anne, for her constant support and early introduction to the world of books with those readings from *The Velveteen Rabbit*; to my sister Eileen for the sensitivity and characteristic insight of her edits; and to my sister Tara for her cheerful encouragement and for the special friendship we have.

The first editors of the first draft were my parents. My father, in his own writing, is the model for me of skill and integrity, and my mother is the literary critic whose judgment matters most. The book owes much, and the author everything, to Leon and Eileen Scully.

I relied most of all on the patience, wisdom, and sheer goodness of my wife, Emmanuelle. I think of this as our book, lived together, and like so much else in life better for being shared with her.

While writing the book, I worked as a speechwriter for Governor and then President George W. Bush. I came to admire him greatly, as a leader and as a man, and I thank him for the privilege.

INDEX